Mindful
Sport Performance
Enhancement

Mindful Sport Performance Enhancement

MENTAL TRAINING for ATHLETES and COACHES

KEITH A. KAUFMAN

CAROL R. GLASS

TIMOTHY R. PINEAU

AMERICAN PSYCHOLOGICAL ASSOCIATION

WASHINGTON, DC

Published by
American Psychological Association
750 First Street, NE
Washington, DC 20002
www.apa.org

To order
APA Order Department
P.O. Box 92984
Washington, DC 20090-2984
Tel: (800) 374-2721; Direct: (202) 336-5510
Fax: (202) 336-5502; TDD/TTY: (202) 336-6123
Online: www.apa.org/pubs/books
E-mail: order@apa.org

In the U.K., Europe, Africa, and the Middle East, copies may be ordered from
American Psychological Association
3 Henrietta Street
Covent Garden, London
WC2E 8LU England

Typeset in Meridien by Circle Graphics, Inc., Columbia, MD

Printer: Sheridan Books, Ann Arbor, MI
Cover Designer: Beth Schlenoff Design, Bethesda, MD

The opinions and statements published are the responsibility of the authors, and such opinions and statements do not necessarily represent the policies of the American Psychological Association.

Library of Congress Cataloging-in-Publication Data

Names: Kaufman, Keith A., author. | Glass, Carol R., author. | Pineau,
  Timothy R., author.
Title: Mindful sport performance enhancement : mental training for athletes
  and coaches / Keith A. Kaufman, Carol R. Glass, and Timothy R. Pineau.
Description: Washington, DC : American Psychological Association, [2018] |
  Includes bibliographical references and index.
Identifiers: LCCN 2017012289| ISBN 9781433827877 | ISBN 1433827875
Subjects: LCSH: Sports—Psychological aspects. | Athletes—Psychology.
Classification: LCC GV706.4 .K377 2018 | DDC 796.01/9—dc23 LC record available at
  https://lccn.loc.gov/2017012289

British Library Cataloguing-in-Publication Data
A CIP record is available from the British Library.

Printed in the United States of America
First Edition

http://dx.doi.org/10.1037/0000048-000

Contents

I

Being a Mindful Performer   9

II

Mindful Sport Performance Enhancement   61

III

IV

Foreword

One never knows who, or even if anyone, will pick up the torch of earlier work or whether some kind of invisible transmission might be taking place that touches something within the hearts and minds of others and inspires a line of inquiry that builds on one's own first steps. In inviting me to write the foreword to this book, the authors shared with me that the direction of their work had been inspired across a gap of decades by early work that I did, in collaboration with Bruce Beall,[1] in training collegiate and Olympic rowers (at Harvard University and at the 1984 Los Angeles Olympics at Lake Casitas and later at the University of California, Berkeley) in mindfulness meditation and its applications to sports performance both on and off the water (see Kabat-Zinn, Beall, & Rippe, 1985; Rippe & Southmayd, 1986). As described in the preface, mindful sport performance enhancement (MSPE) was in part birthed out of that inspiration and out of the authors' enthusiasm for the potential of a truly transformational mind–body-oriented athletic training based on the systematic cultivation of mindfulness. Their integration of mindfulness practices into sports performance in very practical and systematic ways and the study of performance outcomes using rigorous scientific methodologies are major contributions to the field of sports performance.

In ancient Greece and then Rome, where Western sport has its origins, the principle of a sound mind in a sound body was paramount and related to the Greek ideal of beauty so prevalent in classical Hellenic sculpture and in the exquisite languaging within the Homeric oral tradition.[2] The same recognition of the power of the mind to influence the body ran through ancient Greek medicine in the intersecting lineages of Hippocrates and Asclepius (see, e.g., Santorelli, 1999).

---

[1] At that time, Bruce Beall was coach of the Harvard lightweight rowing team and a member of the 1984 U.S. Olympic Team.

[2] This view has been recently subject to scholarly refutation, however; see Young (2005).

Twenty-first-century medicine and health care is now experiencing a resurgence of interest in this ancient wisdom and artistry, namely, the mind's potential influence on the body and on the brain and the role that the intentional cultivation of present-moment attention and the awareness that it gives rise to, known as *mindfulness*, can have in terms of our health and well-being at every level of the organism, including our social interconnectedness. This element of interconnectedness is key with regard to rowing in team boats with up to eight rowers because there are moments both in races and in practice on the water when it feels as if there is only one mind in the boat, a collective mind of total intentionality, and the bodies, the boat itself, and the oars and the water all become one in the effort of that moment, and perhaps the next moment and the next stroke as well, and the next.

One motive force in the growing interest in the clinical applications of mindfulness in medicine and psychology has been the recent advent of new technologies that allow us to look at the real-time activity of the brain in action (although the body, ironically, has to be immobile, encapsulated in a functional magnetic resonance imaging scanner). This technology has catalyzed the emergence of the new science of neuroplasticity and its dramatic implications for learning and performance, driven by training effects anchored in repetition (see, e.g., Wellcome Trust, 2011). Another new field, known as epigenetics, is demonstrating that our lifestyle and behavioral choices, and even the patterns of our thoughts and emotions and our social relationships, often way below the radar of our awareness, can result in vast numbers of our genes being either up-regulated or down-regulated. Such epigenetic regulation has been shown to affect genes involved in inflammatory and cancerous disease processes (see, e.g., Ornish et al., 2008), suggesting that basic biological processes that were once thought to be our genetic fate can be influenced to one degree or another, for better or for worse, by how we actually live our lives, including what we think, how we regulate our emotions, how and how much we exercise, and other lifestyle choices and the quality of our social interactions. A third development, the new science of telomeres and telomerase and their implications for biological aging (Blackburn & Epel, 2017), is also playing a major role in our understanding of the mind's effects on biological processes and our health. All these new disciplines, not even imaginable a few decades ago, have been shown to be positively affected by meditative practices grounded in mindfulness (see, e.g., Kaliman et al., 2014).

It has taken almost 40 years for mindfulness to have made its way into medicine and health care and become widely accepted. Even with all these new methodologies and disciplines now being brought to bear on it, the science of mindfulness is still in its infancy. For that reason, it is necessary to continually exercise caution and skepticism in terms of overstating the evidence for its effectiveness in various domains. At the same time, the evidence accumulated on mindfulness to date points to its being profoundly valuable clinically in the form of various mindfulness-based interventions, such as mindfulness-based stress reduction, mindfulness-based cognitive therapy, and others targeting stress, pain, and chronic illnesses of various kinds, including major depressive disorder and anxiety disorders (Creswell, 2017; Goyal et al., 2014; Segal, Williams, & Teasdale, 2012). Mindfulness is also presently finding its way into K–12 education, higher education, business, the law, and even government (Ryan, 2012; see also Mindfulness All-Party Parliamentary Group, 2015). So it is hardly surprising that it is also finding its way into sport (see Mumford, 2015; see also Wisdom 2.0, 2016).

This book documents all of the emergent trends for bringing mindfulness into the domain of sport in the modern era and evaluates their research base and reported outcomes. The authors also present their own mindfulness-based training program, the eponymous MSPE for athletes and coaches. Although MSPE is still relatively young, as the authors themselves emphasize, there is compelling evidence, just as there was in medicine 40 years ago, that bringing the discipline of systematic mental training into sports at all levels can not only enhance performance and outcomes but also catalyze a greater sense of deep connection and satisfaction and, at least in some cases, the merging of mind and body into a space that, at its higher reaches, transcends the very sense of a separate self who is doing the performing. This experience touches a domain of human performance where what we call *mind* and what we think of as *body* come together in that original beauty of the Greek ideal, embodied in action, in the timelessness of the present moment, an experience that—when it can be put into words at all, which it often cannot, except perhaps in Homeric poetry (see Scarry, 1999, pp. 93–94)—is described as *flow* (Csikszentmihalyi, 1990; see also Lambert, 1998, and Murphy & White, 1978) or *nondoing* (Kabat-Zinn, 2005b). In essence, it is the same phenomenon as when a crew, as described earlier, experiences only one mind and one body in the boat and the boat seems to propel itself through the water, an experience known among rowers as *swing*.

May this book spark widespread interest in mindfulness within the domain of sport and sport performance at all levels in society, from occasional everyday athletic pursuits to the highest reaches of amateur and professional sports, both individual and team-based. And may it equally stimulate a generation of new and increasingly rigorous scientific studies to, as Thoreau said in another context, put a firm foundation underneath our dreams.

—Jon Kabat-Zinn
Northampton, MA

Preface

O ur respective paths to mindful sport performance enhancement (MSPE) began in very different places, and we feel incredibly fortunate to have all come together at just the right time to allow this collaboration to take flight. This book's second author (Carol R. Glass) was a graduate school mentor to the other coauthors at The Catholic University of America (CUA), and a true history of our journey begins with her internship in San Francisco. It was there that she was first introduced to Vipassana meditation by a fellow intern, and they even co-led a group that was truly ahead of its time with its incorporation of this practice. At that point, it was unimaginable that this experience would be pivotal to the development of an innovative mindfulness-based mental training program for athletes and coaches 30 years later. However, her interest in mindfulness continued to evolve through an academic career in clinical psychology focusing on psychotherapy integration and cognitive–behavioral therapy as well as more than 35 years of experience as a practicing psychologist. Her curiosity about sport psychology grew with her son's involvement in elite-level recurve archery. Those countless hours spent attending practices, observing sessions with his coach, and serving as his informal sport psychologist at national championships around the country led to her eventually seeking training as an archery instructor and further inspired her to explore the mental aspects of performance.

Keith A. Kaufman's path began in an undergraduate sport psychology course at the University of North Carolina at Chapel Hill taught by a pioneer in the field, Dr. John Silva. Despite Dr. Silva's legendarily difficult exams, Keith was captivated by this science that combined his great loves, sports and the mind. He showed up at Dr. Silva's office one day and essentially said, "Tell me how I can do what you do," which led to a double major in psychology and exercise and sport science and later to doctoral training in clinical psychology. Keith happened to interview with Carol at CUA just as her son was rising through the recurve archery ranks and her own interest in sport psychology was sparking. Discovering their shared interest led to the birth of what became one of the few sport psychology research labs housed within a

PhD clinical psychology program. As the "mindful revolution" gained momentum in clinical psychology, brainstorming sessions spawned the idea of applying mindfulness to sport performance. To our surprise, little had been written at that time about mindfulness in sport, yet the marriage just made so much sense. Here was a concrete way to teach mental skills crucial to optimal performance, promote mental and physical wellness, and change how athletes approach achievement. It has been a joy for Keith to bring mindfulness not only to his work but also to his own athletic endeavors, which still include soccer, tennis, and distance running.

Since receiving his doctorate almost a decade ago, Keith has continued collaborating with Carol on MSPE research and teaching an undergraduate sport psychology course while establishing a thriving therapy and consulting practice that focuses on the mental training of athletes and others who wish to improve health and performance. Our three initial studies of MSPE with community athletes had just been completed (but not yet published) when Timothy R. Pineau joined our team. Tim came to the lab with nearly a decade of competitive rowing and coaching experience. In addition, while pursuing a double major in clinical psychology and philosophy in college, he nurtured a personal interest in ethics and epistemology, which ultimately led him to the exploration of Eastern philosophical thought. However, Tim did not initially see a way to combine these interests after college and had actually applied to the clinical psychology doctoral program at CUA to pursue psychotherapy integration research. When he interviewed there, Carol asked about his rowing career and began telling him about MSPE. Tim can recall vividly the excitement in the room as they discovered their mutual interests in sport and meditation. This meeting began a fruitful journey, which has led to continued work with Carol and Keith on new MSPE research, and as a clinical psychologist in a college counseling center, Tim works with collegiate athletes and coaches to help them apply mindfulness to their sports and lives.

Our hope is that MSPE and this book help to further interest in research and applications of "third-generation" mindfulness-based approaches in sport, exercise, and performance psychology. We have met so many athletes (and coaches) who know that mental factors such as concentrating, relaxing, and letting go of thoughts and feelings can aid performance but have no idea how to actually do these things under the pressures of training and competition. A notable percentage of these athletes also seem to have a mindset hallmarked by a fear of failure when facing challenges. MSPE provides clear guidance in navigating these challenges, teaching participants how to train key performance facilitators and apply them intentionally within sport and other realms of life, as well as how to shift to a process-oriented (as opposed to outcome-oriented) mentality that can promote higher levels of growth, success, and enjoyment of experiences. Progressive organizations such as The True Athlete Project have begun incorporating MSPE to help improve the culture of achievement in youth athletics, and hopefully this is only the tip of the iceberg as this new way of being is introduced to athletes of all ages and everyone who supports them, including coaches, administrators, parents, trainers, and sport psychologists.

As excited as we are about being at this point in our journey and reaching more people who could benefit from MSPE, we also want to recognize the many individuals along the way who were integral to us getting here. We are deeply grateful to Jon Kabat-Zinn, who took the time to type up his original poster for us that helped serve as the inspiration for MSPE, and to coach Bruce Beall for spending hours on the phone with us in the early days of our work, sharing details of his experience as a rower and coach working with Kabat-Zinn more than 20 years earlier. The assistance of a number of mindfulness experts, athletes, and coaches who agreed to be interviewed for this book is also much appreciated, especially that of Rezvan Ameli. She is Tim Pineau's mindfulness teacher, and he would like to express his sincerest gratitude for her guidance, her insight, and her presence in his life as a true model of a mindful way of living. In addition, our mindful yoga exercise benefitted tremendously from Pamela Kaufman, who developed the yoga routine, and Eileen Twohy, who created the line drawings of the poses.

So many undergraduate and graduate students in our sport psychology lab at CUA provided invaluable help with data collection and entry for MSPE research over the years. We particularly want to thank Lili De Petrillo, Rachel Thompson, and faculty member Diane Arnkoff, who were each deeply involved in early studies of this program.

Also, we are indebted to the current graduate students who consulted with us as we wrote this book, including Josephine Au, Dennis Hoyer, Erin Mistretta, and neuroscience expert Megan Wheeler. Mary Kate Interrante gets special thanks for sharing her experience and observations as a young ballet dancer, and Rokas Perskaudas was indispensable in helping to create the graphic depiction of our FAME profile for athletes and digitally editing the line drawings of the yoga poses. Finally, we are especially grateful to our colleague Claire Spears, who truly went above and beyond to assist in conceptualizing our model and furthering research on MSPE.

Mindful
Sport Performance
Enhancement

Introduction

Kelly was a 38-year-old lawyer and elite distance runner who tended to push herself so hard in races that she'd collapse shortly before the finish line. Jasmine was a 12-year-old middle school and club swimmer who was trying to rediscover a love for her sport while feeling exhausted and unfairly criticized by her coach. Peter was a 21-year-old collegiate pitcher who saw his confidence drop while struggling with accuracy fresh off of Tommy John surgery. Taylor was a 44-year-old collegiate volleyball coach who couldn't get his team to the next level. What do these athletes and coach have in common? They were all striving for something, without full awareness of how to thrive in a present experience they deemed unsatisfactory. And each of them benefitted from training in mindfulness, which helped them to face their respective challenges, embrace process over outcome, and reach new heights in achievement and satisfaction.

Mindfulness is a way of paying attention that entails intentionally being aware of the present moment and accepting things just as they are without judgment. This style of attention is characterized by a sense of equanimity that comes from seeing thoughts, feelings, and sensations as constantly in flux. When able simply to watch such experiences come and go, rather than

http://dx.doi.org/10.1037/0000048-001
Mindful Sport Performance Enhancement: Mental Training for Athletes and Coaches, by K. A. Kaufman, C. R. Glass, and T. R. Pineau

latch on to and overidentify with them, a person has more opportunity to take in the fullness of any given moment. This awareness and acceptance of "what is" ultimately allows for greater responsiveness to the self and environment, providing freedom from the reflexive or automatic reactions that so often guide actions.

Mindful Sport Performance Enhancement

An explosion of interest in mindfulness has spread throughout the field of psychology, including in the domain of sport, exercise, and performance psychology. This book is intended to be a definitive resource on mindfulness and sport, with specific focus on mindful sport performance enhancement (MSPE), one of the leading mindfulness-based mental training programs for athletes and athletic coaches. MSPE evolved in answer to a call for new, more effective interventions within the field of sport psychology. When we were first developing it in 2005, very little consideration had been given to how mindfulness could impact sport performance. A few notable exceptions at that time, each of which is detailed later in this book, were a study by Kabat-Zinn, Beall, and Rippe (1985) that was presented as a conference poster, a 2004 article by Gardner and Moore, and the work of legendary National Basketball Association coach Phil Jackson (1995), who had his championship Bulls and Lakers teams train in mindfulness.

MSPE is a six-session program rooted in the traditions of Kabat-Zinn's mindfulness-based stress reduction and Segal, Williams, and Teasdale's mindfulness-based cognitive therapy, adapted to be unique and specific to athletic populations. Each session includes educational, experiential, discussion, and home practice components, guiding MSPE participants through a structured, easy-to-follow protocol that allows them to learn about mindfulness through their own experience and the experiences of others. Exercises are taught in an intuitive sequence that moves progressively from sedentary practice to mindfulness in motion, culminating in a sport-specific exercise that allows participants to apply the mindfulness techniques from MSPE directly to core skills in their sport (e.g., the putt for golfers, the serve for volleyball players). Special emphasis is also placed on incorporating mindfulness more informally into workouts, practices, and competitions, as well as life beyond sport.

The MSPE protocol can easily be adapted for any sport of interest or for groups (and individuals) representing multiple sports. Our goal with MSPE was to create a program with applicability to any athlete or coach, which teaches not only the fundamentals of this incredibly powerful way to pay attention, but also how to integrate it into real-world training and competitive routines. See Table 1 for an overview of the MSPE protocol.

Over the past decade, we have built a program of research around MSPE with very promising results, studying its impact on coaches and athletes from community, high school, and collegiate settings. Perhaps most exciting are apparent links between MSPE training and the achievement of *flow*, the mental construct often associated with being "in the zone." As word has spread about MSPE, we have received numer-

TABLE 1

Overview of the Mindful Sport Performance Enhancement (MSPE) Protocol

Session	Key concepts	Exercises
Session 1: Building Mindfulness Fundamentals	Defining mindfulness Rationale for MSPE Getting off of automatic pilot	Candy Exercise Diaphragmatic Breathing Sitting Meditation With a Focus on the Breath
Session 2: Strengthening the Muscle of Attention	Overcoming practice obstacles Core performance facilitators Present-moment attention	Body Scan Sitting Meditation With a Focus on the Breath review
Session 3: Stretching the Body's Limits Mindfully	Recognizing the power of expectations The body as a route to awareness	Mindful Yoga Sitting Meditation With a Focus on the Body As a Whole
Session 4: Embracing "What Is" in Stride	Letting go of attachments Acceptance versus resignation	Mindful Yoga review Walking Meditation
Session 5: Embodying the Mindful Performer	Achieving through nonstriving Choice in self-care	Sport Meditation Sitting Meditation With a Focus on the Breath, Body, and Sound
Session 6: Ending the Beginning	Ending MSPE Building an ongoing practice routine	Body Scan review Sport Meditation review

ous requests from around the world for additional information and resources, and new lines of research on MSPE are growing in places as far apart as Tennessee, Iran, and Australia. We thus wrote this book so that sport psychologists, athletes, coaches, psychotherapists with clients who are athletes or performing artists, researchers, educators, and anyone else interested in applications of mindfulness for their own personal fitness or performance can have access to a complete guide to MSPE exercises, materials, and theory. The protocol is presented in its entirety, and no background in psychology, mindfulness, or the sport sciences is required to benefit from the content. Illustrative case studies and reflections on how to get the most from the program as either a participant or a leader are provided to take readers' understanding of MSPE to an even deeper level.

The core performance facilitators targeted in the program are also addressed. Engaging these facilitators helps participants apply the primary characteristics of mindfulness (awareness and acceptance) in a manner that promotes essential self-regulatory strategies (e.g., attention and emotion regulation) and optimal performance experiences, in terms of both achievement and enjoyment. Beyond MSPE itself, this volume explores the concept of mindfulness, reasons why it benefits performance, and strategies for overcoming common barriers to this type of mental training. We also include thorough reviews of the literature on mindfulness and sport to give readers an evidence-based introduction to the science. Because MSPE is one of several empirically based mindfulness interventions available within sport, exercise, and performance psychology, we also offer a broader look at where this movement stands in athletics and other performance realms (e.g., the performing arts) across the globe.

Overview of This Book

This book is divided into four parts, with the nuts and bolts of the MSPE protocol comprising the second part. Part I, Being a Mindful Performer, introduces what mental training in mindfulness involves, as well as the role of mindfulness in sport and promoting optimal performance. Chapter 1 ("Overcoming the Mental Training Paradox") focuses on how to navigate what we call the *mental training paradox*, referring to the widespread phenomenon that, despite general acknowledgment of the importance of the mental game, athletes and coaches rarely dedicate the time to engage in systematic mental practice. Without reconciling this paradox, it is difficult to meet the training recommendations of a program such as MSPE. Chapter 2 ("The Long Past but Short History of Mindfulness in Sport") defines mindfulness, explains how to assess it, and explores the history of the mindful revolution in sport. An in-depth review describes how mindfulness has gained traction in books for athletes as well as in sport psychology interventions and research around the world. Links between mindfulness and performance are considered in Chapter 3 ("Going With the Flow: Mindfulness and Peak Performance"), which discusses theoretical and empirically established connections between mindfulness and crucial performance factors such as flow, attention regulation, and emotion regulation.

In many ways Part II, Mindful Sport Performance Enhancement, is the heart of this book. Chapters 4 through 9 are the MSPE treatment manual, with an entire chapter dedicated to each session of the protocol. These chapters serve as a comprehensive guide, moving the reader through every MSPE concept, exercise, and discussion. Descriptive rationales are provided for each step in the protocol, as are sample scripts of all exercises and examples of discussion questions that could be asked. Recommended home practice assignments and accompanying handouts for every session are available in these chapters and also online, at http://pubs.apa.org/books/supp/kaufman/, and audio recordings of the exercises are available at http://www.mindfulsportperformance.org.

Chapter 4 ("MSPE Session 1: Building Mindfulness Fundamentals") explains how participants are oriented to MSPE and introduces important concepts such as nonjudgment and automatic pilot as well as the first two MSPE exercises focusing on mindful eating and breathing, respectively. Descriptions of the performance facilitators promoted through this mindfulness practice and the MSPE body scan, designed to strengthen bodily awareness and attentional flexibility, occur in Chapter 5 ("MSPE Session 2: Strengthening the Muscle of Attention"). Chapter 6 ("MSPE Session 3: Stretching the Body's Limits Mindfully") presents the MSPE mindful yoga routine, the first incorporation of motion into the training, along with explaining how participants can become more aware of and see beyond their expectations, which are often major determinants of performance.

Chapter 7 ("MSPE Session 4: Embracing 'What Is' in Stride") introduces how participants learn to recognize and work with attachments and limits, as well as the MSPE walking meditation, continuing the progression toward more motive mindfulness practice. Harnessing the power of acceptance and nonstriving are foci in Chapter 8 ("MSPE Session 5: Embodying the Mindful Performer"), as is the most applied MSPE exercise, the sport meditation. This practice encourages the use of movements in a sport as anchors for mindful awareness, thus completing the bridge between the training and actual athletic performance. How to conclude MSPE and help participants build an ongoing practice are covered in Chapter 9 ("MSPE Session 6: Ending the Beginning").

With the protocol unveiled, Part III, Mindful Sport Performance Enhancement: Theory, Research, Practice, and Beyond, takes the reader's understanding of the program to an even deeper level, explaining how and why it works and presenting the evidence base for MSPE, making suggestions for how maximum benefit can be derived, and illustrating implications for new applications in the future. Chapter 10 ("Pathways From MSPE to Peak Performance") explores the performance facilitators cultivated through MSPE, such as concentration (tuning into experience through a present-moment anchor), letting go (getting unstuck from thoughts and emotions), relaxation (identifying and releasing excess tension), establishing a sense of harmony and rhythm (allowing performance to unfold from a still, nonjudgmental mind), and forming key associations that can serve as cues to be mindful. Then, a summary of the research on MSPE to date and proposed future directions are provided in Chapter 11 ("Empirical Support for MSPE").

Chapter 12 ("Tips for Participants: Getting the Most Out of MSPE") highlights the motivational challenges to expect when learning mindfulness and offers suggestions for overcoming those obstacles, based on established behavioral principles and research. Chapter 13 ("Tips for Leaders: Enhancing the Effectiveness of MSPE") describes the essential components and challenges of being an effective MSPE teacher or group leader within the unique domain of athletics. And, as a future direction for the program, Chapter 14 ("Performance Applications Beyond Sport") considers the implications of training musicians, dancers, and actors in MSPE. Existing mindfulness-based interventions in these other performance realms and their empirical support are reviewed to help make the case for expanding MSPE training to other domains.

Finally, to vividly illustrate the MSPE process, Part IV, Case Studies, details the real-life journeys of two participants through the program in their own words. A collegiate baseball player is the subject of Chapter 15 ("Case Study 1: John the Outfielder"), and Chapter 16 ("Case Study 2: Angie the Basketball Coach") focuses on the experiences of a collegiate women's coach.

Programs like MSPE and resources like this book are truly a rarity, and we are excited to be among the leaders of the mindfulness movement in sport, exercise, and performance psychology. We hope that you enjoy the road you are about to embark upon.

BEING A MINDFUL PERFORMER

Overcoming the Mental Training Paradox

1

B aseball legend Yogi Berra famously quipped that "baseball is 90% mental. The other half is physical." Although Berra truly was unique in his ability to make a point through his "Yogi-isms," the sentiment behind this line is one that has been shared by many athletes and sports authorities. For example, in an episode of the Men in Blazers podcast, Cleveland Browns punter Spencer Lanning and Jacksonville Jaguars placekicker Josh Scobee agreed that the percentage of their game that is mental is "104%" (Embassy Row, 2015), and Gia Cillizza (personal communication, January 29, 2015), a highly successful collegiate head field hockey coach, acknowledged that the mental side of the game is "huge." Among sport scientists, Weinberg and Gould (2015) said that a majority of coaches regard sport as at least 50% mental when competition involves opponents of similar physical ability and as much as 80% to 90% mental in certain sports such as golf, tennis, and figure skating. Lynch and Scott (1999) reported asking some of the best elite runners in the United States about the percentage of their daily performance attributable to their level of mental fitness and invariably heard 80% to 90% as well.

http://dx.doi.org/10.1037/0000048-002
Mindful Sport Performance Enhancement: Mental Training for Athletes and Coaches, by K. A. Kaufman, C. R. Glass, and T. R. Pineau

Indeed, sport science appears to support these lofty estimations of the mind's importance. There is ample evidence that psychological, not physical, factors are primarily responsible for the day-to-day fluctuations so characteristic of athletic performance (Weinberg & Gould, 2015). The significance of the mind to performance outcomes may only grow as one rises through the levels of competition and physical capacities (e.g., size, speed, strength) become less distinguishing (e.g., Silva, 1984a). As such, the consistent performance success of transcendent athletes such as Tom Brady or Michael Jordan is probably better explained by their superior mental skills than by any extraordinary physical advantage they may have over their peers.

The Puzzle of the Mental Training Paradox

With popular belief and scientific evidence being in such harmony, one might expect that mental training would be a top priority within the athletic community. However, curiously, this is not the case (e.g., Silva, 1984b; Vealey, 2007). Bruce Beall (personal communication, March 7, 2006), a longtime rowing coach and former Olympian, remarked that coaches like to tell athletes that sport is 95% mental but do not seem to know how to train the mind. Coach Cillizza (personal communication, January 29, 2015) mused that it really is ironic because mental training would be good for the players and the staff. This apparent paradox raises an interesting and crucial question for anyone wanting to undergo or conduct a mental training program in sport: How, in this climate where the mind is widely regarded as important but systematically training it is not, can one create the space and motivation to engage in regular mental practice?

Mindful sport performance enhancement (MSPE) is one of the mental training programs spearheading the proliferation of "third-generation" (sometimes called *third-wave*) mindfulness-based interventions in sport (the "second generation" being traditional cognitive–behavioral approaches). This book provides a comprehensive guide to understanding and using MSPE, along with an introduction to the concept of mindfulness and reviews of the literature on mindfulness and performance. However, before we launch into the details of the program, we believe it is absolutely critical to address this paradox of mental training in sport, why it exists, and how it can be overcome because perhaps the most fundamental factor underlying the efficacy of MSPE is commitment—not just any commitment, but the commitment to practice mindfulness both inside and outside of athletics. Make no mistake, this is no small undertaking. It requires an investment of time and energy as well as a willingness for athletes or coaches to dedicate themselves to something that may be wholly unlike anything they have done before, even if they've previously engaged in other forms of mental training. However, by considering from the start how this commitment can be made, it can open up a world of possibilities for how MSPE can be helpful.

Characterizing Mental Training

Nick Bollettieri, one of the world's preeminent tennis coaches, wrote that, although physical skills are important, mental abilities such as focus, toughness, and quick recovery from setbacks are how the consistent winners defeat their opponents (Ungerleider, 2005). Such abilities, he said, are learnable and worthy of specific training, which defies the common expectation that the mind automatically benefits from physical and tactical training (Ravizza, 1995). Ryan Hilliard (personal communication, January 27, 2015), a high school boys' lacrosse coach, spoke to this expectation, explaining how some coaches think that "with enough [physical] practice, [the body] will develop muscle memory so you don't need mental practice. The mind just takes care of itself." Coach Hilliard admitted he has thought this way himself, and it is one reason why he has not utilized mental training with his athletes.

Various definitions for *mental training* exist, but most of them contain similar elements: the acquisition of psychological strategies through dedicated, methodical, and repeated practice of mental exercises to facilitate effective and healthy functioning in training and competition (e.g., Dosil, 2006; Vealey, 2007; Weinberg & Gould, 2015). Often attached to these definitions in the sport psychology literature are appeals to approach mental training with the same intensity as one approaches physical training (e.g., Dosil, 2006; Lynch & Scott, 1999). After all, few in sport would dispute that physical skills need to be practiced regularly and refined through literally thousands of repetitions (Weinberg & Gould, 2015). Baltzell (2011) noted that people in athletics tend already to be well trained to push themselves physically, technically, and tactically, but many of them are less familiar with the hard work associated with improving in the mental realm of performance. The good news, she added, is that the more consistently one engages in mental training, the more ingrained adaptive mental responses will become in high-pressure situations.

PARACHUTING IN

Thorough reviews of the sport psychology literature have supported the effectiveness of mental training in enhancing athletic performance (e.g., Vealey, 2007). One particularly striking study was conducted by Orlick and Partington (1988), who assessed more than 200 Canadian athletes from the 1984 Olympic Games. Among their findings was that, of the three major readiness factors rated by the athletes (mental, physical, technical), mental readiness provided the only statistically significant link to final Olympic ranking. Mental readiness, these researchers said, results from several learned mental skills that must be practiced continually for an athlete to consistently perform to potential. Furthermore, they concluded that attentional focus and the quality and control of imagery were the most important skills directly related to high-level performance at the Games. Interviews revealed that at least some of these athletes felt that they had already honed their physical and technical skills to perfection up to 4 years before the Games but had not yet learned how to maintain focus in meaningful competitions.

The idea that mental training is its own discipline worthy of study and practice is relatively new to the sport scene. For perspective, during the 1950s, the Soviet Union became the first nation to formally engage in mental training with athletes and coaches, and North America did not catch on until the 1980s (Silva, 2002; Vealey, 2007). It seems reasonable to explain at least some of the stigma that mental training has faced within sport culture by its relative newness, though the passage of time and mounting empirical support have contributed to the lessening of this stigma (e.g., Zillmer & Gigli, 2007). Nonetheless, even those in sport who appreciate its importance tend to regard it as something suited for isolated occasions, when problems arise, and try to "parachute in" mental training in search of a quick fix (Dosil, 2006; Ravizza, 1995; Sinclair & Sinclair, 1994). Of course, such usage goes against the very nature of what quality mental training requires and may produce underwhelming results. Dosil (2006) went so far as to say that, in the majority of cases, dedication to maximum mental development is impractical given sport's current structure.

THE NEED FOR INTEGRATION

For any mental training, including MSPE, to demonstrate its true potential, athletics personnel need to cease parachuting it in and, instead, integrate it into an overall program along with physical and tactical training (e.g., Vealey, 2007). Sinclair and Sinclair (1994) offered one model for providing simultaneous instruction in physical skills and the associated mental skills, suggesting that this combination could benefit learning and retention of the mental skills. In trying to identify solutions to the problem of his coaches not committing to mental training, high school athletics director Dan Checkosky (personal communication, January 21, 2015) highlighted the need for education to help coaches know how to implement it into practices every day, both in and out of season.

The best case example we can turn to for education on this subject is the Soviet Union, which, during the height of its power, developed what is known as an integrated, closed-loop system of training for its athletes. John Silva, a pioneer of sport psychology in the United States, was a member of a 1989 delegation to the Soviet Union and East Germany that had an opportunity to learn about the Soviet system. In a chapter for his 2002 edited book, Silva shared that an important aspect of the Soviet approach was how mental training became embedded in the daily regimen. From the outset, a focus of the system was on understanding and developing psychological principles of performance, which were then applied to athletes competing in national training programs. When these athletes retired from international competition, they returned to the training programs as coaches, completing the closed loop. Silva praised this concept, emphasizing how young athletes were being trained by Olympic medal winners with advanced knowledge of the sport sciences, and he directly linked this system to the incredible dominance of Soviet sport during the mid- to late 20th century (there is a reason the 1980 "Miracle on Ice" U.S. Olympic hockey victory over the Soviet Union is considered among the greatest upsets in American sport history).

For a number of reasons, including obvious political differences, no such system has been developed in the West (Silva, 2002). Looking to the Soviet approach is not an endorsement of state control but rather a way to illustrate the impact mental training can have on performance when it is given the attention traditionally afforded to physical and tactical training. With such integration not being the norm in the current culture of sport, it is important to appreciate the implications of trying to embark upon a program such as MSPE, which requires a significant commitment, and an understanding of the beliefs that perpetuate the mental training paradox.

Factors Sustaining the Mental Training Paradox

The question of what is sustaining the mental training paradox in athletics absolutely fascinates us. Finding the answer seems crucial both for furthering the evolution of sport psychology as a field and, more specifically, for maximizing experiences with MSPE. We thus undertook a thorough exploration of this subject, searching the literature and interviewing a number of authorities across various levels of sport. Three broad explanatory categories were elucidated: perceived lack of time, a knowledge gap, and distrust of the unknown.

PERCEIVED LACK OF TIME

Arguably the most significant impediment to the teaching and practicing of mental skills in sport is the popular sentiment that too little time is available (Weinberg & Gould, 2015). Research on resistance to sport psychology has highlighted the prominent role played by perceived time constraints. For instance, Bull (1991) examined athletes' adherence to a prescribed mental training program and identified beliefs about time limitations as influential to the adherence process. Adherence was generally low, and interviews with the athletes, who notably had volunteered to participate, revealed that they had wanted to do more of the practice but felt unable to fit it into their busy lives. Bull additionally assessed a group of comparable athletes who had chosen not to volunteer for the mental training program and found that 61% of them had labeled insufficient time as the most influential factor in their decision not to participate. Ferraro and Rush (2000) surveyed 20 athletes ranging in status from amateur to professional and similarly concluded that a primary reason these athletes had resisted obtaining sport psychology services was concern about lost time.

Every authority we interviewed about the mental training paradox spoke to the problem of time, providing strong anecdotal support for this explanation as well. Dan Checkosky (personal communication, January 21, 2015) said that, in his experience, people in athletics are not necessarily against mental training. There are "just so many time obstacles" and time is made for what has always been considered most important, that is, the physical. Coaches Cillizza (personal communication, January 29, 2015) and Hilliard (personal communication, January 27, 2015) both described having a compressed practice schedule along with student–athletes who are spread incredibly thin. Therefore, they have focused on what they see as most essential, which includes physical and tactical but not mental training.

Dr. Gary Bennett (personal communication, January 27, 2015), the sport psychology coordinator in a major National Collegiate Athletic Association Division I athletics department, shared his observation that coaches frequently feel there is "no time" to implement mental training with consistency. He empathized with this feeling, saying coaches at that level are "up against the clock and want to use all time available to them for physical training" yet admitted that it can be difficult to "see teams not reaching their potential because of mental mistakes." At the pro level, Ben Olsen (personal communication, February 12, 2015), the head coach of a Major League Soccer team, reported "putting a lot of stock" in mental training but rarely using it, at least in part due to concern that a majority of players would see it as a "waste of time."

One coach we talked to who acknowledged the realities of time constraints in sport but still incorporates mental training "pretty much all the time in [his] regular training sessions" is Edward Brown (personal communication, January 28, 2015), director of an elite academy for soccer goalkeepers. Coach Brown estimated spending 50% to 60% of training time on mental aspects of the game and commented that he is "one of the very few" who does that. He noted that most of his athletes "eat it up" and those athletes and parents who resist tend to espouse the antiquated belief that "if a [player] is not dirty and sweaty, he or she is not working well." The shift in Coach Brown's training approach occurred after he saw that his athletes did not know how to "do" the mental skills that are key to handling the pressures of the position. He found that "the idea of [physical] work, work, work and correcting technique on the fly didn't work for [his] goalkeepers." Coach Brown reflected that his approach has gotten great results, to the point that he can now turn away 60% to 70% of the athletes who want to attend his academy. Yet, when he has spoken to his coaching mentors about the quantity of time he devotes specifically to mental training, they have "gotten upset with [him]," saying that his philosophy is "not right."

Coach Brown's experience of breaking away from a coaching tradition that he realized was flawed may provide valuable insight into addressing the lack-of-time justification for forgoing mental training. There is little doubt that time is precious when it comes to ensuring readiness in sport. However, it seems odd to give the vast majority of this limited resource to domains of training that, as Orlick and Partington (1988) discovered, may already be fairly well established in seasoned athletes—to the exclusion of a domain that could make the crucial difference between performance success and failure. If it is impossible to somehow manufacture more time, as so many authorities in sport claim, perhaps the solution involves a shuffling of priorities. To be clear, we are not proposing the neglect of physical or tactical training through the promotion of mental training but, rather, a more balanced division of available time among these three domains. Reserving even a few minutes daily to build specific mental skills could greatly benefit sport performance (e.g., Lynch & Scott, 1999). Of course, being willing to reprioritize in this way requires knowledge of what mental training is and how to teach it.

A KNOWLEDGE GAP

Another substantial barrier to the proliferation of systematic mental training in athletics is the apparent knowledge gap, which stems from a history of overlooking preparation in this area. Within athletics, there is a great deal of unawareness and misinformation about what training the mind involves as well as how to teach the relevant skills, a fact that sport scientists have become painfully aware of. Silva (2002) lamented that the very people sport psychologists should be serving know little about mental training, how to conduct it, or ways to find someone who can help them get started. He predicted that asking the average coach or athletics director to name five sport psychologists would reveal that they cannot identify a single one. Dosil (2006) echoed this viewpoint, saying that the distance between sport psychologists and their would-be clientele is principally the result of ignorance regarding the potential of mental training, what it consists of, and how it is carried out.

Part of the blame for this knowledge gap has to fall on the sport psychology profession for not promoting its services adequately to target markets. In its defense, sport psychology is one of the youngest branches on the psychology tree, still facing some fairly significant stigma, and psychologists are notoriously uncomfortable with advertising (Fifer, Henschen, Gould, & Ravizza, 2008). However, there is little doubt that the field must do a better job of raising awareness. Much of the remaining responsibility appears to belong to athletics, which has a reputation as a closed-off culture that tends to resist change from the establishment (e.g., Reed, 2013). There seems to be a pattern of coaches teaching the next generation essentially what they have been taught, which may hinder the spread of new ideas such as the importance of learning and integrating mental training. Weinberg and Gould (2015) listed being uninformed as a top cause of the underutilization of mental training in sport.

Most of the administrators and coaches we spoke to also brought up the knowledge gap as an explanation for the mental training paradox. Dan Checkosky (personal communication, January 21, 2015) remarked that training in sports has "historically been about the Xs and Os. It hasn't focused on the mind." Therefore, he continued, coaches "don't have the tools, don't have the knowledge" about mental training to pass along to their athletes. He mentioned the example of a basketball coach instructing an athlete to "focus" before an important foul shot, "but what is the athlete supposed to do with that? The need to focus is common knowledge, but knowledge is lacking about how to teach it. What has been taught is the physical."

Coach Hilliard (personal communication, January 27, 2015) agreed that "you know what you know and can't teach what you don't know." He noted that coaches are required to take certain courses to be employed in his school district and none of those classes address principles of mental training. Coach Cillizza (personal communication,

January 29, 2015) said that "for most coaches my age and older, [the mental] was not part of our training." She continued, "We know that it's important because most of us were athletes and it was important to us too, but many of us were not trained. We may have read some articles, but don't exactly feel positioned [to teach it]." For further context, Coach Cillizza is a relatively young coach, having played Division I field hockey herself in the late 1990s.

Again, Edward Brown (personal communication, January 28, 2015) has found himself somewhat unconventional, this time in terms of his handling of the knowledge gap. He explained how, when he played soccer, his three main coaches all worked with the United States National Team and he was "taught great stuff, but never taught 'the why' on anything [pertaining to his mental game]." As described earlier, Coach Brown has received disapproval from these mentors for his emphasis on mental preparation with his players. Their rationale, Coach Brown said, is that, "for them, it comes down to my coach taught me like this, so it should be this way." For this reason, he observed, "there have been few advances in coaching the [soccer goalkeeper] position since the 1920s," something he is trying to change.

Barry Meuse (personal communication, January 27, 2015), president of and longtime coach within a Little League Baseball organization, expressed a similar desire to move beyond what has always been done. He recently sought guidance on the provision of mental training to his coaches and athletes and indicated that his ambition is to strengthen their "hands, heart, and head." Meuse admitted that it is "the head part I lack knowledge on. I know some basics like it's important to focus while playing baseball, but I don't know how to teach it, or to help my coaches teach it to their players."

What is so refreshing about Meuse's approach is that he knows what he does not know and has actively pursued education. This kind of openness within athletics is essential to bridging the knowledge gap. Equally important is that sport psychologists do more to make educational opportunities available and accessible. Coach Hilliard (personal communication, January 27, 2015) had an interesting suggestion for how to spread credible information about mental training: A school or organization, for example, could provide a Mental Training 101 course to coaches and perhaps offer some type of teaching or coaching recertification credit as incentive for attendance. Including mental training as a standard component of a curriculum for coaches, athletes, and others in sport seems like a sound strategy for promoting awareness of and comfort with these techniques so they are less of a mystery.

DISTRUST OF THE UNKNOWN

The final major explanation we uncovered for the mental training paradox is misgivings about what accessing and exercising the mind will do to an athlete (e.g., Vealey, 2007). This distrust seems to exist on at least three levels: (a) the current knowledge gap often necessitates outside consulting (in the form of a sport psychologist) that exposes athletes to a potentially powerful voice other than the coach's, (b) there is apprehension about going into the mind of an athlete due to concern about what will happen, and (c) the science behind mental training is so young that it is difficult to know what to trust.

Distrust of Outsiders

Silva (2002) addressed this first level of distrust, proposing that, because most Western coaches are not trained in a competitive or educational system that emphasizes and integrates the sport sciences, they are frequently reluctant to allow someone else to have such an influential role with their athletes. Coach Ben Olsen shared this assessment:

> A reason why a coach may believe in mental training, yet still not do it is you have to trust somebody quite a bit. You are entrusting your team to this [sport psychologist] and want to be sure the messages are right, that there are no mixed messages [from what the coach is saying]. I think ego plays into it as well . . . like [asserting] *I* am the coach and don't need help understanding my players. (personal communication, February 12, 2015)

Zillmer and Gigli (2007) identified this brand of distrust as one of the many misconceptions that athletes and coaches have about sport psychology.

Hardy, Jones, and Gould (1996) suggested that this skepticism of sport psychologists could be exacerbated, especially at elite levels of sport, by coaches and athletes getting so used to being approached by outsiders with a personal agenda. Partington and Orlick (1987) interviewed a group of Canadian Olympic coaches and found that two types of sport psychology consultants were viewed as particularly disreputable— what they termed the "shrink" and the "ivory tower" researcher. The shrink type was perceived as seeing personality problems everywhere and his or her services as the only cure. Some coaches were suspicious of such consultants, believing they could foster dependency among the athletes rather than mental strength. The ivory tower researcher type was seen as reliant upon time-consuming assessments that generally provided no useful feedback to athletes and coaches.

It certainly makes sense that coaches want to manage the messages received by their athletes and are wary of outside professionals from a foreign discipline who could be unqualified, out for themselves, or peddling an unhelpful service. However, it seems like the baby is being thrown out with the bath water, so to speak, with mental training being neglected altogether because of this distrust. Even with the reservations they expressed about some types of sport psychologists, there was consensus among the Olympic coaches that high-quality consultants do exist and they possess characteristics such as positivity, confidence, the capability of working with athletes and coaches without being intrusive, and a commitment to assisting in ways that are practical and individualized (Partington & Orlick, 1987),

Distrust of Emotions

In his classic book *The Inner Game of Tennis*, Gallwey (1974) observed that many people gravitate to sport to obtain needed relief from the pressures of life. However, setting lofty standards of excellence for themselves leads to the experience of more frustration and tension while playing rather than less, a pattern reflecting an underlying equation between self-worth and performance that is nearly universal. Gallwey admitted that this is a pretty heavy equation and wondered what else could cause a sport to assume such importance that it elicits conditions such as anxiety, anger, depression, and self-doubt.

Sport breeds emotions, powerful ones that can have a significant impact on performance and well-being. Yet, as Zillmer and Gigli (2007) pointed out, there is a resistance to psychology in much of the athletic community, which prides itself on toughness and is more comfortable with *doing* than getting in touch with feelings. Ferraro and Rush (2000) proposed that this resistance is actually about a fear of facing emotions. Athletes are masters of their bodies but not their emotions and may perceive the release of affect through words, rather than movements, as a daunting task that they would prefer to avoid. Ferraro and Rush added that sport psychology's emphasis on performance enhancement does not fool those in athletics, who know that the tasks involved in mental training are not the familiar physical ones.

Coach Olsen (personal communication, February 12, 2015) listed this discomfort as one of the reasons he does not incorporate more mental training with his team. He said that coaches are generally reluctant to "dive too deep into a player's mind" and believe it is better not to "dissect" what is being thought or felt. If an athlete is struggling mentally, he continued, "Going too deep can be harmful. Sometimes particular players need to think less, rely on instincts, rather than overanalyze who they are, what they are about."

As Coach Olsen suggested, this perspective is not uncommon. However, it made us wonder whether he and other coaches would take the same approach if an athlete were struggling physically or tactically. Would the technique of choice be to avoid training the athlete in these areas out of concern that he or she might get overwhelmed? That is hard to imagine. Perhaps just as those in athletics take pride in their physical and tactical resilience, facing emotions could be pursued as a badge of honor, and one that could yield impressive training gains.

Distrust of Something New

Sport psychology is a young field, which understandably is still experiencing growing pains as it comes into its own (Silva, 2002; Weinberg & Gould, 2015). With the explosion of global communication, there are few places to hide when something goes awry, and unfortunately certain challenges the field has encountered have managed to sour some people in athletics on mental training. Believe it or not, one of the significant issues the field has had is agreeing on what, precisely, the term *sport psychologist* means. As Noren (2014) stated, the title of sport psychologist can be misleading, as the profession uniquely blends two otherwise independent disciplines (psychology and exercise science) that have very different educational requirements. Thus, consumers seeking a sport psychologist do not necessarily know if they are getting a kinesiologist, a licensed psychologist, or someone else.

Silva (2002) traced this confusion back to the 1980s, when many individuals flocked to the field from related professions without adequate training and ended up providing subpar services in a highly public fashion (e.g., surrounding the Olympics). Since that time, efforts have been made to establish standards of entry into sport psychology, with governing organizations such as the Association for Applied Sport Psychology developing a certification process. Although authors such as Stapleton, Hankes, Hays, and Parham (2010) have highlighted competence as an ethical imperative, to some extent the public relations damage has already been done, and the field is still trying to recover. Hopefully, as quality control continues to improve, athletics personnel will more consistently know what they are getting when they hire a sport psychologist, resulting in increased openness to mental training.

It seems worthy of mention that emerging technologies, while exciting in their possibilities, may also be setting back the reputation of mental training. B. Goodman (2015) identified athletes as big users of brain-game applications to gain a mental edge but explained how a startling number of them think these games do not live up to the hype. Scientists investigating the validity of these games appear to agree, and Goodman reported that an international coalition penned an October 2014 open letter to caution consumers that the claims made by brain-game companies are not yet scientifically proven. According to Goodman, brain games have blossomed into a billion-dollar business and one of the fastest-growing segments of the technology market. Thus, there is a need to draw a clear distinction for people in sport between these questionable brain games and the less well-known but more scientifically credible mental training conducted by competent sport psychologists.

As the brain-game phenomenon demonstrates, it is not necessarily difficult to get people in athletics interested in mental training. The problem, as Dan Checkosky (personal communication, January 21, 2015) noted, is "getting them to take action" in a more systematic way. Checkosky was a key figure in bringing MSPE training to his high school, but he acknowledged that it "took six suicides in 4 years to get [us as a department] to go and try this." Athletes were overrepresented among the suicides at Checkosky's school, prompting him and others there to take the more assertive step of introducing mindfulness to better address their athletes' mental health. Hopefully, in the future, greater openness to mental training will not need to be facilitated by crisis, but the reality is that beginning a mindfulness program such as MSPE is a serious undertaking and those looking to do so should know the kind of commitment involved.

Understanding the Commitment Required for Mental Training in Mindfulness

EMBRACING THE THIRD GENERATION

Dealing with the mental training paradox when offering traditional cognitive–behavioral approaches for athletes is already a substantial challenge, and now introducing different "third-generation" mindfulness-based interventions (which we discuss at length in the following chapter) adds further complexity to the dynamic. For years, the emphasis for those coaches and athletes learning about or engaged in mental training has been on controlling and limiting maladaptive thoughts and emotions (e.g., replacing negative thoughts with more positive ones). However, the emergence of ideas such as Wegner's (1994) "ironic processes of mental control," which suggests that attempts to suppress a mental event may paradoxically reinforce it, has ushered in a different way of conceiving mental training. So, just when some in athletics may have been growing more comfortable with established techniques such as self-talk and visualization, the landscape has begun to shift toward the development of additional skills that are departures from the old, such as awareness and acceptance of whatever is happening in the present moment.

In addition to its philosophical underpinnings, the actual practice of mindfulness also looks quite different from traditional sport psychology approaches. Building the capacity to pay attention mindfully, that is, "on purpose, in the present moment, and nonjudgmentally" (Kabat-Zinn, 1994, p. 4), often involves a dedicated contemplative practice. Such practice can entail simply being mindful (i.e., engaging in daily activities with the intention of staying present) or more formal activities, such as meditation. Mentioning the term *meditation* can sometimes evoke strong reactions in athletics. As Dan Checkosky (personal communication, January 21, 2015) said, "Meditation is a word that people [in athletics] don't like to hear." He thought that avoiding this specific buzzword could be important when pitching mindfulness to those in sport. Kabat-Zinn has also acknowledged how polarizing the word *meditation* can be, instead structuring his mindfulness-based stress reduction program and its packaging to minimize the risk of its being viewed as Buddhist, new age, mystical, or flaky (Wylie, 2015). We have made similar efforts with MSPE, as will hopefully become evident as you continue to read this book, by designing our exercises to be directly applicable to what participants encounter in their sport.

NOT PARACHUTING IN

Marks (2008) commented that one way to conceptualize the benefit that mindfulness or related meditation practices can afford those in athletics is to see it as mental efficiency training. He explained how, through the repeated act of attention regulation in contemplative practice, the athletic performer can begin to automate a process of detecting and directing focus to a target stimulus without missing other relevant data from the environment or inside the body. Indeed, research like that done by Brefczynski-Lewis, Lutz, Schaefer, Levinson, and Davidson (2007) has shown that with continued practice over time, meditation may result in a less cognitively active (i.e., quieter) mental state in which tasks performed after meditating may become less effortful (i.e., require fewer cognitive resources without compromising performance). We have heard numerous athletes and coaches say that they aspire to perform with an empty mind, something that is probably impossible given the nature of human thought. What they may be getting at, however, is this idea of enhanced efficiency, of performing with a mind that stays calm and clear even while totally immersed in the chaotic happenings of a sporting event. Gallwey (1974) termed this skill "unfreak-ability" (meaning the opposite of freaking out).

It should be noted that research on the neural correlates of mindfulness is still in its early days, and far more data are needed to establish firm conclusions, but it is easy to get captivated by these glimpses into the potential of the mindful brain (Marks, 2008), which we discuss further in Chapter 3. What we want to highlight here, though, is the less dazzling fine print accompanying these initial findings, which is the need for sus-tained practice to achieve these results. This is where the mental training paradox can become the thorn on the rose.

In his landmark book *Full Catastrophe Living*, Kabat-Zinn (1990) compared the commitment asked of those engaged in mindfulness training with that required in physical training for sport. He noted that athletes preparing for a competition do not practice only when they feel like it or when conditions are ideal. Rather, they work nearly every day, regardless of the weather, boredom, stress, fatigue, or other situational factors. Just as when building the body, having the discipline to persevere in the process is essential to developing mindfulness. In his more recent book *Mindfulness for Beginners*, Kabat-Zinn (2012) characterized this process as the hardest work in the world. He framed it as nothing short of a lifestyle, a way of being, that, if not treated as such, can easily generate the negative and defiant reactions associated with the felt obligation to squeeze yet more out of an already packed schedule.

Talk about not parachuting in! Kabat-Zinn is essentially saying that someone might gravitate to mindfulness to help with something like pain management, stress reduction, or performance enhancement, but seeing it as a means to an end that can just be pulled out when problems flare up will almost certainly be ineffective and likely counterproductive. We echo this sentiment for users of MSPE, particularly given the resistance to mental training that currently exists in sport. For mindfulness training to have maximum benefit, it is crucial to incorporate it into a daily routine (e.g., Kabat-Zinn, 1990), whether it feels necessary at a given time or not. A simile we like to use is that waiting to practice mindfulness skills until you need them is like trying to learn how to swim when you are already drowning. That simply does not work.

This is not to say that MSPE participants must follow our treatment manual to the letter or else it will not benefit them. On the contrary, we repeatedly empha-size making this program your own, fitting it into life in whatever ways work. Undoubtedly, however, some lifestyle change is going to be necessary to make space for daily practice, and participants need to be prepared for that reality. We recog-nize not only the necessity but also the difficulty of this kind of change, and, as such, we share in Chapter 12 a number of tips for MSPE participants to establish a regular practice and to get the most out of the program. Throughout MSPE, we also reference powerful descriptors of the mindfulness training process in performance domains, such as Stanley and Jha's (2009) "mental armor" and Coach Bruce Beall's (personal communication, March 7, 2006) "mental weight lifting," to help inspire the necessary commitment.

SUCCESS STORIES: COMMITTING TO
A CULTURE OF MINDFULNESS

A small number of elite-level teams have been progressive enough to include mindfulness as a key element of training. Perhaps it is not a coincidence that each of these teams has attained at least one championship while committing to this approach and has credited mindfulness as a major ingredient in its success. At this juncture, we hope to whet your appetite for what you will learn in the next chapter about the mindful revolution in sports.

The figure perhaps most associated with bringing mindfulness to his teams is the Zen master himself, former Chicago Bulls and Los Angeles Lakers coach Phil Jackson. Coach Jackson wrote about introducing mindfulness to his players in his 1995 book *Sacred Hoops* and his 2013 book *Eleven Rings*, the latter title, of course, referring to the number of National Basketball Association championship teams he has coached. He explained how, with the Bulls, he developed a routine of having the players sit and meditate for about 10 minutes during practice, wanting them to take a more mindful approach to what was happening on the court and to their relationships with one another. Sometimes, he said, they would extend mindfulness practice to the court itself and run whole practices in silence. He remarked that doing so evoked a level of concentration and nonverbal communication that never failed to astonish him. Coach Jackson shared how, when he took over the Lakers in 1999, they were a highly talented but unfocused group that had been underachieving in the playoffs. He felt that tactical adjustments would not address those players' real problem, which was to quiet the chatter in their minds while trying to play in the heart of celebrity culture, so he began incorporating a similar mindfulness practice with that team.

To help facilitate this training with both the Bulls and the Lakers, Coach Jackson brought in sport psychology consultant George Mumford, who taught mindfulness as a way of life, what he called "meditation off the cushion" (P. Jackson, 2013). As one might expect in this culture of the mental training paradox, the reactions among the players were mixed, with some taking it to heart and others using the sitting time as an opportunity to nap. Coach Jackson noted, however, that one athlete who was impressed with the mindfulness training was Michael Jordan, who believed it helped his teammates get closer to his own level of mental awareness.

The Seattle Seahawks' Pete Carroll is another highly successful coach who has used mindfulness with his team. According to an article by Delehanty (2014), Coach Carroll believes in immersing his players in distractions to train them to quiet their minds in the midst of chaos. He said that mindfulness is the way his team operates, focusing on what is right in front of them as if it is the most important thing in the world. Like Phil Jackson, Coach Carroll brought in a sport psychologist with a strong background in mindfulness to help instill this perspective. Futterman (2015) described how Dr. Michael Gervais spent 3 days per week with the team for the most recent few seasons, floating around and talking with coaches and players about their lives and performances. As with the Bulls and Lakers, not everyone bought in, but assistant coach Tom Cable characterized the team as incredibly mindful and observed his own improved ability to know and get the best from his players (Futterman, 2015). All-pro quarterback Russell Wilson said that this form of preparation helped him to feel more relaxed during games, and all-pro offensive tackle Russell Okung commented that meditation is as important to his success as weight lifting and being out on the practice field (Roenigk, 2013).

One final example is former Chelsea Football Club manager Carlo Ancelotti, who, during his time with that English soccer team, hired sport psychologist Bruno Demichelis to develop a "Mind Room" for his players. Burt (2009) explained that they had constructed a similar space while working together at Italian club AC Milan, and the aim of it was to train players to reach a meditative state in which they could watch themselves make a mistake without experiencing a physiological reaction such as increased heart rate. He quoted Dr. Demichelis as saying that learning how to be aware and accepting of whatever happens in this manner can strengthen players' resilience. Chelsea won both the English Premier League and the FA Cup in the season Dr. Demichelis joined them, and a CBC News story ("Canucks Sued," 2013) cited his belief that the Mind Room was instrumental to those achievements.

Making Mindfulness a Part of Your Training Routine

As the previous examples illustrate, it is very possible to integrate mindfulness training into an athletic culture with great success. The key is to make it a part of what is done on an ongoing basis to prepare for competition, something the Bulls and Lakers, Seahawks, and Chelsea were all able to accomplish in different ways. Coach Olsen (personal communication, February 12, 2015) admitted that it takes a particular kind of coach to make that type of investment in mental training, one whose approach is less concrete, more "analytical." He said he personally wishes he "played for a more unconventional coach like Phil Jackson because [he is] also of that mind . . . [but] even coaches [like himself] that believe in it still don't do it a lot [of the time]." What a powerful articulation of the mental training paradox as it can apply specifically to mindfulness!

MSPE is unique in being one of the first mindfulness-based intervention programs available that was developed especially for sport performers. As you will discover in Part II of this book, the program guides participants step-by-step in cultivating fundamental mindfulness skills and then executing those skills within their athletic endeavors. Our research and experiences with the program have made us quite excited about its potential, and we believe that MSPE can help participants' levels of play and enjoyment reach new heights. However, there is far less chance this training—or any mental training program—will benefit participants if they are not committed to putting in the necessary work.

K. Anders Ericsson, whose efforts have famously become linked with the "10,000 hours" or "10 year" rule for the achievement of expertise, wrote that it is the commitment to deliberate practice that distinguishes elite performers from the masses of others who struggle to meet their performance demands (Ericsson, Krampe, & Tesch-Römer, 1993). As Sinclair and Sinclair (1994) observed, this concept is well understood in athletics with regard to technical, tactical, and physical fitness requirements, but equal resolve must be dedicated to the development of desired mental skills in all practice sessions. Several of Coach Cillizza's field hockey players have taken part in an MSPE training, and she (G. Cillizza, personal communication, January 29, 2015) conveyed her sense that, for a program such as MSPE to be most effective, it has to be integrated by a coach into what is being done throughout the entire season.

Worthwhile change is rarely easy, so we advise beginning to think now about how you can address any biases you might hold related to the mental training paradox or engagement in mindfulness practice and make space for a new way of approaching sport. In the next chapter, we offer an in-depth review of the broader field of mindfulness in sport to provide context for the development of and research on MSPE.

The Long Past but Short History of Mindfulness in Sport

2

A s early as the 1950s, mindfulness was connected to sport by the philosopher Eugen Herrigel in his book, *Zen in the Art of Archery* (1953). Although not an athlete, Herrigel used traditional Japanese archery as a means to advance his journey toward an understanding of Zen. This notable book describes how he integrated breathing into the steps of his shot, creating a rhythmic sequence that he could perform with a kind of effortless strength. Herrigel spoke of becoming empty and rid of the self, becoming as one with the process of shooting an arrow.

Coaches also have espoused mindfulness principles for a long time, without referring to them as such. For instance, in their book *Total Archery*, Lee and de Bondt (2005) argued that mental training to cope with distractions, refocus after errors, and deal with expectations is essential to effective performance. They suggested learning to let thoughts move in and out of the mind, breathe diaphragmatically, and attend to and relax muscle groups as well as accept distractions and move on—all elements of training in mindfulness. Similarly, in interviews with long-time rival coaches Dean Smith and Mike Krzyzewski (Blythe, 2006), both emphasized the importance of being in the present moment during practices and games, focusing on process rather than

http://dx.doi.org/10.1037/0000048-003
Mindful Sport Performance Enhancement: Mental Training for Athletes and Coaches, by K. A. Kaufman, C. R. Glass, and T. R. Pineau

outcome, and letting go of what is uncontrollable—each a key aspect of mindfulness. Yet, none of these coaching stalwarts mentioned mindfulness by name.

Coaches are not the only ones who have been aware of the value of mindfulness concepts for sport. In his 2004 book, *The Golfer's Mind: Play to Play Great*, well-known sport psychologist Bob Rotella talked about the significance of letting go of memories of shots, staying in the present, accepting what happens without judgment, and looking for rhythm in the game. Former tennis player and instructor and now renowned performance psychology author Timothy Gallwey (1981, 1997) highlighted mental skills that allow athletes to achieve peak performance through not overthinking so that the "mind [be] so concentrated, so focused, that it is still" (Gallwey, 1997, p. 8). To quiet the mind, he said, athletes must learn nonjudgmental acceptance of what is, letting go of the tendency to assign value to a performance as either bad or good. Along with this skill comes awareness and observation of what is happening in the present (e.g., the feel of the racket). Awareness and acceptance are at the very heart of mindfulness, yet neither Rotella nor Gallwey specifically branded these principles in that way.

Over the past decade, the term *mindfulness* has become more prevalent in the athletics lexicon as the "mindful revolution" has spread like wildfire throughout the field of psychology and into the world of sport. For example, popular endurance sport author Matt Fitzgerald emphatically stated in his 2010 book that "mindfulness must be trained in running just as it must be cultivated in life" (p. 10), and Sakyong Mipham (2012), an internationally known spiritual leader who has applied the principles of mindfulness to running, made a similar point, calling his fitness program "running with the mind of meditation."

Part of what may be helping the concept of mindfulness to gain traction in sport is that, as discussed in Chapter 1, elite-level teams, from Phil Jackson's Bulls and Lakers to Pete Carroll's Seahawks, have incorporated mindfulness training with striking, title-winning success. In describing his philosophy of mindful basketball, Coach Phil Jackson (1995) wrote,

> To excel, you need to act with a clear mind and be totally focused on what *everyone* on the floor is doing. . . . The secret is *not thinking*. That doesn't mean being stupid; it means quieting the endless jabbering of thoughts so that your body can do instinctively what it's been trained to do without the mind getting in the way . . . completely immersed in the moment, inseparable from what we're doing. (pp. 115–116)

And George Mumford (2015), the sport psychology consultant who gained fame for his work with Phil Jackson's teams, outlined keys to being a mindful athlete: mindfulness, concentration, insight, bringing right effort or diligence, and trust.

The United States Olympic Committee has also become heavily involved in mindfulness training. One of its senior sport psychologists, Peter Haberl (2016), stated that mindfulness is his "guiding paradigm" in helping athletes train for and cope with the stress of performing in the Olympic Games. We had a chance to speak with him about these efforts, and he said that mindfulness is now "pretty much the whole focus" of what he does with his athletes (P. Haberl, personal communication, August 18,

2015). Influenced by the work of Jon Kabat-Zinn, Haberl's training targets skills to build attention and awareness.

In this chapter, we explore the concept of mindfulness, including definitions, assessment, and how it is thought to foster change. We discuss the broader, ongoing mindful revolution and the interventions on which many current mindfulness approaches for athletic performers, including mindful sport performance enhancement (MSPE), are based. Then, we review the history of mindfulness in sport to date, highlighting key empirical contributions from around the world. We feel that the wider context presented here is important in a book about MSPE because it facilitates an understanding of how and why the program was developed, along with its significance to this rapidly emerging field.

What Is Mindfulness?

Mindfulness is derived from a word in early Buddhist scriptures reflecting awareness and presence of mind, whereby impermanent external and internal phenomena are viewed as they exist at a given moment (Chiesa & Malinowski, 2011). As we introduced in Chapter 1, the definition most often used in current psychological applications stems from Eastern traditions and involves intentionally paying attention to the present moment in a nonjudgmental way (Kabat-Zinn, 1994). There is also "an affectionate, compassionate quality within [this] attending" (Kabat-Zinn, 2003, p. 145), as well as an attitude of openness, acceptance, and curiosity (Bishop et al., 2004). Although this conceptualization of mindfulness has Buddhist roots, its applications in modern psychology generally have been secularized.

This Eastern perspective underlies most mindfulness-based approaches to enhancing sport performance (including MSPE) and often suggests formal meditation practice (e.g., from Vipassana and Zen traditions) to strengthen mindfulness skills. However, it is important to note that meditation and mindfulness are not synonymous, just as mindfulness is not relaxation. Mindfulness interventions that do not rely on meditation practice can incorporate cognitive defusion, informal practice of maintaining awareness, and an accepting attitude during daily activities (Hayes & Shenk, 2004). Cognitive defusion helps with the detection of thoughts and seeing them as interpretations rather than literal facts about yourself or the world. For example, an athlete could identify that "right now, I'm having the thought that I can't finish this race," so rather than reflecting an objective truth, it's seen as just a thought. Regardless of what the skills practice involves, the focus of Eastern-rooted mindfulness training is having contact with events in a present-focused, conscious, and nonjudgmental way (Hayes & Plumb, 2007).

Langer (1989) offered a different, social–psychological view of mindfulness as "a flexible state of mind in which we are actively engaged in the present, noticing new things and sensitive to context" (Langer, 2000, p. 220). This engagement entails observing the context in which one acts, actively processing new information, and recognizing that stimuli can be seen from multiple perspectives. This approach focuses primarily on awareness of the situational context and encourages an active reinterpretation of the present moment, whereas the Eastern perspective that underlies MSPE is not goal-directed and puts greater emphasis on internal stimuli and processes (e.g., awareness of thoughts and feelings). Fatemi, Ward, and Langer (2016) discussed the relevance of Langerian mindfulness to flow and peak performance, and we have previously considered how this "mental flexibility" can affect athletes (Pineau, Glass, & Kaufman, 2014).

ASSESSMENT OF MINDFULNESS

Although mindfulness is typically regarded as a moment-to-moment process, most existing measures capture it as a dispositional, habitual trait or tendency to be mindful. A number of scales have been developed to assess dispositional mindfulness, and the Five Facet Mindfulness Questionnaire (Baer, Smith, Hopkins, Krietemeyer, & Toney, 2006; Baer et al., 2008) and Mindful Attention Awareness Scale (MAAS; K. W. Brown & Ryan, 2003) are frequently used in research (see Sauer et al., 2013, for a review). The Langer Mindfulness/Mindlessness Scale (Bodner & Langer, 2001) assesses Langer's construct of mindfulness in four domains.

State mindfulness measures have also been developed to capture the experience of being mindful, such as the State-MAAS (K. W. Brown & Ryan, 2003), the Toronto Mindfulness Scale (Lau et al., 2006), and, most recently, the State Mindfulness Scale (Tanay & Bernstein, 2013).

MECHANISMS OF MINDFULNESS

For someone who does not know what mindfulness is, it is reasonable to wonder how increased mindfulness helps improve psychological functioning. One thought is that these approaches systematically retrain awareness and nonreactivity, leading to defusion and decentering from experiences rather than habitual reactions to them. What comes into the mind (e.g., feelings, thoughts) is observed merely as a psychological event (Fresco et al., 2007), similar to what Chambers, Gullone, and Allen (2009) termed *mindful emotion regulation*; see Z. E. Moore (2016) for a discussion of mindfulness and athletes' emotion regulation. A nonjudgmental attitude lessens the avoidance of inner experience and strengthens both psychological flexibility and distress tolerance (for a focus on mindfulness, distress tolerance, and self-compassion in sport, see Baltzell, 2016b).

Mindfulness-based approaches thus allow individuals to better tolerate or react differently to experiences such as anxiety, whereas cognitive–behavioral interventions may try to reduce the experiences themselves. On the basis of their three-component model of mindfulness, which includes attention, attitude, and intention (why one is practicing mindfulness), Shapiro, Carlson, Astin, and Freedman (2006) proposed that intentionally attending nonjudgmentally and with openness will create what they call *reperceiving*, a significant shift in perspective that may, in turn, help facilitate self-regulation, values clarification, cognitive–behavioral flexibility, and exposure. Research offers a number of psychological processes that could be potential mediators underlying the effects of mindfulness-based interventions on psychological functioning, including self-compassion, psychological flexibility, awareness, decentering and defusion, attentional control, acceptance, exposure, behavioral self-regulation, and values clarification, in addition to reducing cognitive and emotional reactivity (the extent to which stress coupled with mild distress can reactivate patterns of emotions and negative thinking), rumination, and worry (Gu, Strauss, Bond, & Cavanagh, 2015; Keng, Smoski, & Robins, 2011; Kuyken et al., 2010).

Similarly, Z. E. Moore and Gardner (2014), developers of the mindfulness–acceptance–commitment (MAC) approach (e.g., Gardner & Moore, 2007) for enhancing human performance, drew on many of these processes in proposing that a combination of four mindfulness mechanisms results in greater emotion regulation and thus a more flexible approach to performance: enhanced capacity for and regulation of attention, better awareness of internal experience (e.g., thoughts, feelings, body sensations), decentering from internal processes, and fewer automatic connections between cognitions/emotions and behavior.

The Mindful Revolution

The explosion of interest in mindfulness for sport performers derives, in part, from the current fascination with mindfulness throughout the field of psychology and society at large. Mindfulness has become a major media buzzword. For example, a *TIME Magazine* cover story (Pickert, 2014) discussed "The Mindful Revolution," and a *Huffington Post* article immediately followed, proclaiming that *TIME* had hit only the tip of the iceberg (Gregoire, 2014). More recently, *TIME Magazine* released an entire special edition on September 2, 2016, dedicated to mindfulness, reflecting a desire to uncover and explore even more of the iceberg.

Research on mindfulness has also seen exponential growth since the 1990s. Systematic reviews and meta-analyses show that mindfulness training significantly improves psychological outcomes such as stress and anxiety, emotionality, and depression (Goyal et al., 2014; Khoury et al., 2013; Sedlmeier et al., 2012). In addition, mindfulness has been incorporated into successful interventions for physical health, pain, eating behavior, and substance use (e.g., Chiesa & Serretti, 2014; Veehof, Oskam, Schreurs, & Bohlmeijer, 2011)—all relevant for our focus on mindfulness for athletic performers. Overall, research on mindfulness reflects a convergence with a surge of interest in positive psychology, including attention, well-being, and positive interpersonal relating (K. W. Brown, 2015).

This burgeoning interest in mindfulness in the field of psychology is only likely to expand, according to a Delphi poll of an expert panel of mental health professionals (Norcross, Pfund, & Prochaska, 2013). The professionals were asked to rate the extent to which 31 psychotherapy systems would grow or decline over the next decade, and they predicted that mindfulness therapies would see the greatest increase. Readers can refer to several handbooks for a comprehensive overview of the field of mindfulness (e.g., K. W. Brown, Creswell, & Ryan, 2015; Ie, Ngnoumen, & Langer, 2014; Ostafin, Robinson, & Meiers, 2015). In-depth descriptions of the growing array of mindfulness interventions and their empirical support are also available (Baer, 2014; Herbert & Forman, 2010; Roemer & Orsillo, 2008). An edited book by Baltzell (2016a) will be especially helpful for those interested in mindfulness in sport, exercise, and performance psychology.

As the media has embraced the concept, coverage of the mindful revolution has spread to sport as well. Around the time of the Seattle Seahawks' Super Bowl run, reports appeared on how Coach Pete Carroll encouraged players to meditate daily and humorously called this their "ohm team advantage" (Neporent, 2014). Tackle Russell Okung was quoted as saying, "Meditation is . . . it's about quieting your mind and getting into certain states where everything outside of you doesn't matter in that moment" (Roenigk, 2013). Other articles detailed "how meditation won the Super Bowl" (Puff, 2014) and the work of mindfulness coach Michael Gervais, the sport psychologist hired by the Seahawks who has been described as their "best secret weapon" (Gordhamer, 2014).

Numerous other examples are available outside of football. I. Begley (2014) discussed how, after Phil Jackson brought mindfulness to the Bulls and Lakers, his newest team, the New York Knicks, would be "a little more Zen." And Jackson's former player Steve Kerr, now Golden State Warriors head coach, has instilled core values of joy, mindfulness, compassion, and competition in his team (Boyce, 2015), which in 2016 completed the winningest regular season in National Basketball Association history. A list of "Athletes Who Meditate" that appeared in *The Huffington Post* in 2013 included big names in sport such as Derek Jeter, Kobe Bryant, Misty May-Treanor, and Kerri Walsh Jennings. More recently, Angels' pitcher Andrew Heaney talked about how meditation is a "constant presence" in his life, helping him recover from a major injury and Tommy John surgery (Gonzalez, 2016).

Similarly, a newspaper article (Rush, 2014) reported on meditation practiced by college football and basketball teams to improve performance, and another touted mindfulness as one of the ways Olympians stay motivated (Khazan, 2014). In it, Jamie Anderson, snowboarding gold medalist, talked about trying to "do a little bit of yoga and meditate" the night before competition to cope with preperformance anxiety. Another Olympian, marathon medalist Deena Kastor, shared positive psychology tips, including using mindfulness to stay connected to each moment (Sandler & Lee, 2015). Elsewhere, *The New York Times* explored whether mindfulness makes better athletes (Reynolds, 2015), and according to *The Boston Globe*, the Red Sox have a department of behavioral health that plans to emphasize mindfulness (Speier, 2015).

Why Mindfulness for Athletes?

Since first appearing in the 1980s, the psychological literature on mindfulness has focused primarily on mental and/or physical health concerns; significant attention to athletic performers came a few decades later in the mid-2000s. Although athletes and coaches may not necessarily be grappling with the same life issues as are people with clinical disorders, there are many reasons to believe that mindfulness can be just as effective for this generally high-functioning population. As Gordhamer (2014) suggested, "The benefits of mindfulness practice as applied to sports are almost blindingly obvious. Focus, awareness, clarity of thought, and the ability to stay in the present moment are basic skills for any great athlete—and meditator." In Chapter 3, we discuss how the core components of awareness and acceptance inherent in mindfulness may reflect the fundamental characteristics of flow inherent in peak performance.

Birrer, Röthlin, and Morgan (2012) presented a number of factors that can undermine athletic performance (e.g., anxiety, fear of failure), along with nine components and factors of mindfulness that can foster particular skills necessary for peak performance (e.g., attention, acceptance and nonjudgment, emotion regulation, exposure and willingness to endure uncomfortable physical states, nonattachment of happiness to outcomes, less rumination). Ravizza (2002) proposed that an approach based on a view of the athlete as a whole person, grounded in existential philosophy and influenced by Zen and hatha yoga (types of mindfulness practice), could be beneficial for performance enhancement. He specified how such an approach could facilitate freedom, clarification of mission, present focus, letting go of control, and transcending the ego so that athletes can be totally immersed in performance.

In their seminal article proposing a mindfulness- and acceptance-based approach for athletes, Gardner and Moore (2004) suggested that traditional psychological skills training for athletes (e.g., imagery, self-talk, goal setting, arousal control) does not consistently lead to significant performance improvement. Referencing the oft-cited "ironic processes of mental control" (Janelle, 1999; Wegner, 1994), they concluded that trying to suppress or eliminate certain internal processes such as anxiety or negative thoughts might not be necessary and could trigger increases in self-focused thoughts and task-irrelevant attention, along with disruptions in self-regulation. Instead, operating with greater mindfulness may help athletes reduce efforts to control internal experience, change their experience of emotions, and break down literal beliefs in thoughts while boosting focus, awareness, and more efficient responding to performance-related stimuli (Gardner & Moore, 2007).

Two well-established approaches have informed the development of interventions for athletes: mindfulness-based stress reduction (MBSR) and acceptance and commitment therapy (ACT). After discussing these foundational programs, we present mindfulness programs (other than MSPE) developed specifically for sport performers, along with research findings and future directions for the field.

Foundations of Mindfulness Approaches for Sport

MINDFULNESS-BASED STRESS REDUCTION

Jon Kabat-Zinn was a pioneer in developing a systematic, mainstream treatment based on mindfulness meditation. These MBSR workshops were first introduced in the late 1970s, initially focusing on helping medical patients relieve suffering due to pain, illness, and associated stress. The program consists of eight weekly 2- to 2½-hour classes plus an all-day retreat and up to 45 minutes of daily practice of mindfulness exercises. Instruction in various types of meditation enhances the capacity to pay attention while focusing on the present moment (e.g., mindfulness of the breath, body scan, mindful yoga, walking meditation) and to incorporate mindfulness into daily life (Kabat-Zinn, 1990, 1994). Thoughts, sensations, and feelings are observed in a nonjudgmental way, and if the mind wanders, one simply notes where it has gone and gently brings attention back to the point of focus.

MBSR has now been implemented with a large number of diverse populations, and meta-analytic reviews have demonstrated significant benefits with regard to psychological outcomes in adults with health challenges such as chronic medical disease, pain, cancer, and fibromyalgia (e.g., Bohlmeijer, Prenger, Taal, & Cuijpers, 2010; Gotink et al., 2015; Ledesma & Kumano, 2009). Further reviews have targeted psychological health (e.g., Keng et al., 2011). Perhaps more relevant for athletes, MBSR also improves psychological outcomes in nonclinical settings and with healthy adults (Eberth & Sedlmeier, 2012; Khoury, Sharma, Rush, & Fournier, 2015).

Not long after introducing his MBSR approach in an outcome study of patients with chronic pain (Kabat-Zinn, 1982), Kabat-Zinn worked with Olympic and collegiate rowing teams to conduct what appears to be the first empirical test of a mindfulness-based intervention for athletes, which he presented as a poster at the International Sports Medicine Congress in Copenhagen (Kabat-Zinn, Beall, & Rippe, 1985). Kabat-Zinn and colleagues conceptualized this program as a systematic mental training to optimize performance based on mindfulness meditation, arguing that regular meditation practice can deepen concepts emphasized by sport psychologists such as relaxation, concentration, and imagery. Furthermore, they noted that experiences reported by athletes at times of peak performance (e.g., feelings of acute well-being, calm, detachment, being in the present) also are present in meditation and deepen with training. We contacted Kabat-Zinn about his work with the rowers, and he kindly reconstructed his original poster for us. During our correspondence, he commented, "To my mind, it is still as relevant as ever" (J. Kabat-Zinn, personal communication, January 7, 2006), "I hope this serves as a first step" (personal communication, January 22, 2006), and "[retyping the text] brought those wonderful days back in a big and very vivid way" (personal communication, January 25, 2006).

This early application of mindfulness to rowing focused on concentration, letting go of thoughts, relaxation, experiencing harmony and flow between athletes and the boat, and key associations to stay centered. Athletes were taught formal sitting meditation with awareness of the breath and/or the body and were asked to do daily individual practice. Collegiate rowers also participated in weekly 30-minute group meditation sessions followed by discussion and meditated together by the boats on race days. Some Olympic rowers who medaled remarked that the meditation practice had helped them to prepare for and achieve optimal performance. The college rowers performed well above their coach's expectations, improving even more over time. There were also reports among the athletes that the training enhanced their relaxation, concentration, and technique synchronicity while reducing the impact of pain, fatigue, and negative thoughts. Rated as especially important was meditation by the boat before racing, letting go of thoughts, and breath awareness at the start.

Former Olympian Bruce Beall (personal communication, March 7, 2006), who was a member of the U.S. national rowing team and coach of a college rowing team that worked with Kabat-Zinn, shed more light on the nature of this program when we spoke with him as we were developing MSPE. Beall highlighted ways that mindfulness had been most helpful to him and his teams. First, because the mind can "check out" with repetitive activity, paying attention to attention can help athletes learn to be totally present with what they are doing in a given moment, thus helping them change ingrained aspects of technique. Second, Beall commented on the benefits of mindfulness for dealing with experiences of fatigue nonjudgmentally, allowing athletes to push themselves to the limits of their physical abilities. Finally, he offered important suggestions on how to present mindfulness practice to athletes as a "drill for your mind"—just as weight lifting may seem like agony at first, but with practice comes strength. He recalled, "My oarsmen were quite amused when Jon and I started our collaboration, that I was bringing in an expert on chronic pain" (B. Beall, personal communication, February 4, 2006).

It is worthy of note that mindfulness-based cognitive therapy (MBCT; Segal, Williams, & Teasdale, 2002, 2012), an intervention adapted from MBSR as a treatment for recurring depression, was also a major influence on the development of MSPE. MBCT involves learning to observe negative feelings and thoughts in a nonjudgmental, decentered way as mental events rather than facts or reality. It has been found to reduce the likelihood of depressive relapse (see Chiesa & Serretti, 2011; Keng et al., 2011; Kuyken et al., 2016) and has been adapted for other psychological conditions (e.g., Janssen et al., 2015).

ACCEPTANCE AND COMMITMENT THERAPY

Another increasingly popular intervention, ACT (Hayes, Strosahl, & Wilson, 1999, 2011), is based on principles of relational frame theory and encourages people to "get out of your mind and into your life" (Hayes, 2005). No formal meditation training is included, although ACT (pronounced like the word *act*) similarly encourages detached observation and acceptance of thoughts, feelings, and body sensations, relating to them differently without attempting to avoid or change them.

The goal of psychological flexibility (connecting fully with the present moment and behaving in ways that move us toward chosen life directions) is promoted by both acceptance- and change-based strategies based on six interrelated core processes: cognitive defusion, experiential acceptance, mindful contact with the present moment, self as context (the "observing self"), values (desired personal qualities and life directions), and committed action (effective behavior in service of what one values). According to Harris (2009), ACT targets two main psychological processes at the core of human suffering: cognitive fusion ("getting caught up or entangled in our thoughts," p. 17) and experiential avoidance ("the ongoing struggle to avoid, suppress, or get rid of unwanted thoughts, feelings, memories," p. 18). Numerous outcome studies of ACT have demonstrated benefits for concerns such as anxiety, depression, psychosis, addiction, and somatic health problems (see A-Tjak et al., 2015; Keng et al., 2011). ACT is important in the development of mindfulness-based interventions for athletes because of its influence on the MAC approach, which is discussed in the next section.

Mindfulness-Based Interventions for Athletes

After the work of Kabat-Zinn, Beall, and Rippe (1985), nearly 2 decades passed before additional studies of mindfulness-based interventions for athletes were conducted, and even now high-quality research in this area is still in its infancy. Although MSPE remains the focus of our book, we want to acknowledge other directions in practice and research. As reviews of this literature already exist (see Gardner, 2016; Sappington & Longshore, 2015; Wolanin & Gross, 2016), we give just a short description of each program, organized according to the mindfulness approach with which it most closely aligns, with brief references to outcome research. And because people all over the world are now talking about mindfulness for athletes (e.g., Chung, Si, & Zhang, 2013; Jekauc & Kittler, 2015; Solé, Carraça, Serpa, & Palmi, 2014), our aim is to present a global perspective on this emerging branch of sport psychology.

ASSESSMENT OF MINDFULNESS FOR ATHLETES

As mindfulness has spread throughout sport psychology, assessment tools have been developed specifically for athletes, providing a crucial foundation for this growing science. One promising scale is the 15-item Mindfulness Inventory for Sport (Thienot et al., 2014), which determines levels of mindfulness before or during a sport performance and contains subscales for awareness, nonjudgment, and refocusing of attention. A 35-item mindfulness questionnaire for athletes developed in Japan revealed a four-factor model (Amemiya, Yusa, & Sakairi, 2015), whereas a 16-item Athlete Mindfulness Questionnaire consists of subscales that assess present-moment attention, awareness, and acceptance in the context of sport (Zhang, Chung, & Si, 2015). Additional efforts include a revision of the State Mindfulness Scale to assess mindfulness for physical activity (Cox, Ullrich-French, & French, 2016) and a decentering scale for sport (Zhang, Chung, Si, & Gucciardi, 2016).

INTERVENTIONS MORE CLOSELY BASED ON ACCEPTANCE AND COMMITMENT THERAPY

In what may be the first application of ACT principles to sport, Little (1998) designed an intervention for athletes to take a different perspective on their thoughts and feelings, resist attempts to control or suppress them, and engage in behaviors consistent with desired sport performance and effort. Six collegiate fast-pitch softball players received 30-minute training sessions prior to games, including acceptance-based strategies to respond to unwanted feelings and thoughts during competition (Little &

Simpson, 2000). Some athletes increased overall batting average and strikeout recovery and decreased thought suppression.

A handful of years later, the MAC approach was developed. This program has become the most-studied mindfulness-based intervention for athletes to this point, aided by the wide availability of the protocol (Gardner & Moore, 2007).

Mindfulness–Acceptance–Commitment Approach

The MAC program was initially proposed as an acceptance-based behavioral intervention for athletes but has since been conceptualized as a broader approach to performance enhancement. It encourages mindful present-moment attention, acceptance of and willingness to be in contact with internal experience, and full engagement of attention and behavior on valued activities (Gardner & Moore, 2007). The MAC approach, which can be tailored individually to participants, consists of seven modules (see Gardner & Moore, 2007). Although the program can be completed in seven individual or group sessions, additional time may need to be spent with clients who have psychological issues (Z. E. Moore, 2009). The modules include (a) psychoeducation; (b) mindfulness and cognitive defusion; (c) values and values-driven behavior; (d) acceptance of unpleasant thoughts, feelings, and body sensations; (e) enhancing commitment to behaviors consistent with performance values; (f) skills consolidation; and (g) main taining and enhancing practice of these skills. These modules include in-session exercises and discussions as well as between-session assignments designed both to reinforce the skills being taught in each module and to provide material for discussion in subsequent sessions.

A number of case studies have illustrated the MAC approach with adolescent and collegiate athletes as well as an elite powerlifter (Gardner & Moore, 2004, 2007; Schwanhausser, 2009; Wicks, 2012), with improvements in psychological and performance outcomes. Several open trials also have demonstrated the effectiveness of the MAC approach with collegiate athletes (Hasker, 2010; Wolanin, 2004; Wolanin & Schwanhausser, 2010) and in improving psychological flexibility and emotion dysregulation in high school athletes (Gross, Gardner, & Autera, 2012). A randomized controlled study of the MAC approach with female collegiate basketball players found no relative benefits over psychological skills training at posttest but did find significant improvements in hostility, substance use, and emotion dysregulation compared with this active control condition from postintervention to a 1-month follow-up (Gross, 2014; Gross et al., 2016). Finally, 19 recreational golfers trained in MAC showed no significant differences compared with controls but demonstrated significant increases in mindfulness (Plemmons, 2015).

Modifications of the Mindfulness–Acceptance–Commitment Approach

F. R. Goodman, Kashdan, Mallard, and Schumann (2014) adapted the MAC program to offer eight 90-minute sessions over 5 weeks along with hour-long hatha yoga classes. A men's varsity college team reported significantly greater mindfulness and goal-directed energy after the intervention compared with a nonrandomized control group as well as decreases in levels of perceived stress. A modification for junior elite soccer players in

Sweden integrated topics from the MAC approach with group discussions and experiential mindfulness exercises during seven weekly 45-minute sessions (Ivarsson, Johnson, Andersen, Fallby, & Altemyr, 2015). Although findings were not statistically significant, those in the mindfulness group had fewer injuries compared with a randomized active control group.

Si, Lo, and Zhang (2016) addressed the importance of culture with a seven-session mindfulness–acceptance–insight–commitment program for Chinese athletes that integrates "concepts of heart and mind, socially oriented values, insight, and acceptance-based adversity coping" into the MAC approach (p. 238). Six elite synchronized swimmers showed improved mindfulness and psychological flexibility, and an Olympic diver learned to accept and decenter from anxieties. Mindfulness training based on the MAC approach also has led to significantly improved mindfulness, flow, and dart-throwing performance in sport beginners compared with attention controls (Zhang, Si, et al., 2016). In an approach with Olympic shooters in Italy, Bortoli, Bertollo, Hanin, and Robazza (2012) applied action- and emotion-focused strategies derived from a model based in part on the MAC protocol, in which athletes were encouraged to mindfully accept mental and physical distress and focus attention on the core components of their shooting sequence. They showed improved awareness of these core components as well as experiential acceptance of internal distress.

A German version of the MAC approach found significant improvement in emotional control and the accepting-without-judgment aspect of mindfulness compared with waiting-list controls (Heinz, Heidenreich, & Brand, 2010/2011). And in the Middle East, a study with an intervention possibly based on the MAC approach found 20 adult badminton players in Iran significantly increased athletic performance and mindfulness and reduced competitive anxiety compared with a randomized control group (Moghadam, Sayadi, Samimifar, & Moharer, 2013).

In addition to those making modifications to the MAC protocol, sport psychologists around the world have adapted ACT to develop their own approaches for working with athletes.

ACTing SPORT

In Italy, Filimberti, Maffini, and Presti (2013, 2011) developed an intervention to increase psychological flexibility based on the six core processes in the ACT model. The program consists of five 2-hour sessions held with both individual athletes and their teams, in the classroom and outside. Elements include metaphors and experiential exercises such as mindful breathing and a body scan, a sport matrix, cognitive defusion, mindful running, the ACT notion of self as context, contact with the present moment, WARM-ACT (a particular kind of warm-up), and identifying values (e.g., the importance of training).

ACT for Athletes

In Sweden, Lundgren (2015) pioneered a four-session ACT-adapted program with coaches and athletes on an elite ice hockey team, focusing on being present and reacting to what happens on the ice and choosing actions based on their values as players. The program includes exercises and metaphors that help develop an increased acceptance of emotions and thoughts, cognitive defusion, mindful refocusing, and valued action. A nonrandomized control group study demonstrated significant change in experiential avoidance for the treatment group; a more recent randomized controlled trial (RCT) with 40 elite ice hockey players found significant benefits, with 94% saying the intervention had been helpful.

Other ACT-Inspired Sport Interventions Around the World

An ACT-based program developed by Lappalainen and Välimäki in Finland consists of six weekly 1-hour small group sessions that include discussion, mindfulness exercises, and presentation of key issues and metaphors to relate issues to sport experience; coaches also remind athletes of the exercises during practice. A team of 24 female floorball players did not show significantly greater improvement compared with nonrandomized controls (Kettunen & Välimäki, 2014). In Spain, García, Villa, Cepeda, Cueto, and Montes (2004) developed a three-session ACT intervention aimed at accepting bodily states and private events and engaging in valued behavior. Both the ACT and a comparison hypnosis intervention helped 16 adolescent canoeists improve on several performance measures. We eagerly await the results of a randomized trial conducted by Swiss researchers comparing a mindfulness intervention (adapted from ACT, MAC, and MBSR) with psychological skills training and a waiting-list control (Röthlin, Birrer, Horvath, & grosse Holtforth, 2016).

Rodríguez and Rodríguez (2009) conducted four 45-minute ACT sessions with three adolescent male tennis players in Columbia, with graphs suggesting decreases on a measure of psychological inflexibility/experiential avoidance. Yang and Zhang (2014) employed a 5-week mindfulness-based cognitive intervention (consisting of psychoeducation, mindfulness, and a focus on values, avoidance and acceptance, and commitment) with four elite athletes in China; they found significant improvement in anxiety and mindfulness.

Finally, a number of sport and performance psychologists in Australia have used the ACT model in their work with athletes, which is reflected on websites and online postings. For example, Jonah Oliver conducts ACT-based peak performance workshops for Olympic athletes, race drivers, elite tennis players, professional soccer teams, and football clubs, and Joe Ciarrochi, a major figure in the world of ACT, works with professional rugby players.

Mindfulness Interventions for Injured Athletes

ACT has also been adapted for use with injured athletes. Mahoney and Hanrahan (2011) presented four case studies of athletes with anterior cruciate ligament injuries who were introduced to concepts of cognitive defusion, mindfulness, acceptance, and values over a short 4-week intervention. These athletes demonstrated some improvement in accepting private events and committing to rehabilitation behaviors to assist their reentry to sport. Similarly, Perret (2014) employed a 6-week individual ACT intervention that was adapted from a group ACT approach for chronic pain, with additional exercises focusing on values, mindfulness, and defusion. Seven injured athletes were helped to accept their injuries and engage in rehabilitation-adherent behaviors.

MINDFULNESS APPROACHES FOR ATHLETES THAT ARE PRIMARILY BASED ON MEDITATION TRAINING

In addition to Kabat-Zinn, Beall, and Rippe's (1985) early poster presentation, one of the first studies to use meditation with athletes incorporated it as one of eight 1-hour cognitive–behavioral therapy modules for youth volleyball players (Crocker, Alderman, Murray, & Smith, 1988). This mantra-based meditation was based on Benson's (1975) relaxation response. Participants are encouraged to become aware of the breath while silently saying a word such as *one* as they exhale, not dwelling on distracting thoughts and returning attention to the chosen word. As noted previously, Kabat-Zinn's approach to mindfulness meditation has more often been the focus of work with athletes.

Mindfulness Meditation Training for Sport

Mindfulness meditation training for sport (MMTS; Baltzell & Akhtar, 2014) is a 12-session training consisting of two 30-minute meetings per week, with encouragement for daily meditation practice (see also Baltzell & Summers, 2016). Early exercises focus on teaching open awareness in a nonjudgmental way, including mindfulness of the breath, sounds, body sensations, and thoughts. Later sessions guide athletes to focus on the use of self-compassion (caring thoughts for themselves and teammates), concentration exercises, and fostering acceptance of negative mind-states (e.g., labeling emotions while concurrently practicing nonreactivity). All sessions include discussion of how mindfulness skills can be applied to practice and competition.

In a quasi-experimental study, 19 female college soccer players showed a significantly greater increase in mindfulness than did a comparison group of female rowers, whereas controls reported a significant increase in negative affect (Baltzell & Akhtar, 2014). In postprogram interviews, athletes reported that the program had an effect on their relationship with emotions (e.g., increased perseverance and calmness) as well as improved focus on the field (Baltzell, Caraballo, Chipman, & Hayden, 2014). Although it was initially difficult to practice meditation, attitudes changed with continued practice, when a connection could be seen between meditation practice and soccer performance. Athletes also felt that self-compassionate thoughts had an impact on the team and suggested meditation be encouraged before soccer practice.

Mindful Performance Enhancement, Awareness and Knowledge

Building on mindfulness training for active-duty marines, Haase et al. (2015) introduced an intensive 8-week *mPEAK* (mindful performance enhancement, awareness and knowledge) training course with seven athletes from the USA BMX cycling team and found significant improvements in interoceptive awareness and the ability to describe experiences (a facet of mindfulness), as well as increases in insula and anterior cingulate cortical activation, the significance of which is discussed in Chapter 3. The four main 3-hour modules are based on MBSR, with an early focus on interoception (noticing and accepting body experience) and intentional versus automatic ways of responding, and incorporate exercises such as mindful awareness of the body, straw breathing, and sitting meditation. Later modules deal with accepting physical and emotional pain, as well as self-compassion and letting go of perfectionism, and include sitting meditations, an ice bucket exercise, and mindful walking. Six additional 90-minute sessions and 30-minute daily practices over the following 6 weeks help deepen these skills. For a detailed description, see Haase, Kentta, Hickman, Baltzell, and Paulus (2016).

Programs Based on Home Practice Exercises

Aherne, Moran, and Lonsdale (2011) developed a 6-week intervention containing a handout on mindfulness and sport applications, along with instructions and daily text message reminders for home practice (e.g., sitting meditation, standing yoga, body scan). Six Irish college athletes demonstrated significant increases in flow that were not shown by randomized controls.

More recently, Stankovic (2015), working with Baltzell, asked female amateur tennis players to listen to a 10-minute mindfulness exercise four times a week over an 8-week period, with text message reminders to practice. Athletes were taught to focus awareness on breathing and body sensations, nonjudgmentally bring attention back when their minds wandered, and let go of negative thoughts and competition anxiety. They showed significantly improved performance and mindfulness in comparison with active controls. And in Scotland, an exploratory study with six national-level swimmers used CD recordings to practice four mindfulness meditations over an 8-week period, with weekly e-mails. Single-case analyses found that four athletes showed improvements in performance times and three demonstrated large increases in attention efficiency and mindfulness (Mardon, Richards, & Martindale, 2016).

Other Meditation-Based Sport Interventions Around the World

Just as with the ACT adaptations mentioned earlier, programs for athletes based on MBSR are appearing internationally as well. For example, an 8-week adaptation of MBSR for athletes was introduced with elite male soccer players in Portugal (Carraça, Serpa, Palmi, & Magalhães, 2015). The mindfulness group showed significant decreases in psychological inflexibility/experiential avoidance, whereas controls showed significant increases. In Spain, Franco (2009) developed a 10-session flow meditation program for competitive collegiate athletes. ACT metaphors and exercises were integrated with meditation practices drawn from Zen and Vipassana traditions, including a body scan from the work of Kabat-Zinn. In a nonrandomized controlled study, significant improvement was found on measures of resistant personality and sport burnout compared with controls. And Brazilian sport psychologist Aline Wolff (personal communication, May 1, 2016) has included mindfulness in her work with Olympians, has written about mindfulness in sport, and is planning research applying a mindfulness training protocol for multiple sports.

Bernier, Thienot, Codron, and Fournier (2009) developed an intervention based on MBCT with added metaphors derived from ACT, including acceptance (playing golf along with unwanted thoughts) and focusing to commit to each shot. Results of an open trial with seven elite young French golfers showed that cultivating awareness and acceptance helped them perceive negative internal states as part of their experience, reducing their attempts to control or eliminate them, thus allowing for a more efficient psychological mindset. More recently, Bernier, Thienot, Pelosse, and Fournier (2014) worked with seven elite young female figure skaters to teach mindfulness skills (e.g., mindfulness of the breath, body scan), followed by training in attentional focus during skating programs. In general, the girls significantly increased in acceptance as well as awareness in action, and results from two case studies were presented. In another youth mindfulness program, Sant (2015) compared a 4-week mindfulness intervention (with daily practice of exercises such as mindfulness of the breath, mindful movement, and the body scan) to a quasi–randomly assigned control group with 16 adolescent girls on the Scottish national basketball team. Those in the mindfulness program showed significant increases in levels of both mindfulness and resilience compared with controls.

Jouper and Gustafsson (2013) in Sweden developed an intervention based on daily mindfulness and qigong meditation exercises to assist an elite female shooter experiencing burnout; it included three in-person meetings and weekly phone contact. Afterward, she reported becoming more aware of thoughts, feelings, and body sensations and was able to accept them with less judgment and had increased concentration and feelings of well-being. Another study of stress and burnout with junior elite biathlon, cross-country skiing, and shooting athletes in Norway employed sitting meditations with a focus on the breath and body scans. Interviews with six athletes found increased relaxation, awareness, focus, perceived performance, and sleep as well as less rumination after practicing mindfulness (Furrer, Moen, & Firing, 2015).

In China, sport psychologist Xu Shousen has introduced mindfulness techniques with the national badminton team and military pentathlon team and trained two Olympic shooting medalists (Liu & Xu, 2013). For their work with elite shooters in India, John, Verma, and Khanna (2011) developed an intensive 4-week mindfulness meditation training program with 20-minute sessions 6 days a week, which included meditation, a body scan, and focused breathing. Salivary cortisol (to measure stress response) decreased significantly in the mindfulness group but increased in randomized controls. Amemiya and Shoji completed a study with Japanese collegiate high jumpers and throwing athletes using a mindfulness intervention based on MBCT (R. Amemiya, personal communication, December 11, 2015). Also in Japan, Sato and Kuribayashi investigated the association of mindfulness, competitive anxiety, and athlete burnout in collegiate athletes and have plans for future outcome studies (H. Sato, personal communication, November 28, 2015).

Research in Australia (Thienot, 2013) examined a 4-week mindfulness training program consisting of 1-hour group sessions focusing on the enhancement of meta-awareness, acceptance, and refocusing, along with home practice of recorded exercises (e.g., mind–body scan, mindfulness meditation, mindful movement). Fifteen elite swimmers did not improve significantly compared with a (nonrandomized) control group, with findings attributed to lack of practice and the short program, although greater mindfulness practice was significantly related to performance, refocusing, and nonjudgment. Scott-Hamilton, Schutte, and Brown (2016) introduced an 8-week program for competitive Australian cyclists that incorporates group sessions, home practice, and group meetings to practice mindfulness during workouts on stationary bikes. This well-designed RCT found that cyclists in the mindfulness workshop had greater increases in mindfulness and dispositional flow compared with wait-list controls. In addition, athletes with higher adherence to workshop attendance and home practice had significantly greater improvement in mindfulness, flow, pessimistic attributional style, and sport anxiety compared with those with lower adherence (Scott-Hamilton & Schutte, 2016). Finally, Mitchell and Hassed (2016) discussed training Australian Football League players in "practical mindfulness" as part of a program for athlete well-being. This intervention consists of three 45- to 60-minute sessions with brief formal meditations as well as informal mindfulness practice, along with 5-minute daily mindfulness practice supported by mobile apps.

Mindfulness Interventions for Coaches

In addition to the ever-growing number of mindfulness approaches for athletes, a few interventions have been created specifically for coaches, and we recently completed an MSPE study with a group of collegiate coaches (see Chapters 11 and 16 for more details). Coaches are a key stakeholder in the world of athletics, given that they have the power to decide whether to build time into their athletes' sport practice for mindfulness or to encourage their athletes to participate in mindfulness training. Baltzell et al. (2014) suggested that "mindless" coaching could lead to lack of flexibility, worry, not paying attention, and habitual responses that don't consider new information. Mindfulness approaches could thus allow coaches be more present and accepting of whatever their experience might be and improve focus on task-relevant cues.

Mindfulness can help coaches prepare for and get centered before each coaching session and maintain focus and concentration to continually bring the wandering mind back to a focus on the athletes (Passmore & Marianetti, 2007). Mindful coaches can better manage stress and remain emotionally nonreactive with their athletes, who, in turn, can also benefit when coaches model mindfulness techniques of awareness, acceptance, decentering, and being in the moment.

Mindfulness training for coaches (MTC; Longshore & Sachs, 2015) is based on MBSR and MSPE and consists of a 1½-hour group training session followed by 6 weeks of daily home practice. Coaches receive a workbook, guided-meditation CDs, mindfulness practice log, and the option to receive daily text or e-mail reminders. A nonrandomized controlled pilot study of 20 Division I college coaches found significant within-group decreases in trait anxiety and more improvement for MTC versus controls on negative affect. Interviews suggested positive impacts across multiple areas such as self-perceptions of anxiety, emotional stability, mindfulness, coaching behaviors, interactions with athletes, and personal life.

Interviews with three soccer coaches who completed an MMTS program along with their athletes revealed heightened sensitivity to players' emotional and mental states less reactivity to their own emotions while coaching and outside of work, and new ways of interacting with players (Baltzell, Chipman, Hayden, & Bowman, 2015). These results support the charge of Mannion and Andersen (2016) for coaches to develop interpersonal mindfulness (i.e., observing their athletes) as well as awareness of their own internal states.

Future Directions for Research on Mindfulness for Athletic Performers

In their systematic literature review on mindfulness-based interventions for athletes, Sappington and Longshore (2015) concluded that, although studies demonstrate preliminary support for these strategies, there was an "alarmingly small pool of evidentiary support for mindfulness-based therapy with athletes" (p. 236) as well as a need for more methodologically rigorous research. For example, they found only three published RCTs, one of which had poor methodological quality, and seven non-randomized trials.

Evaluations of new interventions often begin with case studies and open trials, followed by small randomized studies with wait-list controls, all of which have their own methodological limitations. The ultimate goal is to be able to conduct large-scale RCTs with methodological rigor, comparing the intervention with others with demonstrated efficacy (active control conditions). As relative newcomers to the field, only in recent years have any mindfulness-based interventions met criteria as empirically supported treatments (e.g., with RCTs, adequate sample sizes, and conducted with treatment manuals by teams of independent investigators), yet many studies lack active controls.

So, considering the amount of progress in research on mindfulness and sport over the past decade, we're off to a good start but still have a long way to go. In addition to RCTs with active comparison groups, it would be interesting to compare mindfulness-based approaches for athletic performers, including programs with and without formal meditation training or those based on MBSR versus ACT, in future research.

Along with more group comparison studies, it is important to examine best practice in program delivery that will help answer some important questions. Are mindfulness-based interventions for athletes best delivered individually, with intact teams, or with groups of athletes from multiple sports? To what extent do programs benefit from being conducted in collaboration with coaches, and how should programs be adapted exclusively for coaches? How can session attendance and adherence to suggested home practice be increased? What are the best ways to build an alliance with athletes who are unfamiliar with mental training or skeptical of something like meditation? Are there specific mindfulness exercises or concepts that are most helpful for athletes in different sports or with different needs? Does the impact of mindfulness skills differ depending on when they are applied (e.g., during practice, before performance, during performance)? What is the optimal length of training, sessions, and home practice? What are the mediators and mechanisms of action in mindfulness-based programs for athletes, and what variables are moderators of change (i.e., who benefits the most)?

Better methods of assessment would also be beneficial, with sessions recorded so that independent assessors can rate adherence and competence carrying out the intervention. Participant expectancy effects before the intervention and compliance with daily practice assignments should be assessed, and future studies could include psychophysiological and brain imaging assessment and objective measures of performance, along with self-report questionnaires. In addition, both short- and long-term follow-up assessments are critical.

All of this, however, is easier said than done. Top quality, scientifically rigorous research is in part a function of the funding available. Gaudiano (2009) found a moderately strong association between methodological quality (of cognitive–behavioral therapy and ACT studies) and the amount of grant funding and suggested that more money likely allows for more advanced methodological procedures. Unfortunately, unlike the large grants going to researchers evaluating mindfulness- and acceptance-based approaches for clinical populations, the funds available to support research with athletic performers tend to be relatively limited. Nonetheless, for mindfulness-based programs in sport to become well-established, creating and disseminating manuals so that independent groups of researchers can investigate these interventions is crucial.

The review provided in this chapter highlights how the proliferation of mindfulness-based interventions in sport simultaneously reflects one of this field's greatest strengths and greatest weaknesses at this juncture. Although there is much enthusiasm about the potential of mindfulness for performance enhancement, there is also a critical need for more consistent, science-backed guidance on how to reach this potential. We hope that the resources offered in this book, particularly the complete MSPE protocol, will play a role in overcoming this weakness. But to set the stage for the MSPE protocol chapters in Part II, we first turn to a discussion of the science behind mindfulness interventions such as MSPE and their capacity to help people achieve peak performance.

Going With the Flow
Mindfulness and Peak Performance

3

Evidence abounds that athletes and coaches believe the mind is important to successful sport performance (e.g., Weinberg & Gould, 2015). One of our coauthors, Timothy Pineau, vividly recalls his college crew coach standing in a launch on many freezing New England mornings shouting, "Rowing is 90% mental—the rest is in your head!" However, as discussed in Chapter 1, this belief is not always accompanied by a thorough understanding of how to do mental training or how it translates into enhanced (ideally, peak) athletic performance.

Sport scientists have recognized for nearly half a century that certain psychological factors seem to facilitate optimal performance states (e.g., Ravizza, 1977). Such states have been identified by many names, including *peak experience* (Ravizza, 1977), *peak performance* (Privette, 1981), *the zone* (Young & Pain, 1999), and *flow* (S. A. Jackson & Csikszentmihalyi, 1999). While these terms are not necessarily interchangeable (Harmison & Casto, 2012), they all refer to a desirable condition that is typically characterized by positive emotions, centered attention, and calmness, as well as feelings of effortlessness and automaticity

http://dx.doi.org/10.1037/0000048-004
Mindful Sport Performance Enhancement: Mental Training for Athletes and Coaches, by K. A. Kaufman, C. R. Glass, and T. R. Pineau

Csikszentmihalyi's (1990) construct of flow has become the term of choice in the sport science literature and has some significant conceptual commonalities with mindfulness, a realization that intrigued us greatly as we were developing and beginning to study mindful sport performance enhancement (MSPE). Flow in sport has been thoroughly described in a number of publications (e.g., S. A. Jackson & Csikszentmihalyi, 1999; S. A. Jackson & Kimiecik, 2008), can be assessed using validated questionnaires (S. A. Jackson & Eklund, 2002), and has been linked empirically to peak athletic performance (S. A. Jackson, Thomas, Marsh, & Smethurst, 2001). This chapter explores the link between mindfulness and flow, with a particular focus on the capacities to regulate attention and emotion, along with a brief review of these capacities' neurological underpinnings.

What Is *Flow*?

Csikszentmihalyi (1990) defined *flow* as the state in which a person gets so involved in an activity and it is so completely enjoyable that nothing else seems to matter. Flow is thought to consist of nine elements (Csikszentmihalyi, 1990; S. A. Jackson & Eklund, 2002): (a) a balance between a challenge faced and the skills required to meet it, (b) the presence of clear goals, (c) unambiguous feedback on the pursuit of those goals, (d) a merging of action and awareness such that the activity almost feels automatic, (e) total concentration on the task at hand, (f) a sense of control, (g) a loss of self-consciousness (lack of self-scrutiny), (h) the transformation of time in the sense that it either speeds up or slows down, and (i) autotelic experience (the activity is intrinsically rewarding). The first three dimensions are considered the prerequisite conditions for a flow experience, and when these are present, an individual is able to experience a state of flow characterized by some or all of the remaining six elements (Swann, Keegan, Piggott, & Crust, 2012), typically resulting in optimal performance. From these descriptions, it is probably easy to understand why flow is such a desirable state for athletes.

Although flow has been well defined, there is still debate regarding whether entering this state is truly controllable, as opposed to a serendipitous experience that just happens sometimes. A majority of athletes have indicated that entering flow is at least partially controllable (Chavez, 2008; S. A. Jackson, 1992), citing how factors leading to flow feel controllable (S. A. Jackson, 1995). If flow is controllable, that would have major implications for the mental training of performers, and this possibility has thus led to research on what might affect the occurrence of flow (Anderson, Hanrahan, & Mallett, 2014; Chavez, 2008; Swann et al., 2012).

Studies suggest that flow results from a complex interaction between internal (e.g., concentration, emotions) and external (e.g., environmental conditions, social support) variables, as well as various factors (e.g., preparation) involved in the lead-up to an activity (Hardy, Jones, & Gould, 1996). Although some of these variables (e.g., weather) are out of a person's control, others (e.g., attention, confidence, preparation, arousal, awareness, adaptability, and the regulation of thoughts and emotions) are not (Anderson et al., 2014; Swann et al., 2012). Interestingly, in their review, Swann and colleagues (2012) found that the same factors identified as facilitating flow also had the potential to disrupt flow. For example, whereas optimal focus, arousal, and confidence can help promote flow, lack of focus, too much or too little arousal, and over- or underconfidence can inhibit it. This finding is important because it suggests that factors leading to flow may exist on a continuum. Thus, making appropriate adjustments along those continua may increase the chances of achieving flow and peak performance.

We contend that flow is controllable, or rather, that the psychological conditions that can lead to flow are controllable. Furthermore, as we explain throughout this volume, we believe that mindfulness training, and in particular MSPE, promotes performance facilitators (covered in Chapters 5 and 10) that enhance athletes' self-regulatory capacities (regulation of attention and emotions), which, in turn, set the stage for flow states and optimal performance.

Flow and Mindfulness

In a clear theoretical link, the primary characteristics of mindfulness (awareness and acceptance) overlap with several elements of flow, such as total concentration on the task at hand, merging of action and awareness, unambiguous feedback, transformation of time, and loss of self-consciousness (Gardner & Moore, 2004; Kaufman, Glass, & Arnkoff, 2009; Pineau, Glass, & Kaufman, 2014; Salmon, Hanneman, & Harwood, 2010). An exploration of the relevant literatures highlights how these constructs could fit together in a meaningful way for athletes. For instance, Wittmann and Schmidt (2014) offered that seasoned meditators' enhanced awareness may help explain why the passage of time can feel so different (e.g., like it is slowing down) during their meditations, and Swann et al. (2012) reported that nearly 30% of athletes endorsed the transformation of time element of flow while performing at their peak.

Also, across five studies of flow in athletes, the most commonly experienced flow elements were concentration on the task at hand and merging of action and awareness (Swann et al., 2012), both of which are strong correlates of mindfulness practice (Chiesa, Calati, & Serretti, 2011; Hölzel & Ott, 2006). In addition, athletes often describe flow experiences in terms that are not easily categorized in the nine flow dimensions but that reflect common effects of being mindful, such as feelings of relaxation and heightened bodily awareness (Bernier, Thienot, Codron, & Fournier, 2009; Chavez, 2008). In light of these findings, it's not surprising that one of the most prolific authors on flow in sport has discussed how an outcome of being mindful in challenging situations can be flow (S. A. Jackson, 2016).

In fact, the mindfulness–flow relationship has been demonstrated empirically, with both nonathletes (e.g., B. A. Moore, 2013) and athletes (e.g., Cathcart, McGregor, & Groundwater, 2014; Kaufman et al., 2009; Kee & Wang, 2008; Pineau, Glass, Kaufman,

& Bernal, 2014; Scott-Hamilton, Schutte, Moyle, & Brown, 2016), and mindfulness-based interventions have been found to increase flow in athletes (Aherne, Moran, & Lonsdale, 2011; Kaufman et al., 2009; Schwanhausser, 2009; Scott-Hamilton, Schutte, & Brown, 2016). In addition, a comprehensive literature review indicated that mindfulness training is a promising way to enhance both sport performance and certain characteristics associated with performance, such as flow (Sappington & Longshore, 2015).

These early findings are interesting and exciting, but much still needs to be learned about the connections between mindfulness and flow and how this link can inform mindfulness-based interventions for athletes (Bernier, Thienot, Pelosse, & Fournier, 2014; Cathcart et al., 2014). There is convincing evidence, however, that the two processes most likely to link mindfulness training with flow are the regulation of attention and the regulation of emotion.

Attention Regulation as a Link Between Mindfulness and Flow

Present-moment attention is a central feature of both mindfulness and flow. Total concentration on the task at hand is one of the nine flow elements (Csikszentmihalyi, 1990), and attentional control correlates highly with the disposition to experience flow (Cermakova, Moneta, & Spada, 2010). Notably, Dormashev (2010) proposed that "prolonged effortless concentration of attention is the principal characteristic of the flow experience" (p. 306).

It is widely accepted that proper attention is essential for optimal sport performance (Boutcher, 2008), which is no easy feat given the complex and often fluctuating attentional demands in sport. According to Memmert (2009), athletes are routinely required to regulate attention by restricting focus to task-relevant targets while disregarding distractions (selective or executive attention), maintaining focus on those targets for extended periods of time (sustained attention), staying on the lookout for new targets that may be important (situational awareness or orientating attention), and shifting or splitting focus between multiple targets (attentional flexibility or divided attention). To put this in the context of normal cognitive functioning, the median length of time during which human focus remains on target is approximately 5 seconds (Weinberg & Gould, 2015). Now, consider the duration of a typical sporting event. It is probably not a surprise that superior attentional capacities consistently differentiate more successful athletes from less successful ones (e.g., Hunt, Rietschel, Hatfield, & Iso-Ahola, 2013) or that indicators of efficient attentional processes (e.g., visual fixation patterns) reliably distinguish expert from novice athletes (e.g., Mann, Williams, Ward, & Janelle, 2007).

This evidence makes a strong case for including mindfulness in training programs for athletes. Developing the capacity to intentionally direct and maintain attention (i.e., attention regulation) is a core feature of mindfulness (Kabat-Zinn, 1990, 2003), and research has shown that mindfulness training can strengthen attentional abilities

(Chiesa et al., 2011; Schofield, Creswell, & Denson, 2015). In fact, higher levels of mindfulness have been related to improvements in all four types of attention described previously (selective attention: van den Hurk, Giommi, Gielen, Speckens, & Barendregt, 2010; sustained attention: Chambers, Lo, & Allen, 2008; situational awareness: Jensen, Vangkilde, Frokjaer, & Hasselbalch, 2012; attentional flexibility: Hodgins & Adair, 2010), which has direct implications for a mindful athlete's propensity to experience flow.

With particular relevance to Dormashev's (2010) contention that prolonged, effortless attention is essential for flow states, Brefczynski-Lewis, Lutz, Schaefer, Levinson, and Davidson (2007) found that meditators with the most experience not only demonstrated superior sustained attentional capacity in comparison with novice meditators but also were able to do so using fewer neural resources. In other words, very experienced meditators engaged in more efficient attentional processing. Although the most advanced group of meditators in this study had extensive experience (more than 37,000 hours) that took many years to accumulate, Slagter and colleagues (2007) came to similar conclusions about increased attentional efficiency when looking at a group of meditators with only 3 months of experience.

Even though these studies were not conducted on athletes, Marks (2008) emphasized the importance of these results when attempting to understand the potential benefits of mindfulness training in sports, and Z. E. Moore (2009) noted that, for athletes, "mindfulness practice may very well facilitate the development of this more economical mode of using and allocating cognitive (in particular) attentional resources" (p. 294). These assertions are further supported by more recent research with athletes (Bijleveld & Veling, 2014) in which working memory capacity, a primary component of attentional processes, was found to reliably predict successful or unsuccessful performance under pressure (i.e., nonchokers vs. chokers). These authors even suggested that their results support the use of mindfulness-based interventions for athletes whose working memory capacity may be negatively impacted by distracting thoughts, which speaks to the potential for mindfulness to enhance attention regulation and thus flow.

Further, Hölzel and colleagues (2011) proposed that the regulation of attention is one of the primary mechanisms of action through which mindfulness enacts change, whereas others have come to similar conclusions in the domain of sports. For instance, Gooding and Gardner (2009) posited that "the positive performance enhancing qualities inherent in mindfulness may be due to its relationship to the self-regulation of attention" (p. 315). Salmon and colleagues (2010) similarly emphasized the importance of self-regulation of attention in sport but added that mindfulness benefits athletes not only through the enhanced capacity to pay attention but also through the generation of a nonjudgmental attitude toward whatever is the focus of attention, which may allow attention to work more fluidly and efficiently.

For example, a focus of attention for athletes is often something that feels negative, such as muscle fatigue, a tactical error, or an opponent perceived to be superior. Athletes who cannot let go of these more difficult points of focus will not be able to use their attention as effectively as will those who can experience whatever happens with acceptance, thus allowing negative reactions to pass and freeing up valuable cognitive and emotional resources. This attitude of acceptance may not only help athletes maintain attentional flexibility but also might help them avoid the performance decrements that can occur when attention is shifted from task-relevant cues (e.g., the movements of an opponent) to self-evaluative cues such as self-critical thoughts (Klinger, Barta, & Glas, 1981). In fact, the potential importance of an accepting and nonreactive attitude for focus has been emphasized by elite pentathletes, who noted that detachment from negative reactions is an important strategy for dealing with the harmful consequences of performance mistakes (Bertollo, Saltarelli, & Robazza, 2009).

This kind of attention regulation would seem to facilitate several elements of flow, such as total concentration on the task at hand, loss of self-consciousness, sense of control, and autotelic experience, perhaps translating into optimal performance. We argue that this impact of mindfulness training on flow elements through attention regulation is a primary rationale for participating in a program such as MSPE, which is designed to instill the ability to perform with full awareness and nonjudgmental acceptance of what is happening. Of course, attention regulation is not the only ability strengthened through mindfulness training, as such interventions also enhance emotion-regulation capacities, which can similarly promote flow experiences.

Emotion Regulation as a Link Between Mindfulness and Flow

Much like athletes' attention, their emotional state is generally understood to have important implications for and can even be predictive of sport performance (Beedie, Terry, & Lane, 2000; Hanin, 2000a). The prevailing sentiment is that positive emotions (e.g., happiness, confidence, optimism, vigor) tend to benefit performance (Vast, Young, & Thomas, 2010), bolster commitment to a sport (Fitzgerald, 2010), protect against exhaustion and burnout (e.g., Chen, Kee, & Tsai, 2008), and, most relevant to this discussion, facilitate flow (S. A. Jackson, Ford, Kimiecik, & Marsh, 1998; Koehn, 2013). Conversely, negative emotions (e.g., anxiety, anger, depression, exhaustion) tend to hurt performance (Hanin, 2010), are associated with overtraining syndrome (Armstrong & VanHeest, 2002), decrease the efficiency of cognitive processes such as attention (Eysenck, Derakshan, Santos, & Calvo, 2007), and limit experiences of flow (S. A. Jackson et al., 1998; Koehn, 2013).

However, the reality seems to be far more complex than simply that positive emotions are good and negative emotions are bad in sport. For instance, higher levels of happiness have been found to correlate with greater cognitive disruption in athletes (Allen, Jones, McCarthy, Sheehan-Mansfield, & Sheffield, 2013), whereas negative emotions such as anxiety, anger, tension, and even depression can benefit performance in certain cases (Beedie et al., 2000; Hanin, 2010; Lane, Devonport, & Beedie, 2012). Athletes themselves also provide inconsistent reports about the roles of their own emotions. Robazza and Bortoli (2003) presented a large group of elite and non-elite athletes with a list of 90 emotions and found that 80% of the items on that list, such as nervous, calm, tranquil, aggressive, and worried, were classified as both facilitative and detrimental to performance. Further, traditionally positive emotions were rated as dysfunctional 39% of the time, whereas negative ones were rated as functional 42% of the time.

Given this lack of clarity on the relation between emotions and performance, several authors have suggested that athletes need to develop their own understanding of how emotions link to performance *for them* (e.g., Hanin, 2000b, 2010). To achieve these individualized optimal emotional states, athletes must engage in strategies to regulate their emotions (Lane, Beedie, Jones, Uphill, & Devonport, 2012; Wagstaff, 2014). Emotion regulation can be quite tricky, however, because competitive sports frequently generate a host of positive and negative emotional reactions, and trying to control their occurrence and intensity can be a futile endeavor that may harm performance. For example, Wagstaff (2014) reported that athletes who attempt to suppress negative emotions may have poorer performances and perceive greater exertion than do those who do not, and McCarthy, Allen, and Jones (2013) claimed that having thoughts of escape during competition (an avoidance strategy) is associated with worse performance.

Such findings are in line with the principle described in previous chapters that attempts to avoid or control emotions can result in more frequent or intense experiences of the very emotions being suppressed (Janelle, 1999; Wegner, 1994). Thus, successful emotion regulation "may arguably focus on adaptive ways of responding to emotional distress, rather than on the control of emotions or dampening of emotional arousal in general" (Gratz & Tull, 2010, p. 111). With this understanding of effective emotion regulation, mindfulness seems like an ideal way for athletes to understand and influence their own unique emotion–performance relationship.

Research on mindfulness in athletes supports the potential usefulness of mindfulness within the classic emotion–performance dichotomy. More mindful athletes tend to have higher levels of positive emotions, such as optimism, and lower levels of negative emotions, such as anxiety (Pineau, Glass, & Kaufman, 2012, 2014), and following MSPE training, athletes have shown increases in positive emotions and decreases in negative emotions (De Petrillo, Kaufman, Glass, & Arnkoff, 2009; Kaufman et al., 2009), which we describe in more detail in Chapter 11. Such results may be particularly significant given the positive association between optimism and flow (Vealey & Perritt, 2015), the negative relation between anxiety and flow (S. A. Jackson et al., 1998; Koehn, 2013), and the mediation of the mindfulness–flow relationship through reduced levels of anxiety and pessimism (Scott-Hamilton, Schutte, Moyle, & Brown, 2016). However, as suggested earlier, although increasing optimism or decreasing anxiety may have utility, it is not the calibrating up or down of specific emotions but rather the capacity to respond adaptively to any emotion (i.e., emotion regulation) that may be most beneficial for athletes.

The acceptance of and willingness to experience any emotion are core components of the emotional balance that is cultivated through mindfulness practice

(Kabat-Zinn, 1990), and it is this acceptance-based approach to internal experience that is thought to account for the advantages of mindfulness interventions over traditional, control-oriented, cognitive–behavioral approaches for athletes (Gardner & Moore, 2007; Kaufman et al., 2009). This idea seems particularly poignant considering that a decreased susceptibility to mood changes in response to environmental factors has been shown to distinguish more successful from less successful athletes (Coker & Mickle, 2000), and higher levels of emotional variability, particularly with regard to negative emotions, are predictive of burnout (Lemyre, Treasure, & Roberts, 2006). In addition, expanding on the initial finding by Walker (2013) that mindfulness is inversely related to burnout, Gustafsson, Skoog, Davis, Kenttä, and Haberl (2015) found that positive and negative emotion mediated this relationship, lending further support to the notion of mindfulness training impacting sport performance, in part, through its effects on athletes' emotions.

The connection between mindfulness and emotion regulation has been demonstrated by a number of studies (e.g., Chambers, Gullone, & Allen, 2009), and emotion regulation is considered one of the main ways in which mindfulness practice produces beneficial effects, in both clinical and healthy populations (Gratz & Tull, 2010; Hölzel et al., 2011) as well as in athletes specifically (Birrer, Röthlin, & Morgan, 2012; Marks, 2008). Relatively little research has examined the role that emotion regulation plays in the achievement of flow states, however. This is surprising given how emotions appear to be crucial to peak performance, and the apparent role of emotions in flow elements such as challenge–skill balance, loss of self-consciousness, sense of control, and autotelic experience (S. A. Jackson & Csikszentmihalyi, 1999). No flow element specifically addresses nonreactivity to emotions, but appropriate self-regulation (e.g., anxiety management) has been cited as a primary psychological mechanism enabling athletes to have peak-performance experiences such as flow (Anderson et al., 2014). In addition, athletes often report sensations of calm when experiencing flow (Chavez, 2008), which may relate to the emotional equanimity cultivated in mindfulness practice. However, such self-reported experiences do not represent the complete picture. Amazing technological advances have made it possible to see how the brain itself changes with mindfulness practice.

The Mindful Brain: Implications for Attention and Emotion Regulation

Thus far, we have presented theoretical and empirically supported rationales for why the attention- and emotion-regulation capacities cultivated during mindfulness trainings such as MSPE may facilitate flow and peak performance. Of course, even with this support, terms such as *mindfulness* and *meditation* can sound "out there" or "new-agey." However, unlocking the hard science of such practices has of late been a major focus for neuroscientists. A growing body of research is showing that mindfulness practice can actually change the brain, altering how different parts of the brain communicate as well as the physical structure of certain brain areas (Davidson et al., 2003; Tang, Hölzel, & Posner, 2015), in particular those that control processes known to be important for successful sport performance (Marks, 2008). Although a comprehensive look at this literature is outside the scope of this chapter (see Tang et al., 2015, for such a review), we want to highlight some of the most relevant findings for athletes, especially as they relate to processes of attention and emotion regulation.

Certain brain structures have been identified as heavily involved in attentional processes, including the anterior cingulate cortex (ACC) and the fronto-insular cortex (FIC), which is composed of the ventrolateral prefrontal cortex and a part of the insular cortex (IC) called the anterior insula (e.g., Fan, McCandliss, Fossella, Flombaum, & Posner, 2005; Posner & Rothbart, 2007). Of these structures, the ACC is particularly important to executive attention, which is the ability to focus attention by ignoring distractions (van Veen & Carter, 2002). Its communication with the FIC and dorsolateral prefrontal cortex (DLPFC) appears to be integral to shifting attention (Kondo, Osaka, & Osaka, 2004; Sridharan, Levitin, & Menon, 2008), which, as described previously, is frequently a necessity for athletes.

Interestingly, many of the same brain areas are involved in emotion regulation, including parts of the prefrontal cortex (PFC), the ACC, and the IC (S. J. Banks, Eddy, Angstadt, Nathan, & Phan, 2007; Diekhof, Geier, Falkai, & Gruber, 2011). The ventromedial prefrontal cortex (VMPFC), also referred to as the orbitofrontal cortex (OFC), seems particularly important for emotion regulation (Diekhof et al., 2011), as it has been found to have strong connections with the amygdala, a brain structure critical for the experience of negative emotions (Zald, 2003). Activation in the VMPFC appears to be inversely correlated with activation in the amygdala when people attempt to regulate negative emotions (Urry et al., 2006), which suggests that the VMPFC is an important structure for modulating the experience of negative emotions. Other prefrontal areas of the brain, such as the DLPFC and the dorsal medial prefrontal cortex (DMPFC), have been found to have a similar relationship with the amygdala and thus are also implicated in emotion regulation (S. J. Banks et al., 2007). Ghashghaei, Hilgetag, and Barbas (2007) emphasized the importance of the connection between these various frontal brain structures (e.g., ACC, OFC, DMPFC) and the amygdala, referring to their interaction as an emotion generation–regulation circuit.

Lending powerful support to the idea that mindfulness training bolsters the capacity to regulate attention and emotion, improved functioning in the DLPFC has been observed in neuroimaging studies of mindfulness meditators (Allen et al., 2012). In addition, experienced meditators have shown greater activation in key frontal structures (e.g., DMPFC and rostral ACC: Hölzel et al., 2007) as well as structural changes (i.e., increased gray matter) in areas associated with attention and emotion regulation (e.g., IC, ACC, and VMPFC) compared with nonmeditators (Fox et al., 2014). Wheeler, Arnkoff, and Glass (2016) further pointed out that even individuals who have high levels of dispositional mindfulness without receiving mindfulness training show some of the neurological hallmarks of enhanced emotion regulation (e.g., downregulation of the amygdala). They also noted, though, that intentional mindfulness practice produces additional benefits, with even beginning practitioners demonstrating neurological changes associated with both enhanced emotion regulation and attentional deployment.

It is worthy of mention that, beyond the neural correlates of attention and emotion regulation, another body of research has indicated that mindfulness training also affects brain structures governing other essential capacities for athletes. For instance, in addition to its role in emotion regulation and attention, the IC has been implicated in interoceptive awareness (Fox et al., 2014), and enhanced bodily awareness is frequently cited by athletes as part of their flow experiences (Bernier et al., 2009; Chavez, 2008). Furthermore, mindfulness training has been found to enhance the somatosensory cortex (Fox et al., 2014), which is the main brain area used to process tactile information. Of particular relevance to athletes, changes in the structure and function of this area in meditators have been associated with higher pain tolerance (J. A. Grant, Courtemanche, Duerden, Duncan, & Rainville, 2010; Zeidan et al., 2011).

We have given just a snapshot of the emerging research showing the brain's incredible ability to adapt. This capacity of the brain to change, both functionally and structurally, in response to the repeated practice of a task (e.g., meditation) is called *neuroplasticity*. Neuroplasticity allows people to alter psychological characteristics (e.g., emotional reactivity) previously thought to be fixed traits (Davidson, 2002), and such neurological adaptations may, in fact, be the essence of what makes mindfulness training effective (Siegel, 2007). This phenomenon has exciting and profound implications for sports. Mindfulness training may be able to enhance brain regions that control attention- and emotion-regulation processes, which, as Marks (2008) noted, are "skills that allow for effective athletic training and make peak performance possible" (p. 220). In this sense, we can view the brain as a muscle and mindfulness programs such as MSPE as a workout regimen to help stretch, tone, and strengthen that muscle, opening the door to a level of performance that may previously have been unattainable.

Incompatibilities of Mindfulness and Flow: The Paradox of Autopilot

This collected evidence demonstrates the strong connection between mindfulness and flow and shows that mindfulness training can strengthen those capacities (e.g., attention and emotion regulation) that are the primary facilitators of flow states. In fact, in athlete samples, the connection has been shown to be so robust that Cathcart et al. (2014) suggested, "One potential explanation for the observed relationships is that measures of flow and mindfulness are in fact assessing the same construct" (p. 137). These authors ultimately concluded that mindfulness and flow are highly related but are distinct constructs with some notable differences. For example, mindfulness is often described as having certain features that definitions of flow do not include, such as openness to and acceptance of all experiences, intentional observation of the transience of experiences, and an explicit focus on the awareness of internal experiences (Bishop et al., 2004).

Other authors have also tried to make this distinction between mindfulness and flow. Dane (2011) proposed that one main difference is that mindfulness tends to encourage a wide breadth of attention (i.e., openness to all experiences), whereas the focus in flow is usually quite narrow (i.e., concentration on the task at hand). However, Marks (2008) cited neurological evidence indicating that a narrow attentional focus is not actually a prerequisite for flow states because both expert meditators and expert athletes demonstrate greater contextual awareness (e.g., breadth of attention) than do their novice counterparts, while still exhibiting optimal performance. In addition, as noted previously, despite athletes' emotional states being significant to their achieving flow (Anderson et al., 2014; Chavez, 2008; S. A. Jackson, 1992), the cultivated nonreactivity that seems to enable mindfulness practitioners to improve their emotion-regulation abilities is not represented among the elements of flow as currently defined. Nevertheless, other correlates of mindfulness not represented among the flow elements, such as calmness and bodily awareness, are often listed by athletes as aspects of their flow states (Swann et al., 2012).

Two other apparent distinctions between mindfulness and flow are worth exploring further: (a) the internal attentional focus of mindfulness versus the external focus of flow and (b) the intentionality of mindfulness versus the felt automaticity of flow. Regarding the former, Josefsson and Broberg (2011) found no differences between the attentional capacities of meditators and nonmeditators (in contrast to much of the extant literature) and concluded that

> mindfulness meditators may have an increased awareness of internal processes and the ability to quickly attend to them but this type of refined attentional ability does not seem to be related to performance on attention tests requiring responses to external targets. (p. 291)

If true, this conclusion would indeed be problematic for athletes, considering the ubiquitous need to attend to external targets in some form across all sports.

It is important to note, however, that even though many mindfulness practices use internal anchors for attention (e.g., the breath), mindfulness is by no means limited to a focus on internal experience and, in fact, many mindfulness training programs, including MSPE, involve exercises that bring attention outside of the body. For example, practitioners can be encouraged to be aware of how they are interacting with their environment (e.g., walking meditation) or to focus attention on external stimuli, such as sounds.

The second distinction, what we refer to as the "paradox of autopilot," seems potentially more significant in our opinion. When describing their experiences of flow, many athletes report a feeling of effortlessness or automaticity, often using the term *autopilot* to capture this sensation (Anderson et al., 2014; Chavez, 2008). Although a number of researchers have commented on this sense of automaticity, some even identifying it as a primary facet of flow (e.g., Rheinberg, Vollmeyer, & Engeser, 2003), there appears to be disagreement in the literature regarding how it is understood. Chavez (2008) suggested that this sense of automaticity is a function of being fully absorbed in the task at hand, connecting it to the merging of action and awareness element of flow. Sheldon,

Prentice, and Halusic (2015) on the other hand, contrasted this automaticity with the sense of absorption one feels in flow—where the absorption has to do with the combination of task engagement and the loss of self-consciousness—while automaticity is about the felt sense of control that results in perceptions of effortlessness. Regardless, there is some possible tension here between mindfulness and flow, because although many athletes frame autopilot as a positive aspect of flow, shifting out of autopilot and intentionally engaging with the world is cited as a benefit of mindfulness training (e.g., Segal, Williams, & Teasdale, 2002).

Sheldon and colleagues (2015) stated that this tension might actually make mindful states incompatible with flow states, such that the self-reflective awareness at the core of mindfulness is likely to interfere with, rather than facilitate, an athlete's ability to get fully absorbed in the task at hand. However, we tend to agree with authors such as Chavez (2008), who have pointed out a connection between absorption and automaticity that would suggest mindfulness could help facilitate flow. We also recognize, though, the complex interconnection between the different elements of flow, and because athletes often report experiencing at least five of the nine elements in any given flow experience (Swann et al., 2012), it seems likely that an interaction of these elements, rather than their simple presence or absence, is what results in this optimal performance state. Thus, with regard to the autopilot paradox, it may be useful to explore ways that mindfulness could potentially affect any element of flow.

It may also be true that the tension between mindfulness and flow is merely semantic. When discussing the "effortless" quality of flow, S. A. Jackson (1996) posited that intentional effort is still present and that athletes are actually describing the lack of tension or strain (e.g., negative emotions) as opposed to the absence of purposeful engagement. Similarly, athletes' use of the term *autopilot* may be reflective of something slightly different from the autopilot many mindfulness teachers talk about. In a mindfulness context, *autopilot* usually refers to a form of mindlessness or automatic behavior in which action is done without awareness of important contextual factors (Langer, 1989, 1997). Thus, decisions come from ingrained habits (which may or may not be helpful), rather than through thoughtful deliberation.

Conversely, while athletes are in flow, their automaticity appears more to reflect a feeling of complete control (Rheinberg et al., 2003) as they tap into knowledge stores developed over years of practice. In fact, what descriptions of flow may really be capturing is the subjective experience of a form of cognitive and neurological efficiency. It is well documented that expert athletes engage in more efficient cognitive and neurological processing than do novice athletes (e.g., Mann et al., 2007; Marks, 2008). In a neuroimaging study examining flow states in athletes, Ferrell, Beach, Szeverenyi, Krch, and Fernhall (2006) found that the importance of efficiency, represented by focused activation in brain areas relevant to performance, may also apply to flow:

> Focused neural activation as a result of a sufficiently practiced activity may provide for an efficient motor-neural pathway in the absence of extraneous mental processing. This would present an explanation for the apparent dichotomy of peak performances with concomitant sensations of ease of effort and no thinking of process. (p. 431)

Such a claim suggests that, instead of being incompatible with the automaticity associated with flow, mindfulness may actually be well suited to facilitate its occurrence. By intentionally tuning in to present-moment experience, which at first does require significant effort and cognitive control (e.g., attention and emotion regulation), the self-regulatory capacities being trained eventually become automatic and effortless themselves (Tang, Rothbart, & Posner, 2012). Marks (2008) said that one way to conceptualize mindfulness programs for athletes is as "mental efficiency training" (p. 230). As such, mindfulness training, such as MSPE, may produce many of its benefits precisely through the enhancement of self-regulation (Hölzel et al., 2011), freeing up valuable resources that can allow practitioners to do more with less.

The idea that the optimal performances associated with flow could be contingent upon maximally efficient internal (e.g., neurological) functioning has significant implications for how and why mindfulness interventions such as MSPE might work. With continued practice of the primary mindfulness characteristics of awareness and acceptance, athletes begin to experience improved regulation of attention and emotion, which, over time, can become their default setting as they deploy these capacities in a way that feels effortless. But the question remains, how do athletes go about actually training these capacities? This is the subject of the next six chapters (Part II of this book), in which we provide the easy-to-follow, session-by-session MSPE protocol, introducing readers to this mindfulness-based approach to mental training.

MINDFUL SPORT PERFORMANCE ENHANCEMENT

II

MSPE Session 1
Building Mindfulness Fundamentals

4

Now that you've been exposed to what mindfulness is and its relevance to sport and attaining peak performance, you have reached the core of this book. The complete mindful sport performance enhancement (MSPE) protocol is provided in these next six chapters. A full chapter is devoted to each session of the training, presenting the main themes, key concepts and rationales, teaching points, exercise scripts, and home practice recommendations for that session. In addition, all handouts that appear in these chapters are available online (http://pubs.apa.org/books/supp/kaufman/), and audio recordings of every exercise can also be found online (http://www.mindfulsportperformance.org). These resources can be used to help guide participants through their practice between or during MSPE sessions as well as after the training has concluded.

Before plunging into the protocol, we think it's beneficial to present a general overview of how the sessions are delivered and how best to prepare for the training. This may also be a good time to revisit the outline of MSPE (see Table 1) presented in the Introduction to this book and/or to look ahead at the bulleted snapshots (see, for instance, p. 65 in this chapter) that begin the description of each session.

http://dx.doi.org/10.1037/0000048-005
Mindful Sport Performance Enhancement: Mental Training for Athletes and Coaches, by K. A. Kaufman, C. R. Glass, and T. R. Pineau

MSPE: Overview and Preparation

The protocol presented here includes content for six 90-minute sessions, delivered weekly to groups of athletes and/or coaches. However, when implementing MSPE, leaders can use their knowledge of sport psychology, mindfulness, and the people they are training to tailor the intervention to participants' unique needs. For example, sessions can be condensed to fit shorter existing time blocks (e.g., 75 minutes, 1 hour), meeting frequency can be adjusted (e.g., meeting every other week), and/or the training can be adapted for use with individuals as necessary (e.g., in counseling or consultation settings). In fact, readers of this book could even use the session descriptions and recorded exercises to lead themselves through the training. Although we provide scripts for all MSPE exercises, in our experience it isn't particularly compelling for a leader to stand in front of a mindfulness group and just read a script word-for-word. Although our intention in offering the protocol in this way is for leaders to stay true to the content of these chapters, we also encourage them to infuse their own style into the discussions and exercises to help the content to come alive for participants.

Taken as a whole, MSPE is designed with a specific progression in terms of how mindfulness is taught. The first two sessions include the largest didactic components, as this is when the concept of mindfulness is introduced, a rationale for the application of mindfulness to sports is presented (Session 1), and the mechanisms of action (i.e., performance facilitators) are explained and linked to sport-specific examples (Session 2). New concepts continue to be introduced throughout the training, but once the foundational knowledge of mindfulness is established in the first two sessions, more in-session time becomes available for experiential practice and discussion. Thus, there is a gradual increase in the amount of formal mindfulness practice throughout MSPE, both within and outside of sessions.

In MSPE, various meditations comprise the formal mindfulness practice and, coinciding with the shift toward an experiential emphasis, exercises transition from sedentary mindfulness to mindfulness in motion. This progression culminates with an applied sport-specific meditation, using core movements in the sport(s) of focus as attentional anchors (see Session 5 in Chapter 8). Numerous present-moment anchors are introduced over the course of the training to build bridges for participants between formal mindfulness practice and everyday activities, in particular their sport performances. In addition, emphasis is also placed on incorporating mindfulness more informally into sport practice, competition, and daily life.

By using these easy-to-follow protocol chapters, a wide range of people—including sport psychologists and consultants, other mental health professionals, athletic coaches, and athletes themselves—can be effective MSPE leaders. However, as we discuss at length in Chapter 13, in addition to familiarity with MSPE, we also think it's essential for leaders to have established the practice of mindfulness in their own lives. Prior experience facilitating groups (if that is the format in which MSPE is being delivered), knowledge of the sport(s) of focus, and awareness of the particular ethical concerns associated with doing mental training in sport are also important.

In terms of potential MSPE participants, we suggest that athletes and coaches of all levels (recreational to elite) and in all sports could benefit, as could people who may not be involved in any particular sport but simply desire to incorporate mindfulness into their exercise routine. The training is intended to be highly adaptable for participants from a single sport or representing various sports. As highlighted throughout these protocol chapters, often via the example of long-distance running, this customization occurs through the insertion of sport-specific details into the didactic, discussion, and experiential components of the training. In addition, as we address in Chapter 14, MSPE could even be adapted for a range of other performers (e.g., actors, musicians). It may be useful for anyone wanting to benefit from MSPE to read Chapter 12 prior to beginning the training to get the most out of the experience.

Session 1 Snapshot

Aims of the first session include developing the group dynamic, introducing mindfulness, and sharing the theoretical basis for MSPE. In addition to being introduced to the science behind why mindfulness (and MSPE in particular) benefits sport performance, it is essential for participants to understand the significance of committing to this form of mental training. Useful parallels can be drawn between physical and mental training, given that participants are likely familiar with the time and dedication required for the former. Like the body, the mind requires versatile, systematic exercise of increasing intensity to cultivate the skills necessary for successful performance, and MSPE provides the necessary structure for how to train in this way.

The main theme of Session 1 is the relevance of mindfulness for sport, which is established through topics such as intentional focus versus automatic pilot, observing what is happening without judgment, and links between mindfulness and the flow state. Components of this session are

- introductions and confidentiality,
- rationales for mindfulness and MSPE,
- candy exercise and discussion,
- diaphragmatic breathing and sitting meditation with a focus on the breath and discussion,
- home practice assignment and distribution of Daily Mindfulness Log, and
- wrap-up and discussion of automatic pilot.

Introductions and Confidentiality

After MSPE leader introductions, participants can introduce themselves, sharing what they hope to get out of MSPE, pertaining to both their sport and other aspects of their lives. It is important for leaders to make clear the need for confidentiality by explaining that people will be disclosing their personal reactions to what is experienced. Agreement to refrain from talking about MSPE discussions with anyone outside of the group is vital to building a sense of comfort and safety that can help maximize benefits.

Rationales for Mindfulness and MSPE

From the beginning, it is crucial that participants understand the nature of MSPE and why it is worth their effort and time. Having the rationale presented in a clear, engaging, and interactive way can help participants develop an intention for their practice, which is an essential element of this type of training (Shapiro, Carlson, Astin, & Freedman, 2006). Leaders can begin this process by introducing the concepts of mental training and the mental training paradox, which we described in Chapter 1. In particular, they can highlight that athletes often spend significant time and energy training to promote their physical conditioning and technical skill but far less time engaged in systematic mental training, despite general agreement on the importance of mental and emotional factors in sport. This paradox is not necessarily due to a lack of interest in strengthening the mind but rather to other factors such as perceptions of insufficient time or lack of knowledge on how to do such training.

MSPE is a mental training program that teaches a range of skills based in mindfulness, which will likely be a new approach for many participants. So, it can be valuable to spend a few minutes exploring what is already known about mindfulness before defining it further. This discussion is the first opportunity for leaders to model a mindful way of being by staying present with participants as they speak and responding in an accepting, nonjudgmental manner. It is also a chance to clear up any misconceptions about mindfulness or meditation. Mindfulness essentially is about paying attention to what's happening right now, in each moment, both internally and externally. This emphasis on attention may be familiar to athletes because coaches have probably been admonishing them to focus throughout their careers.

However, another aspect of mindfulness may be less familiar. Paying attention is just part of it—it's also *how* one pays attention. Examples tailored to the participants' sport(s) may be useful here to illustrate how the style of one's attention can impact performance. Consider this one for runners:

> Imagine a runner in the heat of a race. Lungs are burning, legs are on fire, and an internal mental battle is going on, with one voice saying, "I'm exhausted, I can't do this" and another voice saying, "Just push through this, it's only one more mile." Then, all of a sudden, a competitor comes up from behind and passes.

Leaders can encourage participants to share what would be going on for them as that runner at that moment, looking specifically for comments implying judgments about performance or capability, such as doubts about being able to catch up or worries about the pain associated with speeding up. Participants may notice how their initial reactions might lead them to focus even more on their doubts or worries, which can result in a host of other reactions (e.g., frustration, demoralization) that pull their attention still further away from their performance.

Leaders can point out to participants that such reactions do not help them go faster, and it is here that this other aspect of mindfulness comes in: It's not just paying attention, but paying attention *nonjudgmentally.* Getting so wrapped up in their reactions means they are no longer focused on the task at hand, which is running. Instead, they are focused on their judgments about what is happening, expending their precious mental energy on factors unrelated to present-moment performance. And it is really only present-moment performance that is controllable. To help participants make this connection, leaders can ask them what the runner in this example is actually doing in that moment. In our experience, a range of answers may be offered, but most participants overlook the basic truth that, in this hypothetical moment, the runner is just running. Not losing, failing, or disappointing—just running. Rather than getting caught up in judgments, what if one could simply let them go and notice instead the controllable factors that actually can increase speed, such as the stride or the breath? So often, attention gets stuck in reactions to what's happening or speculations about what hasn't happened yet, rather than being free to observe what's actually happening in that moment.

This kind of example can lay the groundwork for helping participants better understand the potential benefits of mindfulness. To make this type of mental training even more relatable, leaders may find it helpful to draw a parallel to physical training, which is likely much more familiar. The ability to pay attention nonjudgmentally is like a muscle and, for many people, that muscle is weak. MSPE is like strength training for attention; it can increase the capacity for direct focus during performance, which is no easy feat in the distraction-packed sports environment.

Leaders can explain that many exercises in MSPE that build this attention muscle are forms of meditation. *Meditation* can be a somewhat stigmatized term in sport, and MSPE participants may arrive with preconceived ideas of what it involves. It may be useful to urge them to keep an open mind, perhaps pointing out that, even though meditation is rooted in a spiritual tradition, it is not religious in nature, and the skills developed through meditation lend themselves quite well to the achievement of an optimal mind-set while performing, both in sport and in life more generally (e.g., school, work). Within each MSPE meditation, particular anchors for attention are highlighted, and repeatedly directing focus to these anchors provides the "mental reps" for this mindfulness training. Anchors are first used while sitting, but each new exercise incorporates more attentional or bodily movements until ultimately participants are able to execute mindfulness skills while engaging in the movements of their sport.

At this point, leaders can introduce the strong empirical connection between mindfulness and the flow state (reviewed in depth in Chapter 3). Participants may not be familiar with the term *flow* but likely know the concept colloquially as being "in the zone." Leaders can invite them to share any experiences they have had with flow or the zone and then provide a definition of the state, such as episodes of performing as well as or better than ever before that somehow feel effortless. It is important to emphasize that sport scientists understand flow pretty well from decades of research and that some of the key factors associated with it are present-moment attention, a sense of control, and a loss of self-consciousness.

Leaders can tie these elements of flow back to the earlier discussion on mindfulness, making it evident that many of the factors associated with being in flow are taught during MSPE and furthermore that MSPE may increase the likelihood of achieving this optimal-performance state (see the proposed pathways from MSPE to peak performance described in Chapter 10). Additional research linking mindfulness and flow (see Chapter 3), including MSPE studies with athletes that found increases in flow (see Chapter 11), may be worth sharing.

Many former participants have reported also enjoying learning more about the science of mindfulness, such as how it relates to aspects of physical and emotional functioning like healing, immune response, stress reactivity, and overall physical well-being (e.g., Davidson et al., 2003). Studies have also shown structural and functional changes in the brains of those who practice mindfulness, which can enhance abilities such as concentration and emotion regulation (Siegel, 2007). Such findings are contributing to a mindful revolution in sport and other performance domains, and Chapter 2 gave several shareable examples of high-profile, championship-winning mindfulness practitioners from professional, Olympic, and collegiate sports.

Discussing how mindfulness training can be beneficial in participants' specific sport(s) can be an effective way to conclude this portion of the session. It may help to incorporate comments or perspectives from notable figures in these sport(s), if possible, that pertain to mindfulness concepts. The explanation that follows is tailored to runners and serves as an example of what could be adapted to connect with athletes and coaches in other sports.

Leaders can share that running challenges physical and mental limits. Pain, fatigue, boredom, and other sensations can become major distractions. Regretting an error made early in a race or speculating on its impact cannot make that error go away and, in fact, can inhibit doing what is possible now, in the present moment, to help avoid a feared outcome. Similarly, trying to suppress an undesired reaction can have ironic effects, drawing more attention toward the reaction and away from the task at hand, which is simply running. The repetitive nature of distance running makes it very easy for runners to "check out" from their present-moment experiences, which also reduces their ability to make meaningful improvements to their running performance as it is happening. Thus, it is crucial to be able to notice when the mind wanders, to let go of judgmental or irrelevant thoughts, and to refocus attention on the act of running in the moment.

This ability is particularly significant when taking into account exercise science research demonstrating that a primary cause of fatigue and exhaustion in high-intensity aerobic activity is actually mental, not physiological. In other words, during a race when feelings of exhaustion lead to thoughts such as "I don't think I can sprint to the finish," the lack of a sprint has more to do with that thought than with any true physical limit reached. Dr. Timothy Noakes, a well-known exercise scientist, notably said that "the feeling of fatigue *is* fatigue" (Fitzgerald, 2010, p. 7). This is great news for runners because one of the primary aims of MSPE is to teach how to let go of such thoughts so they don't impede performance. In fact, Dr. Thomas Miller, author of *Programmed to Run* (2002) and an expert on the biomechanical and psychological aspects of running, said that this ability to let go is essential to optimal running performance.

Danny and Katherine Dreyer, creators of a method to improve running performance and prevent injury known as ChiRunning (Dreyer & Dreyer, 2004), also talked about the key elements of running optimally. They listed letting go of judgmental thoughts, being able to focus attention, sensing what's happening in the body, breathing diaphragmatically, and staying as relaxed as possible, each of which can be developed through mindfulness training and is taught in MSPE.

It is important to remember, just as adequate physical training is necessary to run a marathon successfully, the mind cannot master these skills without consistent and dedicated practice. MSPE can help to train the mind for peak performance, but it will take commitment to practice, both in and outside of these sessions. Just as time is made for physical workouts, it is necessary to make time for mental ones. Prioritizing something new is rarely easy, so approach this as an opportunity to strengthen the mind, rather than yet another item on a to-do list. It is said that sport is 90% mental, so hopefully this is a chance to learn to run faster by training the mind with the same intensity as athletes train the body.

Candy Exercise

The first exercise done in MSPE uses food as the present-moment anchor. This activity was inspired by the raisin exercise, which has been described by Kabat-Zinn (1990) and Segal, Williams, and Teasdale (2002), among others. Kabat-Zinn said that the raisin exercise is done to relieve participants of their preconceived notions of what meditation is. For a unique twist in MSPE, David Maron (personal communication, July 7, 2011), an experienced mindfulness teacher, recommended the use of candy such as M&Ms rather than raisins. Raisins are not typically regarded as a treat, so using candy can introduce an element of fun to mindfulness, helping make it more accessible. The chocolate center and candy shell of M&Ms also provide a complex texture and a richness that, when savored, stands out in a person's mind. Finally, Maron noted that this exercise highlights the difference between mindful and unmindful eating, so it is helpful to use a food that is often eaten mindlessly and that when eaten in abundance can be unhealthy. The enhanced impact of this exercise when using candy may give participants a powerful example and an effective metaphor for understanding how mindfulness can benefit them in daily life.

For this approximately 7-minute exercise, participants receive two pieces of candy, which they will eat one at a time while paying attention to what they are doing and experiencing, moment by moment. As an alternative to M&Ms, individually wrapped candies (e.g., Peppermint Patties) can be used, and the mindful unwrapping of the candy can be included as part of the exercise. Really, any type of candy can be used, but it is important to take into account allergies or other dietary restrictions of participants and make food substitutions as needed.

Kabat-Zinn (1990) described how, at his clinic, people often comment that they catch themselves automatically moving to eat the next raisin before finishing the one in their mouth, and they recognize that they eat this way normally. When eating mindfully, one is in touch with the food and the process of eating because the mind is not distracted. Awareness of the complexity of eating is increased with recognition of the feedback coming from all of the different senses, the thoughts and emotions generated, and the automatic physical responses triggered (e.g., swallowing, salivating). By applying this kind of awareness to a regular daily activity, this exercise helps participants understand that knowing what is occurring while it is occurring is a hallmark of mindfulness practice.

Before beginning, MSPE leaders can explain that this first exercise involves using food as an attentional anchor and eating in a way that is probably different from what they are accustomed to. They can instruct participants to observe the process of what they are doing and any reactions (thoughts, feelings, sensations) that arise in response.

SCRIPT FOR CANDY EXERCISE

Take two objects out of the bag as it is passed around the room. Do not eat them yet. For now, set one of these objects aside and hold the other in the palm of your hand. I want you to look down at this object and view it as if you have never seen such a thing before. See the shape. Is it perfectly proportioned or lopsided? Notice the colors and the way the light hits its surface. Pretend that this object is totally foreign to you. Let your eyes slowly and carefully explore every part of it. *(Pause for 5 seconds.)*

Feel the object resting in your hand, and sense its weight. Now, feel its texture, perhaps as you slowly turn the object over with your fingers. If, at any point while doing this, you find yourself asking questions such as, What's the point of this? What's this weird exercise we're doing? or When can I eat this? then just note these questions as thoughts and gently escort your attention back to the object in your hand.

Now, smell the object, perhaps holding it just beneath your nose. With each in-breath that you take, see if you can find the object's unique scent. Notice what thoughts or memories arise when you take in that particular smell and just let those thoughts glide in and out of your mind as you return your awareness to the object. *(5 seconds)*

Now, take the object between your thumb and index finger. As you hold it, bring it toward your face, but do not place it in your mouth. Observe what reactions begin to occur. Do you feel your mouth start to water? Do you sense a desire to eat this thing? Once you have noted any reactions, bring the object away from your mouth once again.

Take another careful look at the object. Then, slowly begin moving the object toward your mouth once more, maybe noticing how your hand knows just where to go or any physical reactions to the object's approach. Close your eyes and gently place the object in your mouth and, without chewing, explore how the object feels sitting on your tongue. Let it just sit there. *(10 seconds)* When you feel ready, slowly, with full awareness, begin chewing and observe the taste. Pause for a moment as you chew, noticing how the conditions in your mouth and the consistency of the object are changing. If pieces get stuck in your teeth, observe the sensations of your tongue getting them out.

Notice when you feel the urge to swallow, perhaps sensing how strong or automatic this urge can be. And, as you swallow, see if you can track the process as the object leaves your mouth. Try to sense how you are reacting to having eaten this object. What thoughts does eating this particular object, with this particular taste, bring to your mind? Can you notice within yourself a desire or a craving for more? As best you can, bring a gentle curiosity to these observations. Be with this experience fully: physically, mentally, and emotionally. *(10 seconds)*

Now, take the second object, the one you had set aside earlier, and place it in the palm of your hand. I want you to again proceed through these same steps, consciously seeing, feeling, smelling, and then tasting the object before swallowing it, and noting any changes that occur in your body. In this instance, however, go through these steps in your own time, observing any thoughts or reactions that come to mind and then, as best you can, letting them go and gently, mindfully escorting your attention back to the object. *(10 seconds)*

Reflect on how this one object can be experienced so differently and so much more deeply. Recognize your ability to experience life richly, and notice how all that is needed are a few calm, mindful moments. When you have finished, please open your eyes.

DISCUSSION OF CANDY EXERCISE

After the candy exercise, participants are given a chance to discuss their experiences and reactions. It is important for leaders to model responding mindfully to any observations, questions, or concerns raised. They can facilitate this discussion by asking open-ended questions such as the following, allowing 2 to 3 minutes for each:

- What were your experiences while eating these objects?
- What types of thoughts went through your mind during the activity?
- How was this way of eating different from the way you usually eat?

Leaders can then take the opportunity to tie the mindfulness skills practiced in the candy exercise back to the sport(s) of focus. The following description (informed by Segal et al., 2002) has been tailored to runners but should be customized to fit the sport of interest.

As exemplified by this exercise, much of what is done in MSPE involves bringing awareness to present-moment activities. Practicing this kind of awareness will make clearer how much time is spent passively receiving experiences and how mindfulness can allow for a more active participation in life. More freedom, control, and choice are available by becoming more fully aware of thoughts, feelings, and sensations. Recall the example of getting passed by a competitor in a race. Getting wrapped up in judgments about how much the rest of the race will hurt or how badly the race is going makes it quite difficult to focus on what can actually help performance in that moment. In fact, attending to these kinds of self-evaluative thoughts actually can be a significant distraction, generating unnecessary stress and tension that could further harm performance. But, letting go of those thoughts and remaining in touch with the action of running as it is happening (e.g., stride, arm motions, breathing) can provide the chance to take control of the performance, maybe to tweak form and/or energy expenditure, and perhaps catch that competitor.

This is a good time to say a bit more about what is meant by being "in touch with" an activity as it's happening. Sometimes people hear that phrase and think they are being asked to self-instruct their way through or micromanage an experience, which is not the style of attention developed in MSPE. Rather, the program is designed to strengthen the ability to just observe, to be present with and aware of what is occurring, without getting lost in reactions and judgments that so often detract from experience and performance. In other words, eating a piece of candy mindfully or running with awareness of form does not mean relearning the steps involved in eating or running. This training is about approaching these familiar activities with a fresh, nonjudgmental, observing mindset, which can enhance one's experiences of them.

Diaphragmatic Breathing and Sitting Meditation With a Focus on the Breath

The next present-moment anchor introduced is the breath. Participants learn about using this anchor through two exercises: 3 minutes of diaphragmatic breathing and then a 9-minute sitting meditation with a focus on the breath. Recommendations and examples from Kabat-Zinn (1990, 1994) and the Mindfulness of the Breath script found in Segal et al. (2002) informed the development of this sitting meditation exercise.

INTRODUCTION TO DIAPHRAGMATIC BREATHING

Kabat-Zinn (1990) referred to the sitting meditation as the heart of formal mindfulness practice, and it is a central component of MSPE. When discussing the importance of the breath, he explained how it is beneficial to breathe in a particular way, a technique known as belly or *diaphragmatic* breathing (as opposed to chest breathing, which is usually rapid and shallow). According to Kabat-Zinn, when breathing diaphragmatically, one relaxes the belly as much as possible. Then, as the breath comes in, the belly can expand slightly in an outward direction as the diaphragm pushes down on the abdomen from above. The diaphragm is able to push down further when the belly is relaxed, so the in-breath is a bit longer and the lungs fill with more air. A little more air is then expelled on the out-breath, so that the cycle of breathing is slower and deeper. To practice this technique, it may be helpful to put a hand over the belly and observe its movement as air flows in and out.

Kabat-Zinn (1990) further suggested that being mindful of one's breathing can help to calm the body and mind. Giving the mind only one thing to keep track of, instead of the range of stimuli it usually finds to preoccupy itself with, may enhance the ability to concentrate. Deep breathing also has measurable physiological benefits, decreasing sympathetic nervous system activity, which governs the fight–flight–freeze response, and increasing parasympathetic activity, which governs the "rest and digest" response (Pal, Velkumary, & Madanmohan, 2004). In addition, breathing down into the belly enables the intake of more air than does shallow chest breathing, allowing athletes not only to reduce symptoms of stress but also to consume more of the oxygen their muscles need to perform.

It is noteworthy that instruction in diaphragmatic breathing is inherently change-focused (i.e., there is a correct way to breathe), which, in some ways, is incongruent with the acceptance-based nature of mindfulness practice. Although diaphragmatic breathing is beneficial, feeling that it is necessary to breathe in this way may be counterproductive. So, before the sitting meditation is introduced, MSPE includes a brief diaphragmatic breathing exercise for participants to build some initial comfort with its execution. The ultimate intent of this exercise is to allow the sitting meditation to be free from change-oriented language so that participants can simply notice whatever is present, even if that is chest breathing. It will likely take repeated exposure for participants to master diaphragmatic breathing skills, so this short exercise will be practiced at the start of each subsequent MSPE session, and leaders are encouraged to issue reminders throughout the program to incorporate this way of breathing into informal mindfulness practice.

When introducing the diaphragmatic breathing exercise, leaders can survey participants to see if anyone has heard of this type of breathing and then define it for them. It may be helpful to emphasize particularly the differences between chest and belly breathing, the range of benefits that diaphragmatic breathing can produce, and the need for consistent practice to build comfort.

SCRIPT FOR DIAPHRAGMATIC BREATHING EXERCISE

To begin, sit up tall with your feet planted firmly on the ground, and imagine each of your vertebrae stacked one on top of the other, all the way up your spine, with your head resting comfortably atop your shoulders. You can close your eyes if you'd like, or, if you prefer, you can leave them open slightly, allowing your gaze to rest unfocused on a spot on the floor a few feet in front of you. Many of us can develop the habit of breathing into our chest and tightening our abdomen as we move throughout the busyness of our lives, so it may take a few moments to find a comfortable rhythm of belly breathing. Allow the muscles in your abdomen to relax, letting your stomach expand and deflate as you breathe down into your belly. You may find it helpful to place one of your hands, palm open, on your belly, just above the belly button. See if you can sense your hand rising and falling with the rhythm of your breathing, and see if you can intentionally take in more air with each in-breath. Notice any changes that occur by breathing into your belly in this way. You can leave your hand on your belly as long as you like, or, when you feel at ease maintaining a gentle awareness of the breath traveling down into your belly, you can place your hand wherever feels right to you. *(Pause for 1 minute.)*

Now, take one more deep, full inhalation, and then imagine that your belly button is trying to reach all the way back to your spine as you slowly and completely exhale. When you're ready, you can open your eyes and return your attention to the world around you.

INTRODUCTION TO SITTING MEDITATION WITH A FOCUS ON THE BREATH

Leaders can explain that the next exercise also involves the breath, but this time the focus is slightly different. For this exercise, a *sitting meditation*, the breath is used as an attentional anchor, much like the candy was used earlier. The breath is an especially convenient and effective anchor because it is always present. If you're alive, you're breathing. Despite its literally vital importance, breathing is something that typically doesn't get much attention, yet each breath presents a fresh opportunity to practice mindfulness and strengthen the mind.

Leaders can instruct participants that, for about the next 9 minutes, the task will be simply sitting and observing the process of breathing. But unlike the previous exercise, this one is not about altering the breath. In fact, exactly the opposite is true. For this exercise, participants just notice the sensations associated with the breathing cycle, whatever they might be in a given moment. It is important to emphasize that it is absolutely fine to notice chest breathing. There is no need to make any changes; rather, they merely observe what is occurring as they breathe.

It may be useful for leaders to point out that this exercise might sound simple, but it actually requires significant patience and concentration. Participants will find that they cannot focus their attention on the breath for very long without their minds being pulled away by something else, such as thoughts about the rest of their day or judgments about the meditation (e.g., whether they are doing it "right"). That's perfectly natural; it is just what minds do. Encourage participants to notice each time that their attention has wandered and then simply escort it back to their breath. The essential skill here is not to maintain perfect focus on the breath but rather to notice when the mind has wandered and then to bring it back to the breath, without being self-critical. A great sports analogy is to compare this practice with doing reps in the weight room. Each time participants notice the mind wandering and return it to their anchor, they're strengthening the mental muscles of attention and letting go. When first trying the breathing meditation, participants can often be quite negative and self-critical when they find their minds wandering a lot, even though this is a very natural occurrence. So, letting go also means noticing and accepting such judgments and gently bringing attention back to the breath.

SCRIPT FOR SITTING MEDITATION WITH A FOCUS ON THE BREATH

To begin, sit tall, with your spine straight, your ears over your shoulders, and your chin slightly tucked toward your chest. The idea is to adopt a posture that is comfortable and erect. Place your hands wherever feels right to you, maybe on your knees or in your lap. Lay them with the palms facing upward and allow the muscles in your fingers to relax. You may find it helpful to gently close your eyes, but if you would rather keep them open, let your gaze fall unfocused to a spot on the floor about a foot in front of you. *(Pause for 10 seconds.)*

Now, bring your attention to the tips of your toes. From there, allow your attention to slowly rise up through your whole body with each in-breath. As your attention passes through each body part, see if you can notice any tension being held by your muscles. If you do notice tension, you can sit with that experience or you can gently tense that area of your body as you breathe in and relax as you exhale, leaving behind loose muscles as your attention rises a bit more in your body on the next in-breath. As you continue to breathe, imagine that each inhalation is taking in a cool, peaceful, relaxing feeling that is slowly permeating your being, from your toes to the top of your head. *(10 seconds)*

Your breath is your anchor. It is always present. No matter where you are or what you are doing, your breath is with you. It is happening right now, in this moment. Each time you breathe, let your breath remind you that you are alive, right here, right now. Notice now the rhythm of your breath as it flows naturally. You do not need to try to breathe more deeply or at a different speed. Allow your breath to do what it always does and just observe this process. Feel the air as it enters your lungs and fills your abdomen. Notice the brief pause just before you exhale, then let go of this breath. Pay close attention to each moment of the breath, from the in-breath, to the pause, to the out-breath. One continuous flow. Each breath keeps us alive. Each breath is vital to us. Yet we always let it go. We are always breathing. We are always letting go. *(10 seconds)*

As you watch your breath, it might be helpful to settle your attention on the physical sensations you are feeling. Notice the feeling of expansion in your torso as you inhale. And notice your muscles relax with the sense of gentle deflation as you exhale. These feelings may be centered in your chest or in your belly. Wherever you notice them is perfectly fine. Or notice the feelings in your nostrils and on your upper lip, perhaps feeling the coolness of the air entering your nose and the sensation across your upper lip as the air flows back out. Allow these sensations to fill your field of awareness as you sit with your breath. They do not need to be different; they do not need to be changed. Right now, for this breath, they are exactly what they need to be. *(10 seconds)*

You will find, as you sit with your breath, that your attention wanders away, perhaps getting caught up in the endless flow of thoughts and feelings that we all have each day. This is perfectly natural. Minds wander; that is just what they do. When you notice your mind has wandered from the breath, you may have a reaction such as "I am terrible at keeping my focus" or "I must be doing this wrong." Rest assured, this is not the case. You are also not doing anything wrong by having these judgments. They are perfectly natural too. But, as best you can, try to let such judgments of your experience just pass out of your mind. In realizing that your attention has wandered, you are truly present. You are noticing something right here and right now. You are seizing the opportunity to observe what your mind is doing in this very moment.

If you notice your thoughts being drawn away, maybe by the memory of where you have been or in anticipation of where you are going next, see if you can acknowledge where your mind has gone, appreciate that it might be important to you, and then gently bring your attention back to your breath. The past has come and gone, and the future has not yet arrived. Give yourself the gift of this moment. Let those thoughts about other times go; let them pass through your mind. Your thoughts are like clouds, and you are like a mountain. Just as the harshest storm clouds may batter a mountain, they always pass by in time, but the mountain remains. Recognize this inner, imperturbable calm that resides in us all. When you notice that your mind has left the breath and followed a thought, congratulate yourself, for you have taken advantage of a valuable opportunity. Thank yourself for your patience and understanding as you, again and again, bring your attention back to the anchor of your breath, tuning into your present-moment experience. *(1 minute)*

Now, begin to draw this experience to a close. Feel where your hands are positioned on your body; feel the points of contact between your body and the chair or ground. Maybe wiggle your fingers and toes, seeing what sensations arise. Observe any feelings that may have been generated by this practice. Take three deep breaths as you sit with these feelings, letting them be just what they are. *(10 seconds)* When you are ready, gently open or refocus your eyes, and bring your awareness back to the world around you.

DISCUSSION OF DIAPHRAGMATIC BREATHING AND SITTING MEDITATION WITH A FOCUS ON THE BREATH

After the sitting meditation, participants are given a chance to discuss their experiences and reactions to these two breathing exercises. It is very important for leaders to respond to any observations, questions, or concerns mindfully. They can facilitate this discussion by asking open-ended questions such as the following, allowing 2 to 3 minutes for each:

- What was it like to practice breathing diaphragmatically?
- What did you notice while you were doing the sitting meditation?
- How did you let thoughts go and bring attention back to the breath?
- How might this kind of breath work affect your sport performance?

Common reactions to this initial mindful breathing practice may be reflected in statements such as "I feel like I'm not doing it right" or "I can't keep my focus." If such comments are made during this discussion, leaders can demonstrate how to apply a mindful attitude to these reactions. For instance, leaders could note that participants feeling like they are not doing it correctly is a judgment and then could point out that they were not doing it "right" or "wrong." They were simply breathing, nothing more, nothing less. And although participants may be frustrated by the experience of a wandering mind, leaders can help reframe this experience, highlighting that everyone's mind wanders and the fact that the participants are noticing this happening means that they are being aware and present, which is exactly what the sitting meditation is intended to help them do.

Home Practice

After completing the mindfulness exercises for Session 1, leaders can review the information that follows to indicate the role and importance of home practice in MSPE. Connecting mindfulness home practice with participants' physical training in their sport(s) may be an effective parallel to make here by asking, "Who here does physical training just once a week?" We have never had anyone answer this question affirmatively, as athletes tend to recognize that if they trained their bodies only once a week, they would fail to develop valuable physical attributes such as strength and endurance. Leaders can suggest that the same basic principle is true for mental training. Practicing mindfulness only once a week likely won't bring much benefit, which is why daily home practice is recommended.

FORMAL PRACTICE

Participants are asked to complete at least one formal mindfulness exercise on each of the days between MSPE sessions. When going over the home practice this initial time, leaders can define what is meant by formal practice, which refers to setting aside specific time to do one or more of the exercises. Over the course of the program, this means anywhere from 3 to 40 minutes of daily practice, if possible. Longer exercises come later in the program, when participants are more used to this type of skills practice, much like how physical training builds up to more intensive workouts. As mentioned at the beginning of this chapter, it can be helpful to provide participants with recordings of the formal practice exercises to guide their home practice, which can be accessed online (http://www.mindfulsportperformance.org). To promote practice and self-monitoring, each week give participants a copy of the Daily Mindfulness Log (adapted from Segal et al., 2002) to complete between sessions (Handout 1; see Exhibit 4.1). On this form, they keep a daily record of the type and duration of their mindfulness practice as well as observations about their daily practice that they wish to note. It can be useful for participants to bring their completed logs to subsequent sessions to serve as a reference during group discussions.

For this week, formal home practice involves practicing the 3-minute diaphragmatic breathing exercise three times and the 9-minute sitting meditation three times. As Segal et al. (2002) suggested, it is a good idea to remind participants that breathing can be used as a tool, like an anchor, to bring stability to the body and mind when one deliberately chooses to become aware of it. They can try to notice how the breath

EXHIBIT 4.1

Handout 1: Daily Mindfulness Log

Please record your daily mindfulness practice in the log below. Feel free to note anything that you observe during your practice so we can discuss it at the next mindful sport performance enhancement session.

Week #: _____

DATE	MINUTES	WHAT I PRACTICED	OBSERVATIONS

Note. From *Mindfulness-Based Cognitive Therapy for Depression: A New Approach to Preventing Relapse* (p. 290), by Z. V. Segal, J. M. G. Williams, and J. D. Teasdale, 2002, New York, NY: Guilford Press. Copyright 2002 by Guilford Press. Adapted with permission.

changes with fluctuations in mood, thought, and body posture. With the sitting medita-tion, the goal is not to control the breath but to watch and feel it with a sense of interest, gently letting go of thoughts when there is recognition that attention has wandered.

By engaging in mindfulness practice each day, participants will be strengthening their "attention muscles." This is a new and exciting way to train for their sport, and hopefully the first session has them interested in seeing what will happen going forward. Leaders can remind participants to be open to whatever unfolds as a result of their regu-lar practice and that simply taking time to focus on the breath will likely help them to relax tense muscles, deal with powerful emotions (e.g., fear, anger), and improve aware-ness of various other aspects of their lives, which can be crucial to athletic performance.

It is also important to acknowledge that participants all have very busy schedules and that adding an extra daily activity can sometimes be hard, even if it is just for 3 min-utes. Spending a few moments here brainstorming how to create space for mindfulness practice can help with adherence. If no participants mention it, leaders can suggest identifying a specific time to practice each day, possibly even recording that time on a schedule or calendar. Some mindfulness teachers say that the morning is the best time to meditate because the day's events have not yet come into full swing and the mind often isn't yet revved up. So, participants may want to set their alarm a few minutes early each morning to fit in this practice. Of course, any time is a good time to practice mindfulness, so if the morning doesn't work, making time before lunch, after dinner, before bed, or whenever works is just fine. However, participants should consider that practicing at a time when they are likely to fall asleep may limit the benefits obtained because attention is not being trained while asleep. Leaders can also help participants think about where they'll do their mindfulness practice, encouraging them to choose a quiet, private setting.

INFORMAL PRACTICE

In addition to doing formal home practice each week, participants are invited to engage in informal mindfulness practice. Leaders can explain that informal practice involves seizing opportunities to pay attention mindfully while in the midst of daily life, bringing this style of focus to whatever is happening at a given moment—for example, while driving a car, eating a meal, taking a shower, walking to practice, working out, or preparing to compete. Whatever the activity, there is an opportunity to strengthen mindfulness skills by tuning in to the present.

An acronym to remember for informal practice is STOP (Stahl & Goldstein, 2010), which stands for Stop, Take a few breaths, Observe what's happening, and then Proceed. When participants check in with themselves in this way, their connection to what is happening is enhanced, allowing them to experience more richly and respond more effectively, both inside and outside of their sport. It is also a great opportunity to practice and reinforce the habit of diaphragmatic breathing. Participants can be reminded that the T in STOP can actually mean "take a few diaphragmatic breaths."

Similar to how participants can schedule their formal practice, leaders can sug-gest setting alerts or alarms, such as on a phone or calendar, as reminders to STOP at certain moments during the day. Having such reminders may be particularly important this first week, when participants are initially trying to instill the habit of informal practice. Leaders can also consider giving participants a rubber band to wear on their wrist throughout the week. Especially if participants are not used to wearing a rubber band on their wrist, this tool can serve as an effective, low-tech alternative to alarms, as the texture of a rubber band naturally creates a feeling of friction on the skin as one engages in regular daily activities (e.g., pulling something out of a pants pocket). This sensation can serve as a reminder for participants to STOP each time they notice it. Using a rubber band also helps to reinforce the simile of attention being like a rubber band (introduced in the next session), which can always snap back to center when it wanders.

Wrap-Up

Segal, Williams, and Teasdale (2002, 2012) conclude their first session with a brief summary of being on automatic pilot, and a similar approach is taken in MSPE. Leaders can initiate this discussion by asking, "Who has ever gotten into a car and driven somewhere, and when you get to where you're going, you don't remember the drive there? Or, you intended to go one place, but after several minutes, you realized that you were heading someplace else?"

Of course, driving is not the only time that people go on automatic pilot. It is common to get so absorbed in thoughts that much of what's going on elsewhere is missed. When someone is on automatic pilot, life is not really being lived to its utmost because there is no choice about how to live in each moment. It's likely that the wrong direction or location traveled to while on automatic pilot involves a route previously traveled many times. When the mind gets caught up in some stream of thought, what tends to emerge is a familiar habit, such as driving to a frequented place. This is the essence of automatic pilot. When not paying attention, people fall back into old habits (which may not be adaptive) without awareness of being stuck in judgments and worries. In his 2012 book *Mindfulness for Beginners*, Kabat-Zinn compared this type of experience to being in a straitjacket of automatic reactions.

Freedom can be gained by honing awareness skills and learning to experience each moment right now, as it is happening. What has begun in this session is using the anchors of food and the breath to harness this power, which can be crucial to successful sport performance. Actually seeing what is happening, while it is happening, enables choice in how to respond.

It can be helpful at this point to revisit the sport-specific example introduced earlier in the session to make clear the connection between autopilot and sport performance. For instance, leaders could point out that when a runner gets passed by a competitor, it would be easy to get lost in reactions (e.g., doubts, worries) if the mind is on automatic pilot. But mindfulness provides an alternative. The runner can tune in and see what is actually happening in that moment: running, just running. Having this awareness can free up that runner to choose to let go of the reactions and focus

EXHIBIT 4.2

Handout 2: Summary of MSPE Session 1

Takeaways From Session 1

- *Mindfulness* means paying attention to the present moment, nonjudgmentally (i.e., noticing and letting go of feelings, thoughts, and physical sensations, rather than getting lost in them).
- There is a theoretical and empirical connection between mindfulness (as taught in MSPE) and the optimal-performance state known as *flow* or being "in the zone."
- MSPE uses meditations and specific present-moment anchors to train mindful attention in sport and other performance situations.
- Benefitting from a mental-training program such as MSPE means prioritizing mindfulness practice along with physical and tactical training.
- It is possible to strengthen the capacity for present-moment attention by doing daily activities (such as eating) mindfully.
- Breathing diaphragmatically can reduce stress, increase oxygen consumption, and easily be incorporated into daily informal mindfulness practice.
- Observing that the mind has wandered and then nonjudgmentally escorting it back to a present-moment anchor (e.g., the breath) represents the mindfulness "reps" that build skills such as focus and letting go.
- STOP (stop, take a few breaths, observe, proceed) is a helpful acronym to remember for informal mindfulness practice.
- Mindfulness helps reduce the tendency to be on automatic pilot, thus enhancing connections to what is happening and providing choice in how best to respond.

Daily Home Practice for the Week After Session 1

- Do the 3-minute diaphragmatic breathing exercise three times.
- Do the 9-minute sitting meditation with a focus on the breath three times.
- Seize opportunities to STOP and pay attention mindfully during daily activities.
- Record this practice on your Daily Mindfulness Log and bring it with you next session.
- If one will not be provided, remember to bring a mat, blanket, or towel to the next session.

---

on the true task at hand, which is running more efficiently. Leaders can emphasize that it is through their daily practice that participants will build the skills needed to display this kind of mental strength and ultimately run faster.

Before they leave, participants are given a copy of Handout 2 (see Exhibit 4.2), which provides a convenient summary of the important takeaway points covered in this session as well as a list to remind them about home practice for the upcoming week. Finally, leaders can invite participants to bring a towel, yoga mat, or blanket to Session 2 and all subsequent sessions (unless leaders are able to provide them), because certain exercises will involve being on the floor.

MSPE Session 2
Strengthening the Muscle of Attention

5

Session 2 highlights five core performance facilitators targeted in mindful sport performance enhancement (MSPE). The strengthening of these facilitators stems from the development of awareness and acceptance (defining mindfulness characteristics), with their intentional deployment (i.e., self-regulation) ultimately leading to flow experiences and peak sport performance (see Chapter 10 for further explanation of this model). This session continues to emphasize the importance of attention, and the new exercise, the body scan, involves directing attention to various body regions, noticing sensations there, and then letting them go.

Session 2 Snapshot

Components of this session are

- diaphragmatic breathing exercise,
- discussion of home practice and overcoming practice obstacles,
- core performance facilitators targeted in MSPE,
- body scan and discussion,

http://dx.doi.org/10.1037/0000048-006
Mindful Sport Performance Enhancement: Mental Training for Athletes and Coaches, by K. A. Kaufman, C. R. Glass, and T. R. Pineau

- sitting meditation with a focus on the breath and discussion,
- home practice assignment and distribution of Daily Mindfulness Log, and
- wrap-up and discussion of present-moment attention.

Diaphragmatic Breathing Exercise

Starting with this session, each meeting will begin with the 3-minute diaphragmatic breathing exercise from Session 1 (see Chapter 4) to help with letting go of whatever was consuming attention before arrival and transitioning to a focus on MSPE.

Discussion of Home Practice and Overcoming Practice Obstacles

Many common themes emerge when first building a mindfulness practice. Thus, discussion of the home practice is extremely important, as it provides a chance to explore and learn from these issues, which are likely to persist as practice progresses. We allot 5 to 10 minutes for processing the home practice at the start of Session 2 and all future sessions.

Some typical reactions to the first week of home mindfulness practice include having difficulty finding time to practice, feeling bored during practice, fearing the exercises are being performed incorrectly or misunderstood, judging that the practice did or did not work based on outcome (e.g., falling asleep), and struggling to slow down the mind (Segal, Williams, & Teasdale, 2002, 2012). Participants often have shared such reactions in MSPE, and it is important for leaders to respond to whatever themes arise mindfully (i.e., with nonjudgmental acceptance). For instance, if during an exercise participants are questioning whether they are doing it correctly, leaders can respond by saying that this is a common concern and it's great that they have noticed such thoughts. It is not necessary to suppress or eliminate them; rather, participants can choose to acknowledge them simply as events in the mind and let them go. Mindfulness is just about noticing what is; there is no right or wrong. This attitude can actually be quite liberating once participants move beyond a felt need to be correct or even perfect.

As we mentioned in Chapter 1, perhaps the most common obstacle to building a mindfulness practice is perceived lack of time, so this issue is very likely to come up in the initial home practice discussion. Leaders can acknowledge how typical this challenge is and remind participants that mental training works just like physical training in the sense that commitment to regular, systematic workouts is the best way to develop strength. Rather than making mindfulness practice an obligation or an item to check off a list, it can be seen as a choice to nurture oneself and one's ability to perform.

Leaders can also stress that the home practice assigned in MSPE is meant as a suggested guideline for best practice. But what is most important is participants giving themselves a daily dose of formal and/or informal mindfulness training, even if that means, for example, sitting for 3 minutes rather than 10 minutes. No matter how busy life is, it is hard to argue that there aren't even just a few moments to devote to being present during a day. There really is no way to get around the simple fact that participants will get out of MSPE what they put into it, so creating some room to practice is essential. It may be helpful for leaders to brainstorm further with participants on how to make time for formal and informal practice outside of the sessions, perhaps inviting participants who did practice regularly to share what strategies worked for them.

Leaders can encourage participants to take ownership of these discussions, emphasizing that, just as with the home practice, the more they participate in sessions, the more they are likely to get out of this training. Mindfulness is best learned experientially, so exploring their practice and listening to what others have to say will help enhance their understanding. Listening mindfully is a wonderful way to practice being present and can be contrasted with the ubiquitous automatic pilot experience, for example, missing critical information in a class or a meeting while "zoning out." It is ideal to hear from everyone in the group, but nobody should ever be forced to speak. However, leaders can note that it is just fine to say, for instance, "I don't want to share" or "I didn't do the home practice" as a form of participating and that being present with the discussion in this way is enough to benefit the group.

It may be helpful for leaders to remind participants that they can reference their daily log during this discussion and that recording their practice during the week can be an effective way both to stay on track while establishing a new training routine and to observe how practice experiences change over time. Having trouble recording practice at first (e.g., forgetting, not seeing the value) is not unusual, so again it may be useful to invite those participants who did have some success with this endeavor to share what strategies worked for them.

Core Performance Facilitators Targeted in MSPE

As we explore in detail in Chapter 10, MSPE targets five core performance facilitators that may ultimately increase the likelihood of an athlete achieving an optimal-performance state. We adapted our descriptions of these performance facilitators from the foundational work presented by Kabat-Zinn, Beall, and Rippe (1985). To help participants further develop an intention for their practice and understand how MSPE can improve their sport performance, leaders can review these facilitators, perhaps incorporating the theoretical and empirical support provided in Chapter 10 and tailoring their explanation to the sport(s) of focus. We will continue to use the example of long-distance running to illustrate how these facilitators can be discussed.

The first performance facilitator is *concentration*. It is crucial for runners to be able to focus their minds while running. It is so easy to get distracted or caught up in reactions to what is happening (e.g., worry, fatigue, pain, elation) and then contact is lost with what is actually happening, which is running. When not paying attention to the act of running, a runner has a harder time getting the most out of the experience by, for example, making adjustments that could help performance.

In the first session of MSPE, it was explained how directing attention to present-moment anchors can help strengthen focus. The breath was the primary anchor in that first session, but as the program progresses, it will become clear that many additional anchors, such as the stride, foot plants, arm motions, and other aspects of form, are available while running. The repetitive, cyclical nature of running provides a variety of great anchors, which are always present. Remember, being aware in this way does not mean reinstructing oneself on how to run. It simply involves noticing what is happening while running without getting swept away by reactions to the experience. One is switching off of automatic pilot, a state in which reactions occur out of habit and there is no control over actions, and thus harnessing the incredible power of awareness to complement physical execution, so the choice can be made to run better.

The second facilitator is *letting go*. The mind is always going, always analyzing, assessing, judging, projecting, and criticizing. Thus, the mind is popularly compared to a wild elephant, moving after whatever entices it. Some call it "monkey mind" because it is constantly jumping from place to place. As this process is occurring, some reactions can feel so compelling that they are believed as hard truths.

For instance, a runner might begin to experience pain and think, "I can't go on." Such a reaction can usurp attention and, if unchecked, could become the reality, leading to slowing down or giving up. There is no doubt that running is physically taxing and often produces sensations that are uncomfortable. Of course, sometimes pain is actually signaling something more serious than the discomfort associated with exertion, such as an injury. In such instances, it is essential that athletes listen to these signals and stop what they're doing rather than let go of pain and continue on (see Chapter 10 for further discussion of this topic). However, it's possible that the enhanced bodily awareness that comes from mindfulness practice may actually help athletes to better distinguish between these different types of pain. The main point to emphasize here is that when the pain is effort-based, there is a big difference between simply noticing its presence versus reacting to it in such a way that it creates potentially inaccurate beliefs about one's limits.

Letting go of such reactions is not about preventing them from arising at all while running, which would likely be impossible. The mind is never empty, but it is also never completely at the mercy of its "wild elephant" nature. The mind can be conceptualized instead as a rubber band with the ability to stretch in all different directions but always snapping back to the present. Noticing the mind wandering and then bringing it back to a present-moment anchor is practice in letting go and accepting "what is."

The third facilitator is *relaxation*. Many people become tense before or while they are running (recall the example from Session 1 of a runner getting passed by a competitor), and excess tension can have a negative impact on performance. Muscle tension may disrupt bodily coordination and waste precious energy. In addition, tension can impact cognitive processes essential for optimal performance, as heightened physiological arousal has been linked to decrements in working memory functioning, which is needed for focus and decision making.

Although the goal of mindfulness training is not to relax (a common misunderstanding), relaxation is a common effect of being mindful. This happens in at least three ways. One is through the practice of diaphragmatic breathing, a well-established method for inducing the body's relaxation response. A second way is by letting go. Tension often has a snowballing effect, and a way to break that vicious cycle is by returning attention to the present moment, allowing it to be exactly what it is. A third way is by noticing what is happening in the body and releasing excess and unnecessary tension, permitting the body to work as efficiently as possible.

Each of these first three facilitators contributes to the fourth: *establishing a sense of harmony and rhythm*. Learning to observe the mind and body in a nonjudgmental way can facilitate running with a still, quiet mind, which is untangled from the distracting reactions that accompany sensations such as pain, fatigue, worry, or boredom. As the MSPE program progresses, participants move beyond focusing on a single anchor and stretch their capacity to concentrate on a greater breadth of stimuli. For example, runners can begin to connect with the totality of the running experience, noticing how each movement is an integral part of a much larger endeavor, which includes their thoughts, breath, and entire body. There are also connections to teammates and competitors, with everyone needing the Earth itself as a surface on which to run.

By allowing a given moment to be exactly what it is without needing to change it, runners can experience a harmony, both within themselves and with their surroundings, which can allow performance to unfold more seamlessly, facilitated by the mind rather than hindered by it. In essence, strengthening this ability can help runners perform more consistently at their peak, minimizing the day-to-day ups and downs that can be so frustrating and perplexing.

Finally, the fifth facilitator is *forming key associations* between identified cues and the application of the other four facilitators (concentrating, letting go, relaxing, and establishing rhythm). Anything can be used as a cue, as long as it is available when the reminder to be mindful is needed. In MSPE, the choice of cue can be up to the individual or determined collectively by the group. One example might be a runner using crossing the start line, particular mile markers, the halfway point, identified landmarks, and/or the finish line as alerts to direct attention to a present-moment anchor such as the breath or stride. It may be useful to establish cues outside of the sport environment as well, such as at home, school, or work. Forming key associations is an important way to encourage informal mindfulness practice.

Body Scan

Kabat-Zinn (1990) described the body scan as a powerful technique for reestablishing contact with the body and cultivating moment-to-moment awareness. It is effective for developing both concentration and flexibility of attention. He claimed that the idea in scanning the body is to feel each region focused on and to linger there, with the mind right on it or in it. Participants breathe into and out of each region a few times and then let go as their attention moves on to the next region. As they let go, the muscles in that region literally let go too, lengthening and releasing much of the built-up tension. According to Kabat-Zinn, the intent when practicing this exercise is to maintain awareness in every moment, a detached witnessing of the breath and body, region by region, while scanning from the feet to the head.

Like the sitting meditation, the body scan is a sedentary exercise. However, attention is quite mobile in the body scan, as focus shifts from region to region. The 30-minute body scan used in MSPE was developed for athletes and informed by the work of Kabat-Zinn (1990) and Segal et al. (2002). When introducing the body scan, leaders can explain that this exercise involves focusing attention on different parts of the body, starting down at the toes and working up to the top of the head. As participants focus on each body region, they can notice what sensations are there, observe any reactions to those sensations, and then let them go as they move on to the next region. Leaders can remind participants that if they find this exercise hard or frustrating, they can just notice that reaction and try to let it go as well.

Leaders can further share that this exercise commonly facilitates relaxation. It is all about enhancing communication between the body and mind so that participants can better observe what's happening in each body region. Participants may find that when they let go of each region, they also let go of the tension that might be stored there. This ability is very important for performance, as being able to release excess tension can allow the body to work more efficiently. In fact, it is not uncommon for participants to get so relaxed during a body scan that they drift off or even fall asleep. So, leaders can remind them to try to keep a still but sharply focused mind because their attention is not being trained when they are asleep.

SCRIPT FOR BODY SCAN

Position yourself comfortably on the floor, perhaps on a towel or mat, lying on your back with your arms next to your body, your palms facing upward, and your eyes gently closed. Or if you'd rather not close your eyes fully, allow your eyelids to shut partially and let your gaze rest, unfocused, on a distant point above you. Notice sensations in the places where the back of your head, your shoulder blades, your buttocks, your calves, and your heels are making contact with the ground. Very slowly, lift your arms up over your head and stretch your body, reaching out with your toes and your fingertips as far as you can at this time. Feel the muscles in your arms, abdomen, and legs elongate as you reach away from your body in these two opposing directions. *(Pause for 2 seconds.)* And let go. Now, stretch your left arm and your right leg, and feel the sensations coming across your entire body. *(2 seconds)* And let go. Now, stretch your right arm and left leg, reaching as far as your body presently allows, feeling the sensations that arise. *(2 seconds)* And let go. Slowly bring your arms back to your sides, palms up, and, again, take a moment to notice the points of contact between your body and the ground.

Now, direct your attention to your breath. Allow the muscles in your abdomen to soften and relax, letting that region expand and deflate as you breathe down into your belly. If you notice chest breathing, that's ok too. Just try to breathe naturally, letting the pace and depth of your breaths find a comfortable, steady rhythm. As you breathe in this way, see if you can notice the sensations in your torso as it fills with air on the in-breath and then deflates on the out-breath. Notice the ever-present process of letting go with each exhalation.

We are about to tour the entire body with our attention. The goal here is not to relieve tension or to relax your muscles, although this may happen along the way. If you do enter a relaxed state, it is still important to remain awake and alert while on this journey. Our intention is to notice the variety of sensations that occur in our bodies at each moment, to acknowledge these sensations with our full attention, and then simply to let them go. So, make every effort to remain awake and aware during this scanning of the body.

If a particularly intense sensation calls for your attention at some point on this journey, it is not necessary to resist it. Listen to that call, and take a moment to direct your attention to it. Welcome the sensation into your experience. Acknowledge and appreciate this communication from your body. Once you have heard what your body has to say, gently let go of the intense sensation and bring your attention back to where you are in your tour.

With your next inhalation, direct your attention down to your left foot. Imagine your attention is like a laser beam, an intense, directed point of focused awareness. With this focused awareness, begin to scan the toes on your left foot. If you can, try to follow the contours of each toe. Maybe you can notice the slight sensation of pressure where your toes touch each other, how your socks or shoes feel against the pads of each toe, or, if your feet are bare, how the air feels as it surrounds your toes. As best you can, approach these sensations with an open curiosity, as if you are noticing these subtle sensations for the first time. If you are having trouble noticing anything in your toes at this time, that is okay too. Just let your experience be whatever it is at this moment. *(10 seconds)*

Imagine that the sensations you are experiencing are like a rising tide, blanketing the shore of your consciousness. Now, as you exhale, let go of these sensations you have noticed, allowing the tide to flow back out to sea, leaving your field of awareness bare to receive what new sensations may come. And, as you let go, gently shift the beam of your attention to the bottom of your left foot. As you breathe in, explore, in turn, the sensations in the ball of your foot, the arch, and the heel. Can you notice any difference in the feelings present at the top and bottom of your foot? Is there tension or discomfort in these well-used, important muscles? To whatever you may find, bring an attitude of warmth and acceptance. *(10 seconds)*

On your next exhalation, observe the retreating tide of these sensations as you let them go from your field of awareness and shift your attention up your left leg to the ankle, calf, and knee. Allow your focused attention to move up your lower leg, exploring the skin, penetrating the muscles. Is there any tightness, any tingling you can sense? Can your attention find its way into the joints of your ankle or knee? What are you sensing there? Allow a stillness to fill your being as you listen with careful intention to what your body is communicating. *(10 seconds)*

On your next exhale, let go of this region. Allow your laser beam of attention to move to your _____ *(Insert in sequence the body parts listed in the next paragraph.)*. With awareness and intention, scan this body part, maybe even imagining that you are breathing into it, so that it expands and deflates with your breath.

As best you can, notice each sensation, powerful or subtle, that rises and falls moment-by-moment. Allow each sensation to maintain a place in your field of awareness, without judging and without wanting it to be any different than what it is. Then, as you exhale, let it go. With every breath, you are letting go, allowing these sensations to pass through your mind, as your attention moves on through the tour of your body. *(5 seconds)*

Insert the following body parts in sequence, as noted in the previous paragraph:

- upper left leg
- right toes
- right foot
- lower right leg
- upper right leg

Pause to read this paragraph before proceeding to hip and pelvic region. At times, you may find your inner stillness disrupted by chatter the mind tends to generate. Your attention may be drawn away from the sensations within a region of the body by a thought, a memory, or a plan for the future. This is natural and to be expected. Our minds are very busy, and no fault or blame is to be placed when the mind wanders. That is just what minds do. Acknowledge what has drawn you away, and gently bring your attention back to the region you are focusing on at this moment. *(5 seconds)*

- hip and pelvic region
- lower back
- abdomen
- chest
- shoulders
- upper left arm
- left forearm
- left hand
- upper right arm
- right forearm
- right hand

On your next exhale, let go of this region. Allow your laser beam of attention to move to your neck and facial muscles. These muscles help us speak, laugh, eat, and express ourselves without words. We use them all the time, and they can hold a great deal of tension. Notice your jaw. Is it clenched at all? Perhaps your tongue is pressed up against the roof of your mouth. Or maybe your eyes are closed just slightly tighter than they need to be. If you notice any of this tension, you can allow yourself to release it, letting it drain out with each exhalation, as you continue to explore the sensations around your face. Can you feel your ears? The top of your head? The point of contact between your head and the ground? Just note what's there, letting the sensations rise and fall along with your breath. *(10 seconds)*

Now, take a moment to allow the focused beam of your attention to relax and expand. Let this laser point become an expansive, shining light. Permit it to flood over your entire body, as you become aware of all its sensations happening at once. *(10 seconds)* As you breathe, feel the hum of life that comes from the endless motion within us, from the blood flowing through our vessels to the constant movement of each tiny cell. Just float in the sea of your inner stillness, and allow this moment to be exactly what it is. Quiet and calm.

(1 minute) Now, take a final deep breath, gently wiggle your fingers and your toes, open or refocus your eyes, and bring your attention back to the world around you.

DISCUSSION OF BODY SCAN

After the body scan, participants are given a chance to discuss their experiences and reactions to this exercise. It is important for leaders to respond mindfully to observations, questions, or concerns raised. They can facilitate this discussion by asking open-ended questions, such as the following, allowing 2 to 3 minutes for each:

- What was your experience of the body scan?
- What thoughts or feelings did you notice?
- What do you feel like now that the body scan is complete?
- What applications might the body scan have to performance in your sport?

Common reactions of participants to the body scan include thoughts about how they looked, parts of their bodies they wanted to change, or feelings of awkwardness when focusing on the body in this manner (Segal et al., 2002, 2012). Some participants may also have difficulty staying awake or find that feelings of physical discomfort distract them from proceeding through the scan. Such experiences present an opportunity to teach that, through awareness and an attitude that "whatever arises is okay," it is possible to begin relating quite differently to thoughts, feelings, and sensations.

Sitting Meditation With a Focus on the Breath

The 9-minute sitting meditation with a focus on the breath from Session 1 (see Chapter 4) is repeated, providing an opportunity for additional group practice and discussion. Like doing reps in a weight room, this repeated practice helps to build up the mental muscles. Participants can be reminded to use the breath as their anchor. The idea is simply to observe the breath and, when the mind wanders, gently escort it back to this anchor.

SCRIPT FOR SITTING MEDITATION WITH A FOCUS ON THE BREATH

Use the script from Chapter 4.

DISCUSSION OF SITTING MEDITATION WITH A FOCUS ON THE BREATH

After this exercise, participants are given another chance to discuss their experiences and reactions. It is very important for leaders to respond mindfully to any observations, questions, or concerns raised. They can facilitate this discussion by asking open-ended questions, such as the following, allowing 2 to 3 minutes for each:

▪ What thoughts, feelings, or reactions did you have during this meditation?
▪ How would you describe your attention during this exercise?
▪ What differences, if any, did you notice between this practice and your home practice?

Home Practice

Another copy of the Daily Mindfulness Log is distributed for the upcoming week of home practice. Leaders can remind participants to bring their completed daily log to the next session. Home practice for Session 2 again includes both formal and informal practice.

FORMAL PRACTICE

It may be helpful to introduce the formal home practice for this week by talking further about training the mind with the same intensity with which one trains the body. The description that follows is tailored for runners but can be adapted for any sport.

Leaders can pose the question "Who trains by doing only long, easy-paced runs?" Most likely, nobody does, and the follow-up question can be asked: "Why not?" Leaders can emphasize that training needs to be varied in order to improve multiple aspects of physical performance. Running requires different attributes, such as endurance, speed, and strength, so runners do hills, sprints, and more, in addition to their longer runs. Mindfulness training can be thought of in the same way. Practicing only one type of meditation may not be sufficient to develop the versatility of mental performance being trained in MSPE.

Going forward, participants are thus asked to practice different combinations of exercises every week. Just as a coach might create specific plans for physical training, MSPE is a mental training regimen. As discussed earlier, it is important that everyone does their best to follow the guidelines for home practice to optimize the effectiveness of MSPE. For this week, the formal home practice includes doing the body scan one time and the sitting meditation with a focus on the breath five times (if a recording of the body scan will be provided, leaders can inform the participants about how to access it and integrate it into their practice).

As with last week, one formal exercise is done each day. The body scan takes about 30 minutes, so it may be important to be strategic about when this longer exercise is done to be sure there is ample, uninterrupted time. Even if 30 minutes or 9 minutes (length of the sitting meditation) aren't available, remember that what is most crucial is getting some daily dose of formal mindfulness practice.

It might be helpful for leaders to offer tips for doing the body scan at home, such as the following, which are based on suggestions from Segal et al. (2002, 2012). First, even if it is hard to focus or stay awake, keep at the practice, seeing if it's possible to embrace experiences in the moment. Second, this is a longer exercise, so be kind and patient if the mind wanders frequently; just continue to bring it back to whatever body part is the current anchor. Third, try to approach this practice with an open mind, regardless of how the in-session experience was, because each iteration can be different and there is no right way to do it. And, finally, see if the primary motive for practice can be doing the body scan for its own sake, as opposed to seeking to get something out of it. Often, trying to generate a particular outcome, such as relaxation, makes that outcome more elusive.

INFORMAL PRACTICE

Leaders can remind participants to continue incorporating informal mindfulness practice into their daily routine. Participants can keep using the STOP acronym (stop, take a few breaths, observe, proceed; Stahl & Goldstein, 2010) and take diaphragmatic breaths when they pause. Also, they can stick with or develop new reminders such as alerts (e.g., on a calendar or phone) or a rubber band. There are so many convenient ways to issue reminders, and participants should feel free to experiment with what works best for them. As talked about earlier in the session, forming associations within the athletic environment can also be highly effective. Participants can be encouraged to come up with possible cues as part of their home practice, and leaders should devote a few minutes to brainstorming how cues can be developed over the next week.

Wrap-Up

The regular practice of mindfulness exercises such as the sitting meditation and body scan can provide many opportunities to notice when the mind has drifted away from the present moment and then gently, but firmly, bring it back. Engaging in these "reps" can help MSPE participants better connect with each moment of their lives, including when they are performing, potentially enriching their experiences. Leaders can remind participants that it is perfectly natural for the mind to wander during this practice; it is not a sign of error or weakness. In fact, only through the awareness of this wandering can they come to experience the difference between autopilot and true presence.

The major task this week is just to notice. In particular, participants can be encouraged to notice how frequently they observe when their mind has drifted, and when they notice this, they have the opportunity to intentionally reconnect with a present-moment anchor. These experiences are successes, not failures. Leaders can reiterate to participants that there is nothing wrong with their mindfulness abilities, even if

EXHIBIT 5.1

Handout 3: Summary of MSPE Session 2

Takeaways From Session 2

- Five core performance facilitators, which follow from the promotion of awareness and acceptance, are targeted in mindful sport performance enhancement (MSPE). When deployed intentionally, these facilitators can potentially lead to flow and peak performance. They include the following:
  - *Concentration:* Use present-moment anchors (e.g., the breath or parts of your body) to direct your focus. In sport, this can be achieved by anchoring attention to specific aspects of technique.
  - *Letting go:* Our reactions to experiences (and our reactions to those reactions) can interfere with performance. By noticing the mind wandering and directing it back to an anchor, you are practicing letting go.
  - *Relaxation:* Although not a specific goal of mindfulness, relaxation is a common effect of these practices. Learning to notice and release excess tension can help performance.
  - *Establishing a sense of harmony and rhythm:* Integrating concentration, letting go, and relaxation, you can connect to the totality of athletic experience and find an effortless rhythm in what you are doing.
  - *Forming key associations:* Generating meaningful cues within and outside the performance environment can help remind you to be mindful.
- The MSPE body scan involves shifting attention around different regions of the body, noticing what is there and then letting go. This practice is helpful for building attentional focus and flexibility as well as releasing excess muscle tension.
- Incorporating different mindfulness exercises into your practice can help build the range of mental skills needed for optimal sport performance.

Daily Home Practice for the Week After Session 2

- Do the 30-minute body scan one time.
- Do the 9-minute sitting meditation with a focus on the breath five times.
- Seize opportunities to STOP (stop, take a few breaths, observe, proceed) and pay attention mindfully during daily activities.
- Record this practice on your Daily Mindfulness Log and bring it with you next session.
- If one will not be provided, remember to bring a mat, blanket, or towel to the next session.

their attention wanders away a thousand times. Much like in sport, this practice is not about being perfect but about staying committed to continuing to build one's mental muscle. Seizing opportunities to reconnect with the present moment is the essential work that may allow participants to derive benefits from MSPE for athletic performance and everyday life. Exhibit 5.1 (Handout 3) includes a summary of the main points shared in MSPE Session 2 and home practice for the upcoming week.

MSPE Session 3
Stretching the Body's Limits Mindfully

6

Session 3 of mindful sport performance enhancement (MSPE) introduces bodily movements into the practice to help participants connect to sensations of motion with awareness and acceptance. The main theme of the session is understanding the roles of expectations and limits, and a mindful yoga exercise is taught to illustrate how these factors can be transcended. In this yoga exercise, participants dwell at the boundaries of how far the body can stretch, without attempting to change them, and let go of any reactions that arise.

Session 3 Snapshot

Components of this session are

- diaphragmatic breathing exercise,
- discussion of home practice and recognizing the impact of expectations,
- mindful yoga and discussion,
- sitting meditation with a focus on the body as a whole and discussion,

http://dx.doi.org/10.1037/0000048-007
Mindful Sport Performance Enhancement: Mental Training for Athletes and Coaches, by K. A. Kaufman, C. R. Glass, and T. R. Pineau

- home practice assignment and distribution of Daily Mindfulness Log, and
- wrap-up.

Diaphragmatic Breathing Exercise

This session begins with the 3-minute diaphragmatic breathing exercise from Session 1 (see Chapter 4) to help participants transition into being present with today's MSPE training.

Discussion of Home Practice and Recognizing the Impact of Expectations

Participants can spend 5 to 10 minutes sharing their experiences with mindfulness practice during the week. Again, leaders can encourage everyone to share, and it is important that they respond mindfully (i.e., with nonjudgmental acceptance) to anything raised. If participants need assistance generating discussion, they can reference their Daily Mindfulness Logs to help them recall the details of their practice, and leaders can pose open-ended questions, such as the following:

- What differences, if any, did you notice between practicing the body scan at home and doing it during our previous session?
- How have your reactions to the sitting meditation changed over the past 2 weeks?
- What types of informal mindfulness practice did you engage in?
- How have you made time to practice the MSPE exercises?
- What cues did you come up with to facilitate forming mindful associations?
- How have you noticed yourself applying what you've learned in MSPE, either while engaging in your sport or during other activities?

Comments about home practice, especially after only a few weeks of training, create important opportunities for leaders to provide education on certain integral mindfulness concepts (Segal, Williams, & Teasdale, 2002, 2012). For example, statements such as "I get distracted too easily," "I don't feel relaxed," or "I can't stop my mind from wandering" are all connected by the theme of expectations. In this context, the word *expectation* refers not to predicted outcomes but rather to beliefs about what an experience should or needs to be (or should have been) or what is expected of oneself. When these rigid expectations of what should be do not match what is happening, that tends to produce a sense of distress. This process can be particularly problematic if the expectations held are unreasonable or unrealistic.

In MSPE practice, for instance, participants may expect that they *should* be able to sustain focus on an anchor throughout an entire exercise, and failing to do so can generate such reactions as frustration or disappointment. However, they need to recall that the nature of the mind is not to stay focused in this way (hence the term *monkey mind*) and that, in fact, a crucial aspect of this practice is seizing opportunities to get "mindfulness reps" by noticing when the mind has wandered and directing it back to an anchor nonjudgmentally.

Needing or expecting something to be other than it is, especially when that something is not fully controllable (like the nature of the mind), can lead to undeserved, nonconstructive blame of the self and others. Siegel (2007) suggested that the real clinical benefit of mindfulness is that by learning to accept "what is," this form of tension is resolved. Athletics tends to promote an outcome orientation, which can leave people with little tolerance for deviations from what *should* be. However, somewhat ironically, the process of simply observing and accepting, rather than the direct pursuit of specific outcomes, facilitates the achievement of desired results, and this lesson is learned repeatedly through mindfulness practice.

Leaders can invite participants to consider situations they've faced in their sport(s) when they thought something *should* have been different than it was, such as falling behind a competitor judged to be inferior, having worries, or feeling fatigue or pain. In such situations, what was the impact of *shoulding*? Was it helpful or did it make them feel worse? In truth, it is a waste of precious resources to focus on what should be happening but is not. When something undesirable is happening, having the capacity simply to recognize and accept it as true in that moment (as opposed to any future moment) is a much more effective response than shoulding.

Mindful Yoga

Kabat-Zinn (1990) indicated that hatha yoga is one of the most powerful methods for connecting with the body through mindful awareness, both because of its ability to transform physical limits and because of how good it usually feels to practice it. He defined *mindful yoga* as gentle stretching and strengthening, done slowly, with moment-to-moment awareness of breathing and the sensations that accompany shifting the body into various postures or poses. Kabat-Zinn said that mindful yoga may help the body become more relaxed, strong, and flexible and is another way in which individuals can learn about themselves and come to experience themselves as a whole. Similar to the body scan and the sitting meditation, mindful yoga ideally is practiced without striving or forcing, accepting the body in its current state from one moment to the next.

This last piece is really important, and Kabat-Zinn (1990) made a specific comparison to how athletes train to further this point. He remarked that athletes often try to identify and then eclipse their limits in an effort to "get somewhere" (i.e., push past the limit), whereas the spirit of mindful yoga is to discover and be with where the limit is at that moment without trying to change anything. Kabat-Zinn proposed that such acceptance can illuminate how boundaries are not fixed and prevent the distress that typically comes with relentless striving.

The MSPE yoga protocol was designed specifically for this training by a 500-hour certified yoga instructor (and sister of our coauthor), Pamela Kaufman. We recommend that leaders play an audio recording of the yoga script during the session (found online at http://www.mindfulsportperformance.org) so that they are free to guide participants through the poses. It may also be helpful to provide participants with images of the poses (see Figure 6.1, available online at http://pubs.apa.org/books/supp/kaufman/) for their reference in session and when doing home practice. This exercise is the first chance participants have to practice being mindful while engaged

FIGURE 6.1

MSPE Mindful Yoga Poses.

in active bodily movements, with the physical sensations themselves serving as the anchors for attention, and represents an important step in MSPE's progression.

It is also worthy of note that the mindful yoga exercise is the longest MSPE exercise (the routine we provide lasts about 40 minutes). If leaders have time constraints, they can shorten the routine, but any pose involving movements on one side of the body, followed by the same movements on the other side of the body (e.g., warrior I), should be kept intact. This particular routine is intended for individuals with any level of yoga experience.

When introducing this exercise, leaders can make it clear to participants that this exercise is appropriate for beginners and that they will be guided through the poses. It might also be helpful to inquire about any past experiences with yoga. As participants share their initial thoughts, leaders can highlight any expectations or preconceived notions regarding, for instance, what yoga is, the types of people who do it, personal yoga abilities, or the outcomes of yoga and encourage them to approach this activity with an openness to whatever is experienced.

Leaders can then provide a bit of background on yoga, explaining that it comes from an Eastern tradition that is becoming increasingly popular in Western culture as a form of exercise, stress relief, and a way to promote overall health. Although yoga may indeed have these benefits, at its core it is a nonstriving meditative practice, like other mindfulness exercises. These exercises are not about reaching an expected outcome, such as increasing flexibility or relaxation, but are about observing what is happening nonjudgmentally. So, although many people practice yoga, they are not necessarily doing mindful yoga.

Participants can be informed that MSPE's version of mindful yoga involves a progression through a series of poses while noticing the accompanying physical sensations. These sensations are the anchors for attention, and it is important to observe them for what they are without judging them as good or bad. While doing the stretches, one can tune into the body's current perceived limits, dwelling there without striving to push through them or anxiously backing away from them. By doing so, it is possible to observe how limits change naturally with this practice over time. Participants can be encouraged to let go of judgments of limits as bad or unacceptable, which is akin to the process of *shoulding* discussed earlier (e.g., "I should be more flexible"), and instead try to stay open to simply experiencing their body in the moment.

Leaders can further point out that, like the body scan, mindful yoga is an excellent way to connect the mind and body. Matt Fitzgerald (2010), a leading author on how the mind–body connection can improve running performance, recommended yoga for precisely this purpose. He claimed that many people, even athletes, do not take sufficient time to listen to their bodies. This poor communication can lead the mind to forget how to talk to the muscles, making it much harder to, for example, relax when there is excess tension. Like the body scan, mindful yoga can help reestablish these mind–body connections, allowing participants to be more aware of what is happening in their bodies while they perform and to manage crucial factors such as muscle tension. Of course, yoga is different from the body scan because it involves practicing mindfulness in motion and represents a key step toward attending mindfully while competing in sport.

After hearing this background information, participants can make several rows with their yoga mats (or whatever they brought), allowing for ample space to stretch. It may also be prudent to invite them to skip any stretch that would be contraindicated (e.g., due to an injury).

SCRIPT FOR MINDFUL YOGA

This mindful yoga exercise combines simple body movements called *poses* or *postures* with relaxation. It is important, during this exercise, to take full responsibility for your own body and to do only what you feel capable of. Feel free to skip any movements and poses that seem inappropriate for where your body's limits are right now.

During this exercise, try to pay full attention to how your body is feeling in each moment. It might be helpful to ask yourself questions such as, What sensations am I feeling now? Where in my body am I feeling them? What qualities do these sensations have?

The goal of this yoga exercise is not to get anywhere in particular but, rather, to develop greater awareness of and sensitivity to yourself, becoming conscious of your body's limits and staying at them long enough to experience and begin to accept them. Try not to force yourself to be any different than you presently are, but know that, with regular practice, you may notice your limits start to change on their own.

Centering

Come to a comfortable seated position. Take a moment to turn your gaze inward. Begin to notice where you are right now, in this moment. Take a deep breath in. As you exhale, feel your sit-bones ground down into the floor. Inhale. Exhale. Just breathe, feel, and experience this moment in time. *(Pause for 5 seconds.)*

Gently begin to scan your body, starting from the tips of your toes and working your way up to the crown of your head. Notice areas where the body feels tight or filled with tension. Notice areas where your body feels agitated or longing to move. Notice areas where your body feels heavy or lethargic. Notice areas where your body feels spacious and at ease. Try not judging whatever it is that you notice. Simply observe what you find, perhaps saying to yourself, "Hmm, that's what that feels like today," and gently continue with your full-body scan. As you come to the crown of the head, notice your thoughts. Where do they want to go? Simply notice them, and let them pass through your mind. *(5 seconds)*

Bring both hands to your belly, placing your hands flat against your stomach, just above your belly button. Notice the sensations of your breath. Observe the expansion of your belly with each inhale and the falling of the belly with each exhale, being fully present with yourself. Slowly begin to deepen your breath, inhaling to the count of five, exhaling to the count of five. *(10 seconds)* Keeping one hand on your belly, bring the other to your chest, right above your heart. We are going to work with the *three-part yogic breath*. As you inhale, feel the belly fill with air, then the area right below the ribcage, and, finally, the chest. As you exhale, press the air first from the chest, then the ribcage, then, finally, from the belly. Continue with this three-part breath, inhaling through the belly, ribcage, chest, exhaling through the chest, ribcage, belly. *(10 seconds)* Gently bring both hands back to your belly. Notice any shifts that may have occurred in the pattern of the breath or within your body. *(5 seconds)*

Bring your hands together in front of your heart, palms facing each other, and take a moment to create an intention for your practice: for example, nonjudgmentally listening to the signals of your body or being fully present with your thoughts. Make your intention something that is personally meaningful.

Warm-Up

Slowly, with full awareness, come to your hands and knees. *(5 seconds)* As you inhale, drop your belly forward as you arch your back, sticking your tailbone up toward the sky. *Cow pose.* As you exhale, round your spine, drop your head, tuck your tailbone. *Cat pose.* Inhale, lift the head, drop the belly, lift the tailbone. Cow. Exhale, round the spine, press the mat away with the palms of your hands as you drop the head and tuck the tailbone. Cat. Take a few more cat/cow movements. Pay careful attention to the sensations as your body shifts between these postures. In the background, as best you can, try also to maintain awareness of your breath entering and leaving your body. Allow the breath to lead your motion. *(10 seconds)*

Come to rest again on your hands and knees. Inhale as you slowly lift your right arm out to the side. Notice the muscles in the shoulders and arm that engage to allow this motion. As you exhale, thread that arm underneath you, bringing your right shoulder and your right cheek to the mat. *Thread the needle.* Hips stay lifted and are not resting on the heels here. Take three deep breaths and feel the sensations of this pose. Notice the contact points between your shoulder and cheek against the ground. Notice any constriction that may be present in the belly, and as best you can, release this tightness with each exhalation. *(5 seconds)* Gently rise back up and thread the needle to the other side, bringing the left shoulder and the left cheek to the mat. Take three deep breaths here and tune into the feeling of this pose. *(5 seconds)*

Rise back to the hands and knees, tuck your toes, lift your hips up and back for *downward facing dog*. It's okay if your heels do not touch the ground, but continue to feel the sensation of the heels falling toward the ground, allowing the hamstrings to lengthen. Spread your fingers wide, with your middle finger pointing directly in front of you. Relax the shoulders. Roll the upper arms away from you so that the shoulder blades roll toward the outer edges of the back. As you hold this pose, notice the sensations it creates in your hamstrings and low back. With these sensations held in your awareness, imagine yourself sending your breath into these muscles as you inhale. Imagine these muscles filling along with your belly, gently expanding with the in-breath, and, as you exhale, feel their gentle deflation as you let go. Now, bend one knee as you stretch through the heel of your opposite foot. *(5 seconds)* Switch sides. Take three deep breaths here to wake up your hamstrings and calves. *(5 seconds)*

Slowly walk your feet forward to meet your hands, bending your knees as much as you need to. When you arrive, hang forward in a *standing forward bend*. Allow the head to be relaxed on the neck, maybe shaking it yes, shaking it no. Take a few breaths here, and notice how you can go deeper and deeper into the pose with each out-breath. Experience the subtle letting-go that happens with each exhalation. *(5 seconds)* Now, bend your knees deeply, and slowly roll all the way up to *mountain pose*. Notice what you are feeling as your body moves, engaging the various muscles that flex and relax to change your positioning. Glance down and make any adjustments required to bring your feet parallel to the sides of the mat. *(5 seconds)* Relax your shoulders, feeling them fall away from the ears. Come back to your intention. If you find yourself questioning why you are doing this exercise or having thoughts about past events or where you are going next, gently escort your attention back to this moment. *(10 seconds)*

Standing Practice

As you inhale, lift your arms out to the side and up overhead, palms facing up. As you exhale, arms reach out to the side, palms facing down as you dive forward over your legs. Bend your knees so that your hands come to the mat. Gently step your right foot back to a *lunge*. Come to your fingertips. Line your fingers up with your left toes. Bring your left knee so it is directly above your left ankle. Relax your shoulders away from your ears. Glance back at your back leg. Bring the right heel directly over the ball of the right foot. Lengthen through the right leg. Allow the right leg to support the left. Take three deep breaths, listening to the messages your body is sending you in this stretch. If you can, again imagine yourself breathing into this stretch, feeling the gentle expansion of your muscles as they fill with your breath and their gentle deflation as you let go of your breath. Notice what reactions you may be having to this sensation. As best you can, watch these thoughts rise up, and allow them to pass through your mind, leaving no more of an imprint than light does as it passes through water. On your next exhale, step your left foot back to meet your right. Downward facing dog. *(5 seconds)*

Slowly come forward to *plank pose*. Your shoulders are over your wrists and your heels are over the balls of your feet. Your body is in one long line, just like a plank. Hips and belly are not falling toward the floor. Hug your belly button in and back toward the spine. Take a deep breath here. *(5 seconds)* As you exhale, slowly lower your knees to the mat, then, hugging your elbows in toward the body, lower all the way down to your belly in one smooth motion, keeping your body in one long line. Try not to drop the hips, the belly, or the chest. Release the toes, pressing the tops of the feet into the mat, bringing the hands next to the chest so the elbows point behind you, and gently lift the chest for *baby cobra*. *(5 seconds)*

Tuck the toes, bend the knees as you lift the hips up and back for downward facing dog. *(5 seconds)* As you inhale, lift the right leg up and back behind you for *down-dog split*. Step the right foot forward to a lunge. If the right foot does not make it all the way up on the first step, hold the ankle with your hand and bring it forward. Over time, you may notice your limits gradually changing. Once again, line up your fingers with your right toes. Activate your back leg, bringing the back heel over the ball of the foot. Relax the shoulders. Take three deep breaths here, directing those breaths, breathing into these muscles. *(10 seconds)* Now, gently step your left leg forward. Take as many steps as you need to get there. Slowly roll all the way up to mountain pose. Notice the consequences of having done this series of movements. *(5 seconds)*

Inhale and raise your arms up overhead. As you exhale, dive forward over your legs. Step your left foot back to a lunge. *(5 seconds)* Step your right foot back to downward facing dog. *(5 seconds)* Slowly come forward to plank. Feel your core activate. Even though it's tempting to hold your breath here, breathe into the pose. *(5 seconds)* Lower your knees to the mat; do not shift your hips back. Slowly lower all the way down to the mat. Keep your hands by your chest as you lift to baby cobra. Feel the tops of the feet press into the mat, as the legs activate, supporting the lower back. *(5 seconds)* Bend the knees; shift back to downward facing dog. *(5 seconds)* Lift the left leg up and back behind you. Gently step it forward to a lunge. Use your hands to help you if your foot does not come all the way forward, recognizing your current limits as they are. Step your right foot forward to meet your left. Hang here. Shake your head yes, then no. Feel your hips shift forward as your weight moves into the balls of your feet. If it feels okay, bring the palms of the hands to the back of the calves, the ankles, or the floor behind you. *(5 seconds)* Gently release. Bend the knees deeply as you slowly roll all the way up to mountain pose. Come back to your intention, being totally present with and accepting of the sensations occurring in your body. *(5 seconds)*

Lift the arms up overhead and dive forward over your legs. Step your right foot back to a lunge. *(5 seconds)* Slowly lower your right knee to the mat, mindful of any sensations there. Release your back toes. Bring your hands to your left thigh. Take a moment here to find your balance. *(5 seconds)* Gently lift your arms up overhead, palms facing each other. Relax your shoulders. With each inhale, imagine the gentle inflation of your muscles in use. With each exhale, release the front of the right hip toward the floor a little bit more. Take five deep breaths here, experiencing with concentration what this feels like. *(20 seconds)* Slowly release your hands down to frame your left foot. Allow the feeling of the mat as it touches your fingertips to enter your awareness. No sensation is too small to be noticed. Tuck your back toes and lift your right knee off the mat for your lunge. *(5 seconds)* Step the left foot back, into downward facing dog. *(5 seconds)* Come forward to plank position. *(5 seconds)* Lower your knees to the mat, hug the elbows in, and lower all the way down. Lift the chest as the tops of the feet press into the mat for baby cobra. *(5 seconds)* Bending the knees, shift back to downward facing dog. *(5 seconds)* Lift the right leg up and back behind you for down-dog split and step it forward to a lunge, allowing yourself to make any adjustments as necessary. And, as you move through these poses, as best you can, notice the sensations not only of each pose, but of movement itself. The waves of muscle contractions, the air against your skin when your body is in motion, and the subtle tingling in your muscles when the movement has stopped. Now, lower the left knee to the mat. Release the back toes. Bring your hands to your right thigh as you find your balance, then slowly lift your arms up overhead, palms facing each other. *(5 seconds)* As you inhale, find length in your spine, without lifting the shoulders. As you exhale, feel the front of the left hip release toward the floor. Take five deep breaths here. *(20 seconds)* Slowly lower the hands to frame the right foot. Tuck the back toes and step or drag your left foot forward. Just hang here. *(5 seconds)* Bending your knees deeply, slowly roll up, one vertebra at a time, maintaining an awareness of your ever-present breath, and coming back to the mountain pose. *(5 seconds)*

Inhale and raise your arms up overhead; exhale and dive forward. As you inhale, lift your spine halfway up so the crown of your head is pointing directly in front of you. *(5 seconds)* Interlace your fingers behind your back and fold forward, reaching your hands toward the back of your head. Try not to lock your elbows here. Continue to feel the sensation of the shoulders releasing down the back, even as you activate between the shoulder blades. Slowly release the hands and hang. *(5 seconds)* Step your right foot back to a lunge. *(5 seconds)* Step your left foot back to meet it, in downward facing dog. *(5 seconds)* Come forward to plank. *(5 seconds)* Lower your knees to the mat, hug the elbows in, and lower all the way down. As you inhale, press the tops of the feet into the mat as you lift the chest. *(5 seconds)* Relax the shoulders. Bend your knees as you lift your hips up and back into downward facing dog. *(5 seconds)*

Lift your right leg up and back behind you for down-dog split and step it forward to a lunge. *(5 seconds)* Step your left foot in just a few inches, bringing your left heel to the mat. Slowly rise up to standing. *(5 seconds)* Bend into your right knee as your arms rise up overhead, palms facing each other. Your torso is facing forward. If you are tight in the hips, simply step the left foot out to the left a bit more. Bring the left toes to face the left front corner of the mat. This will free up the left hip so that the hips can face forward, parallel with the front of the mat. Your back leg is straight, while your front knee is bent and directly over your front ankle. *Warrior I* pose. Take a moment to see where your awareness is. What are you noticing? What physical sensations? What thoughts or reactions? As best you can, observe the entirety of your experience. Welcome all that arises, acknowledging the complex workings of the mind and body, while always escorting your awareness back to the anchor of your breath. *(5 seconds)* Now, slowly straighten through your right leg and step your left foot in a few inches closer to your right. *(5 seconds)* Interlace your fingers behind your back and gently fold over your right straight leg as you reach your hands toward the back of your head. Try not to lock your knees or your elbows here. Notice a nice stretch through the right hamstring as you breathe into this muscle. Continue to press through the outer edges of that back foot, keeping the back leg active. *(5 seconds)* Slowly rise up. *(5 seconds)* Step your left foot back a few inches. Bend into your right knee as your arms come up overhead to find warrior I. *(5 seconds)*

Bring your hands together in front of your heart as you step your feet even wider apart, bringing your left foot parallel to the back of your mat and opening your hips to the side for *warrior II*. Open your arms out to a T, shoulder height, with the palms facing down. Your right knee is still over your right ankle. Feel the inner thighs rolling away from each other. *(5 seconds)* Slowly straighten the right leg and bring the right foot parallel to the front of the mat so that both feet are facing the same direction. *(5 seconds)* Interlace your fingers behind your back and hinge forward from the hips into a *wide-leg bend*, reaching the hands toward the back of the head. Press into the inner and outer edges of the feet here. As you exhale, feel your hamstrings release as you let go of your breath. *(5 seconds)*

Release your hands toward the floor and hang. *(5 seconds)* Begin to walk your hands around to frame your right foot. Release your left heel from the ground to find a *low lunge*. *(5 seconds)* Step your right foot back to meet your left. Downward facing dog. *(5 seconds)* Come forward to plank. *(5 seconds)* Lower your knees and lower all the way down to the mat. Baby cobra. Chest lifts, feet press into the mat. *(5 seconds)* Shift back to downward facing dog, being fully aware of this moment. Perhaps notice the warmth that has been generated by the movement of your body. Take a moment to quickly scan your muscles, from your feet to your head, while your awareness maintains a constant connection with your breath. *(5 seconds)*

Lift your left leg up and back behind you for down-dog split and step it forward to a lunge. *(5 seconds)* Step your right foot in just a few inches, bringing your right heel to the mat. Slowly rise up to standing. *(5 seconds)* Bend into your left knee as your arms rise up overhead, palms facing each other. Your torso is facing forward. If you are tight in the hips, simply step the right foot out to the right a bit more. Bring the right toes to face the right front corner of the mat. This will free up the right hip so that the hips can face forward, parallel with the front of the mat. Notice also what reactions you may have to any tightness you observe. It is not something that needs to be changed. Your back leg is straight, while your front knee is bent and directly over your front ankle. Settle back into warrior I. *(5 seconds)* Slowly straighten through your left leg and step your right foot in a few inches closer to your left. Interlace your fingers behind your back and gently fold over your left straight leg as you reach your hands toward the back of your head. Try not to lock your knees or your elbows here. Feel a nice stretch through the left hamstring. Continue to press through the outer edges of that back foot, keeping the back leg active. As you breathe here, feel the air being sent to all your active muscles and all the points of contact with the ground. *(5 seconds)* Slowly rise up. *(5 seconds)* Step your right foot back a few inches. Bend into your left knee as your arms come up overhead to find warrior I. *(5 seconds)* Bring your hands together in front of your heart as you step your feet even wider apart, bringing your right foot parallel to the back of your mat and opening your hips to face the side of the mat for warrior II. Open your arms out to a T, shoulder height, with the palms facing down. Your left knee is still over your left ankle. Feel the inner thighs rolling away from each other. *(5 seconds)* Slowly straighten the left leg and bring the left foot parallel to the front of the mat so that both feet are facing the same direction. Interlace your fingers behind your back and hinge forward from the hips into a wide-leg bend, reaching the hands toward the back of the head. Press into the inner and outer edges of the feet here. As you exhale, feel your hamstrings release as you let go of your breath. *(5 seconds)* Slowly release your hands toward the mat and hang. *(5 seconds)* Walk your hands around to frame your left foot to find your low lunge. *(5 seconds)* Step your left foot back to downward facing dog. *(5 seconds)*

Lower your knees to the mat and your hips to your heels for *child's pose*. Your arms can be out in front of you or down by your sides. Allow your belly to be soft and the muscles around the eyes and jaw to relax. Take three deep breaths, fully permitting yourself to experience being just as you are, right now, in this moment. Follow these breaths as they rise and fall within you. *(20 seconds)*

Reach your hands out in front, spread your fingers wide, and tuck your toes as you lift your hips up and back for downward facing dog. *(5 seconds)* Lift your right leg up and back behind you for down-dog split and step your right foot forward into a lunge. *(5 seconds)* Step your left foot up to meet it and hang. *(5 seconds)* Now, bend your knees and slowly roll up to mountain pose. Come back to your intention. Notice how your body is feeling. *(5 seconds)*

Seated Cooldown

Inhale, bring your arms up overhead, and dive forward. *(5 seconds)* Slowly walk your feet back to downward facing dog, bending your knees as much as you need to. *(5 seconds)* Lower your knees to the mat and come to sit on your shins. With careful awareness, shift your weight into either hip so that you can bring your legs around in front of you. Stretch your legs long and flex your feet, so your toes are pointing toward the sky. As you inhale, lift your arms up overhead, lengthening through the spine, and, as you exhale, hinge forward from the hips to fold over your legs into a *seated forward bend*. Try not to round your spine. The goal is not to touch your toes but to release the hamstrings. Often you do not need to fold very far to feel this release. You may sense some tightness in your hamstrings and low back in this pose. There is no need to push beyond these boundaries. Whatever your body can do in this moment is just right. *(5 seconds)* Slowly roll up. Bring the soles of your feet together with your knees out to the side to find *bound angle pose*. Take a deep inhale as you find length in the spine. As you exhale, do a *seated twist* to the right, bringing your left hand to the outside of your right knee and your right hand behind you. Relax the shoulders. Allow the head and the neck to be a natural continuation of the spine. There is no need to pull yourself beyond what is comfortable. *(5 seconds)* Gently come back to the center and twist to the left. *(5 seconds)* Return to the center and take a deep inhale as you lengthen through the spine. As you exhale, fold forward. Think of opening your heart toward your feet, again, working to keep the spine long, without rounding. Notice a slight hinging in the hips. Feel the stretch in your inner thighs. Breathe into this stretch. *(5 seconds)* Slowly roll up and onto your back. *(5 seconds)*

Hug the knees into your belly and gently rock from side to side, massaging your lower back, before making your way into final relaxation, *corpse pose*. *(5 seconds)* Lie flat on your back with your arms down by your sides, palms facing up. Allow your legs to be long, feet rolling open to the sky. Allow your breath to be natural and your eyes to gently close. Relax your body, taking in the benefits of your practice today. Let go of your thoughts about what you have just asked your body to do or where you need to go next, and simply be present with yourself, in the here and now. Perhaps congratulate yourself for having taken the time to do this exercise, recognizing how you are working toward building greater strength and flexibility, both in your body and in your mind. *(1 minute)*

When you feel ready, bring small movements back to your fingers and your toes, and hug your knees into your belly as you gently roll onto your right side before pressing up to a comfortable seated position. Take a deep breath in and a deep breath out, feeling the flow of your breathing. Briefly scan your body, noticing any shifts that may have occurred during this exercise. Come back to your intention, either taking it with you today or letting it go, allowing it to become what it will, inside of you and out in the world. Take one more deep breath in and gently bow forward to seal your practice. Namaste.

DISCUSSION OF MINDFUL YOGA

After the mindful yoga, participants are given a chance to discuss their experiences and reactions. It remains important for leaders to respond mindfully to any observations, questions, or concerns raised. They can facilitate this discussion by asking open-ended questions such as the following, allowing 2 to 3 minutes for each:

- What were your experiences during this mindful yoga practice?
- What does your body feel like now that the mindful yoga practice is complete?
- What was it like to dwell at your body's limits?
- What applications might this yoga practice have to performance in your sport?

Sitting Meditation With a Focus on the Body as a Whole

For this exercise, the sitting meditation done in Sessions 1 and 2 is expanded and now lasts for about 14 minutes. The new portion guides participants in extending their awareness beyond the breath to include a focus on the body as a whole. This expansion was informed by Segal et al.'s (2002) sitting meditation with mindfulness of the breath and body.

Leaders can explain to participants that this sitting meditation is similar to the one practiced to this point but a bit longer and with an additional anchor for attention. Much as upping weight at the gym helps the body to get stronger, expanding on meditation exercises in this way can build up mental muscle. They can remind participants that it is natural for the mind to wander during this kind of practice. The key remains noticing when this is occurring and then returning attention to the anchor, like a stretched rubber band snapping back into place.

The recording of this script (available at http://www.mindfulsportperformance. org) includes the entire 14-minute exercise. The full script starts with the first six paragraphs of the Script for Sitting Meditation With a Focus on the Breath from Session 1 (see Chapter 4) and then continues with the introduction of the new anchor in the next five paragraphs.

SCRIPT FOR SITTING MEDITATION WITH A FOCUS ON THE BODY AS A WHOLE

Your field of awareness has been filled with the experience of your breath. Now, allow your awareness to expand beyond the sensations associated with the rising and falling in your torso and the air flowing in and out of your nose.

Begin to take in the sensations from the rest of your body. Maybe you can feel your heart beat in your chest or the pulsation in your legs or your arms as your heart completes each contraction. Perhaps you can feel a slight tingling in your fingertips, the sensation of the air on places where your skin is bare, or the feeling of your clothes resting against your skin. Your body is sensing all the time. As best you can, notice this vast array of sensations as your entire body hums with life. *(Pause for 10 seconds.)*

Using your attention, explore your body with a gentle curiosity. Maybe you notice the pressure of contact where your body touches your seat, or where your hands are resting on your body. And, as you explore, note the changes in the boundaries of your awareness. Can you, in the same moment, be aware of the rhythm of your breath, the feeling of your clothes on your skin, and the tension in your muscles? If possible, allow your attention to settle on the full, rich experience of your entire body in this moment. *(10 seconds)*

If you are noticing that your mind is drawn to one sensation in particular, in just one part of your body, that's fine. That is not a failure or a mistake. That is your body communicating with you. Maybe you notice tightness in a particular muscle, an itch, or even a sensation of pain or discomfort. Take a moment to explore the sensation. It is asking for your attention. As best you can, welcome it into your experience. These kinds of sensations are a part of what makes your life so rich. *(5 seconds)* Also, notice your mind's reaction to this sensation. Do you feel the desire to shift in your seat or to scratch the itch? You may choose to respond to this desire or not. If you do respond, observe the process of this response in its entirety, maybe even noting how often we react to such desires so automatically that we miss the complexity of these experiences. If you do not respond, then just allow your attention to rest on the sensation, observing how it changes, how its intensity rises and falls.

These sensations are like waves on the ocean. Though they may swell to enormous heights, they eventually dissipate. They are just on the surface and cannot disrupt the immensity of the calm sea below. *(5 seconds)* Once you have observed this sensation and have respectfully acknowledged your body's communication, let it go, allowing your attention to expand, taking in the entirety of your body in this moment. *(1 minute)*

Now, begin to draw this experience to a close. Feel where your hands are positioned on your body and the points of contact between your body and the ground. Notice any feelings that may have been generated by this practice. Take three deep breaths as you sit with these feelings. *(10 seconds)* When you are ready, gently open or refocus your eyes, and bring your awareness back to the world around you.

DISCUSSION OF SITTING MEDITATION WITH A FOCUS ON THE BODY AS A WHOLE

After this sitting meditation, participants are given a chance to discuss their experiences and reactions. Again, it is important to respond mindfully to any observations, questions, or concerns that are raised. Leaders can facilitate this discussion by asking open-ended questions such as the following, allowing 2 to 3 minutes for each:

- What did you experience during this expanded sitting meditation?
- What was it like to add another anchor into the sitting meditation?
- How is your ability to direct and return attention to an anchor changing?
- How might a focus on your body as a whole benefit your sport performance?

Home Practice

Another copy of the Daily Mindfulness Log is distributed, and leaders can remind participants to bring their completed daily log to the next session. This might also be a good time to hand out the line drawings of the yoga poses (see Figure 6.1), if not already done. Home practice for Session 3 again includes formal and informal practice.

FORMAL PRACTICE

This week, mindful yoga is incorporated into the home practice, and participants are asked to complete the routine one time before the next session. The full MSPE yoga routine takes about 40 minutes, so it is advisable for participants to plan ahead and select an ample window when there is minimal chance of being interrupted. In light of yoga's intricate and potentially unfamiliar movements, it could be helpful to tell participants how to access a recording of the script and to remind them to reference the handout provided with images of the poses.

Leaders can suggest that, when doing mindful yoga at home, participants pay careful attention to how any limits observed in this session might be shifting with additional practice. Leaders can reiterate the point made earlier that simply noticing and being with limits as they are, and letting go of any felt need to change them, may actually allow those limits to extend over time. It may be useful to offer a sport-specific example of how such a process can unfold. For example, with long-distance runners, perhaps they've experienced feeling like a new target distance or personal-best time was quite daunting, but with continued training, they saw themselves accomplishing feats that felt unimaginable at the outset.

Also, participants are asked to do the 14-minute sitting meditation with a focus on the body as a whole five times this week, and they can be told how to access the recording of this exercise. Leaders may also want to reemphasize that, even though another anchor has been added to the sitting practice, the intention is still the same: maintaining awareness of the target anchor and then, when the mind wanders, directing it back to that anchor nonjudgmentally.

Finally, leaders can point out that there is a bit more to do for home practice this week. There's still only one formal exercise a day, but the exercises have gotten a little longer. It might be effective to again highlight the parallels between participants' physical and mental training, using examples from their sport. For instance, just as long-distance runners would gradually increase their weekly mileage when starting to train, it is also necessary to increase "mental mileage." The MSPE exercises introduced are meant to help develop a range of skills that reflect major aspects of mindfulness and ultimately allow participants to apply them in competition. Although it is important to up the training load, leaders can remind participants that these formal home practice assignments are only what's recommended to get the most out of the program. What is most essential is getting a daily dose of mindfulness practice, even if time is limited.

INFORMAL PRACTICE

Leaders can also remind participants to continue incorporating informal mindfulness practice. They can keep using STOP (stop, take a few breaths, observe, proceed; Stahl & Goldstein, 2010) and take diaphragmatic breaths when they pause. In addition, they can stick with or develop new reminders for informal practice such as alerts (e.g., on a calendar or phone) or a rubber band and be encouraged to continue identifying cues that serve as key associations in their sport and daily lives. It may again be helpful to brainstorm how cues can be developed over the next week.

Wrap-Up

Segal et al. (2002, 2012) conclude their fourth session by reminding their participants to stay present and use the body as a way to awareness. Session 3 of MSPE wraps up in a similar spirit. This endeavor can be as basic as remaining mindful of posture and thinking about what sensations the body is experiencing at a given time. It is important to be in the body as it moves, as it twists, as it reaches for something. Repeated practice at bringing attention back to the anchor of bodily sensations and letting them be just what they are without judgment or expectation is an essential part of cultivating mindfulness and moving beyond current limits. It is also a key to translating awareness from formal meditation practice to daily life.

So, as the session ends, leaders can distribute Handout 4 (Exhibit 6.1) and reflect on the progression over the past 3 weeks from the sitting meditation to the body scan to mindful yoga. As MSPE moves forward, the body is used more and more as an avenue toward greater awareness—essential practice to being able to apply mindfulness to sport performance. Although all exercises can help establish connections to what is happening in the body at a given moment, yoga does this while the body is in motion. And this progression will continue in future sessions.

EXHIBIT 6.1
Handout 4: Summary of MSPE Session 3

Takeaways From Session 3

- The main theme of the session is understanding the roles of expectations and limits.
- There can be a tendency in mindfulness practice, sport performance, and other situations to have limited tolerance for something that doesn't match what we think *should* be happening. Such expectations of ourselves or others often lead to nonconstructive blame and produce distress. Somewhat ironically, letting an experience be what it is, even if unpleasant, may be a more likely route to achieving a desired result.
- Practicing yoga mindfully means paying attention to the experience of the body while moving into and holding poses. Part of what that involves is recognizing limits and accepting them for what they are, neither bad nor good. Such acceptance is key to experiencing how limits change over time.
- Much like in physical training when weight might be added over time to build fitness and different exercises strengthen different abilities, the meditations in mindfulness sport performance enhancement (MSPE) are getting longer and more varied.
- The sitting meditation with a focus on the body as a whole adds a new anchor that helps participants practice expanding the scope of attention, whereas mindful yoga incorporates physical motion, moving mindfulness practice toward mindful sport performance.
- Paying attention to the body mindfully is a wonderful way to strengthen the mind–body connection and can be done throughout the day as the body twists, bends, and stretches with the natural movements of daily life.

Daily Home Practice for the Week After Session 3

- Do the 14-minute sitting meditation with a focus on the body as a whole five times.
- Do the 40-minute mindful yoga one time.
- Seize opportunities to STOP (stop, take a few breaths, observe, proceed) and pay attention mindfully during daily activities.
- Record this practice on your Daily Mindfulness Log and bring it with you next session.
- If one will not be provided, remember to bring a mat, blanket, or towel to the next session.

MSPE Session 4

Embracing "What Is" in Stride

7

S ession 4 of mindful sport performance enhancement (MSPE) builds on paying mindful attention while the body is in motion. This session's main theme is attachments, in particular how they relate to expectations and how to respond to them mindfully (i.e., through acceptance). The walking meditation is introduced, during which participants observe the physical sensations of walking and practice moving forward without striving, letting go with each step.

Session 4 Snapshot

Components of this session are

- diaphragmatic breathing exercise,
- discussion of home practice and attachments,
- mindful yoga and discussion,
- walking meditation and discussion,
- home practice assignment and distribution of Daily Mindfulness Log, and
- wrap-up and discussion of acceptance versus resignation.

http://dx.doi.org/10.1037/0000048-008
Mindful Sport Performance Enhancement: Mental Training for Athletes and Coaches, by K. A. Kaufman, C. R. Glass, and T. R. Pineau

Diaphragmatic Breathing Exercise

This session begins with the 3-minute diaphragmatic breathing exercise from Session 1 (see Chapter 4) to help participants transition into being present with today's MSPE training.

Discussion of Home Practice and Attachments

Participants can spend 5 to 10 minutes sharing their experiences with mindfulness practice during the week. Again, leaders can encourage everyone to share, and it is important that they respond mindfully (i.e., with nonjudgmental acceptance) to anything raised. If participants need assistance generating discussion, they can reference their Daily Mindfulness Logs to help them recall the details of their practice or leaders can pose open-ended questions such as the following:

- What differences, if any, did you notice between practicing the mindful yoga at home and practicing it during our previous session?
- How have your reactions to the sitting meditation been evolving now that we've practiced it for 3 weeks and begun to expand it?
- What types of informal mindfulness practice did you engage in?
- How have you made time to practice the MSPE exercises?
- What cues did you develop to facilitate forming mindful associations?
- How have you noticed yourself applying what you've learned in MSPE, while either playing your sport or engaged in other activities?

Leaders may notice certain themes in what is shared, including feelings of annoyance, frustration, and/or disappointment regarding mindfulness practice not going as planned. Or, because the load has increased, there may be reactions to how much practice time is being requested. Leaders can explain that such experiences may, at first, seem like negative outcomes, but they actually provide rich material through which the nature of mindfulness can be explored further. For instance, perhaps participants can consider what kinds of expectations may be present that are contributing to these reactions. As discussed in the previous session, when realities don't match expectations of what should be, distress is a common result.

It may be useful to take an even deeper look at expectations and what might cause them to take hold, highlighting how one of the primary factors that gives expectations their power is *attachment*. In this context, attachment can be understood as an underlying belief about what is "good," "bad," "right," or "wrong," which can result in rigid expectations. For instance, being attached to the idea that losing is bad can generate the expectation that "I should always win." This expectation not only is unrealistic but also can feed into a spiral of frustration, self-blame, and anxiety when the "bad" outcome (i.e., a loss) occurs. Paradoxically, holding on to such feelings can increase the likelihood that performance will suffer further, leading to more losses.

Reactions to mindfulness practice itself can provide a wonderful illustration of how attachments function. For example, if participants report frustration with being asked to do more minutes of home practice during the week (e.g., feeling it is a waste of time), leaders can explore potential attachments underlying this reaction, such as to a belief about the (lack of) value of this kind of training (it's "bad" or the "wrong" way to train), to other activities that feel sacrificed to make room for mindfulness practice (something else is "better"), or to assumptions about how much time is available (it's "wrong" to be asked to do one more thing). Similarly, annoyance, disappointment, or even happiness with the perceived quality or consistency of practice can relate back to needing to categorize something as bad or good. Leaders can point out that being mindful means there is no bad, good, right, or wrong. There is simply "what is," and each experience presents the chance to be nonjudgmentally present with whatever is happening.

Starting to recognize where attachments exist, that it is possible to separate from them, and that doing so can provide a new level of freedom and choice are important takeaways for participants. Adhering to unexamined attachments is another way one can remain on automatic pilot, a concept discussed in Session 1. If participants are attached to the belief that their schedules are full and thus being asked to do any additional thing is bad, then they may conclude automatically that practicing mindfulness for 40, 15, or even 5 minutes is too much to accommodate. However, being able to pause and then observe how this belief could inhibit their ability to think more flexibly about the reshuffling of priorities can empower participants to see beyond their initial reaction and make room for this practice, if they choose. For instance, perhaps a few minutes of evening unwinding time could be spent doing a sitting meditation or yoga poses, rather than watching television or going on the Internet.

Leaders can expand this discussion to include attachments within the sport(s) of focus by asking participants to consider whether they have any beliefs regarding how they should train to be prepared for competition or results they need to achieve in a competition to feel satisfied. For instance, a long-distance runner may be attached to the belief that giving up is bad and so has the expectation that she should persevere through anything. Although, in some instances, this mentality may lead to dedicated training and consistent maximal effort in competition, it may also lead this athlete to ignore signs of pain and chronic exhaustion that can signal overtraining syndrome or even result in some of the common overuse injuries for runners (e.g., shin splints, runner's knee, plantar fasciitis). Among the consequences of such outcomes could be weeks or months of not being able to train or compete, which would likely feel far worse to this athlete than staying attuned to her body, letting go of the need to never give up, and taking it easy at times. Participants can be invited to imagine how being aware of this attachment and separating from it could change this scenario.

In light of the mental training paradox discussed in Chapter 1 and the particular bias that may exist toward techniques such as meditation, it also might be useful to address any attachment to the idea that focusing on anchors such as the breath or the body cannot improve performance like running, lifting weights, or studying film can (i.e., it's not the "right" way to train). Leaders can acknowledge that this way of thinking is common in sport, where physicality has long been the emphasis, but also make clear that this is an opportunity to break from such an attachment and therefore give themselves a powerful new way to train.

Mindful Yoga

The mindful yoga routine from Session 3 (see Chapter 6) is repeated here to provide another chance for group practice and discussion. Leaders can encourage participants to attend nonjudgmentally to their experiences as they move into and hold the poses as well as to observe their body's limits and how those limits might be changing with continued yoga practice. Kabat-Zinn (1990) described how, no matter one's physical condition, being aware of and working at current limits helps those limits to fade over time. And, like limits, thoughts about what is achievable do not have to be fixed, if one is able to listen to feedback from the body. Generating a sport-specific example to illustrate this concept could be helpful. For instance, when runners first start training, perhaps they think that 1 mile is their limit until they successfully work up to it. Then, maybe 2 miles seems like the limit until they work up to that distance, then 3, then 4, and on and on, and then 1 mile no longer feels like such a significant challenge.

SCRIPT FOR MINDFUL YOGA

Use the script from Chapter 6. Leaders can remind participants that the anchors in this yoga exercise are the sensations that arise as they progress through the poses. They can observe their current limits for what they are and dwell there without pushing through or stepping back from them. Again, leaders may wish to play the audio recording of the yoga script so that they are free to guide participants through the poses, to make any needed adjustments to the routine if there are time constraints, and/or to invite participants to skip any poses that would be contraindicated by injury.

DISCUSSION OF MINDFUL YOGA

After the mindful yoga exercise, participants are given a chance to discuss their experiences and reactions. It is very important for leaders to continue responding mindfully to any observations, questions, or concerns raised. They can facilitate this discussion by asking open-ended questions such as the following, allowing 2 to 3 minutes for each:

- What did you experience during this mindful yoga practice?
- What differences, if any, did you notice while practicing the mindful yoga today?
- What did you observe about your body's limits as you held any of the poses?
- What applications does this yoga practice have to your sport performance?

Walking Meditation

Continuing the MSPE progression of incorporating more and more movement into mindfulness practice, the next exercise introduced is the walking meditation. This activity involves focusing intentionally on the sensations generated by walking (Kabat-Zinn, 1990) and is another technique that can help participants become more aware of their physical experiences in a given moment (Segal, Williams, & Teasdale, 2002). Kabat-Zinn highlighted *nonstriving* as a main concept for the walking meditation, which, in this context, means moving without trying to get anywhere in particular. In other words, the focus is on the process of walking, rather than where one is walking to, and thus it is sufficient for participants just to be with each step, recognizing that they are where they are and attempting to be there completely.

Kabat-Zinn (1990) described mindful walking as having full awareness as one foot contacts the ground, the body's weight shifts into it, the other foot lifts and moves forward, and then it, in turn, comes down to make contact with the ground. He suggested that directing the gaze straight ahead can help practitioners to deepen their concentration and that, although it eventually can be practiced at any pace, it may be most effective to start at a slower pace than ordinary walking to get used to moving in this way.

The MSPE walking meditation lasts for approximately 11 minutes and was informed by the work of Kabat-Zinn (1990) and Segal et al. (2002). In addition to focusing on the physical sensations associated with walking, participants are encouraged to observe the various connections within the body and between the body and the environment that are apparent when walking. As with other MSPE exercises, an essential component is noticing when the mind has wandered away from its anchor and then nonjudgmentally bringing it back. Although it is a formal practice, this exercise also lends itself quite well to informal mindfulness practice, once participants get comfortable with the technique (Kabat-Zinn, 1990).

When introducing the walking meditation, leaders can explain that this exercise continues the progression toward applying mindfulness while one is engaged in increasing amounts of movement. It provides participants with another way to practice concentrating on present-moment experience, letting go of thoughts and emotions as they arise, and releasing excess tension while in motion. In addition, with a more explicit focus on the interconnections within and outside of the body, the walking meditation invites participants to notice the sense of harmony and rhythm that can exist while in motion. The intentional practice of these performance facilitators ultimately helps participants to achieve a full integration of mindfulness into sport performance.

In this activity, the main attentional anchor is the collection of sensations associated with walking, but other foci are incorporated as well, such as the breath and awareness of bodily and environmental connections. Participants may also notice a somewhat ironic effort at nonstriving when, even though they are moving, the idea is to focus on just where they are at this moment. To help emphasize this point, leaders will have participants walk in a circle (either clockwise or counterclockwise). As such, participants are instructed to line up in a circle, all facing in the same direction, with adequate space between each person. Leaders can mention that the exercise begins by standing in place and then speed is increased gradually to give ample opportunity to get used to moving in this way. They can also remind participants of the benefits that may come with this kind of practice, such as the ability to notice and then let go of distractions or excess tension while moving.

SCRIPT FOR WALKING MEDITATION

Take a moment to notice your breath and your posture as you stand. Observe the placement of your feet, the bend in your legs, the curve of your spine, and the angle of your neck. Now, with a deliberate intention, gaze down at your feet. Slowly, with careful attention, arrange your feet, starting with your left foot, so they are parallel, slightly less than shoulder width apart. *(Pause for 5 seconds.)* As you settle your weight evenly in your feet, move your attention up to your knees. Take a moment to bend and straighten your legs slightly, without moving your feet, noticing the flexing and relaxing of the muscles that surround your knees. After a few bends, settle into a comfortable standing position. Now, roll your shoulders up and back as you take a deep breath, and as you do, place your head squarely atop your shoulders, then allow your shoulders to relax. As you do this, feel your back straighten and your chest expand. Sense the peaceful calm that comes with a tall, dignified posture. Allow your arms to find a comfortable and relaxed position, maybe hanging down by your sides or with your hands gently clasped behind your back. Again, notice your posture as you stand, and allow your gaze to settle on a spot several feet in front of you on the floor.

Once you are comfortable in your stance, gently direct your attention to the soles of your feet. Notice the sensations at the points of contact with the ground. Feel the pressure on the balls and the heels of your feet. Notice the tilt in the foot, how there is slightly more pressure along the outside of each foot than on the inside. Notice the constant shifting of your weight as your stabilizer muscles flex and relax, keeping you upright and balanced.

Now, without lifting your feet off the floor, begin to shift your weight from your left foot to your right foot, and continue shifting, back and forth. Notice the changing sensations in your feet as the pressure of contact drains out of one foot and fills the other. Notice the flow of this pressure as you shift, like pouring water back and forth between two glasses. *(15 seconds)*

As you continue to shift your weight, allow your field of awareness to expand. Notice the tension generated in the calf muscle of the leg holding your weight. Observe the flexing and relaxing of your quadriceps, the gentle rhythm of the tilting of your hips, and the subtle sway of your shoulders as your weight flows back and forth, from leg to leg. Even the simple motion of shifting your weight from foot to foot reverberates through your entire body. Even the smallest actions cascade far beyond what we usually notice. *(5 seconds)*

Maintain the slow rhythm you have created, but now begin to lift each foot off of the floor, one at a time, as the weight flows out of each leg. Allow the muscles in your foot and calf to relax as you lift each foot. Notice how your toes hang down as you lift your leg. They are the last part of the foot to leave the ground and the first to reestablish contact. Make your movements slow and deliberate, giving yourself the opportunity to feel every sensation. Notice the wave of pressure as your foot comes in contact with the ground, starting at the toes and flowing through the ball of the foot, the instep, and finally to the heel. *(15 seconds)*

Now, as your weight shifts to your left foot, pause with your right foot off of the ground. Direct your attention to your right leg, and very slowly begin walking. Feel the tension created in the upper thigh as you lift each leg off of the ground, and pay careful attention to the bottom of each foot as it makes contact with the ground. As you continue taking slow steps forward, feel the wave of pressure move through your foot, starting with your heel. Notice how the pressure increases on your heel as your weight begins to shift from your back leg to your front leg, and notice how that pressure flows through the outside of your foot, to the ball of your foot, and finally to your toes as you take another step forward. Notice the intricate, coordinated sensations between your feet as you walk, placing each step with careful intention. Observe how even the slightest relief of pressure from your back foot pours that pressure into your forward foot. Feel the gentle rhythm of this process, noticing every small step in the sequence. *(20 seconds)*

Recognize the interconnectedness of every motion. As you continue to walk in this intentional way, allow your awareness to expand beyond your feet and legs. Feel the muscles in your lower back tensing as you step forward. Feel the muscles in your neck as they stabilize your head on your shoulders. Feel the air against your face as you move through it. Feel the gravity of the earth pull you down with each footfall. Every movement you make establishes connection after connection after connection. When you walk, allow yourself to take in the entirety of this connective process. Not only do these motions reverberate through your body, but you move the air that surrounds you and push off the earth below you. A single step cannot exist by itself. To take a single step you need muscles and tendons to move your body, you need the earth to walk on, and the earth needs space to float through. With every step you are connected to the infinite space that surrounds you. *(5 seconds)*

With your attention comfortably settled on the sensations associated with each slow, deliberate step, allow your pace to gradually increase. As best you can, continue to notice the waves of pressure as they move through your feet when you reach your regular walking pace and all the various sensations throughout your body when you exceed your regular walking pace. Observe how the experience of walking changes as your speed increases, while also observing the ways the experience stays the same. If you notice your mind wandering, be thankful for this connection to the present moment and gently escort your attention back to the soles of your feet, allowing your field of awareness to again expand through your whole body and to the greater connections associated with each and every step. *(1 minute)*

Now, begin to slow your pace back down and come to a stop. Do a quick scan of your body, from your feet to the top of your head, taking in the sensations generated by this practice. *(5 seconds)* When you're ready, take a deep breath and full exhalation, and bring your attention back to the world around you.

DISCUSSION OF WALKING MEDITATION

After the walking meditation, participants are given a chance to discuss their experiences and reactions. It remains very important for leaders to respond mindfully to any observations, questions, or concerns raised. They can facilitate this discussion by asking open-ended questions such as the following, allowing 2 to 3 minutes for each:

- What thoughts, feelings, and sensations did you notice while walking in this way?
- How was it to move forward while still trying to focus on the present moment?
- How did this experience compare to that of other MSPE exercises?
- What applications might this exercise have to performance in your sport?

Home Practice

Another copy of the Daily Mindfulness Log is distributed for the upcoming week of home practice, and leaders can remind participants to bring their daily log to the next session.

FORMAL PRACTICE

The 11-minute walking meditation is the primary formal practice for this week. Participants are asked to complete it four times before the next session. Because of the number of chances participants are likely to have to practice walking mindfully, it might be a good idea to provide a recording for this exercise, so participants can use it while out and about. Leaders can remind participants that the walking meditation is a nonstriving activity, so the idea is to remain fully present with each step, allowing it to be exactly what it is.

In addition, participants are asked to do the body scan one time and mindful yoga one time before the next session. As before, leaders can remind participants that these exercises are a bit longer, so it may be useful to identify well in advance an ample window of time when they are not likely to be disrupted. Leaders can also spend a few moments discussing participants' reactions to this home practice assignment, looking for any responses (e.g., concern about finding time for two longer exercises) that may reflect underlying attachments (e.g., mindfulness practice is not a priority because it's not the "right" way to train for sport).

INFORMAL PRACTICE

Leaders can also remind participants to continue incorporating informal mindfulness practice into their daily routine. For instance, they can continue to use STOP (stop, take a few breaths, observe, proceed; Stahl & Goldstein, 2010) and take diaphragmatic breaths when they pause. Also, participants can stick with or develop new reminders such as alerts (e.g., on a calendar or phone) or a rubber band and can be encouraged to continue thinking of and using cues that serve as key associations in their sport and daily lives. It may again be helpful to spend a few minutes brainstorming how cues can be developed over the next week.

Wrap-Up

Segal, Williams, and Teasdale (2002, 2012) concluded their fifth session with a discussion of the nature of acceptance or allowance, particularly as it relates to dealing with unpleasant experiences. After the ability to notice experiences (i.e., present-moment awareness), such as reactions to the body's limits during mindful yoga, is strengthened, the next step in mindfulness training involves deciding how to relate to whatever enters awareness (e.g., a thought, feeling, physical sensation). Relating with acceptance (i.e., letting an experience be what it is) can help promote peace and relaxation, as opposed to automatic and often maladaptive reactions. Instead of getting wrapped up in fighting what is happening, perhaps because it generates an unpleasant reaction, acceptance allows for a freeing of attention and energy to actually see, understand, and, when appropriate or possible, take direct action to address the root of a current experience.

This session of MSPE, with its emphasis on awareness of and separation from attachments, wraps up with a similar message. In this discussion (as we also describe in Chapter 10), it is important to explain how acceptance is a mindful response to attachments and to differentiate acceptance from resignation, as this is a common point of confusion. Leaders can suggest to participants that when they observe themselves feeling upset about a particular condition or outcome, they can consider the attachment(s) that produced this feeling. Such awareness can lead to the next step of integrating mindfulness into their way of being, namely, bringing an attitude of acceptance to whatever the situation is. Doing so does not mean they have to like what is happening or that they are resigned to it continuing, but rather that they are letting things be what they are in the moment, even if unpleasant. Acceptance is really about empowerment, in the sense that it can help one to tolerate the truth of whatever is occurring rather than react emotionally to a feared future so one can make accurate and intentional choices about how to respond in the present moment. In contrast, no choices are available while stuck wishing things would be different.

Offering a sport-specific example here may be helpful. For instance, recall the runner discussed in Session 1 who got passed during a race. Several negative reactions could arise in this situation, leading the runner to think with resignation, "I'm going to lose this race." This thought is quite different from the more accurate one, "My competitor just passed me," which exemplifies accepting the truth about the situation in the present moment, with no predictions of what's to come. Getting passed in one moment does not mean an inevitable outcome that the race is lost. Accepting "what is" right now and letting go of unpleasant thoughts and emotions that arise in reaction to the fact that current experience doesn't match what is desired can permit runners to seize the moment. They can thus refocus attention on actual running in that moment and remain in control of the process of the performance, which ultimately is what determines the outcome and can potentially lead to a different future.

EXHIBIT 7.1

Handout 5: Summary of MSPE Session 4

Takeaways From Session 4

- The main theme of this mindfulness sport performance enhancement (MSPE) session is *attachments*, particularly how they relate to expectations and how to respond to them mindfully (i.e., with acceptance).
- An attachment is an underlying belief about what is "good," "bad," "right," or "wrong" and can result in rigid expectations.
- We can get so attached to a condition or outcome as necessary or unacceptable that when things don't go as they "should" we experience significant resistance or distress. Such attachments can, for example, inhibit the ability to reshuffle priorities and make time for mindfulness practice or adversely affect the way we perform in our sport.
- While continuing to practice mindful yoga, pay careful attention to how the body's limits may be changing over time.
- The walking meditation continues the progression toward incorporating mindful attention into sport performance. The primary attentional anchor involved is the collection of sensations produced by walking, though the breath and connections both within the body and to the environment also are foci. An emphasis during this exercise is on *nonstriving*, that is, letting a particular moment be what it is without trying to get anywhere else.
- Acceptance is a way to respond to attachments mindfully and is *not* synonymous with resignation. Tolerating the truth of "what is" empowers us to choose how to respond in the moment, which can potentially lead to a different future.

Daily Home Practice for the Week After Session 4

- Do the 11-minute walking meditation four times.
- Do the 30-minute body scan one time.
- Do the 40-minute mindful yoga routine one time.
- Seize opportunities to STOP (stop, take a few breaths, observe, proceed) and pay attention mindfully during daily activities.
- Record this practice on your Daily Mindfulness Log and bring it with you next session.
- If the leader has suggested it, remember to bring any sport equipment with you to the next session (to use during the sport meditation) and/or wear appropriate shoes.

At the close of the session, leaders can distribute the weekly handout summarizing what was covered and home practice for the upcoming week (Handout 5; see Exhibit 7.1). Of note, the next session contains the most applied, sport-specific MSPE exercise, so participants can be invited to bring any equipment that leaders wish to incorporate into this practice (leaders may look ahead to the next chapter to plan accordingly). Also, depending on the sport(s) of focus and the movements involved in the sport meditation (e.g., running), it may be important to ask participants to wear appropriate shoes.

MSPE Session 5
Embodying the Mindful Performer

8

ession 5 of mindful sport performance enhancement (MSPE) focuses on the full integration of mindfulness into sport. The main theme is nonstriving, which was introduced in the previous session, and is expanded upon here to include its applications to athletic performance. Over the course of MSPE, participants have brought mindful attention to their experiences, beginning while seated and then while increasingly in motion. In Session 5, this style of attention is brought into the sport(s) of focus through the identification and use of sport-specific, present-moment anchors. This sport meditation is the final piece of the bridge between formal mindfulness practice and mindful sport performance. In addition, a lengthier sitting meditation is done, which includes both a new anchor and a period of silence (as opposed to guided meditation).

Session 5 Snapshot

Components of this session are

- diaphragmatic breathing exercise,
- discussion of home practice and nonstriving,

http://dx.doi.org/10.1037/0000048-009
Mindful Sport Performance Enhancement: Mental Training for Athletes and Coaches, by K. A. Kaufman, C. R. Glass, and T. R. Pineau

- sport meditation and discussion,
- sitting meditation with a focus on the breath, body, and sound and discussion,
- home practice assignment and distribution of Daily Mindfulness Log, and
- wrap-up and discussion of the role of choice in self-care

Diaphragmatic Breathing Exercise

This session begins with the 3-minute diaphragmatic breathing exercise from Session 1 (see Chapter 4) to help participants transition into being present with today's MSPE training.

Discussion of Home Practice and Nonstriving

Participants can spend 5 to 10 minutes sharing their experiences practicing mindfulness during the week. Again, leaders can encourage everyone to share, and it is important that they respond mindfully (i.e., with nonjudgmental acceptance) to anything raised. If participants need assistance generating discussion, they can reference their Daily Mindfulness Logs to help them recall the details of their practice, and/or leaders can pose open-ended questions such as the following:

- What was it like to incorporate the walking meditation into your home practice?
- What did you experience with the body scan and mindful yoga this week?
- What types of informal mindfulness practice did you try?
- What cues did you develop to facilitate forming mindful associations?
- How have you noticed yourself applying what you've learned in MSPE, while either playing your sport or engaged in other activities?
- How have you made time to practice the MSPE exercises?

Leaders should be prepared to respond to certain themes in the reactions of the participants, such as continued resistance to the time and effort required for daily practice or indications of using mindfulness to achieve an outcome such as relaxing or reducing pain. To address such comments, leaders can refer to how mindfulness involves both awareness and acceptance and explore the power of acceptance a little more deeply.

Acceptance was discussed in the previous session as a mindful response to attachments and a route to empowerment. As described by Segal, Williams, and Teasdale (2002, 2012), one of the greatest challenges in building mindfulness is being accepting of situations without having a hidden agenda of fixing them. Through this home practice discussion, participants can consider whether they truly are beginning to accept "what is" without needing to change it (e.g., "Ok, I'm stressed right now") or if they are using mindfulness to alter what they've discovered (e.g., "I'm stressed, so I should meditate to relax").

This idea, that mindfulness is about nonstriving and many of its benefits stem from intentionally not trying to go anywhere other than the present, can be difficult to conceptualize, perhaps especially for those people who are bombarded by pressures to achieve and advance. Competitors, such as athletes and coaches, who often are trained to focus on reaching and even eclipsing desired outcomes, may have particular trouble embracing nonstriving, so it is crucial for leaders to allot ample time for this discussion.

Because exercises like the sitting meditation, body scan, and mindful yoga can lead to desirable conditions like relaxation, participants may have begun using them to strive toward these ends. However, working to accept present-moment experience in order to change it is not really accepting present-moment experience! Admittedly, this notion is a bit of a brain twister, so it may be important to examine it more with participants, possibly providing an example. For instance, using mindful breathing to relax may have some benefits, but such striving might actually limit the full experience of being mindful because actions still are being guided by an unexamined attachment to outcomes. In this case, by using mindful breathing to relax, the attachment is to the belief that stress is "bad" and its removal is "good."

Acceptance involves simply acknowledging that events are unfolding exactly as they are supposed to. Nothing needs to be done to "fix" them, which is the essence of nonstriving. This principle suggests that more relaxation can come about through accepting that stress is present than by trying to reduce it with a particular technique. Meditating to relax implies an attachment to the belief that stress needs to be removed and an expectation that mindfulness practice should induce relaxation. Imposing such requirements actually can generate more stress, whereas just meditating with the stress, letting it be what it is, can allow for the freedom to let go and relax.

Achieving through nonstriving may seem somewhat paradoxical to participants, especially in the context of MSPE, because they might have understood the basic premise of the program to be using mindfulness to improve performance. In fact, the name *mindful sport performance enhancement* appears to suggest that mindfulness will be used to enhance sport performance. This certainly is the result we predict will follow the training, with mindfulness leading to sport-related benefits. However, being mindful in order to perform better would thus focus on the same goal as does the control-oriented psychological skills training used in traditional sport psychology interventions and therefore shares some of the same limitations.

Leaders can explain that this "do X to cause Y" mentality is commonly applied in sport (and other achievement realms) and relates to the learned assumption that actions always are done for a purpose, to reach some goal or objective. The powerful attachment to this way of being, however, can be extraordinarily limiting. So, even though this may have been their initial understanding of MSPE, it is our hope that participants will eventually come to understand and embrace the nonstriving attitude of mindfulness, allowing them to experience the freedom and the new possibilities that come with full acceptance of the present moment.

Leaders can use sport-specific examples to illustrate this point. For instance, runners commonly experience pain, resulting in a variety of reactions. Thoughts such as "This hurts so bad, I need to stop" can impact performance significantly, if treated as fact. Unless the runners are injured and thus truly need to stop, such thoughts come from an attachment to the notion that pain is bad and so always needs to be reduced.

These types of reactions convey messages about the limits of abilities, which may not objectively be true. While running, isn't it possible to feel quite sore and yet continue on? Understanding where these messages come from and accepting them merely as thoughts, feelings, or sensations, and not necessarily reality (i.e., decentering), is a key to lessening the harm they can do to performance.

What might this acceptance look like? Mindful runners who notice pain could think to themselves, "This hurts so bad and I want to stop, but that's just a reaction to my pain. I can notice my pain, accept that I am in pain at this moment in time, and still continue to run." By accepting this pain as just a part of the present moment, with nothing needing to be fixed (again assuming there is no injury that would make it advisable to stop), these runners can break away from an attachment to pain as something needing to be removed and continue with the process of running, putting themselves in a better position to achieve success.

A question that often comes up is, "Does embracing nonstriving mean that I can't have goals?" It is important for leaders to make clear that there is nothing wrong with having goals, which are wonderful ways to generate and sustain motivation. In fact, having goals and nonstriving actually can coexist nicely. It all comes down to how goals are framed. For instance, the goal of winning a competition could be framed as "I would like to win" or "I need to win." The former is more of a preference, which does not necessarily have to result in negative reactions if the desired outcome is not achieved. The latter, however, has a rigidity that might make it difficult to let go of any thoughts or feelings that come up after a loss. The insertion of needing to win also entails some follow-up thoughts (e.g., "I need to win, and if I don't I'm a failure") that will likely cause significant distress if things don't turn out as predicted.

With regard to the pursuit of goals, as Kabat-Zinn (1990) explained, backing off of striving and instead focusing on the acceptance of current conditions exactly as they are is actually the best way to achieve goals. With patience, movement toward goals takes place naturally. This movement is inherent in emphasizing process over outcome. With long-distance running as an example, one can imagine a runner who ran an excellent race, maintaining the pace she had planned, feeling focused and self-assured, letting go of distracting thoughts and sensations, and putting forth maximal effort all the way to the finish line—and yet she still lost. Focusing on the outcome might leave this athlete feeling demoralized and frustrated, blinding her to all of the aspects of her race plan that she executed well and leading to increased levels of anxiety approaching her next race. However, by focusing on the process, this athlete can feel satisfied with her performance, holding in mind both the things she felt she did well and the areas she might want to change for next time. Her ability to appreciate how she ran (rather than just the outcome, which she has far less control over) may actually enhance her sense of confidence, efficacy, and motivation as she trains for her next race.

Leaders may take this opportunity to reiterate the point from the conclusion of Session 4 (see Chapter 7) that acceptance is not synonymous with resignation. As this example illustrates, accepting the realty of the situation (i.e., that she lost the race) does not entail this runner accepting that she is a bad competitor or that she will have a losing season. On the contrary, her ability to accept the totality of what happened and to let go of such predictions can free up mental and emotional resources and allow her to make more intentional, and likely more helpful, choices moving forward.

Sport Meditation

Participants have been working to develop a mindful style of attention while engaged in progressively greater amounts of bodily movement, and that progression culminates here with the sport meditation. This exercise uses the physical sensations generated through core motions in athletes' and coaches' sport(s) of focus as present-moment anchors. This concept of using sport-specific sensations as anchors for attention fits with rowing coach Bruce Beall's (personal communication, March 7, 2006) recommendation that by focusing on elements of technique, athletes can sustain concentration on their form and become a type of self-coach, potentially aiding performance. The idea is that being nonjudgmentally present with what is happening while moving in sport is an effective way to separate from the reactions (e.g., worry, fatigue, pain) that can so easily hijack attention, undermine control, and prevent immersion in the task at hand, all of which inhibit flow and optimal-performance states (Csikszentmihalyi, 1990).

As mentioned in Session 1, it is very important to differentiate between mindfully observing a present-moment anchor (e.g., sensations of movement) and micromanaging or overanalyzing well-learned skills. Whereas mindfulness can free up attentional resources to be directed to where they are most needed, focusing on step-by-step instruction about how to do something that is already a well-trained skill can waste those resources and disturb the efficiency gained with expertise. Being mindful of core motions in a sport (i.e., observing them for what they are while they are occurring) can maximize control of the performance process, but such control is not possible when attention is wrapped up in the mental directives more typical of a novice first attempting to learn the skills.

It may also be important to note here that while this exercise uses the motions of a sport as anchors for attention, we are not suggesting that participants should attempt to meditate during competition. There is a difference between being mindful and practicing mindfulness, but through this sport-specific practice of mindfulness, participants become better able to be mindful when performing in their sport.

Ideally, the sport meditation is practiced while participants move through the identified core motions of their sport, and as such, leaders need to be thoughtful about how and where this meditation can take place. For instance, a running meditation may require a larger space, possibly an outdoor track or a large gym. And, if a leader plans to guide the meditation, it may be advisable to have participants run in several lines, with the leader following in back so that his or her voice projects forward. In contrast, a meditation that focuses on the sensations of the golf swing can likely be done in a much smaller space, though additional equipment (e.g., golf clubs) may be necessary. In addition, in certain circumstances (e.g., if a participant is injured) it may be more appropriate to practice this meditation using visualization of the movements. To illustrate how leaders can introduce this meditation, we use the example of running. Adaptations are necessary to fit other sport(s) of focus.

Leaders can explain that MSPE has been working toward helping participants integrate mindfulness skills into their sport performance. The sport meditation represents the culminating step in that effort, as participants will now have the opportunity to run mindfully. Running can be "a form of dynamic meditation" (Miller, 2002, p. 41), and its cyclical nature provides a number of anchors for present-moment attention. For instance, the sensations associated with the feet hitting the ground or the arms swinging are constantly accessible while running.

During this exercise, participants will be running as their attention is directed to various bodily movements. The sensations generated by these movements are the present-moment anchors, and participants are also invited to notice their reactions to these sensations. The purpose of this exercise is not to receive instruction on how to run, to perfect form, or to maximize speed. Rather, the purpose is simply to be present with the body and mind while running, letting go with each stride. Participants can regard the prompts to tune in to their movements as a general guide, and if their movements are somehow different from what is described, that is perfectly fine. They can just pay attention to what is true for them. Running mindfully can allow for recognition of factors that disturb performance. Accepting that these factors exist, without judging them as "bad," can provide the freedom to choose to run more effectively.

As with previous exercises, participants can be reminded to direct their attention back to the anchors when they find their minds wandering, like a rubber band snapping back to its center. Examples of several sport meditation anchors are provided in the next section. A full script of a 14-minute running meditation is also included, and an audio recording of it can be found online (http://www.mindfulsportperformance.org).

ANCHOR SELECTION

Leaders can choose the anchors for the sport meditation in advance or select them in collaboration with participants during this session. In either case, participants can be encouraged to personalize their anchors while practicing the sport meditation outside of the session. If MSPE is being administered to a group of participants representing multiple sports, it is advisable to identify anchors that are applicable to as many of the sports as possible. Provided next are sample anchors for two sports, running and golf, and the running anchors are then used in the script for the sport meditation. These are meant as illustrative examples and, of course, would be adapted to fit the sport(s) of focus. For instance, the running anchors could be modified to incorporate stick handling in lacrosse or dribbling in soccer, whereas totally different anchors would be chosen for the serve in volleyball or tennis.

Running Anchors

Recommendations by running experts such as Dreyer (2001), Hahn (2004), and Miller (2002) informed the selection of these anchors, which include

- *The breath.* Notice the breath, which perhaps is diaphragmatic.
- *Gaze.* Observe head position and gaze direction, which perhaps is straight ahead.
- *Shoulders.* Scan the shoulders and maybe release any excess tension on the exhale.
- *Arms and hands.* Notice sensations associated with arms swinging and hands gripping.
- *Legs.* Observe sensations associated with hips rotating, knees bending, and muscles flexing.
- *Feet.* Experience each foot plant and the shifting of weight that occurs.
- *Posture.* Expand awareness to the whole body and how it is being held while running.

Golf Anchors

If golfers do not have a club with them, they can progress through this exercise as if they are actually holding one. Such an adaptation can be made for any sport requiring equipment or if safety and/or space are concerns. The full golf swing can be divided into several phases (e.g., Newell, 2001), which provide powerful anchors:

- *Addressing the ball.* Notice sensations associated with the stance over the ball and holding the club with the head resting on the ground behind the ball.
- *Backswing.* Observe sensations associated with a rotation of the club head back and up all the way to the top of the backswing, the shift in body weight, and movements in regions such as the pelvis, shoulders, arms, elbows, and wrists.
- *Downswing.* Notice the sensations associated with the club head changing direction as it follows the reverse of the path it took during the backswing, paying particular attention as the club approaches and moves through the hitting zone.
- *Follow through.* Observe the sensations associated with continuing to rotate the body so the club head travels up and over the shoulder.

SCRIPT FOR SPORT MEDITATION (EXAMPLE OF A RUNNING MEDITATION)

We now take the mindfulness skills that we have learned and apply them directly to your running. As in many of the other meditations we have done, you will use your body to help keep you connected to the present moment. Although every individual runs a bit differently, we will use several common elements of running form as anchors for our attention. In addition to these specific movements, also try to maintain awareness of the sense of connectedness between all of your body parts. Recognize how each muscle and each motion play its unique parts in creating the greater whole that is your running. *(Pause for 5 seconds.)*

Now, begin running at a slow and relaxed pace, allowing your muscles to warm and stretch. As you run, allow your field of awareness to be filled with each of the following elements in turn. Also, keep in mind that this exercise, in itself, is not about maximizing speed or effort but about noticing the sensations in your body as you run, allowing all that arises through this experience to come and go without judgment. As you explore each component of your form, as best you can, allow your attention to remain expansive, taking in the entirety of your body and all of its sensations. *(5 seconds)*

First, take a moment to notice your breath. Are you breathing into your nose? Your mouth? Either way, there is no need to change it; just observe the natural experience of breathing as you run. Notice also where your breath is going. Breathing down into your belly, rather than into your chest, can allow your lungs to more efficiently get needed oxygen to your muscles. It can also help keep the body relaxed, saving you precious energy. As best you can, in the background of your awareness, maintain a gentle focus on your breath, perhaps periodically wondering to yourself, without any self-blame or reproach, but simply with a kindhearted curiosity, "Where is my breath going right now?" If you notice that you are not breathing into your belly, congratulate yourself on this connection with the present moment, and if you choose, you can then give your body the gift of belly breathing. *(5 seconds)*

Once you have found a comfortable rhythm with your breath, allow your attention to shift to the placement of your head and the direction of your gaze. How is your head positioned? Is it sitting squarely atop your shoulders? If so, or if not, what does it feel like? Where is your gaze directed? Perhaps notice how looking out ahead of you a short distance or toward the horizon helps align your neck with your spine, allowing the muscles in your neck to stay loose and relaxed. Take a moment to explore with your attention the muscles in your forehead, cheeks, and jaw. Tension can sometimes reside in these places. Breathe with whatever you are experiencing and, on your next exhalation, allow your forehead to soften, your cheeks and jaw to slacken, letting any tension go. *(5 seconds)*

Next, allow your attention to shift down to your shoulders. Notice their positioning. Are they hunched up toward your ears? Are your shoulder blades pinched back behind you? Muscle tension can cause fatigue and can make running more difficult. If you notice any tension or tightness, explore this sensation for a moment, and on your next exhalation, allow the tension to drain from these muscles. Feel your shoulders drop with each exhalation, and let your shoulders stay loose as they gently sway back and forth with each stride you take. *(5 seconds)*

After you have scanned your head, neck, and shoulders, allow the focus of your attention to move down to your arms and hands. Notice the angle of your elbows, the rhythm created by the swinging of your arms. Observe how your arms are moving. Are they out away from your body, or do they brush up against you? Are your fingers loose and relaxed, or are your fists tight and clenched? Feel how the motion of your arms works in synchrony with your legs, propelling you forward. As you breathe, see if you can allow your hands to relax, perhaps cupping them gently as if you were holding something small and delicate in your palms. Let your arms bend comfortably at the elbows. Permit your arms to swing rhythmically by your side, forward and back, between your waist and chest. Feel how this motion incorporates itself into the momentum of your body. *(5 seconds)*

Next, allow your attention to move down to your lower body. Notice the sensations in your hips as your legs swing back and forth. Feel the gentle alternation of flexion and relaxation in your quads and hamstrings as each leg switches from the driving leg to the recovering leg. Pay particular attention to the sensations in your feet, ankles, and knees as each foot contacts the ground. Notice what part of your foot hits the ground first, how your weight transfers through your foot with each step. Observe how high your knees come up with each stride and where you place your foot under your body with each step. *(5 seconds)* If you find any especially powerful sensations in any of these locations, allow yourself to note them and then let them fade gently into the background of your awareness. *(5 seconds)*

As we proceed, try to remain conscious of your breath going down into your belly. Allow the focus of your attention to now come to the soles of your feet. As each foot hits the ground, see if you can follow the sequence of pressure that travels through it. Observe your foot falling under your center of gravity with each stride. As each foot hits the ground, notice how the first point of pressure may be in your midfoot, just behind the outside of your little toe. If so, as your weight moves forward, the pressure may shift to the ball of the foot and then to the heel. Finally, as your center of gravity moves beyond the planted foot, the pressure may shift to your toes as you push off of the ground, propelling yourself forward, allowing gravity to pull you down into your next step. Take some time to maintain a focus on this progression of pressure, from the ball of the foot at the foot plant, to the heel as your weight settles on your foot, and then to the toes as you push off the ground. This progression of pressure through your foot may happen very quickly, and, if you find it difficult to feel the sequence, that is okay. As you continue to focus your attention, you may find that, over time, you are able to notice finer details of your experience. If you find that your particular sequence of contact is different than this, that is okay too. Just notice your sequence and do your best to follow it, whatever it is. *(5 seconds)*

Now that you have scanned through these aspects of form in turn, allow your awareness to expand to your body as a whole and the sensations of running itself. Notice your posture. What does it feel like? Is your stance tall and erect or something different? Perhaps see if you can sense your body leaning forward slightly, how this lean comes from your ankles rather than your hips or back, and how it creates a subtle sense of falling into each step. Let the full experience of running wash over you. *(5 seconds)* Recognize the trust and acceptance so inherent in running. Just as breathing is a constant process of letting go, so too is running. You connect to the ground with each step, but to move forward you must let that connection go, let gravity take over, let the process be exactly what it is in each moment. *(5 seconds)*

If you find your mind wandering while you run, drawn away from the sensations in your body, perhaps by thoughts of where you need to go, what you need to do, or how fast you need to do it, that is just fine. Noticing this is a wonderful opportunity, and you can kindly congratulate yourself for taking advantage of it. This is part of your experience. This is neither good nor bad, it just is. Once you have noticed that your mind has gone elsewhere, you may, with a mindful intention, bring your attention back to the anchor of your breath and the sensations of your stride. Although many moments have come and gone, and many are still to come, the moment that is right now is the only moment in which you live, the only moment in which you have control. It is a wonderful and generous thing to give yourself the opportunity to be in this moment, to truly experience your life and the wonders of running. *(1 minute)*

Now, begin to slow your pace and gradually come to a stop. *(10 seconds)* Once you have stopped, close your eyes, take some deep breaths, and notice any sensations in your body after having done this exercise. *(5 seconds)* When you are ready, gently open your eyes and bring your attention back to the world around you.

DISCUSSION OF SPORT MEDITATION

After the sport meditation, participants are given a chance to discuss their experiences and reactions. It remains very important for leaders to respond mindfully to any observations, questions, or concerns raised. They can facilitate this discussion by asking open-ended questions such as the following, allowing 2 to 3 minutes for each:

- What did you notice while practicing this sport meditation?
- How did this experience compare to your experiences of other MSPE exercises?
- What was it like to apply mindful attention to executing skills in your sport?
- How might using this style of attention impact the way you compete?

Sitting Meditation With a Focus on the Breath, Body, and Sound

This exercise returns to the sitting meditation, with some added elements. The previous iteration (incorporating a focus on the body as a whole) done in Session 3 (see Chapter 6) is expanded to include awareness beyond the breath and body to the sounds heard in the surrounding environment, such as the ticking of a clock or distant chatter. Participants are encouraged to notice these sounds and their reactions to them, trying to let them be what they are without judgment.

Another new feature is a 3-minute period of silence at the end of the exercise. Other MSPE meditations have been mostly guided. A voice can provide a helpful cue to return to an anchor, which may be especially useful to novice meditators. However, this guidance can also give the mind something to do, potentially reducing its tendency to get bored or distracting it from perceived discomfort, which are themselves experiences that can offer some of the richest opportunities for mindfulness practice. Kabat-Zinn (1990) claimed that during the sitting meditation, it is at the point that the mind has had enough with the boredom or discomfort that "self-observation gets particularly interesting and fruitful" (p. 64).

With the added anchor of sound and the period of silence, this sitting meditation is somewhat longer than the others, lasting about 21 minutes. The MSPE version of this exercise was informed by the work of Kabat-Zinn (1990) and Segal et al. (2002). Leaders can introduce this exercise to participants as a way of continuing to strengthen the primary characteristics of mindfulness (awareness and acceptance). Building on the earlier sitting meditations, this one stretches the mental muscle further by adding the new anchor of environmental sounds and a period of silence at the end. Leaders can explain that such longer exercises, which pose fresh attentional challenges, can help get attention into the kind of shape that will be required during a sport performance, which usually lasts much longer than a few minutes. If participants notice themselves feeling uncomfortable, bored, or restless, they can acknowledge these reactions with an attitude of acceptance, perhaps considering what attachments might be present. For example, sensations of restlessness may be rooted in an attachment to the idea that movement is necessary to feel productive and that not feeling productive is "bad." Whatever reactions are observed, participants can just note them and then direct attention back to their anchor.

The audio recording of this exercise (see http://www.mindfulsportperformance. org), contains all 21 minutes of this exercise (i.e., the expansion of attentional anchors from the breath to the body to environmental sounds). However, because the first two thirds of this material is covered in earlier scripts, what is presented next is only the new portion (the focus on sounds and the period of silence). This exercise thus starts with the first six paragraphs from the Sitting Meditation With a Focus on the Breath script in Session 1, continues with the first four paragraphs from the Sitting Meditation With a Focus on the Body As a Whole script from Session 3, and then finishes with the following material.

SCRIPT FOR SITTING MEDITATION WITH A FOCUS ON THE BREATH, BODY, AND SOUND

Your field of awareness has been filled with the sensations in your entire body. Now, allow your awareness to expand once again. Invite the sounds all around you into your awareness. As best you can, continue to follow the rhythm of your breath and the flow of life within your body, while also noticing the noises occurring all around you, perhaps appreciating how complex each and every moment can be. Maybe you can hear a distant conversation, the hum of some electric device, the ticking of a clock, the chirping of birds, or the buzz of traffic. Just as you did earlier with your body, explore these sounds with a gentle curiosity as they enter your awareness. *(Pause for 5 seconds.)* Observe any reactions you have to the sounds, noting what thoughts and feelings arise, but without holding onto them. These sounds are part of your experience right now, in this moment, and need not be changed. *(10 seconds)*

Maybe you find yourself wishing that these sounds would change, linger, or go away. Such reactions are a wonderful opportunity for you. Try to notice them, and recognize how your thoughts have taken you into a desired future, to a time and an experience that has not yet and might not occur. Our thoughts often take us into the future and away from the lives we are living right now. Congratulate yourself when you notice this happening because, in that moment, you are awake, you are aware, you are present. You are giving yourself the opportunity to fully and truly experience your life. And, with this recognition, gently bring your attention back to your current experience: the rising and falling of your abdomen with your breath, the sensations flowing throughout your body, and the sounds that compose every one of our complex and unique moments of life. We will now sit in silence with this awareness, noting the natural wandering of the mind, and you can congratulate yourself on your reconnection to the present moment as you bring your attention back again and again to the anchor of your breath, your body, and the sounds around you. *(Allow for 3 minutes of silence.)*

Now, start to draw this experience to a close. Gently bring your attention back to the tips of your toes. Allow your attention to again rise up through your body with each in-breath, scanning each area of your body for sensations that may be lingering. *(10 seconds)* Notice those sensations that let you know where your body is. Feel where your hands are positioned on your body and the points of contact between your body and the ground. Observe what this moment is like, right here, right now. Notice feelings that may have been generated by this practice. Take three deep breaths as you sit with these feelings. *(10 seconds)* When you are ready, gently open or refocus your eyes, and bring your awareness back to the world around you.

DISCUSSION OF SITTING MEDITATION WITH A FOCUS ON THE BREATH, BODY, AND SOUND

After this sitting meditation, participants are given a chance to discuss their experiences and reactions. It remains very important for leaders to respond mindfully to any observations, questions, or concerns that are raised. They can facilitate this discussion by asking open-ended questions such as the following, allowing 2 to 3 minutes for each:

- What did you experience during this further expanded sitting meditation?
- What was it like to add the anchor of sound into the sitting meditation?
- What were your reactions to the silent portion of this sitting meditation?
- How might this type of practice benefit your sport performance?

If responses to the question about the silence indicate preferences for guided meditations for reasons such as "A voice keeps me focused" or "I don't get bored as easily," then this may be a valuable opportunity for leaders to highlight the latent attachments present: for instance, attachment to the priority of "staying focused," as opposed to observing the natural activities of the mind, or to the need to "stay busy," rather than accepting the experience of being bored.

Home Practice

Another copy of the Daily Mindfulness Log is distributed for the final week of home practice, and leaders can remind participants to bring their daily log, as well as any equipment and appropriate shoes needed for the sport meditation, to the next session.

FORMAL PRACTICE

Formal practice for this week centers on the two new exercises, the sport meditation and the sitting meditation with a focus on the breath, body, and sound. Participants are asked to practice the sport meditation four times during the week and can be encouraged to experiment with other potential anchors in their sport(s). The Sport Meditation script presented in this chapter takes about 14 minutes to complete, but participants can be flexible with how long they practice this meditation depending on the anchors involved. They are asked to do the 21-minute sitting meditation two times during the week. Even though the training has reached the point of applying mindfulness directly to sport performance, it is still important to keep building the fundamentals.

INFORMAL PRACTICE

Leaders can also remind participants to continue incorporating informal mindfulness practice into their daily routine. They can keep using STOP (stop, take a few breaths, observe, proceed; Stahl & Goldstein, 2010) and take diaphragmatic breaths when they pause. In addition, they can stick with or develop new reminders such as alerts (e.g., on a calendar or phone) or a rubber band and can be encouraged to continue thinking of and using cues that can serve as key associations in their sport and daily lives. It may again be helpful to spend a few minutes brainstorming how cues can be developed over the next week.

Wrap-Up

Segal et al. (2002, 2012) end their penultimate session with a discussion of self-care, stressing that the benefits of cultivating a mindful attitude extend beyond enhanced awareness of the present moment. This type of practice can also help with responding mindfully, based on what is learned from awareness. As Session 5 of MSPE wraps up, participants can be prompted to consider what they have learned about themselves since the beginning of the program and how they might apply that knowledge to improve the quality of their experience in athletics and in their lives more broadly. They can work toward accepting that some things in life are difficult while making a conscious effort to incorporate more of what brings them joy.

This idea can be tied back to the concepts of acceptance and nonstriving discussed earlier and can lead into a discussion of choice. At this point, MSPE participants hopefully have begun to notice how staying present in each moment allows them to experience life events more fully and/or to learn something new about themselves. For example, maybe they have found that certain activities in their sport (or elsewhere) bring them pleasure, whereas others tend to be more stressful or draining. They can use this awareness to choose to inject greater joy and wellness into their lives, a power they don't have when functioning on automatic pilot.

Of course, there will always be tasks that feel obligatory or that are not particularly enjoyable, perhaps such as completing a challenging drill in practice or making a public speech. Becoming more mindful can enable accepting rather than fighting such realities while empowering choice to do more activities that feel good when those opportunities arise. Both this acceptance and this choosing can promote personal wellness.

For example, after getting home from an intense practice, someone might choose to read a good book or listen to a favorite song, which brings pleasure and allows for some recovery from the stress experienced. Contrast such a choice with how it might

EXHIBIT 8.1

Handout 6: Summary of MSPE Session 5

Takeaways From Session 5

- The main theme of the session is nonstriving, which involves intentionally not trying to go anywhere other than the present moment.
- It is still possible to have goals while practicing nonstriving, and, in fact, nonstriving may be the most effective way to reach goals. This concept is part of the path toward acceptance.
- The sport meditation is the final piece of the bridge from mindfulness practice to mindful sport performance. Core movements in the sport(s) of focus are selected as present-moment anchors.
- There is a significant difference between being nonjudgmentally present with the sensations of movement and micromanaging or overanalyzing well-learned skills, with the former being a possible route to an optimal-performance state.
- The sitting meditation with a focus on the breath, body, and sound is a further expansion of this fundamental mindfulness practice. The longer duration and period of silence are new challenges intended to stretch the mental muscle even further.
- Acceptance can allow for a mindful response to any given situation. As you learn more about yourself, you can choose to engage in practices that will bring you greater joy, satisfaction, and wellness.

Daily Home Practice for the Week After Session 5

- Do the sport meditation four times (length will depend, in part, on the anchors chosen).
- Do the 21-minute sitting meditation with a focus on the breath, body, and sound two times.
- Seize opportunities to STOP (stop, take a few breaths, observe, proceed) and pay attention mindfully during daily activities.
- Record this practice on your Daily Mindfulness Log and bring it with you next session.
- Bring any equipment and/or shoes to review the sport meditation next session.

feel to come home from that practice and then immediately, on automatic pilot, jump from activity to activity that "has" to get done, such as checking e-mail or getting ahead on tomorrow's work, or flip on the TV and "zone out" for a while, only to later regret that "lost" time. That's not to say that things such as checking e-mail or watching TV are counter to effective self-care, but any activity done on autopilot, even a supposedly relaxing one, may not be particularly rejuvenating when someone is not intentionally choosing to do it or is not present with the experience as it is happening. Leaders can invite participants to consider setting aside specific time this week to do something intentionally that they have learned helps them feel good and then to see what impact that choice has on their next sport performance. As the session concludes, Handout 6 (Exhibit 8.1) can be distributed.

MSPE Session 6
Ending the Beginning

9

The last session of mindful sport performance enhancement (MSPE) provides an opportunity to reflect on the training and to consider how an ongoing mindfulness practice can be established. No new concepts or exercises are introduced in this session. Rather, the body scan and sport meditation are reviewed to observe how experiences of them have evolved.

Session 6 Snapshot

Components of this session are

- diaphragmatic breathing exercise,
- discussion of home practice (for the week and over the course of MSPE),
- body scan and discussion,
- sport meditation and discussion,
- wrap-up and discussion of experiences in MSPE, and
- practicing beyond the conclusion of MSPE.

http://dx.doi.org/10.1037/0000048-010
Mindful Sport Performance Enhancement: Mental Training for Athletes and Coaches, by K. A. Kaufman, C. R. Glass, and T. R. Pineau

Diaphragmatic Breathing Exercise

This session begins with the 3-minute diaphragmatic breathing exercise from Session 1 (see Chapter 4) to help participants transition into being present with today's MSPE training.

Discussion of Home Practice (for the Week and Over the Course of MSPE)

For this final home practice discussion, participants can share their experiences with mindfulness practice during the week, as well as over the course of the entire training. The last session of a mindfulness program is a wonderful time to observe what has been learned and how practice experiences have changed (Segal, Williams, & Teasdale, 2002, 2012). Again, leaders can invite everyone to contribute and it remains important that they respond mindfully (i.e., with nonjudgmental acceptance) to anything raised. Up to 15 minutes can be allotted for this discussion, and if participants need help generating dialogue, leaders can prompt them to reference their Daily Mindfulness Logs or by asking some open-ended questions such as the following:

- What was it like to incorporate the sport meditation into your home practice?
- How did you experiment with different movement anchors in your sport?
- What were your experiences practicing the further expanded sitting meditation?
- What cues did you develop to facilitate forming mindful associations?
- What changes have you noticed in your reactions to doing the home practice over the course of MSPE?
- How have your impressions of meditation evolved over the course of the training?
- Which MSPE exercises particularly resonated or did not resonate with you?

Leaders can conclude this final home practice discussion by reviewing a central message about mindfulness emphasized throughout the program. Being fully present with each moment and accepting whatever is happening without judgment may sound simple, but it takes a lot of mental discipline to put into practice. Many people are constantly bombarded by messages to *do*, implying that simply *being* is not enough. Yet, hopefully participants have found during this training that, somewhat paradoxically, just being can allow for real change.

Leaders can also highlight two important points about practicing daily. First, participants may have established a firm foundation of mindfulness through MSPE, but cultivating a mindful way of being takes much longer than 6 weeks. This is only a gateway to beginning a continued commitment to being mindful in their sport and broader life. Daily practice, even if only for a few minutes, is still necessary to continue enhancing the characteristics of awareness and acceptance that are central to mindfulness and from which the benefits of MSPE stem. And second, mindfulness practice will be most powerful when it is tailored to each individual. In other words, participants can think about how to personalize their practice to incorporate a mix of techniques that work best for them. These ideas are discussed more at the end of the session.

Body Scan

Kabat-Zinn (1990) said that revisiting the body scan late in a mindfulness training provides a sense of coming full circle. In our experience leading MSPE programs, we have observed that with a deeper understanding of mindfulness, participants frequently have a different experience of the body scan in this final session, sometimes in a powerful way. Such change can be a window into how their experience of their bodies has evolved over these weeks, which may, in turn, help strengthen their motivation to make the body scan a part of their ongoing mindfulness practice.

As discussed throughout MSPE, developing mindfulness may benefit performance by helping participants accept present-moment experiences, even if unpleasant, without getting lost in the often false assumptions about what the experiences mean or whether they are "good" or "bad." Of course, to accept what is happening in the body, one must first be aware of what is happening in the body. In coming back to the body scan, leaders can reiterate that this exercise is a technique for building this awareness and strengthening the mind–body connection.

Leaders can instruct participants to try to keep an open mind during this practice because it is quite possible that their experience will be different at this point in the training. As a reminder, this exercise involves taking an attentional tour of the body, noticing what sensations are present in each region before letting go and moving on. When the mind wanders, participants can simply note where it went and then direct attention back to the anchor.

SCRIPT FOR BODY SCAN

The Body Scan script from Session 2 (see Chapter 5) is again used for this 30-minute exercise.

DISCUSSION OF BODY SCAN

After doing the body scan, participants are given a chance to discuss their experiences and reactions. It remains important for leaders to respond mindfully to any observations, questions, or concerns raised. They can facilitate this discussion by asking open-ended questions such as the following, allowing 2 to 3 minutes for each:

- What did you experience during this practice of the body scan?
- How were your reactions today different from when you first did the body scan?
- How did you react to the length of this exercise at this point in the training?
- How might regular practice of this exercise impact your sport performance?

Sport Meditation

In this session, participants get another opportunity to practice and share their reactions to the sport meditation. Leaders can review the instructions and rationale (see Chapter 8), feeling free to incorporate themes that came up in the earlier discussion of home practice. They may choose to review the movement anchors used in the previous session or identify new ones in collaboration with the participants. Leaders can also remind participants that the intention of this exercise is to be as present as possible with the mind and body while moving in this way and that there is a difference between intentional awareness of well-learned motions and micromanaging them. As is done throughout MSPE, when the mind wanders from the anchors, participants can direct it back without judgment, just like a rubber band snapping back into place. Reactions such as "This feels awkward" or "This feels great" can be observed with an attitude of acceptance and let go of as the mind returns to the anchors.

If any participants find themselves moving differently from what the prompts in this meditation indicate, that is perfectly okay. They can attend to whatever is true for their own form, continuing the personalization of this work. It may be important for leaders to acknowledge that it can take a lot of practice before this way of performing feels comfortable, but often many benefits are associated with applying this style of attention. As noted in the previous session, it is also necessary for leaders to be thoughtful about how and where the sport meditation is conducted depending on the sport(s) of focus, and visualization (e.g., if a participant is injured) or simulation (e.g., if equipment is not present) can be substituted for actual physical skill execution when warranted.

SCRIPT FOR SPORT MEDITATION

Use the Sport Meditation script in Chapter 8 as a foundation for this exercise.

DISCUSSION OF SPORT MEDITATION

After the sport meditation, participants are given a chance to discuss their experiences and reactions. It remains very important for leaders to respond mindfully to any observations, questions, or concerns raised. They can facilitate this discussion by asking open-ended questions such as the following, allowing 2 to 3 minutes for each:

- What differences did you notice when practicing the sport meditation this time?
- How was moving in this way different from how you usually move in your sport?
- How might regular practice of this exercise impact the way you perform?
- What are some ways to make this exercise your own as you keep practicing it?

Wrap-Up Discussion

At the end of this session, time is reserved for participants to reflect on their experiences during the MSPE training and how the lessons learned can be incorporated into their preparation and performance going forward. Although the discussion at the start of this session was focused on the home practice specifically, this later discussion is an opportunity to share broader reactions to the training. The feedback provided can be invaluable to both leaders and participants as they consider best practice for themselves beyond this program. If necessary, leaders can pose open-ended questions such as the following to help spur dialogue:

- What are some of the major lessons you are taking from MSPE?
- How closely did this training match your initial expectations?
- What changes, if any, have you observed in yourself over the course of this training?
- What are the obstacles to continuing to incorporate mindfulness into your life?
- How has this mindfulness training affected you as a performer?
- What was it like to dedicate this kind of time to a mental training program?

After this discussion, leaders can summarize some of the main concepts from MSPE, emphasizing how cultivating a mindful style of being, encompassing awareness and acceptance, can enrich participants' performances and day-to-day lives. By becoming more aware and accepting of "what is," participants can strengthen performance facilitators such as concentration, letting go, relaxation, finding harmony and rhythm, and forming key associations, which allow them to engage in more effective self-regulation that sets the stage for optimal performance experiences (i.e., the model proposed in the next chapter). Tremendous power is available to enhance experience by taking oneself off of autopilot, recognizing and letting go of limiting expectations and attachments, ceasing to fight the reality of whatever is happening, and understanding that one moment in time does not guarantee a particular outcome. Allowing a process to unfold without trying to make it something other than it is, even if it is undesirable or unpleasant for a time, may be the most effective way to maximize control over a situation and reach a goal.

Leaders can explain that this MSPE program truly is only an introduction to mindfulness for athletes and coaches. It typically takes much longer than 6 weeks to transition to this way of being. By sustaining a regular, personalized practice, participants can continue to work toward becoming mindful sport performers, experiencing all the benefits that this can bring.

Continuing Practice Beyond MSPE

Leaders can distribute Handout 7 (see Exhibit 9.1), which reviews tips for continued practice. Maintaining a systematic mindfulness practice in the absence of weekly sessions is a challenge faced by all participants. An analogy we like to use to highlight the importance of regular practice is comparing learning mindfulness to learning how to

EXHIBIT 9.1

Handout 7: Tips for Continued Practice

1. *Find a time.* We make time for certain activities every day that we can't imagine skipping. If we make time for mindfulness practice each day, it too will become part of a daily routine. Many people find that the morning is an ideal time to practice because it tends to be quieter then and the practice can set a nice tone for the day. However, any time that works for you is fine.
2. *Make a commitment.* Mindfulness practice is most effective when done every day. Start out by committing to some sort of formal and informal practice daily for 2 weeks, for however many minutes you choose. Then, see how this routine is working and make any necessary adjustments. Ideally, mindfulness practice is an endeavor of choice, not merely another obligation done out of habit or checked off a to-do list. To reinforce this choice, it may be helpful to experiment with choosing not to practice for a time and noting the consequences.
3. *Create a space.* Identify a specific place to do mindfulness practice each day and make it special. Put a personally significant reminder of your intent to practice in this place. Making a space can also mean opening yourself up to an entirely new form of training, other than the physical and tactical training that is likely to be more familiar.
4. *Make it personal.* Mindfulness practice is a highly personalized experience, so it's important to develop a routine that works for you. As crucial as it is to build a commitment to mindfulness practice, even with the best of intentions you may not always have as much time to practice as you would like, so remaining flexible enough to make it your own is essential. Of course, no matter how busy we get, it is hard to argue that we don't have at least a few minutes to stop and be present. Like physical training, mental training needs to be a personal priority to be effective. You can continue to use the audio recordings of the exercises (available at http://www.mindfulsportperformance.org).

---

swim. The act of swimming is composed of many discrete skills (e.g., kicking, pulling), and it is only when these skills are well learned and integrated that one is swimming. But, there is a need to practice these skills before getting thrown into the deep end. One can't learn how to swim when already drowning! Similarly, with mindfulness, component parts (e.g., awareness, acceptance) come together to create a mindful way of being. And these too need to be practiced regularly so that when one is thrown into the deep end (e.g., faces a stressful situation), there isn't a need to worry about learning to swim while drowning—the skills will already be there.

Before the group disbands, it can be useful to decide on a pattern of practice for at least the next several weeks. Leaders may wish to encourage brainstorming this topic, perhaps inviting everyone to contribute at least one suggestion. They can also share specific tips like the ones in the following list, which are expanded upon later (see Chapter 12) in this book. These tips were informed by the works of Ameli (2014), Kabat-Zinn (1990), and Segal et al. (2002, 2012).

1. *Find a time.* Most people make time to brush their teeth and check their e-mail at least once a day, and it may be hard to imagine going a day without doing

so. Of course, the choice is available not to do these activities, but there would be consequences, such as getting cavities or missing important messages. If time is made for mindfulness practice each day, it too will become part of a daily routine, ultimately becoming something unimaginable to go a day without. The morning is an ideal time to practice and can help set a nice tone for the rest of the day. But, in truth, any time works because there is no bad time to be present.

2. *Make a commitment.* Mindfulness practice is most effective when done daily. However, this doesn't mean that it is necessary to do a 30-minute body scan every single day from now on. That would be a pretty daunting ambition! Instead, athletes and coaches can be encouraged to make a commitment to doing some sort of formal and informal mindfulness practice every day for the next 2 weeks, for as many minutes as they choose. Then, after those 2 weeks, they can see how that routine is working for them and make any needed adjustments. The most important part is making a reasonable commitment and then using experience to inform decisions going forward. What that commitment actually looks like is up to each individual. Ideally, regular mindfulness practice is an endeavor of choice, not just another chore or obligation done out of habit or checked off of a to-do list. But, to make this choice, one needs to feel personally motivated, which normally comes from actually experiencing the effects of mindfulness. To highlight these effects, it can sometimes be useful, after a period of regular practice, to commit to not practicing for 1 to 2 weeks and observe what happens. As with not brushing one's teeth or checking one's e-mail, the consequences of not practicing may quickly become apparent.

3. *Create a space.* Designate a specific place for mindfulness practice, and make it special. Try to practice there each day, ideally at a time when there won't be interruptions. It may be useful to include reminders in this location of why this practice is important, such as a trophy, a slip of paper with a personal-best time, or a photo from a past performance. This recommendation can have a more figurative meaning as well, in the sense of creating space for a kind of training that may feel very different from the likely more familiar physical and tactical training.

4. *Make it personal.* MSPE includes a variety of exercises, and some probably resonated with individuals more than did others. Mindfulness practice is a highly personalized experience, so it's important that people develop a routine tailored to them. On certain days, time really may be limited, so it might feel impossible to practice. That's just fine. As valuable as commitment is, flexibility is also needed. Although it's generally recommended to do some kind of formal practice for 20 to 30 minutes per day, practicing for 5 minutes or even 1 minute is great, if that's all that is possible. Daily dosage is what's most crucial, which is likely something participants already know from their physical training. It is no different with mental training.

Finally, we recommend that leaders make themselves available to participants for consultation after the end of MSPE training to address any questions or concerns that arise with continued practice. Options might include phone calls, video conferencing, e-mail, or in-person meetings. Having a plan for follow-up is critical for any mental training program, perhaps especially for one such as MSPE in which the concepts learned may be so new.

Now that you are familiar with the nuts and bolts of MSPE, Part III of this book explores our conceptualization of how and why it works, as well as the empirical support to date. In addition, we offer suggestions for ways to maximize its effectiveness (for both participants and program leaders) and potential applications to performers outside of sport. This exploration begins in the next chapter, which unveils our model for how MSPE facilitates peak performance.

MINDFUL SPORT PERFORMANCE ENHANCEMENT: THEORY, RESEARCH, PRACTICE, AND BEYOND

Pathways From MSPE to Peak Performance

10

The previous six chapters provided a detailed description of each mindful sport performance enhancement (MSPE) session, outlining the nuts and bolts of this mindfulness training program. Although the concrete steps toward becoming a mindful sport performer may be clear, we recognize that the specific mechanisms leading from mindfulness practice to peak performance might still feel somewhat abstract. Thus, this chapter presents our conceptualization of how MSPE enhances performance by developing the primary mindfulness characteristics of acceptance and awareness. These characteristics allow for the intentional deployment of five core performance facilitators, thus strengthening attentional and emotional self-regulatory capacities, which in turn lead to optimal psychological states (e.g., flow) and ultimately peak performance (see Figure 10.1).

It is important to note, however, that this model likely oversimplifies the interrelations of these constructs. For instance, although no arrows represent this, the performance facilitators may mutually influence each other and, as such, it is their integration that truly reflects a mindful way of performing. It also seems possible that some of the connections proposed are actually bidirectional. For example, increased mindful awareness likely generates enhanced

http://dx.doi.org/10.1037/0000048-011
Mindful Sport Performance Enhancement: Mental Training for Athletes and Coaches, by K. A. Kaufman, C. R. Glass, and T. R. Pineau

FIGURE 10.1

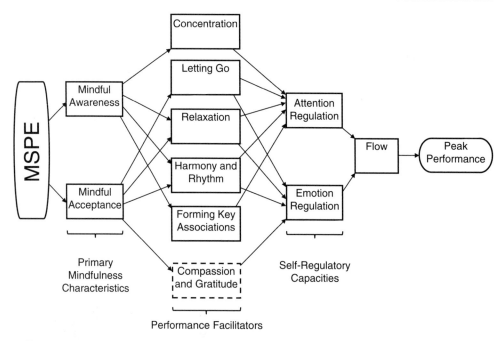

Proposed pathways from mindful sport performance enhancement (MSPE) to peak performance. *Compassion and gratitude* is not one of the primary performance facilitators but is included as a potential mechanism through which MSPE can influence emotion regulation and performance.

concentration, whereas the intentional application of concentration in a specific situation could help to strengthen mindful awareness. We hope future research will test and expand upon this model, which we find to be a useful guide to understanding the way we think about MSPE.

In Kabat-Zinn, Beall, and Rippe's (1985) poster describing the early use of mindfulness with athletes, they included in their rationale a list of five specific applications of meditation training to rowing. They explained how a technical aspect of the rowing stroke (e.g., movement of the oar handle) was used to center concentration on the present moment. Experiences such as fatigue, pain, and fear could be recognized merely as thoughts and let go of. The rowers learned to attend to abdominal breathing during their performances to promote relaxation and were shown how to find harmony and flow by nonjudgmentally observing the broader connections between themselves and their actions. Finally, meaningful cues were developed so that the rowers began to make key associations between points in their races and being mindful.

We saw that these applications could create a readily understandable framework for how the awareness and acceptance fostered by formal meditation practice could put athletes in an optimal performance mindset. Thus, we adapted them for our MSPE protocol and discuss them in Session 2 (see Chapter 5) as part of the rationale for the training. However, one of the notable changes we made was to rename *experiencing harmony and flow* to *establishing a sense of harmony and rhythm*, which serves to distinguish Kabat-Zinn's use of the word *flow* from Csikszentmihalyi's (1990) flow construct described in Chapter 3. Certainly, it seems reasonable to expect that improved capacities to concentrate, let go, relax, find rhythm, and utilize cues to be mindful could all facilitate a flow state, so we think this distinction is important.

In the following sections, we discuss each of these performance facilitators in depth, link them to particular MSPE exercises, and elucidate the range of benefits that MSPE participants may see when they incorporate them into their performances. At the end of this chapter, we also include a brief discussion of another important aspect of mindfulness practice—compassion and gratitude—which is woven into the language of MSPE exercises and discussions.

Concentration

Many definitions of *mindfulness* exist, and most of them share an emphasis on attention (Carmody, 2014), specifically how we direct attention, and for all of the different forms of meditation, the ability to regulate attention is integral (Ivtzan & Hart, 2016). Like Kabat-Zinn's mindfulness-based stress reduction, MSPE uses the practice of various meditation exercises as the building blocks of mindfulness. As described in Chapter 3, athletes face a number of attentional challenges during performances, such as being able to direct, sustain, and shift focus and pick out what is most important amidst a litany of distractions. Athletes who are less aware are more likely to miss opportunities or to make mistakes (Toner, Montero, & Moran, 2015). Or if they are too narrowly focused on a specific goal, they can miss unexpected but important cues (Memmert & Furley, 2007). These potential pitfalls are referred to as *mindlessness* and *inattentional blindness*, respectively, and mindfulness training has been shown to counteract both of them (e.g., Langer, 2014; Schofield, Creswell, & Denson, 2015). The central role of appropriate concentration in mindfulness, meditation, and sport performance is why we are emphasizing it as the first core performance facilitator in MSPE.

Early in the first session, MSPE begins helping participants hone their ability to concentrate by introducing the concept of attentional anchors to the present moment. One of the initial anchors used is the breath, which is consistent with how meditation generally is taught (Carmody, 2014). Every MSPE exercise highlights a particular anchor, with other examples including bodily sensations, environmental sounds, and ultimately movements integral to the athletes' sport(s). Also, education on the importance of concentration and how to strengthen it through mindfulness is provided throughout the program. Participants learn, for instance, that if they are not tuned in to the present (i.e., are operating on autopilot), they are robbed of the freedom to act intentionally and are instead governed by ingrained habits, which are not necessarily conducive to performance or well-being. Building up the capacity to direct attention to the present moment and to be with whatever is happening nonjudgmentally can restore the power to choose how to respond in a given situation. Exercising such choice can promote a sense of control, regardless of what is occurring, which you may recall is one of Csikszentmihalyi's (1990) elements of flow.

A review of how enhanced attention regulation can facilitate flow was presented in Chapter 3, but other potential benefits are worthy of mention here as well. It has been well documented that intentionally directing attention to one's actions is essential to the development of expertise (Ericsson, 2006). What has become known as the "10,000-hour" or "10-year" rule suggests that it can take 10,000 hours or 10 years of practice to reach mastery across a variety of domains such as sports, business, and music.

Ericsson, whose work has become associated with this rule, stipulated that these are not magic numbers. The total amount of practice is far less important than the quantity of deliberate practice, which he defined as the "engagement with full concentration in a training activity designed to improve a particular aspect of performance with immediate feedback, [and] opportunities for gradual refinement by repetition and problem solving" (Ericsson, 2013, p. 534). Thus, intentional, sustained awareness of present-moment actions seems crucial to becoming an expert at something, which is precisely the style of concentration learned in MSPE. Moreover, once expertise is attained, this ability to maintain awareness of one's actions may facilitate performance improvement even further (Toner & Moran, 2015). After a task is learned to the point of automaticity, the ability to control or adjust that skill can decrease, resulting in a performance plateau (Ericsson, 2006; Sutton, 2007). Toner et al. (2015) reviewed performance errors (e.g., mistakes in planning, lapses in skill execution) that can occur as a result of automaticity and found that maintaining awareness of actions can allow athletes to avoid or alter these dysfunctional automated processes.

However, automaticity can be helpful to athletes to the extent that it increases mental efficiency, freeing up cognitive resources for strategic (rather than technical) aspects of performance (A. M. Williams & Ford, 2008), and the automaticity that comes from the synchrony of action and awareness is often included in descriptions of flow (e.g., Chavez, 2008). Because both automaticity and intentional concentration seem important to performance, it has been proposed that learning to shift between automated and consciously controlled processes is necessary for athletes to reach their peak (Toner et al., 2015). Mindfulness practice has been associated with the attentional flexibility needed for this mental shifting (A. Moore & Malinowski, 2009) and been shown to help reduce the impact of interfering information and make conscious previously automated behaviors (Chong, Kee, & Chaturvedi, 2015).

In addition, Toner et al. (2015) suggested that cultivating bodily awareness may enhance already expert-level performance, particularly when athletes are trying to relearn skills (e.g., after an injury) or correct their technique (e.g., Gray, 2004). Several MSPE exercises use aspects of the body as attentional anchors to strengthen this form of concentration and help athletes avoid the pitfalls of excessive automation. It is important to note that this process is not about analyzing or micromanaging an experience but rather maintaining a "bare awareness" of it as it unfolds (i.e., observing the thoughts, feelings, and sensations that arise with the experience, without judging them and without following any of the associations that may stem from them). For example, a runner attending to the legs mindfully while striding is not giving self-instruction on how to stride but is observing the process of the stride and is therefore able to choose to make an adjustment if he or she notices something interfering with the effectiveness of the movement. This distinction is emphasized throughout MSPE, as participants may need time to discover how to allow a well-learned process to unfold while remaining nonjudgmentally aware of what is happening. Achieving this equanimity involves not only concentration but also other performance facilitators such as letting go and relaxation.

Letting Go

Although not every current definition of mindfulness is rooted in Eastern philosophical thought (e.g., Langer, 1989), that is the tradition from which MSPE has emerged, and thus some of its underpinnings are important to understand. One tenet of this tradition is that dissatisfaction stems from our cravings or our attachments (Gethin, 1998). For instance, we are often attached to the felt need to hold on to things that we experience as positive and avoid or push away the things we experience as negative. However, fulfilling this need is impossible for two reasons. First, everything in life is impermanent. Even when we experience things that make us feel good, whether for a moment (e.g., a cool breeze on a hot day) or a long time (e.g., a loving partnership), there is still always an ending. Thus, our desire to hold on to these things will inevitably result in dissatisfaction when we reach that ending. Second, we do not have control over the world, or at least not as much as we would like. We cannot control the wind on a hot day or if and when a tragic accident or illness will take a loved one. No matter how hard we might try or how ardently we might wish, we cannot totally avoid negative experiences nor can we make positive experiences last forever. Therefore, we are bound to continually reexperience dissatisfaction.

This may sound pessimistic, but as many authors have pointed out, a true understanding of Buddhist philosophy suggests exactly the opposite (e.g., Gethin, 1998; Nhat Hanh, 1998). When one recognizes this perpetual cycle of dissatisfaction and its source (e.g., impermanence), the opportunity exists to experience life differently. Herein lies the power of letting go as we conceptualize it in MSPE. By accepting the nature of life and understanding the ways in which reactions to experiences, rather than the experiences themselves, cause distress, MSPE participants learn to let go of expectations and attachments, allowing things to be just as they are. This can be both empowering and liberating. By directing attention inward and observing reactions to experiences and then reactions to those reactions, participants come to see that, with practice, they can let go of the reactions that pull attention away from the present moment.

To illustrate how this process can unfold in sport, imagine a collegiate lacrosse player stepping onto the field to play the first game of her junior-year season, going against an opponent that her team has lost to every time they have played them for the past 2 years. In the present moment, the only thing happening is that she is about to play lacrosse. However, instead of this neutral, factual description, she is thinking about those past matchups and even some of the specific plays she made, or failed to make, accompanied by feelings of regret, shame, and doubt. She is also thinking about the future: how hard she expects this game to be as well as the frustration that will come with losing yet again. This player then projects even further, picturing how this loss could lead to a losing season, how upset her coach will be, how the talented freshmen will not want to return next season, how next year will thus be even harder, and how she'll end her college career with bitter disappointment. And this all happens before the game has even started! Once the game begins, she becomes aware that she is anxious and distracted and gets angry with herself for being this way, which pulls her focus even further away.

You'd probably agree that this player does not sound poised to have a great game. But what if she could break out of this cycle, let go of her imagined future and associated judgments, disengage from her apparent attachment to the belief that she needs to win in order to feel like playing lacrosse is "worth it," and reconnect with her experience in the present moment, which is simply playing lacrosse? What if, when she sees these reactions arise, she could recognize that they are merely thoughts and feelings, not reality? She could then more easily focus on the task at hand, immerse herself in playing, and give herself the opportunity to perform at her best.

This notion of acceptance and letting go may be the precise antidote for the potentially damaging impact of Wegner's (1994) "ironic processes of mental control" on sport performance as discussed in Chapter 2. More broadly, acceptance of one's experience is also a primary mechanism of action through which mindfulness practice influences mental health (Coffey, Hartman, & Fredrickson, 2010). There is great power in realizing that thoughts and feelings are transient, just like all of our experiences, and furthermore that the connections we observe among our thoughts, feelings, and behaviors are not necessary or absolute.

Take the classic sports scene of a basketball player about to perform in a pressure-filled, end-of-game scenario (e.g., attempt a last-second foul shot). He might have the thought, "I need to make this shot or I will let my whole team down," which could bring anxiety about this dreaded outcome and extra muscle tension that can interfere with shot execution. It is probably difficult to imagine being in this type of situation without experiencing such anxiety and tension. However, the application of mindful acceptance, aspects of which have been referred to as "decentering" (Sauer & Baer, 2010), "decoupling" (Levin, Luoma, & Haeger, 2015), "defusion" (Hayes, Strosahl, & Wilson, 2011), and "reperceiving" (Shapiro, Carlson, Astin, & Freedman, 2006), could allow this athlete to have an entirely different experience.

He could come to see that the event in the present moment (i.e., taking a foul shot) is no different from all of the other times he has taken a foul shot, when he did not experience the same thoughts, emotions, or tension. By disconnecting the actions, thoughts, and feelings, he can recognize that his reactions are not an objective aspect of this task, let them go, and concentrate instead on the foul shot itself. This letting go has profound implications for athletes with regard to emotion regulation, the benefits of which we described in Chapter 3, and it can also help with managing other possibly disruptive experiences such as fatigue and pain.

In their poster, Kabat-Zinn, Beall, and Rippe (1985) listed how applications of letting go could extend beyond thoughts to physical sensations, including fatigue and pain. We similarly highlight in MSPE how participants can improve their performance by relating differently to such physical experiences. Renowned exercise scientist Timothy Noakes (2012) explained that his field has assumed for a long time that fatigue and exhaustion are purely physiological phenomena, determined by factors such as lactic acid buildup that govern the functioning of the muscles. However, researchers have started identifying the significant role the mind plays in these occurrences. In fact, many of these findings are incompatible with physiologically based models of fatigue (Noakes, 2000), and it has been suggested that fatigue is actually a complex emotion rather than a physiological sensation (Noakes, 2012). He even referred to fatigue symptoms as "illusionary," writing that "the winning athlete is the one whose illusionary symptoms interfere the least with the actual performance" (Noakes, 2012, p. 9). In line with this idea, it has been found that perception of effort (a mental phenomenon), rather than any physiological marker, best predicts exhaustion (Marcora & Staiano, 2010). From this perspective, it seems plausible that one way in which mindfulness may help athletes manage fatigue and exhaustion is through the same mechanisms that help them regulate their responses to other emotions, such as anxiety.

Unlike fatigue, however, pain is thought to be more physiologically based. Pain is an ever-present aspect of training and competition, particularly when athletes are performing at higher competitive levels, and an athlete's interpretation of that pain could be detrimental to performance (O'Connor, 2016). Some kinds of pain in sport occur naturally as a result of intense effort, and others are indicative of serious injury (O'Connor, 2016). It is essential for athletes to be able to distinguish between the two, as it is not advisable to push through pain related to an injury. However, accepting effort-based pain as part of sport can reduce the suffering associated with it, potentially aiding performance. MSPE participants are introduced to this notion, and there is significant evidence to back it up.

At around the same time that Kabat-Zinn was working with athletes, he was also engaged in research on mindfulness for chronic pain. He found that patients reported reductions in their subjective experiences of pain, mood disturbance (i.e., emotional reactivity to the pain), and use of pain medication following mindfulness training, and most of these changes persisted for years after the training (Kabat-Zinn, 1982; Kabat-Zinn, Lipworth, & Burney, 1985; Kabat-Zinn, Lipworth, Burney, & Sellers, 1986). Much like the current conceptualizations of how mindful acceptance works (e.g., decentering, decoupling), Kabat-Zinn (1982) said that a process of "uncoupling" the sensations of pain from the emotional reactions to pain was essential.

More recent controlled studies using healthy participants have also found reductions in pain sensitivity after mindfulness training (e.g., Zeidan, Gordon, Merchant, & Goolkasian, 2010), whereas other research has found that people who meditate exhibit a higher pain threshold than do nonmeditators (J. A. Grant & Rainville, 2009). Evidence indicates that these alterations in pain perception are the result of structural and functional neuroplastic adaptations in response to meditation (J. A. Grant, Courtemanche, Duerden, Duncan, & Rainville, 2010; Zeidan et al., 2011) and that these changes are unique to the practice of mindfulness when compared with placebo pain-relief strategies or sham meditation practices (Zeidan et al., 2015).

What seems to be unique about mindfulness practice is the active cognitive reappraisal of one's experience, that is, attending to something with a nonjudgmental, nonevaluative attitude (Zeidan et al., 2015). Acceptance appears to help individuals separate their experiences of pain from their reactions to pain, thus allowing them to tolerate pain without feeling the need to change their behavior to stop the pain. In fact, participants who receive mindfulness training have been shown to persist longer during a painful activity than do those who do not, despite still reporting "very much pain" (Gutiérrez, Luciano, Rodríguez, & Fink, 2004).

This body of research has significant implications for athletes. Given the ubiquitous experience of fatigue and pain in sports and their potentially detrimental effects on performance, mindfulness training (and particularly the performance facilitator of letting go) can help athletes regulate fatigue as they do other emotions, tolerate higher levels of pain, and persist in activities even while feeling pain and discomfort. These outcomes, of course, are in addition to the multitude of other benefits athletes can obtain from accepting and letting go of their constant stream of internal experiences, detaching from irrelevant stimuli to refocus on the task at hand.

MSPE exercises help to strengthen the ability to let go, as participants are guided throughout to observe their inner experiences without judgment and to practice letting go of whatever they notice (e.g., passing thoughts in the sitting meditations, somatic sensations in the body scan, reactions to dwelling at physical limits during yoga), so that they can free attention and redirect it to a particular present-moment anchor. MSPE also provides education on how acceptance can work in sport situations, addressing, for example, the impact of expectations in Session 3 (see Chapter 6) and unexamined attachments in Session 4 (see Chapter 7).

Also during Session 4, an important distinction is made between acceptance and resignation. There exists an apparent "goal paradox" when teaching mindfulness to athletes and coaches, as mindfulness is a nonstriving practice, whereas striving toward goals (e.g., winning) is practically the definition of competitive sports (Birrer, Röthlin, & Morgan, 2012). Many participants we've worked with have asked a version of the totally understandable question "If I'm supposed to accept whatever is happening, then when I'm losing, I just need to be ok with that?" We tend to respond by pointing out that the assumptions underlying this question represent the possible pitfalls of being outcome-oriented. Participants are typically describing a situation in which they are in the midst of competing and not in the lead. However, a win or a loss is an outcome, and if the competition is still happening, the winning or losing has not yet occurred. So, in actuality, they are assuming they are going to lose in the future based on reactions to what is happening in the present. This kind of assumption holds significant danger, and even researchers who are not approaching sport from a mindfulness-based perspective recognize it. In talking about the phenomena of close finishes in a footrace, Noakes (2012) claimed that

> somewhere in the final section of the race, the brains of the second, and lower placed finishers accept their respective finishing positions and no longer choose to challenge for a higher finish. Once each runner consciously accepts his or her finishing position, the outcome of the race is decided. So just as a single athlete must "decide" to win, so too must the rest of the top finishers decide the opposite—specifically that they are not going to win. (p. 8)

We fully agree with the basic point being made here, although we disagree with Noakes's use of the word *accept* because, from our perspective, what he really is referring to is *resignation*. In his example, the lower-place finishers resign themselves to the feared predicted outcome and, in doing so, assume that they cannot do anything to affect their present circumstances. Mindfulness allows practitioners to see how they make these future predictions and how they experience an emotional reaction in response to their feared future rather than their true present. They also realize that these reactions interfere with their ability to focus, and they take meaningful action in the present that could contribute to creating a different future than the one they fear. So, a concise answer to the type of question from MSPE participants mentioned previously might be

> No, when you notice that you're not in the lead, you don't simply resign yourself to a future in which you lose. Instead, you accept the fact that your current experience does not match your desires, let go of the unpleasant thoughts and emotions that arise in reaction to that, and refocus your attention on your actual performance in the moment.

This answer may not satisfy all of the participants' concerns when they are confusing acceptance with resignation. To do that, they will need to experience the paradoxical reality that arises from the regular practice of mindfulness, that by letting go of striving toward goals, it actually becomes easier to achieve them. Being aware and letting go of striving necessitates letting go of the worries, regrets, and self-doubt that striving often entails and that causes so much of our stress and tension. Thus, participants who consistently practice concentration and letting go become equipped to more fully apply relaxation, the next performance facilitator.

Relaxation

Meditation practices have long been associated with relaxation (e.g., Benson, 1975). Empirical investigations have documented the relaxation response in certain types of meditation through physiological markers such as heart rate variability (e.g., Wu & Lo, 2008) and neurological activity (e.g., Lazar et al., 2000) as well as through the subjective experiences of meditation practitioners (e.g., Morone, Lynch, Greco, Tindle, & Weiner, 2008). Several meditation-related activities, including basic diaphragmatic breathing (Pal, Velkumary, & Madanmohan, 2004) and yoga (Ross & Thomas, 2010), have also been shown to induce relaxation.

As we mentioned in Chapter 2, however, relaxation and mindfulness are not synonymous, and research has indicated that relaxation is not always an outcome of all types of mindfulness practice (Lumma, Kok, & Singer, 2015). Sport psychologists often erroneously assume that an explicit goal of mindfulness is relaxation (Z. E. Moore, 2016). Rather, relaxation exercises generally are change focused, with the goal of reducing tension, whereas mindfulness exercises do not aim to decrease arousal or promote relaxation. "Rather, mindfulness training seeks to develop an openness and acceptance of all internal states as normal and transient" (Z. E. Moore, 2016, p. 41) and neither good nor bad, which, in itself, can be liberating and stress-relieving. So, even though mindfulness practice is not done to relax, the practice can be relaxing, making the potential physical, emotional, and cognitive benefits of relaxation relevant to discuss.

From a physiological perspective, relaxed muscles are more efficient at absorbing oxygen, whereas unnecessarily tense muscles create resistance for an athlete, leading to wasted energy (Dreyer & Dreyer, 2004). It has been suggested that optimal control of muscle tension improves skill execution and helps athletes to conserve energy (Sime, 2003). Perhaps not surprisingly, then, relaxation techniques are included in many sport psychology interventions and, just to give a few examples, have been found to predict superior performance in golfers (Bois, Sarrazin, Southon, & Boiche, 2009) and world rankings in elite freestyle skiers (Dupee, Werthner, & Forneris, 2015), bolster the performance of Taekwondo practitioners (Ottoboni, Giusti, Gatta, Symes, & Tessari, 2014), and reduce burnout (Goodger & Jones, 2012).

This discussion of relaxation brings to mind our previous example of a basketball player about to take a foul shot at the end of a game, when the coach might pull him aside and advise, "Just relax." We use this image frequently when leading MSPE groups to highlight the fact that even though the importance of staying calm under pressure may be nearly universal in sport, most athletes have never actually been taught how to relax in such situations. The abilities learned in MSPE can fill this void, so the player knows what to do and/or the coach knows what to instruct, beyond the obvious. For instance, maybe a player could recognize that he is focusing on the one possible future involving missing and all the negative consequences that could come from it, which, as he can tell from his bodily sensations, is driving up his level of arousal. With that nonjudgmental awareness, he is able to refocus on the present-moment anchor of his breath and engage his diaphragm, simultaneously centering his mind on the moment at hand (involving a shot he's executed successfully many, many times) and triggering his body's relaxation response.

This is just one example, but relaxation helps sport performance in many ways. First, it is a primary mechanism through which athletes can regulate their levels of anxiety and arousal, which is crucial for performing under pressure effectively (Weinberg & Gould, 2015). According to Weinberg and Gould (2015), the key is finding optimal levels of anxiety and arousal, which reflects sufficient intensity without losing concentration or coordination. One of the most popular representations of the relationship between arousal and sport performance is the inverted-U hypothesis, also known as the Yerkes–Dodson law (Yerkes & Dodson, 1908), which indicates that more arousal helps performance to an optimum point, after which further arousal starts to hurt performance. The optimum point varies, depending on the task being performed (e.g., it generally will be lower for a golfer than for a powerlifter). Critics have questioned the simplicity of this hypothesis, and an alternative view has emerged suggesting that (a) optimal anxiety does not always occur at the midpoint of the continuum and varies from person to person and (b) optimal anxiety is a bandwidth rather than a single point (Weinberg & Gould, 2015). In other words, this latter view says there is an individual *zone* of optimal functioning (IZOF; Hanin, 2000b), and Hanin's IZOF model has been well supported in empirical studies (Weinberg & Gould, 2015).

Relaxation also seems to aid performance through its impact on working memory (WM). WM refers to our ability to hold and manipulate the information necessary to engage in complex cognitive tasks, such as reasoning (Baddeley, 1992). Although attention and WM are considered separate entities, there is significant overlap between them (Gazzaley & Nobre, 2012), and their functioning is intertwined (Awh, Vogel, & Oh, 2006). Indeed, WM capacity appears to be a predictor of attentional control (Kane & Engle, 2003).

It has been proposed within theories of distraction (e.g., Eysenck, Derakshan, Santos, & Calvo, 2007) that anxiety interferes with performance by causing a shift in focus away from the task at hand to either internal (e.g., self-doubt) or external (e.g., a noise) task-irrelevant stimuli. This shifting requires the allocation of precious WM resources, resulting in less attention available for the task at hand and increased likelihood of performance decrements or choking (Englert & Oudejans, 2014). Research has supported these theories, finding that athletes with higher WM capacity perform better in high-pressure situations (Bijleveld & Veling, 2014). These authors thus suggested that mental skills training that can reduce the impact of distraction may be especially useful for athletes with a lower WM capacity.

WM also appears related to effective decision-making, which itself has been proposed to directly affect outcomes in sports (Bar-Eli, Plessner, & Raab, 2011). Athletes routinely need to make decisions "on line" (i.e., under pressure, as a play is in motion) in a dynamic, complex, and unpredictable environment, where attending to and processing all of the relevant stimuli to make fast and correct decisions requires WM resources. Johnson (2006) said that one reason expert athletes exhibit superior decision-making (compared with novices) could be that "expertise 'frees' mental resources that may effectively increase working memory capacity or attention, which could thus be modeled by an increase in number of dimensions attended in a given period of time" (p. 642). Supporting this contention, Furley and Memmert (2012) found that athletes with higher WM capacity are better able to focus on tactical decision-making and adapt to a situation.

So, how does relaxation help WM? Studies have demonstrated that anxiety can impair WM functioning (e.g., Ashcraft & Kirk, 2001), which is significant given the previously cited research indicating that relaxation can reduce anxiety. In line with this notion, Mikicin and Kowalczyk (2015) found that relaxation training improved athletes' performance on a prolonged, cognitively demanding task. With specific regard to mindfulness-based strategies, mindfulness training has been shown to improve WM capacity (Jha, Stanley, Kiyonaga, Wong, & Gelfand, 2010) and prevent stress-related WM impairments (J. B. Banks, Welhaf, & Srour, 2015). In addition, a systematic review found that yoga can improve executive functioning (Gothe & McAuley, 2015), which is an aspect of cognitive functioning strongly linked to WM (McCabe, Roediger, McDaniel, Balota, & Hambrick, 2010). Also, it has been hypothesized that the established link between mindfulness practice and enhanced decision-making abilities (Sun, Yao, Wei, & Yu, 2015) may be due, at least in part, to the positive impact relaxation has on WM.

All of this is not to say that mindful relaxation alleviates all tension and anxiety. Anxiety is always going to be present to some extent in competitive sports and can even facilitate performance under certain conditions (e.g., Jones, 1995). So, when we are talking about relaxation in MSPE, what we are really referring to is the ability to identify and release *unnecessary* tension. Of course, as Kabat-Zinn (1990) pointed out, people cannot release tension that they don't know is there. A lack of bodily awareness is particularly problematic for athletes, as it can result not only in unnecessary tension but also in loss of efficiency and increased risk of injury (Fitzgerald, 2010). The MSPE exercises that use bodily sensations as attentional anchors (e.g., the body scan and mindful yoga) may be especially important in this regard, echoing Fitzgerald's (2010) suggestion that yoga is a highly adaptive practice to help restore mind–body communication. Managing excess tension is a prime example of what can result when performance facilitators work together. MSPE participants learn to concentrate and let go of distractions to direct attention into their bodies, allowing them to notice any unnecessary tension and then, if they choose, to release that tension (i.e., relax). This focused, relaxed state is an integral component of optimal performance and sets the stage for the next performance facilitator.

Establishing a Sense of Harmony and Rhythm

Kabat-Zinn, Beall, and Rippe (1985) described the application of harmony and flow to rowing as

> [an] emphasis on allowing one's performance to unfold out of stillness of mind, from a cultivated state of detached observation, beyond fatigue, pain, and fear. Also, on experiencing one's individual effort and self as an integrated part of a collective effort and intention, as if the athlete and the boat were a single organism.

As explained earlier, Kabat-Zinn, Beall, and Rippe's use of the word *flow* was not in reference to Csikszentmihalyi's (1990) construct but rather to what the process of performing mindfully can feel like. In many ways, what they were capturing is the manifestation of the other performance facilitators being put into action, a phenomenon that may very well relate to flow as Csikszentmihalyi (1990) defined it. Kabat-

Zinn, Beall, and Rippe's harmony and flow seem to get at the sense of performance feeling effortless that is reported by many athletes as typical of flow (Chavez, 2008), the feeling of union with the environment that often is associated with peak experiences in sport (Ravizza, 1977), and the unity with an athletic partner that has been identified as facilitating flow states (S. A. Jackson, 1992). Regardless of these semantic differences, athletes can experience a range of benefits when they allow their performance to unfold from a state of detached observation. To maximize clarity in MSPE, we've renamed this performance facilitator *establishing a sense of harmony and rhythm*.

The idea that there is a certain feel to superior performance characterized by the presence of rhythm has a long history in the sport and exercise literature (e.g., S. Hanley, 1937), and its significance becomes clear when one considers the degree of coordination across multiple levels required for successful performance. Millar, Oldham, and Renshaw (2013) offered that intrapersonal (interaction of aspects of athletes' internal functioning, such as muscle activation), interpersonal (interactions between the actions of two or more athletes), and extrapersonal (interactions between athletes and the environment) coordination are all necessary.

As did Kabat-Zinn, Beall, and Rippe (1985), we use the sport of rowing to illustrate. Research on the rowing stroke, a highly complex athletic skill, supports the importance of intrapersonal coordination. For instance, it has been found that practicing the stroke results in enhanced coordination and efficiency of muscle activation (Lay, Sparrow, Hughes, & O'Dwyer, 2002) and that more coordination between the temporal sequencing of the stroke differentiates highly skilled from less-skilled rowers (Den Hartigh, Cox, Gernigon, Van Yperen, & Van Geert, 2015).

There is also evidence of the need for interpersonal coordination. The synchronization of rowers within a crew, and not simply the size, strength, or skill of the individual athletes, is a main determinant of boat velocity (Baudouin & Hawkins, 2002), and synchronous training (as opposed to solo training) has been found to increase the pain threshold of rowers (Cohen, Ejsmond-Frey, Knight, & Dunbar, 2010). Further, rowing takes place in a dynamic environment, as the boat is affected by numerous external factors (e.g., wind), highlighting the importance of extrapersonal coordination. Millar et al. (2013) discussed the interaction between rowers' actions and environmental cues (e.g., the speed of water passing the boat) and how these cues help rowers improve coordination at both the intrapersonal and interpersonal levels.

Since Kabat-Zinn, Beall, and Rippe's (1985) foundational work, other studies have supported the notion that mindfulness training can positively impact these levels of coordination. At the intrapersonal level, mindfulness practice (ranging from brief inductions to ongoing regimens) has been shown to improve coordination and balance (Burschka, Keune, Oy, Oschmann, & Kuhn, 2014; Kee, Chatzisarantis, Kong, Chow, & Chen, 2012). At the interpersonal level, Haas and Langer (2014) found that even simple instructions about approaching a conversation in a mindful way can increase synchronicity between people. Finally, because the environment of sport is such a complex, interactive system (Davids et al., 2014), attentional flexibility, which has been linked to mindfulness (Hodgins & Adair, 2010; A. Moore & Malinowski, 2009), is needed for athletes to attend and respond effectively to their surroundings (i.e., extrapersonal coordination).

It certainly makes sense that achieving coordination across these levels (i.e., a sense of harmony) would help an athlete feel a sense of rhythm during performance, and MacPherson, Collins, and Obhi (2009) even stated that "feeling the rhythm or temporal structure of a movement may be the only necessary strategy when attempting to produce peak performance" (p. 58). The particular kind of rhythm targeted by MSPE is effortless. We propose that for something to feel effortless, it has to unfold from a still mind, rather than one that is self-consciously judging or speculating on the past or future. So, a mind must be fully concentrating on the task at hand, letting go of irrelevant distractors, and releasing excess tension. It is the integration of these other performance facilitators that creates a sense of effortless rhythm, giving athletes the chance to take in the entirety of their performance in a given moment, fluidly responding and adapting to the constant flux of their internal and external environments. In addition, this state entails an openness to experience that has been associated with increased creativity in nonathletes (Langer, 1989) and athletes (Memmert, 2007), and creativity has been tied to superior sport performance (Memmert, 2011) as well as flow (Csikszentmihalyi, 1996).

It could be argued that any mindfulness exercise may enhance a sense of harmony and rhythm, but we contend that meditations emphasizing a broadening of attention most explicitly train this ability. In MSPE, the movement-based exercises, such as the walking and sport meditations, involve such broadening. Participants are invited to expand their focus beyond a single anchor (e.g., the breath) to the entirety of a motive experience, taking in the coordinated movements of the body and the harmony between their bodies and their environment. This kind of practice can help participants find an effortless rhythm and sense of connection in their sport and their daily lives. As we discuss in the next section, the fullest potential of MSPE may exist in this pervasive application of mindfulness.

Forming Key Associations

The final performance facilitator is somewhat different than the previous four, in the sense that it helps participants put the others into practice. Session 1 of MSPE (see Chapter 4) concludes with a discussion of autopilot and how our lives can be lived without full awareness, governed simply by habit with our minds removed from the present, often worrying about the future or regretting the past. Doing formal mindfulness exercises provides the opportunity to practice being in each moment intentionally. However, in some ways, formal practice is limited. We may sit with a clear intention to concentrate on the present, taking in the richness of our moment-to-moment experiences, letting go of distractions, and welcoming in a sense of relaxation—for 10 minutes. But, what about the other 950 minutes or more of our waking day? Spontaneously recognizing that we are on autopilot is a skill that develops only over time and with practice. After all, if you were aware that you were on autopilot, then you wouldn't be on autopilot! So, the question becomes, how can we become more aware of when we aren't aware?

The ability to form key associations can help answer this question. We encourage MSPE participants to choose or create cues in their environment that can act as reminders to be mindful. That way, they do not have to rely entirely on the spontaneous emergence of their awareness, especially in highly stimulating, distracting, and emotional situations such as sport. Ideally, participants choose cues that are relevant to or a part of their training, competitions, or daily life. For instance, runners could use passing a landmark on a training run, standing on the start line of a race, and/or brushing their teeth in the morning as reminders to scan their bodies briefly and release any excess tension. Establishing associations between these cues and behaving mindfully can help participants build consistency in practicing what they learn in MSPE. Over time, this systematic practice can translate into a default mode of mindfulness. In this way, MSPE helps individuals become mindful performers, not just performers who practice mindfulness.

We believe this distinction is quite meaningful because it highlights the importance of regular mindfulness practice, both formal and informal. When we say "formal," we are referring to practice done in a particular location, at a specific time, and for a predetermined duration (e.g., a body scan done each morning, in a quiet corner of one's bedroom, for 20 minutes). "Informal," on the other hand, means being mindful during the activities of daily life, such as while washing dishes, going for a run, or practicing or competing in one's sport.

There is evidence that the amount of time one practices mindfulness may impact the effectiveness of mindfulness-based interventions (e.g., Carmody & Baer, 2008; C. Crane et al., 2014), although it is important to note that not all studies have supported this contention (Vettese, Toneatto, Stea, Nguyen, & Wang, 2009) and the vast majority of this research has focused on formal practice (Morgan, Graham, Hayes-Skelton, Orsillo, & Roemer, 2014). Interestingly, some evidence suggests that even though it can be difficult for participants to maintain a regular formal practice after mindfulness training, they are more likely to continue to engage in informal practice (de Zoysa, Ruths, Walsh, & Hutton, 2014).

Mindfulness-based interventions with both formal and informal practice components have been found to be more effective than interventions that focus solely on informal practice (Hindman, Glass, Arnkoff, & Maron, 2015), but informal practice has been associated with a range of benefits, including decreases in stress and negative affect and increases in positive affect (Dobkin & Zhao, 2011; A. W. Hanley, Warner, Dehili, Canto, & Garland, 2015). In fact, Morgan and colleagues (2014) found that the amount of informal practice, but not formal practice, following a mindfulness training predicted improvements in worry, anxiety, and quality of life for up to 1 year. Thus, although the amount of research looking at informal practice is limited, the available data indicate that it can be a crucial and beneficial component of mindfulness training.

MSPE places a significant emphasis on informal practice while also incorporating formal exercises that are easily translatable to sport situations. The importance of informal practice is introduced in Session 1 of MSPE and returned to in each subsequent session. Just as with formal practice, participants are encouraged to increase their amount of informal practice each week to seize as many opportunities as possible to be mindful. Forming key associations is an important element of this, and, in Session 2, participants begin considering cues that could work for them. These cues can be environmental (e.g., the half-court line), temporal (e.g., the beginning of every play), or even a word or phrase. Participants are encouraged to make these cues their own and to imbue meaning in them beyond simply as reminders to breathe or relax. For example, coauthor Tim Pineau worked with a lacrosse team that came up with the phrase "hold the rope" as a mindfulness cue. The coach or any team member could say, "Hold the rope," and then every other team member who heard it would repeat the phrase as a reminder to stay present.

For this team that Tim trained, "hold the rope" also became a reminder of their bond: that no matter how vulnerable a particular player might feel, they knew that every other team member was holding on to the other end of their rope. Thus, this key association was also inviting in feelings of support, trust, and compassion for one another, reminding them of how grateful they were to be a part of the team. This example highlights another aspect of mindfulness training worthy of mention that, although not considered one of the primary performance facilitators promoted in MSPE, can nonetheless have a profound impact.

Compassion and Gratitude

At present, there appears to be limited interest in exploring the effects of compassion and gratitude in sport, despite their identification as positive emotions commonly experienced by athletes (Lazarus, 2000). There is, however, plentiful research elsewhere looking at gratitude and compassion (for the self and others), both of which appear to increase following mindfulness training (Davis & Hayes, 2011; Fredrickson, Cohn, Coffey, Pek, & Finkel, 2008). Some authors have suggested that self-compassion is inextricably linked with mindfulness (Neff, 2003), and Hölzel et al. (2011) pointed out that "meditation is typically practiced with an intention—implicit or explicit—to cultivate self-compassion as well as compassion toward other beings" (p. 550).

Although the research is sparse, what is known about athletes and gratitude is noteworthy. Athletes who experience more feelings of gratitude, both overall and regarding their sport specifically, report less burnout, higher self-esteem, and greater satisfaction with their teams and lives (Chen & Kee, 2008; Chen & Wu, 2014). It has also been proposed that a gratitude-based group intervention may be uniquely suited to help college athletes manage the stressors inherent in balancing their lives as student–athletes (Datu, 2013). These findings suggest an important link between gratitude and well-being for athletes, which echoes the connection between gratitude and a range of well-being indicators (e.g., positive social relationships, physical health) found in other populations (Wood, Froh, & Geraghty, 2010).

Somewhat more attention has been directed toward the impact of compassion, especially self-compassion, on athletes. It has been found that female athletes with higher levels of self-compassion exhibited lower levels of maladaptive self-evaluative processes, such as shame, social physique anxiety, and fear of failure, as well as higher levels of adaptive self-evaluative processes, such as authentic pride (Mosewich, Kowalski, Sabiston, Sedgwick, & Tracy, 2011). In addition, Mosewich, Crocker, Kowalski, and DeLongis (2013) found that a self-compassion intervention helped female athletes reduce self-criticism, rumination, and concern over mistakes. These studies support Reis et al.'s (2015) conclusion that female athletes with higher levels of self-compassion generally have more healthy reactions (e.g., behavioral equanimity) and fewer unhealthy reactions (e.g., catastrophizing thoughts) to difficult sport situations.

People in athletics should take note of these findings because self-criticism is a main component of maladaptive sport perfectionism (Anshel & Sutarso, 2010) and can interfere with goal progress in athletes (Powers, Koestner, Lacaille, Kwan, & Zuroff, 2009). However, some athletes may perceive self-criticism as necessary because they believe it motivates them to improve and keep their edge (Ferguson, Kowalski, Mack, & Sabiston, 2014). Thus, self-compassion at times is equated with passivity or resignation and therefore seen as undesirable or even threatening. This perception harkens back to the utility of drawing distinctions between acceptance and resignation, and there is also empirical evidence that debunks this view.

For example, Breines and Chen (2012) found that, in nonathletes, self-compassion was actually associated with greater motivation for and effort toward self-improvement after failure. For athletes, Ferguson and colleagues (2014) discovered not only an association between self-compassion and well-being but also that self-compassion was negatively related to passivity and that athletes reported believing that self-compassion could improve their capacity to persevere through difficult situations. Further, Kageyama (2014) concluded that "the research suggests that harsh self-criticism only increases passivity, procrastination, and fear of failure, and that self-compassion may actually be the key to maximizing our potential" (p. 31).

We believe that feelings of gratitude and compassion are naturally generated when one takes on a more mindful perspective, and we explicitly encourage such feelings throughout MSPE. The intention of self-compassion is interwoven throughout in-session discussions of acceptance and is also evident within the language of each exercise, as participants are guided to be kind to themselves and let go of any judgments when, for instance, they notice their minds wandering.

The movement-based meditations (e.g., mindful yoga, walking meditation) emphasize gratitude by encouraging participants to appreciate all that their bodies do for them and the simple fact that they can move. In the sport meditation, gratitude is similarly focused on one's capacity to engage in his or her sport. Depending on the sport, gratitude may also extend to teammates, and even opponents, because it is only with the collaboration of every individual involved that a team is formed and a sport is played.

Despite our intentional integration of compassion and gratitude into MSPE, we do not explicitly define it as a primary performance facilitator, partly because, as alluded to previously, our experience has shown that many athletes don't respond well to terminology that feels too soft or touchy-feely. In fact, well-known sport psychologist and meditation teacher George Mumford was asked whether he used the terms *mindfulness* and *compassion* with athletes, and he responded that he can now use the former because of the growing popularity of the concept, but with regard to the latter he said, "No, that's too much" (Delehanty, 2016, p. 54). Even without designating compassion and gratitude as a primary performance facilitator, we still view it as an integral element of mindfulness training, adding to the ways in which MSPE can benefit individuals in both their sport and their lives.

Conclusion

In reviewing the five performance facilitators promoted in MSPE, along with associated empirical support, we have attempted to provide an overview of our conceptualization of how mindfulness is applied in practice and the path through which MSPE can help athletes and coaches translate the power of mindfulness into athletic success. However, even though these factors were presented individually, it is essential to reiterate that they are not taught or practiced one at a time. It is their combination and integration, which comes from the mindful state of being that MSPE helps to instill, that can ultimately promote flow and peak performance. However, that integration itself requires time, dedication, and practice.

MSPE is one vehicle for that practice, providing the infrastructure for any athlete or coach to establish a mental training program that is as rigorous and effective as their physical and tactical training. Over the past 10 years, MSPE has evolved as we've sought to discover the best ways to help participants bring all of these concepts and practices together. In the next chapter, we review this evolution as well as the empirical support that MSPE has gained as an emerging leader in the field of evidence-based mindfulness mental training programs for performance enhancement.

Empirical Support for MSPE

11

E vidence-based practice in psychology can be supported by a range of research designs, including qualitative research, effectiveness studies of interventions delivered in more naturalistic settings, and efficacy research such as randomized controlled trials (RCTs; American Psychological Association, Presidential Task Force on Evidence-Based Practice, 2006). In Chapter 2 of this book, we presented an overview of current knowledge on mindfulness in sport, focusing on approaches other than mindful sport performance enhancement (MSPE). Clearly, more research in this area, especially more methodologically rigorous studies, is needed to say that current mindfulness interventions for athletes and coaches (including MSPE) have very strong empirical support.

Even with research on mindfulness in sport still being in its relative infancy, we are encouraged by the growing body of promising results supporting MSPE. Sharing these results and suggesting directions for future MSPE research are the foci of this chapter. Three studies from our lab demonstrated early support for MSPE's efficacy with adult community athletes. More recent research, involving use of an expanded MSPE protocol, has included collegiate long-distance runners, mixed-sport groups of college athletes (in an RCT),

http://dx.doi.org/10.1037/0000048-012
Mindful Sport Performance Enhancement: Mental Training for Athletes and Coaches, by K. A. Kaufman, C. R. Glass, and T. R. Pineau

intact teams within a university athletics department, college coaches, and teams of high school athletes. Other researchers from around the world have also begun to evaluate the program, including the True Athlete Project, a nonprofit organization in the United States, which has used MSPE with elementary school athletes to assist in efforts to change the culture of youth sport.

Initial Studies With Community Athletes

MSPE FOR GOLFERS AND ARCHERS

For the first study of MSPE (Kaufman, Glass, & Arnkoff, 2009), we had planned to conduct RCTs of MSPE with adult archers and golfers from the local area. Unlike with previously existing mindfulness programs for physical and psychological issues, such as the eight-session mindfulness-based stress reduction intervention whose participants may be highly motivated to address painful aspects of their lives, we doubted that prospective MSPE athletes would have the desire or time flexibility for eight weekly meetings. So, we originally designed MSPE to be a four-session group program, meeting once weekly for 2½ hours. As you will see, both the structure and the applications of MSPE have evolved as our work has continued.

Extensive recruitment efforts over the course of many months, which included contacting members of archery clubs in five states and advertising in dozens of golf pro shops, resulted in a smaller-than-expected sample of 10 archers and 19 golfers. Both the recruitment struggles and scheduling challenges that emerged with those athletes who did sign up required a shift in research design. Thus, the archers received the training in spring 2006, and two groups for golfers were run that summer. A total of seven archers and 14 golfers completed a series of pre–post (trait) and during-training (state) questionnaires assessing factors such as mindfulness, flow, anxiety, perfectionism, confidence, mindfulness practice, and sport performance.

Overall trait mindfulness (i.e., as an enduring disposition) and optimism (as an aspect of sport confidence) increased significantly for the archers, whereas a facet of mindfulness (describing experiences) rose significantly for the golfers. Although the archers increased in confidence and decreased in thought disruption and somatic sport anxiety, with the small number of athletes in this study, these changes emerged statistically as only near-significant trends. Other trends, such as an increase in the flow dimension of loss of self-consciousness, were found for the golfers.

Significant increases in state flow were observed for those athletes who completed the between-session state flow measure each week. Also, significant increases in the decentering (openness to experience) aspect of mindfulness were found for those who completed the weekly state mindfulness measure. When pretraining levels of mindfulness were controlled for, post-MSPE trait mindfulness had a correlation of .43 with the number of sessions attended (only a near-significant trend given the sample size), suggesting a benefit from attending more sessions.

Regarding changes in sport performance, over the course of MSPE the golfers' average 18-hole scores decreased, but not significantly. This lack of significance was not surprising because only three golfers reported at least one round score for each week of the training. Unfortunately, we didn't see a way at that time to assess performance change for the archers in a standardized way because they engaged in various forms of weekly practice and competition involving different numbers of arrows shot, target distances, and even target sizes.

Even with these limitations, valuable insights into how the athletes felt MSPE had impacted their sport performance were obtained from a program evaluation form. Feedback suggested that the training had positively impacted their sport performance, with an average rating of 6.62 on a scale from 1 (*not at all successful*) to 10 (*very successful*). The mean rating of how satisfied the athletes were with their performance after MSPE was 7.00, and they expected to be even more satisfied in the future (8.48 expected in 1 year and 9.00 in 5 years). In addition, open-ended questions on this form revealed that approximately three quarters of the athletes who responded expected MSPE would improve their performance quality and/or enjoyment in the future, and one third described that MSPE had affected their sport performance by allowing them to become more focused on the task at hand.

MSPE FOR LONG-DISTANCE RUNNERS

For the second MSPE study (De Petrillo, Kaufman, Glass, & Arnkoff, 2009), the protocol was adapted for long-distance runners, incorporating recommendations from books on the psychology of running (e.g., Dreyer & Dreyer, 2004) and an interview with coach Bruce Beall (personal communication, September 20, 2006), who, as described in Chapter 2, had experience delivering a mindfulness-based intervention to endurance athletes. The revised manual focused more on the use of mindfulness within repetitive endurance sports to deal with fatigue, pain, and boredom. Recruitment occurred in the fall of 2006 and targeted adult runners from local clubs and teams who competed in races ranging from 1 mile to marathon distances. Scheduling limitations again impacted our design, and only 40% of the runners could be randomly assigned to either an intervention or a waiting-list control group. Twelve runners completed at least three of the four MSPE sessions in the intervention group, as did 10 runners from the waiting-list control.

Few significant differences were found between conditions over the 4 weeks of MSPE, although for the intervention group, worry, perfectionism, and best-mile time were all moving in a beneficial direction. When all 22 athletes were combined, we found significant increases in mindfully attending to activities in the moment and significant decreases in aspects of perfectionism and sport anxiety. There was also a near-significant trend toward improvement in sport concentration disruption and task-related worries. Overall state mindfulness, particularly decentering, also increased significantly from the first to fourth session.

Although no significant changes in self-reported running performance were found over the 4 weeks of the program, 81% of the athletes indicated at posttraining that they expected their running to improve further with continued mindfulness practice, and 80% said they had applied skills they learned to deal with life stressors. In fact, several runners contacted principal investigator Lillian De Petrillo after the training to report improvements in their running performance following additional mindfulness practice. One male runner said he was able to implement what he learned during several races and obtained personal bests, exceeding even his "highest hopes." Another runner commented that by using mindfulness, she was able to maintain superior focus and effort, helping her to run better and enjoy her sport more than ever before. Other participants explained how, after MSPE, they found themselves with a greater inclination to try new and more challenging routes, such as running through mountainous trails.

LONG-TERM FOLLOW-UP WITH ARCHERS, GOLFERS, AND RUNNERS

Given the results and encouraging posttraining feedback in these first two studies, it was crucial to follow up with these athletes to see what had unfolded a year after their respective MSPE training. We had also been wondering whether it was reasonable to detect significant changes, particularly on trait factors, after only 4 weeks of being introduced to an entirely new approach to mental training. Thus, the original participants were contacted for a follow-up assessment (Thompson, Kaufman, De Petrillo, Glass, & Arnkoff, 2011). Four archers and eight golfers (57%), as well as 13 runners (59%), chose to participate.

Almost 92% of these archers and golfers and 77% of these runners reported at least occasional mindfulness practice in the year following MSPE, for an average of 17.5 and 32.5 minutes a week, respectively. The most frequently practiced exercise was mindful breathing (sitting meditation), but yoga, the body scan, and sport meditation were also done. Lack of available time and lack of motivation were identified as the largest obstacles to maintaining a regular mindfulness practice. Interestingly, duration of weekly mindfulness practice was significantly correlated with reductions in sport-related worries ($r = -.79$) and showed a near-significant trend for the correlation with improvement in the runners' mile times ($r = -.60$).

Archers and golfers showed significant reductions in task-irrelevant thoughts and overall thought disruption during sports from pretest to follow-up, with a trend toward reduction in sport-related worries. The 10 athletes who completed the measure of trait mindfulness at all three time points showed a near-significant increase in overall mindfulness as well as the specific mindfulness facets reflecting the ability to describe experiences and act with awareness. Runners showed significant increases in acceptance without judgment and significant decreases in the concentration disruption aspect of sport anxiety as well as ratings of anxiety and stress. They also demonstrated a near-significant change in overall trait mindfulness.

To determine if the athletes had experienced improvement in their sport performance, the best scores they had attained in the 12 months prior to and following MSPE were compared. Although golfers' performance did not improve significantly, there were interesting findings for the other athlete groups. For this study, we were able to create a standard metric to make the archery scores comparable, calculating them as a percentage of the total possible score for each performance, and the four archers showed a near-significant trend toward performance improvement in their outdoor competitions (from 74.68% to 82.05%). The runners' reported best mile times in the 12 months after MSPE were significantly faster than their times prior to and during the MSPE training. In addition, the runners' performance improvement was significantly associated with increases in mindfulness (accepting without judgment) and decreases in sport anxiety. On a scale from 1 (*not at all*) to 5 (*a great deal*), the runners indicated moderate confidence that MSPE had impacted their sport performance (mean rating of 2.75).

When athletes were asked to describe any changes in how they felt about their sport since before MSPE began, 30% of the responses indicated a better understanding of mental aspects of sport (e.g., "I know that focus and concentration is a big part of playing well"), 30% indicated superior confidence (e.g., "increased confidence in competition"), and 20% indicated greater relaxation (e.g., "I feel more relaxed"). Furthermore, answers from 78% of the archers and golfers and 33% of the runners as to why any such changes occurred identified mindfulness and related mental strategies (e.g., "I can move ahead faster after a poor shot") as the reason. In addition, when asked about the impact of MSPE outside of sport in other life domains, 57% of the athletes mentioned the benefits of mindfulness skills for anxiety and/or stress reduction (e.g., "meditation or other mindfulness practices can calm") and 14% reported an improved capacity to focus (e.g., "I seem able to ignore distractions better"). Also, that summer we received an e-mail from an archer who spoke to the benefits of MSPE for his competitive mindset:

> I just completed shooting in the national senior Olympics on Tuesday. My exposure to your seminar and the [recordings] were put to full use. The field temperature on the second day was over 124 degrees. . . . [I] was in first place by 1 point going into the second day of competition. I survived equipment troubles and the heat to win by a margin of 19 points. I am positive the second-place shooter lost in his head game.

Studies With Collegiate Athletes

MSPE FOR A UNIVERSITY CROSS-COUNTRY TEAM

From these early studies, it was apparent that a longer program might be even more beneficial for athletes to learn these new skills, apply them to sport performances and life, and demonstrate changes on trait measures of factors such as anxiety. Any mindfulness-based intervention is hopefully only a beginning to a long-term practice, but we thought it would be advantageous to add more sessions while still maintaining respect for the busy schedules of our participants. Tim Pineau took the lead on our next MSPE study in fall 2011 (Pineau, 2014), expanding the protocol length to six

90-minute sessions weekly, substantially developing the themes for each session, adding specific questions to include in discussions, and creating original scripts for all of the exercises. Audio recordings of MSPE exercises, as well as line drawings of the yoga poses, were also created to guide the assigned home practice.

We recruited two National Collegiate Athletic Association Division I cross-country teams (one as a control group) to test this expanded intervention. Although in many ways this design was an improvement on previous research, a number of unanticipated methodological issues limited the program's effectiveness (e.g., lack of coach involvement or a private space to hold the training, university budgetary cuts affecting the team). Given the circumstances, we did not find significant results. Although this study was statistically disappointing, it provided critical lessons that informed and strengthened our work going forward and that are detailed in Chapter 13.

MSPE FOR COLLEGIATE DIVISION III STUDENT–ATHLETES FROM MULTIPLE SPORTS

In collaboration with Claire Spears and with the support of the university's athletics department, an RCT of the six-session MSPE program was conducted in fall 2014 with mixed-sport groups of Division III varsity athletes who had volunteered for the training and consented to participate. The MSPE protocol was again updated and expanded, more closely reflecting the current program presented in Chapters 4 through 9 of this book. One change was the addition of significant content on incorporating informal mindfulness into home practice, such as the STOP acronym (stop, take a few breaths, observe, proceed; Stahl & Goldstein, 2010), as a way of practicing mindfulness in daily life as well as on the field of play.

Sixty-nine student–athletes were randomly assigned to either one of two 6-week MSPE groups starting in early September or a waiting-list control condition that received the program in one of two groups starting in late October. Of these participants, 55 attended at least one session and 49 of these athletes (41 women and eight men) completed both pre- and postintervention measures; the 20 who attended at least five sessions were deemed treatment completers. Athletes from a wide range of sports, including cross-country, track, swimming, tennis, soccer, lacrosse, field hockey, baseball, football, and volleyball, were represented. Assessments were conducted before and after the first groups, after the control athletes received training, and at the end of the school year. Both self and coach ratings were used to assess performance. Participants were asked to practice exercises on 6 days during the week and reported practicing an average of 3.42 days.

Outcome Results

Analyses comparing the intervention and control groups showed a significant interaction of condition and time (C. R. Glass, Spears, Perskaudas, & Kaufman, 2016). Although controls reported a significant increase in depressive symptoms over time, the intervention condition did not (symptoms actually decreased slightly). In light of the significant academic and social stressors faced by college athletes on top of academic demands (Humphrey, Yow, & Bowden, 2000), these students could be at heightened risk for depression (Wolanin, Gross, & Hong, 2015) and MSPE may be a promising approach for preventing escalations in these symptoms. Furthermore, although MSPE is not a substitute for psychological treatment for clinical depression, "mental training for athletes" might be viewed as more acceptable and less stigmatizing than psychotherapy, thus providing preventative support for any at-risk student–athletes, who might be hesitant to seek mental health treatment.

Once waiting-list control athletes received the intervention, comparisons of pre- and posttraining scores for all 49 athletes showed significant increases in overall dispositional flow as well as on three flow dimensions of challenge–skill balance, merging of action and awareness, and loss of self-consciousness. In addition, significant decreases were found in the worry aspect of sport anxiety. A more in-depth look at the 20 treatment completers was also of key interest. Despite the smaller sample size, significant improvements were found on a much larger number of measures. In addition to the changes already mentioned, athletes also increased in the clear goals dimension of flow and two facets of mindfulness (reflecting attention to present-moment experiences and allowing thoughts and feelings to come and go without reacting to them), with a near-significant trend for improvement in the ability to describe experiences in words. Finally, self-rated sport performance was significantly higher at the end of the MSPE training, along with overall life satisfaction. These results suggest that the athletes who completed the program experienced far greater benefits than did those who started MSPE but attended fewer than five sessions, which means a full dose of MSPE may be necessary to reap optimal benefits.

The follow-up assessment was completed at the end of the academic year by 37 (76%) of the athletes who attended at least one session. All gains were maintained, with near-significant trends for additional increases in self-ratings of overall athletic performance as well as overall mindfulness and the facet of describing experiences in words.

Because between-session mindfulness practice is thought to be integral in producing the benefits of mindfulness-based interventions (Grow, Collins, Harrop, & Marlatt, 2015; Vettese, Toneatto, Stea, Nguyen, & Wang, 2009), we also examined associations between amount of mindfulness practice and key outcomes. Among participants who attended at least one MSPE session, those who practiced mindfulness more frequently during the week showed greater increases in both flow and the attention- and emotion-regulation aspects of sport performance (e.g., concentration, mental toughness, ability to "keep one's cool" in the midst of stressful athletic situations). Thus, participants who more often practice mindfulness on their own may experience greater benefits, and future research should continue to investigate whether a certain amount of between-session mindfulness practice is needed to produce optimal outcomes for MSPE. In addition, greater enjoyment of weekly mindfulness practice was associated with improvements in stress, psychological inflexibility, and flow over the course of the intervention.

Qualitative Results

A coding system was developed to evaluate open-ended responses from athletes in this study, with excellent interrater reliability in identifying key themes (Mistretta, Glass, et al., 2016). Around half of the participants chose to fill out a post-MSPE program evaluation, which contained a number of open-ended questions. When asked more generally what they liked most about MSPE, the most frequent responses (32%) related to learning new mindfulness skills and exercises (e.g., "Learning different methods I can use to practice mindfulness in a way that fits me," "yoga," "breathing exercises"). A similar number dealt with obtaining psychological benefits related to nonjudgment, increased focus, and self-awareness (e.g., "Learning how to stay more focused on the moment and not dwell on mistakes or the future"), along with reductions in stress or worry (e.g., "It allowed me to relax more"). Other common answers (23%) spoke to aspects of the group such as liking the group discussions and the enthusiasm and helpfulness of the leaders, and 9% described sport-related benefits (e.g., "Learning different ways to control my stress towards sports").

When asked specifically how MSPE was helpful for their sport, 41% addressed how mindfulness skills facilitated greater mental focus, letting go of emotions, mental toughness, and increased awareness and self-confidence (e.g., "I think I found a way to let go of things if I'm not doing them well in a game or practice"). An additional 23% mentioned dealing better with stress (e.g., "It helped me to relax more during games"). Finally, 9% alluded to improvements in sport performance (e.g., "Pushing myself beyond what I thought was my limit"), and an additional two athletes had not found MSPE to be beneficial or applied it to their sport.

A third question asked about benefits seen in their everyday lives outside of sport. The most common response (45%) mentioned psychological benefits such as staying in the moment, letting go of negative feelings, developing different perspectives, and feeling more peaceful and focused (e.g., "It enabled me to be able to think about only what I'm doing at that moment and not worry about other things in my life"). Anxiety reduction, such as "staying relaxed in times of stress," was listed by 36% of the athletes. Other athletes (18%) did not find it helpful in this context or had not used mindfulness in their everyday lives.

Approximately a third of the participants responded to a question asking what they disliked about the training. Quite a few answers (53%) spoke to situational factors such as the scheduled length or time of the sessions, which were held on Sunday evenings (e.g., "It's our only day off from practices and a prime homework time"), with 33% describing issues relating to the group format (e.g., "There were too many people," "talking very often about personal experiences"). Only 13% of the answers were specific to the MSPE program, such as that the concept of mindfulness was hard to get used to or that some sessions were boring.

Program Evaluation Ratings

Most (75%) of the athletes who responded to posttraining rating scales indicated that they were at least somewhat sure they would continue practicing mindfulness (with 40% very confident), and 70% were at least somewhat sure that they would continue to incorporate mindfulness into their everyday lives. Finally, when asked to rate whether they would recommend this mindfulness program for other collegiate athletes, 70% replied in the affirmative (i.e., with a rating of 4 or 5 out of 5), with an additional 25% saying that they would "possibly" recommend MSPE training. The average strength of recommendation was 3.90, suggesting that overall the mindfulness training was well received (Mistretta, Glass, et al., 2016).

Additional Feedback

We also received unexpected e-mails from coaches and athletics administrators, sharing their perceptions of MSPE's efficacy. One head coach e-mailed us to say, "I know this isn't an official evaluation, but this week [one of your participants] has had a great week of practice. She told me she's using her 'breath as an anchor' and it is really helping her focus" (P. Waas, personal communication, October 29, 2014). That academic year, the university's athletics program achieved its highest-ever ranking in the National Association of Collegiate Directors of Athletics Sports Directors' Cup and was named the best overall athletics program in its conference. And the university's athletic director told us, "You all helped a number of our coaches and student–athletes recalibrate themselves to produce an even higher level of performance. That's got to go into your summary somewhere. . . . It WORKED!" (S. Sullivan, personal communication, May 22, 2015). He had likewise written us earlier to say that the mindfulness training for the athletes was not only well received but also very impactful.

ADAPTING MSPE FOR TEAMS AS PART OF A UNIVERSITY ATHLETICS PROGRAM

Although we were excited to see these positive results with mixed groups of athletes, we continued to be interested in applications of MSPE training with intact teams. In October 2015, the coach of a women's team at the Division III university where Tim Pineau had recently started working approached him about mindfulness training for her athletes. After making some adjustments to the protocol to accommodate the team's schedule (e.g., abbreviating the body scan and yoga routine in the second and third sessions), Tim provided six 1-hour MSPE sessions during their preseason and added a follow-up meeting just before their first game. FAME profile measures (defined and described in the section that follows) were completed, as were self- and coach ratings of athlete performance, and participants consented to having measures used for research purposes.

The university athletic director later invited Tim to discuss mindfulness with all of the university's coaches. Following that meeting, three more coaches reached out to him with interest in having their teams trained in MSPE, with one men's team receiving MSPE concurrent with the first few weeks of their spring season and two other men's teams scheduling an initial meeting with plans for the full intervention the following fall. What is particularly exciting about how this has unfolded is that it illustrates the potential for how MSPE can be implemented within an athletics department. For instance, the athletic director has even discussed the possibility of finding ways to offer MSPE to the university's athletes more broadly. Having the support of coaches and administrators is absolutely crucial. As we discuss in other chapters, our view is that MSPE is most effective when it is integrated into the culture of a team or department. In this instance, coaches have done the training along with their athletes and were involved in each session. They also consulted with Tim about how to incorporate mindfulness into their daily training, practice routines, and workouts and collaborated with him to create sport-specific meditations.

In addition to these advantages that come with such institutional support, offering MSPE in this way helps to address some common methodological concerns in sport psychology research, including the early research on MSPE. Namely, the recruitment process becomes dramatically streamlined, continued contact with the teams after the completion of the program offers the chance to look at the long-term impact of MSPE, and having repeated opportunities to offer MSPE in a consistent setting allows for the combination of data from different iterations to examine the impact of MSPE with a much larger sample size. Of course, the use of intact teams presents other challenges for conducting RCTs, which highlights the importance of pursuing multiple avenues of research.

Preliminary analyses of the results from the two teams that received MSPE (32 total athletes) are extremely promising (Pineau, 2016). After the end of the six sessions, athletes demonstrated significant increases in trait mindfulness, the refocusing aspect of sport-related mindfulness, flow (including a majority of the flow dimensions), and self-rated performance, as well as significant decreases in experiential avoidance and sport-related anxiety (particularly worry and concentration disruption). At a post-season follow-up (2–3 months after the conclusion of the training), all of these gains were maintained except on a flow subscale and a mindfulness subscale, and some additional improvements were also evident. Specifically, a significant reduction in somatic anxiety was found, as well as significant increases in total sport mindfulness and in coach-rated performance.

Beyond these quantitative results, one team had the winningest season in their program's history, whereas the other had their winningest season in over a decade, making it to their conference championship tournament for the first time and achieving more individual athlete accolades (e.g., rookie of the week, all-conference honors) than ever before. Of note, both teams had losing records the previous year.

The FAME Profile

When discussing Tim's work with the university athletics department, we mentioned that he had MSPE participants complete FAME profile measures. Because FAME features prominently in our more recent research and can be a useful tool to anyone wanting to research or administer MSPE, we'd like to offer some further explanation of what FAME is here. FAME was born out of the desire to give useful feedback to MSPE participants on how crucial mental performance factors changed from the beginning to the end of the training. The profile we developed asscsses Flow, Anxiety, Mindfulness, and Emotion regulation (FAME). Using published norms on these factors, graphs can be used to illustrate pre- versus postprogram *z* score change. Examples of FAME profiles appear at the end of the case studies that conclude this book.

For constructing a FAME profile, we recommend using well-validated measures of these four constructs. Among the measures we have used are the Dispositional Flow Scale-2 (S. A. Jackson & Eklund, 2002, 2004), Sport Anxiety Scale-2 (Smith, Smoll, Cumming, & Grossbard, 2006), Five Facet Mindfulness Questionnaire (Baer, Smith, Hopkins, Krietemeyer, & Toney, 2006), and Mindfulness Inventory for Sport (Thienot et al., 2014) as well as the Difficulties in Emotion Regulation Scale (Gratz & Roemer, 2004). We have also considered using briefer flow and mindfulness measures (e.g., Philadelphia Mindfulness Scale; Cardaciotto, Herbert, Forman, Moitra, & Farrow, 2008) and have used the Acceptance and Action Questionnaire-II (Bond et al., 2011) as a measure of experiential avoidance, substituting this construct for emotion regulation as the *E* in the profile.

Study With Collegiate Coaches

At the time of the RCT described previously, several coaches approached us about doing MSPE training. With support from the athletic director, a group was run in spring 2015, including seven Division III coaches (five women and two men) representing basketball, volleyball, baseball, lacrosse, and fitness. Five of these coaches consented to be in a study and completed both pre- and postprogram FAME profile measures.

Although statistical findings were limited with so few participants, the coaches showed significant improvements in overall flow as well as on the transformation of time flow subscale (Hoyer, Glass, Spears, & Kaufman, 2016). However, they also demonstrated unexpected declines in the dimension of mindfulness reflecting attention to activities in the moment and increases in the concentration disruption aspect of (but not overall) sport anxiety. Only one of the coaches was in-season during this training, so most of them had no opportunity to apply mindfulness in their primary coaching setting. Although it was not part of the original research design, we recognize that a follow-up asscssment would have been helpful, as previous research on the mindfulness–acceptance–commitment (MAC) approach with athletes (e.g., Gross, 2014) has shown significant improvements from postintervention to a 1-month follow-up that were not present right after the program had ended.

Comments on a posttraining questionnaire nonetheless indicated that coaches had really enjoyed the training and especially "loved the discussions." They felt MSPE had helped them be "more aware of my surroundings and my own thoughts" and "better focused for meetings after competition" and had "brought awareness to how much I am judgmental on myself and don't need to be." They also were looking forward to using mindfulness in their upcoming season, suggesting having their teams do "10 minutes of mindfulness before [watching] film" and that they would "[use] awareness to keep them in the moment" as well as use the breath to focus. On a scale from 1 (*not at all*) to 5 (*very*), the coaches' average rating was 4.2 when asked how confident they were that they would continue to incorporate mindfulness into their coaching.

A year later, we heard from one of the assistant basketball coaches that she had spent "a lot of time talking about mindfulness" with her team, sharing the digital mindfulness exercises with her athletes, hanging mindful posters on the locker room walls, and offering mindful quotes on the bus before games. She added that many benefitted, so that "instead of focusing on the things they were doing wrong, they noticed that they should just go out there and play!" and were able to calm down instead of panic (B. Crites, personal communication, April 4, 2016).

Studies With Youth Athletes

MSPE FOR HIGH SCHOOL TEAMS

Given the increasing interest in mindfulness for children and adolescents, we were excited when a local school district interested in promoting student–athlete mental health approached Keith Kaufman in fall 2014 about offering MSPE trainings. He thus provided a pilot program at one of the high schools to 12 female athletes (nine soccer and three field hockey players) and their head coaches. Eight of the soccer players completed FAME measures as research participants.

The findings from these questionnaires were striking, given the small sample size and the fact that weather-related school closures had forced MSPE to be condensed into five sessions (Mistretta, Kaufman, Glass, & Spears, 2016). These athletes showed significant increases in overall sport mindfulness as well as in the awareness aspect of mindfulness. Emotion regulation difficulties, particularly the dimension of nonacceptance of emotions, decreased significantly. A near-significant trend was found for decreases in total sport anxiety, most notably in somatic anxiety. A similar near-significant trend was found for increases in overall dispositional flow but with significant increases in the challenge–skill balance and clear goals dimensions.

Since then, Keith has offered MSPE training at a second high school in the same school district, once with the boys' lacrosse and softball teams and once with the field hockey team. Although no data were collected, our sense is that having the field hockey coach be part of the training (the other coaches were not) made a big difference in terms of how her team engaged and ultimately benefitted from the training. The field hockey coach remarked to Keith how she'd heard the athletes using terminology from MSPE on the field during practice and games to help each other with regulation of attention and emotions, and she wanted to build on that, something she would not have been able to do if she had not been present for the sessions.

MSPE FOR ELEMENTARY SCHOOL STUDENTS: THE TRUE ATHLETE PROJECT

In 2015, elementary school athletics director Sam Parfitt brought together a group of international expert athletes, coaches, and sport psychologists to consider how to improve kids' experiences of sport through a mind–body–spirit approach (e.g., incorporating tai chi, sensory awakening techniques, meditation, mindfulness, and sport psychology). The stated goal of his nonprofit organization, the True Athlete Project (TAP), is to change the culture of youth sports through the practice of mindfulness (Cook, 2015). Keith Kaufman has been involved as a consultant to the project, which offers sport-specific meditation classes; workshops; and retreats for athletes, educators, and coaches. In late 2015, TAP piloted a 6-week MSPE training with a group of 47 fourth- and fifth-graders during their regular physical education class times, with some modifications to the language and length of exercises to accommodate time constraints and the age of participants. After the program, children's mean acceptance and mindfulness scores increased significantly, whereas levels of anxiety decreased significantly (S. Parfitt, personal communication, March 27, 2016). Parfitt added that they received "a lot of fantastic comments from the parents," who were pleased that their children had this opportunity, and there were reports of kids practicing mindfulness in the hallways, in the car, after dinner, and even of the kids teaching their siblings.

Parfitt (personal communication, March 28, 2016) additionally passed along some comments participants had made regarding their MSPE experiences. One fourth-grade girl reported,

> I like mindfulness because it helps me focus on important stuff, not minor details. If I feel a lot of feelings at once, and I'm confused, your mindfulness training helps me sort it out. It feels like I'm in my own world, and I can hear nothing but my own thoughts, and everything seems to be clearer.

A fifth-grade boy offered,

> I like mindfulness a lot. I like it because it calms you down and helps you refocus on the task at hand. In the walking meditation, I challenge myself by looking around and then refocusing. I feel like I'm not really here, but I can feel everything going on around me. It really helps me with running. I can focus on my stride and I remember to breathe. It also helps me with my homework!

Other kids said, "I still get nervous at swim meets, but now I don't let it get the better of me," "I feel like I'm floating in a cloud," "I feel like a weight lifted from my head and I'm free," and "I feel like I've transformed. This is going to help me so much" (True Athlete Project, 2015).

Studies Around the World

Over the past several years, we have gotten inquiries about MSPE from people around the world and have shared our protocol with colleagues in Brazil, Holland, Iran, and Australia as well as in the United States. For example, psychologist Cheree Murrihy at Monash University in Melbourne, Australia, and her colleague Maria Bailey, a psychologist and tennis coach, contacted us in 2015 to say they were interested in using our MSPE program. They plan to conduct training with youth tennis players and collect pre–post data on the effectiveness of the program. We hope that the dissemination of the MSPE protocol in this book will support and encourage even more research with athletes and coaches from different countries and cultures.

Future Directions for MSPE Research

As we reviewed in Chapter 2 and pointed out again at the beginning of this chapter, the literature on mindfulness-based interventions for athletic performers is sorely in need of studies that are more methodologically rigorous. In addition to using well-validated outcome measures, it is important to have programs led by well-trained and experienced individuals, with manualized replicable treatments, checks for treatment adherence, objective measures of sport performance, and perhaps brain imaging and psychophysiological assessments. For the future, studies with larger samples conducted by new investigators are crucial, as is the inclusion of both short- and long-term follow-ups and in-depth qualitative (as well as quantitative) research.

Large-scale RCTs with methodological rigor comparing MSPE with other active treatments with demonstrated efficacy (e.g., psychological skills training based on cognitive–behavioral therapy and other mindfulness-based interventions such as the MAC approach) are clearly an important direction for the future. Other important questions concern what both the "active ingredients" and moderators of change are in MSPE (i.e., do athletes with certain characteristics benefit more than others?), to what extent the inclusion of formal meditation practice is crucial for the program to have an impact, and whether similar or different processes (e.g., increases in trait mindfulness, decentering, experiential acceptance) mediate change in MSPE compared with other mindfulness-based approaches for athletes. Further investigation of the mechanisms of change involved in MSPE and tests of our conceptualization of the role of the five core performance facilitators (discussed in Chapter 10) will help to revise and expand upon this model.

However, it is also important to conduct more effectiveness studies in real-world athletic settings (e.g., with high school teams, within college athletic departments) where rigorous controls may be less possible but where the success of MSPE can be tested under conditions similar to how applied sport psychologists or coaches will implement it. Single-subject designs involving training a participant one-on-one in MSPE could also more closely resemble real-world applications. In addition, adapting

MSPE for use with other types of performers such as musicians and actors would be a valuable contribution (see Chapter 14).

Mindfulness is now increasingly introduced for children in elementary and middle schools. Teachers across the United States and around the world have received training in mindfulness to be able to introduce it into their classrooms, and organizations have gone directly into the schools to teach mindfulness to students (as well as to teachers, administrators, counselors, and parents). In addition, more and more books and research on mindfulness for children and adolescents are appearing (e.g., Kallapiran, Koo, Kirubakaran, & Hancock, 2015; Willard & Saltzman, 2015). In light of this growing interest, continuing to adapt MSPE for use with youth recreational and elite athletes is an important future direction.

As we stressed earlier, questions also exist regarding best practice in program delivery. Do participants benefit to a similar degree from MSPE training conducted in group format versus individually? Is MSPE more effective with intact teams where attendance is required versus groups with interested participants who may represent a range of sports? How important is coach involvement in MSPE? Are certain mindfulness exercises or concepts in MSPE most helpful based on participants' specific sports (e.g., coactive vs. interactive), needs (e.g., recovering from injury), or the particular times they are applied (e.g., during practice, before performance, during performance, after a game)? How many training sessions and how much home practice is needed for participants to experience significant change, and how is adherence to home practice best assessed?

The MSPE protocol provided in this book will assist sport psychologists and other researchers to continue to add to the empirical literature on its efficacy and effectiveness. Of course, we also recognize that any research is valid only insofar as the program is followed and implemented as intended. As such, equipping MSPE participants and leaders with tools to get the most out of the program could significantly help the cause of demonstrating the true potential of this intervention, and the next two chapters address how maximum benefit can be achieved.

Tips for Participants
Getting the Most Out of MSPE

12

Having reached this point in the book, our hope is that you are getting excited about how mindful sport performance enhancement (MSPE) could enhance experiences in and outside of sport and have even started thinking about ways to build a mindfulness practice of your own (if you don't have one already). Perhaps you are considering incorporating MSPE or mindfulness into your work with athletes or are an athlete who wants to complete the training personally. Our intent in this chapter is to give you a sense of the kinds of motivational challenges to expect when learning mindfulness skills, while offering specific suggestions for overcoming those challenges.

We absolutely want to nurture any enthusiasm you might be feeling, but we also caution that, as when learning anything else in life, the road to mindful performance typically takes time and effort. Meditation practice has been characterized as simultaneously simplicity itself and the hardest work in the world, necessitating a high degree of motivation (Kabat-Zinn, 1994, 2005a). So, without the willingness and commitment to make the necessary investment, this endeavor can become just like any other activity that had once sparked your interest but is now gathering dust in your proverbial closet. In his bestselling *Magicians* series, Lev Grossman (2011) spoke to this familiar

http://dx.doi.org/10.1037/0000048-013
Mindful Sport Performance Enhancement: Mental Training for Athletes and Coaches, by K. A. Kaufman, C. R. Glass, and T. R. Pineau

pattern of initial motivation fading upon realization of the actual effort involved in skill development, through the musings of his protagonist on learning to fence:

> The beginning, the laying down of the fundamentals, was always the worst part, which he supposed was why so few people did it. That was the thing about the world: it wasn't that things were harder than you thought they were going to be, it was that they were hard in ways that you didn't expect. (pp. 97–98)

Peter Haberl (personal communication, August 18, 2015), a senior sport psychologist with the United States Olympic Committee who has made mindfulness training a big part of what he does with his athletes in Colorado Springs, highlighted the importance of such transparency to a program's success, explaining how "mindfulness is often misunderstood. It is hard work and takes effort to acquire the skills and use them in competition. People tend to be looking for a 'quick fix,' but mindfulness is not that."

As we discussed in Chapter 1, resolving the mental training paradox that currently exists in sport psychology is essential to harnessing the power available through MSPE and may take special resolve when dealing with something outside-the-box and often stigmatized, such as meditation. To date, mindfulness experts from across the spectrum have been remarkably consistent in their recommendations on cultivating a robust practice, with the big three tips being (a) find a time, (b) make a commitment, and (c) create a space (e.g., Ameli, 2014; Kabat-Zinn, 1990). Finding a time involves identifying a daily window for practice, making a commitment means selecting a challenging but reasonable goal for practice you can recommit to periodically, and creating a space entails making room for practice in your life both literally and figuratively.

We share these tips about sustaining practice at the conclusion of MSPE (see Chapter 9) but explore these suggestions here at a deeper level. Surprisingly, given how much has been written recently about mindfulness, few links to behavioral science principles have been offered when guiding participants on how to build a high-quality sustainable practice. Thus, we delved into the literature on habit, willpower, intrinsic motivation, deliberate practice, and mindset to provide meaningful tools for constructing a practice, staying with it, and ultimately getting the most out of MSPE. In addition, we spoke with several highly regarded mindfulness experts and sport psychologists on this topic and include their perspectives as well.

Finding a Time

Rezvan Ameli (personal communication, August 28, 2015), a clinical psychologist, mindfulness teacher, and author of *25 Lessons in Mindfulness: Now Time for Healthy Living* (2014), commented that "making time to practice is the hardest part" of learning mindfulness. This statement is consistent with our observation that perceived lack of time is the most common explanation given by MSPE participants for why they do not practice, both during the training and in the months after it ends (e.g., Thompson, Kaufman, De Petrillo, Glass, & Arnkoff, 2011). In her *TIME Magazine* cover story on the "mindful revolution," Pickert (2014) suggested that because we live in an era of technological hyperconnectivity, where it can feel impossible to take breaks or fully inhabit a task at hand, there is a perpetual sense of not having enough time to accomplish all that we want or need to do. She proposed that mindfulness can provide an antidote to this perspective, precisely because its practice challenges us to slow down, unplug, and make time for the kind of focused attention necessary for the optimal experience of an activity. Of course, this antidote only has potency if we can meet that challenge and actually prioritize mindfulness practice.

We have little doubt that people already have crowded schedules, and being asked to add another item to one's to-do list can feel quite daunting. As a solution to this problem of perceived lack of time, Kabat-Zinn (1990) advised mindfulness practitioners to establish a *conscious intentionality*—in other words, a purposefully set goal to practice each day regardless of mood, energy level, or other obligations. Interestingly, Kabat-Zinn compared this brand of determination with that employed by athletes in their physical training. He claimed that, just as with top athletes preparing their bodies for competition, intentional scheduling and priority rearrangement is required to free up the time needed for mindfulness practice. For this reason, he noted that participating in a mindfulness training program can sometimes increase stress in a person's life in the short run, a phenomenon we have also observed in our MSPE groups.

One piece of conscious intentionality that we wish to emphasize is the importance of writing an intention down and posting it in a salient location (e.g., the space established for your mindfulness practice). Taking these steps can help an intention feel more tangible and provide a useful prompt so that it does not get swept away in the flood of daily activities. Research suggests that prompts are most effective when certain guidelines are followed: They are specific, visible, and available immediately before a target behavior is needed; remind users of the desired consequences; and trigger behavior that can be followed by reinforcement (van Houten, 1998).

An element of conscious intentionality that Kabat-Zinn has discussed (e.g., 1990, 1994, 2012) is identifying a particular time that works best for mindfulness practice and then protecting it. He has recommended the early morning as an ideal time for meditation because the rush of the world has not yet launched (Kabat-Zinn, 1994) and suggested adhering to the chosen time for a minimum of 6 months to allow this new habit to take hold (Kabat-Zinn, 2012). Tara Brach (personal communication, September 29, 2015), a world-renowned psychologist, author, and teacher of mindfulness meditation, similarly spoke to the importance of "getting a habit going so you can just assume that [the practice] is a part of your life" by "each day, dedicating at least a short time to simply paying attention to your moment-to-moment experience." She shared the example of a woman who had struggled to find time to practice but prepared tea every morning and eventually was able to use the moments while waiting for her tea to cool to get in touch with her present moment. Although a longer practice later developed, "it was important that [the woman] realize that even a few short moments could begin to bring her back to presence." This use of tea-making as a prompt for mindfulness practice brings to mind the Premack Principle, which states that engaging in a higher-probability act (drinking tea) after performing a lower-probability one (practicing mindfulness) can reinforce and strengthen the lower probability (less frequent) behavior (Premack, 1965). Whatever opportunities an individual can seize to be present are "perfect" and "count as daily practice," Brach said.

Repeating mindfulness practice behaviors to the point that they become habitual appears to be a key to overcoming the barrier of perceived lack of time, so we are now going to dig further into the science of habit formation. For this discussion, it is important to keep in mind the difference between the automaticity associated with executing mindfulness habits and the "mindlessness" of performing activities without any attention or awareness (i.e., autopilot).

HABITS

As Tara Brach (personal communication, September 29, 2015) explained, "the science is out there in terms of what [mindfulness] can do for you," but the mind is not "designed to have this [type of practice] be easy. Evolutionarily, [especially] when we get stressed, [meditating] is the last thing we want to do. It takes bravery to pause and be with [what] we habitually avoid." Part of what she meant by *bravery* in this context is the ability to overcome our default tendencies when trying to install a new behavior, something that can be quite difficult or scary early on in the process, even when we know that the new behavior is good for us. Charles Duhigg (2012) wrote what has become a definitive source on the science of habit formation, *The Power of Habit: Why We Do What We Do in Life and Business*, in which he claimed that there are literally dozens of behaviors we ought to perform every day that never catch on as habits. He cited the example of applying sunscreen, saying it is common knowledge that dabbing a bit of sunscreen on your face each morning significantly lowers the odds of skin cancer, yet fewer than 10% of Americans engage in this routine. One focus of Duhigg's book is on trying to understand why this strange phenomenon is so prevalent, and his explanation may be useful to MSPE participants as they try to establish a habit of mindfulness practice.

Duhigg (2012) described habit formation as a three-step process, or loop, in the brain. First, there is a cue, which triggers the brain to respond. Then, there is a routine, which is a physical, mental, or emotional response to the cue. Finally, there is a reward, which helps determine whether a particular loop is worth remembering for the future. Over time, this loop becomes increasingly automatic and the cue and reward become linked, so that a powerful sense of anticipation or craving emerges. According to Duhigg, the craving ultimately drives the loop (and can do so even to the exclusion of common sense), so one must deliberately fight against it to disrupt the pattern. To most effectively engage in this battle, he recommended keeping the familiar cue and reward but both inserting a new routine and understanding the craving that is propelling the system. Duhigg cited the example of smoking cessation: Smokers identify the cues and rewards they associate with cigarettes and then choose a new routine that gives a similar payoff, which can make it more likely that they will quit.

So, what are the implications for MSPE participants struggling to make time for mindfulness practice? Well, odds are that some entrenched habit loops are impeding their capacity to make a fully conscious choice in certain circumstances (similar to the impact of attachments as we discuss in MSPE). As a participant, perhaps you can examine your daily schedule to see where being mindful might better deliver the reward (e.g., relaxation, focus, positive emotions) you are craving. For instance, maybe one of the first things you see each evening upon coming home is your computer screen, which prompts you to sit and unwind for a bit by checking your e-mail and social networking accounts. In this case, the screen is your cue, wanting to unwind is the craved reward, and checking your accounts is the routine you are using (likely without even thinking about it) to achieve that state. A potential problem with this routine, however, is that online engagement of this nature tends to be stimulating rather than relaxing and exerts a powerful hold over users. This can lead to spending more time online than intended, sometimes further exacerbating stress (Hair, Renaud, & Ramsay, 2007).

Recognition that the cued routine is not producing the desired reward could free you up to substitute mindfulness practice as a new, more effective routine. Suddenly, a time slot and clear incentive are available. To help with this transition, Duhigg (2012) advised deliberately planning for the cue and the preferable response, which is often called *developing implementation intentions* (e.g., Gantman, Gollwitzer, & Oettingen, 2014). This process is very similar to what we talk about in MSPE as *forming associations*. Rezvan Ameli (personal communication, August 28, 2015) described how helpful visual or auditory reminders can be to mindfulness practitioners, such as chimes that can be set to go off on a computer. So, knowing that you will see your computer screen and that you are trying to build a routine of mindfulness practice, perhaps you could schedule such a chime to ring on your computer at around the time you usually arrive home. Thus, you are promoting a different habit loop that maintains the cue and reward but involves a new routine that actually brings about what is craved. Repetition of this plan will strengthen the connections between habit loop components, eventually making it feel easier and more natural to choose to practice mindfulness.

WILLPOWER

Duhigg (2012) suggested that a critical factor in being able to choose a new routine over a default one is willpower. Baumeister (2002) characterized willpower as analogous to self-regulation, operating like a strength or energy reserve. As Baltzell (2011) explained, the limits to this energy reserve are why it can be so difficult to get ourselves to consistently do what we know we "should" to benefit our health and performance. In other words, it is why we cannot "just do it," as Nike urges (Baltzell, 2011). Willpower depletes with even brief and minor self-control exertions (Baumeister, 2002) and may drain still faster when the endeavor is challenging or unfamiliar (Baltzell, 2011), as is often the case when altering a habit loop. The good news, as Baumeister observed, is that the resources expended by acts of self-control do slowly replenish, most notably through rest and the experience of positive emotions.

The takeaway here is that making time for mindfulness practice consistently enough for it to become habitual requires sufficient willpower. Thus, it is important to monitor willpower level because, once it runs out, it will be very hard to fight against the default routine in place (e.g., checking your online accounts in the previous example). Perhaps this is one reason why Kabat-Zinn has found it so effective to target early morning hours for meditation. Willpower has had a chance to regenerate with sleep, and there has not yet been much need to exert self-control. If a later hour is preferred, it might be strategic to allot time for a regenerative activity before settling into practice. In our groups, we have seen that the odds of finding a time to practice go way down when participants try to cram it in while leapfrogging through daily obligations.

Whereas the construct of willpower has been criticized for being too dispositional (someone either has it or doesn't) and thus potentially undermining of self-control efforts (e.g., Thoresen & Mahoney, 1974), more recent conceptualizations have compared its functioning to a muscle (e.g., Baltzell, 2011; Baumeister, 2002) that can be strengthened. Duhigg (2012) proposed that the optimal way to strengthen this "muscle" is to make willpower itself into a habit through the use of inflection points. He defined *inflection points* as times when unexpected obstacles emerge; if one plans for how a desired routine could follow such an obstacle, willpower is taxed less when the obstacle arises. This conservation occurs because it is easier to respond to something when you already know what to do. Duhigg shared the example of employees who are taught to recognize inflection points such as overwhelmed customers and then to follow preestablished protocols for calming them. Thus, the desired routine (store protocol) follows more seamlessly (drains less willpower) from the unexpected circumstance (customer melting down).

With regard to mindfulness practice, maybe an MSPE participant could choose ahead of time how to respond upon waking up in the morning and not feeling like meditating or, returning to our earlier example, how to respond upon arriving home and hearing the computer chime but recalling the need to write an urgent e-mail. Preparing in this way can allow the habit of willpower to protect a mindfulness practice from all of the demands that can so easily intrude.

One other way to reduce the load on our willpower muscle is to remember that finding time for mindfulness practice is a personal choice, not an imposition coming from the outside. Feeling you "should" or "have to" practice to please another likely will deplete willpower far more quickly and result in not practicing, whereas taking ownership of this practice as something you want to do for your own reasons will make the decision much easier (Duhigg, 2012; Standage & Ryan, 2012). The nature of one's motivation to learn mindfulness is a strong determinant of what can ultimately be gained from MSPE and is the subject of our next recommendation.

Making a Commitment

Kabat-Zinn (1990) described the attitude necessary to optimize the experience of his mindfulness program as *engaged commitment*, which means choosing to practice every day, no matter the conditions, just for the sake of practicing because it is what you want to do for yourself. He shared his observation that some people have resistance to the idea of doing something only for themselves with no ulterior purpose, which is perhaps an artifact of the Puritan ethic. Yet, it is exactly the prioritization of self that enables us to commit fully to establishing a practice. The word *selfish* has earned such a negative connotation that we have witnessed MSPE participants become visibly uncomfortable when this notion has arisen in group discussions. It therefore seems important to differentiate selfishness in the sense of disregarding or exploiting others from simply acknowledging that you, your well-being, and your success are quite important and deserving of being a priority. Without the latter brand of selfishness, how can you adequately take care of yourself or get the most out of your efforts?

In his book *Drive: The Surprising Truth About What Motivates Us*, Pink (2009) indicated that behavioral science has identified three main drives powering human behavior: biological urges such as hunger and sex, the external environment in the form of rewards and punishments, and our internal desire to do a task merely because we enjoy it. He suggested that this third drive, often referred to as *intrinsic motivation*, is the secret to highest level performance toward a chosen goal. Interestingly, this secret is one we appear to know when we are young and primarily motivated by having fun and personal growth, as Ewing and Seefeldt (1989) found regarding participation in sports. However, as we get older, the consequences of our endeavors, such as winning, praise, and money, become more alluring.

Summarizing the prevailing sentiment on this topic in sport science research, Pink (2009) claimed that intrinsically motivated people usually achieve more than do their reward-seeking counterparts, largely because a predominantly extrinsic (external) focus neglects the key ingredients to "genuine" motivation: autonomy, mastery, and purpose. In fact, contrary to early hypotheses viewing intrinsic and extrinsic motivation as additive (the more of each the better), it appears that, in many cases, the more a person is extrinsically motivated, the less that person will be intrinsically motivated (e.g., deCharms, 1968; Weinberg & Gould, 2015). For example, Deci (1972) found that people who were rewarded with money for participating in an interesting activity ended up spending less time doing that activity than did people who were not paid.

The implications for MSPE participants are clear. Successfully committing and recommitting to goals pertaining to the development of a mindfulness practice routine involve overcoming hangups about being selfish and getting in touch with personal reasons for wanting to learn these skills. These reasons may be independent from externally derived values or outcomes, such as from a coach, parent, teammate, or even a mindfulness instructor. Connecting with this personal motivation makes it much more likely that a routine will be fulfilling and thus resilient. To further illustrate what an intrinsically motivated mindful athlete or coach looks like, we explore each of the three factors that Pink (2009) identified as essential ingredients to genuine motivation: autonomy, mastery, and purpose.

AUTONOMY

When one looks at children, it is evident that the nature of human beings is to be curious and self-directed, but this disposition gets challenged with the rise to prominence of extrinsic motivators (Pink, 2009). The importance of feeling empowered to make our own choices is captured in a well-supported model of motivation called *self-determination theory* (SDT; Deci & Ryan, 1985), which lists autonomy as the most crucial of basic human needs. SDT describes a continuum of motivation based on level of autonomy, ranging from autonomous (intrinsic) to controlled (extrinsic). In general, autonomous motivation has been linked with better learning, performance, persistence, productivity, and well-being as well as less burnout (e.g., Buckworth, Dishman, O'Connor, & Tomporowski, 2013).

Within SDT's continuum of motivation are gradations of extrinsic motivation, varying in the degree that a motive is reflective of one's interests and values. The least autonomous type is called *external regulation*, which occurs when someone has no personal investment in an activity that is done merely as a means toward an end. The most autonomous type of extrinsic motivation is called *integrated regulation*, which happens when a person recognizes the social value of an activity but has also found personal value in it and sees it as congruent with his or her other life values. According to SDT, as one moves toward internalization (i.e., toward greater autonomy), the quality of motivation improves (e.g., Buckworth et al., 2013; Rigby, Schultz, & Ryan, 2014). This knowledge seems to be embedded in the mindfulness literature, as Kabat-Zinn (2005a) identified the quality of motivation (i.e., the degree of ardor brought to it) as the most significant support for a mindfulness practice.

We think that considering the commitment made to mindfulness practice from an SDT perspective could be quite useful for MSPE participants. Yes, being purely intrinsically motivated is ideal, but the reality is that most people probably choose to pursue MSPE to get something else out of the training. As Tara Brach said (personal communication, September 29, 2015), the Western ego is programmed to be directed toward the external benefits of mindfulness practice, and that is not necessarily a bad thing. Mindfulness practitioners can "begin with a focus on losing weight, increasing mental focus, or reducing stress, and discover in the process the deeper benefits of becoming more intimate with themselves and . . . others."

Baltzell (2011) coined the term *motivational flexibility* to describe the ability to shift between intrinsic and extrinsic motivation purposefully as necessary, shifting between doing an activity simply for the joy of it and doing an activity because it will help achieve some valued extrinsic goal. This last piece is the key for MSPE participants to remember. It is perfectly natural for extrinsic motives (e.g., gaining a competitive advantage, wanting to please a coach) to be an element of the commitment to practice mindfulness, but it is very important for those motives to be as internalized as possible (e.g., finding personal value in pleasing your coach), so that both a sense of autonomy and the overall quality of motivation to practice are maximized.

MASTERY

Pink (2009) explained that the opposite of autonomy is feeling controlled. Feeling controlled breeds compliance, whereas autonomy generates engagement. It is this engagement (also highlighted by Kabat-Zinn) that feeds the second element of genuine motivation, which is mastery, the desire to get better at a personally meaningful task. Pink did not romanticize mastery. Instead, he characterized it as a long, grueling process that involves a ton of work and sometimes little to show for it over stretches of time. Most strikingly, he compared mastery to an asymptote, which you can approach but never quite reach. So, for truly motivated people, both the quest for and elusiveness of mastery are attractive. In other words, for the intrinsically driven, it is more about the pursuit and process than the realization of outcome.

Psychologist K. Anders Ericsson has conducted groundbreaking research on the pursuit of expert performance, and his work has shed new light on what facilitates mastery. As discussed in Chapter 10, mastery does not automatically happen through the accumulation of experience. Rather, it is the result of sustained (sometimes up to 10 years for the highest levels of achievement), intentional engagement, with full concentration (sounds very mindful), in an activity to improve one's performance, or what Ericsson called *deliberate practice* (Ericsson, Krampe, & Tesch-Römer, 1993). The notion that expertise develops gradually over a long period, up to a decade, is cited throughout achievement domains such as sport (e.g., Epstein, 2013). Ericsson and colleagues specified that deliberate practice is hard, and not always fun, but is a highly effective way to journey toward expertise.

The message here to MSPE participants is that finding value in being mindful as an end in itself, and thus wanting to improve these skills to the point of expertise (like they already may desire to do in their sport), is an extremely powerful way to commit to a mindfulness practice. The process involved, as highlighted by Peter Haberl (personal communication, August 18, 2015), is not a quick or easy one, so patience and discipline are required, likely over a period of several years as Ericsson's work suggests.

Rezvan Ameli (personal communication, August 28, 2015) shared that a barrier she "comes up against a lot" as a mindfulness instructor is the "culture of immediate gratification" in our society. She stated that "by definition, [mindfulness training] is a slow process. It's important to educate people about [this truth] very quickly, that this is a growing process." Tara Brach (personal communication, September 29, 2015) similarly said that one of the biggest reasons she sees people abandoning their practice is the feeling of not doing it right or of not getting what they "should" out of it. George Mumford has become well known through his work with some of Phil Jackson's National Basketball Association (NBA) championship teams, and he claimed in his 2015 book that one of the major challenges in mindfulness training is resisting the assumption that, if there are no immediate results, it does not work. He compared the process of mindfulness training to planting seeds in the sense that, when they first sprout, they are under the surface, invisible to the naked eye, but, with proper attention and care, they can grow and eventually bear fruit.

Even though deliberate practice is not necessarily fun, there is something to be said for trying to enjoy the process of learning a new skill set. Kabat-Zinn (1990) linked this capacity to maintaining the *beginner's mind*, a mind that remains open and curious, willing to see everything as if for the first time. Pink (2009) commented that, as beginners, kids tend to use their brains and bodies to probe and obtain feedback from their environments in an endless pursuit of mastery, but, for some reason, this pattern diminishes as we get older. He described a conversation he had with flow expert Mihaly Csikszentmihalyi, who attributed this phenomenon to the adult perception that pursuing an activity just for the joy of it, what he has termed *autotelic experience*, is childish and therefore something to feel ashamed of. Recognizing this potential bias and reconnecting with the pleasures of growth and mastery can help MSPE participants truly engage in this training.

PURPOSE

Pink (2009) claimed that autonomous people pursuing mastery perform at very high levels. However, those individuals who do so in the service of some greater objective can achieve even more. The most deeply motivated, productive, and satisfied people, he said, attach their ambitions to a cause with significant personal meaning. This line of thinking suggests that an MSPE participant who, for example, is seeking to become more mindful and improve the quality of his or her life may commit to this way of being more effectively than might a participant ultimately looking for an extrinsic reward such as someone else's approval. It may be particularly important for generally high-functioning individuals such as athletes to identify a meaningful purpose of their mindfulness training. As Rezvan Ameli (personal communication, August 28, 2015) mentioned, "getting started in practice is never easy and there is not [necessarily] that desperation [in athletes]" that one can see when bringing mindfulness to a group that, for example, is suffering from debilitating, chronic pain.

As one goes through and beyond MSPE, it may therefore be important to consider carefully what goals have the most value (i.e., why are you doing all of this?). Gantman et al. (2014) called such a process *mindful goal selection*, consciously deciding on and committing to an intention. Kabat-Zinn (1990) described it as a necessary step of finding a personal vision, with no wrong place to begin. As Rezvan Ameli (personal communication, August 28, 2015) said, "there is no one recipe for all. Wherever you start is perfect." Reiterating an earlier point, the one guideline we strongly suggest adhering to is writing goals down, whatever they are, and posting them somewhere visible. Doing so has a way of solidifying them and can serve as a helpful reminder of purpose while on the long road toward skill development. It might even be beneficial to redraft goals periodically, such as at the beginning of the training, following the last session, and after a few weeks of post-MSPE practice, to keep the commitment fresh and salient.

Creating a Space

Creating a space for mindfulness practice is a recommendation that can have multiple meanings. It can literally mean finding a physical location to do daily practice, such as a place in a home or office. Important considerations for choosing a location include having consistent access to it, feeling comfortable and safe in it, and being able to limit the likelihood of disturbances while practicing there. It can also be helpful when creating this space to find ways to make it special or personally meaningful, for instance by posting reminders of your intention to practice (e.g., a sticky note with your personal-best competition time or placement). Although we feel making a physical space can be important to the development of a regular practice and we highlight this in our tips for continued practice in the final MSPE session, this recommendation can also have a more figurative meaning, in the sense of opening oneself up to learning something entirely new and different. This latter meaning—cultivating an attitude that makes an inner space for mindfulness—is our focus here.

Kabat-Zinn (1990) suggested that the attitude brought to the practice of mindfulness will, to a large extent, determine its long-term value. Skepticism is natural and often even beneficial, as long as individuals are open to trying their best and seeing what happens. It is when the mind is open and receptive that learning and change occur. Peter Haberl (personal communication, August 18, 2015) indicated that this idea has heavily influenced his work, and he encourages Olympic-level athletes to approach mindfulness training with a skeptical but open-minded attitude.

A very common question that comes up in any training program, whether in sport or in another domain, is "Am I doing it right?" Certainly, MSPE participants ask this question all the time, and we like to respond by saying, in mindfulness, there is no right or wrong. There is only *what is*. Kabat-Zinn (1990) similarly wrote that his briefest response to this question of doing it right is that, if a person is aware of what is happening, then he or she is doing it right, no matter what the circumstance. This notion that there is no right way to practice mindfulness can be quite liberating once participants wrap their minds around it. However, we have observed that, at least at first, it can be disconcerting for participants when they are overly concerned with being correct or avoiding a mistake, as many of us tend to be in achievement-oriented situations. As alluded to earlier, Tara Brach (personal communication, September 29, 2015) does a lot of work around such judgments in her trainings because she has seen that they are the biggest reason people quit. Echoing this sentiment, Salmon, Santorelli, Sephton, and Kabat-Zinn (2009) said that paying nonjudgmental attention to the practice of mindfulness itself—in other words, applying a mindful attitude to participating in a mindfulness training—makes it less likely that doubts or feelings of inadequacy about performance will adversely affect adherence to the training.

Making this kind of open-minded, nonjudgmental space for mindfulness practice can be a major facilitator of getting the most out of MSPE. Pink (2009) linked this mindset, which prioritizes learning over result, to the pursuit of mastery. Psychologist Carol Dweck has emerged as a leading researcher on achievement motivation, specifically the role that one's mindset plays in excellence. In her 2006 book, she differentiated a fixed mindset, characterized by beliefs that abilities are carved in stone and achievement situations bring the threat of inadequacy, from a growth mindset, in which preexisting talent is just a starting point for development through effort and learning. She said that the passion for stretching oneself and hanging in, even or especially when it is not going well (sounds a lot like dwelling at limits as we describe it in MSPE), is the hallmark of the growth mindset and leads to superior coping with challenges, belief in effort, resilience in the face of setbacks, and greater odds of success. The good news, according to Dweck, is that mindsets are just beliefs and beliefs are changeable. Thus, when operating from a fixed mindset and saying things such as "This has to work" or "I can't do this right," one has the choice to step back from it, see oneself and one's budding mindfulness skills as works in progress, and reapproach practice in a way that emphasizes growth and learning (Dweck, 2006).

An article by McGinn (2015) detailed how Michael Jordan and Kobe Bryant shifted their mindsets, making a space for mindfulness in their careers while working with George Mumford. Jordan had just quit baseball and returned to the NBA when Mumford introduced him to a more mindful way of leading his team. Initially, Jordan was quite skeptical, but he gradually began to understand the significance of learning to focus and perform in the present moment. Through the work he was doing, Jordan started to play more unselfishly, and the Chicago Bulls players realized how Mumford's approach was transforming the dynamics of their team. Now, Mumford recalls Michael Jordan as one of his best students.

When coach Phil Jackson moved from Chicago to the Los Angeles Lakers in 1999, he similarly had that team work with Mumford, and the same pattern of player skepticism followed by acceptance emerged. With guidance from Jackson and Mumford, meditation became an essential part of game preparation for Kobe Bryant and his then-teammate Shaquille O'Neal. According to a memorable quote from Roland Lazenby, a veteran NBA writer who authored biographies of both Jackson and Jordan, "There weren't a lot of things that Shaq and Kobe agreed on, but they both agreed on the effectiveness of George Mumford" (McGinn, 2015).

Jackson built dynasties with the Bulls and Lakers, and the space made for Mumford and mindfulness training was key. The journeys of these teams illustrate the success that can come from remaining open-minded, nonjudgmental, and growth-oriented regarding this different manner of training in the face of perfectly natural skepticism. As individuals are progressing through and beyond MSPE, we suggest examining attitudes toward the practice and seeing where additional room can be made for this new, and in some ways unconventional, method of preparing for and being in one's sport.

Conclusion

MSPE has the potential to change fundamentally the ways in which participants train and perform, allowing them to reach greater heights in athletic achievement and enjoyment. However, as when learning any new skill set, it is necessary to work at it to see real benefit. If enthusiasm wanes as this reality sets in, or it is a struggle to incorporate mindfulness into a daily routine, please know that this is quite common. We encourage participants to keep at it and to find a time, make a commitment, and create a space using the principles laid out in this chapter.

One of the reasons we designed MSPE as a group intervention is that it can often be easier to accomplish these objectives while part of a supportive community. A consistent observation that came up in our discussions with mindfulness experts such as Rezvan Ameli and Tara Brach is how helpful having a community can be for finding accountability and the discipline to practice. So, at any point, it may be advisable to link up with a group, a few friends, or even just one practice buddy who can help you along this path (and vice versa).

In the next chapter, we turn the tables and explore how MSPE leaders can be most effective in delivering the training.

Tips for Leaders
Enhancing the Effectiveness of MSPE

13

T his chapter begins with a cautionary tale of an experience we had training a team of collegiate runners in mindful sport performance enhancement (MSPE) that went poorly. In many ways, this experience provides
a checklist of what not to do when leading MSPE groups. We share
it here because the mistakes made and the obstacles that arose highlight
several of the lessons we have learned along the way about how best to
implement MSPE, as well as what is necessary to be an effective MSPE leader.
This example reflects the myriad skills required to be, all at once, a mindfulness practitioner, a mindfulness teacher, a group leader, an expert on sport
and performance, and (in this instance) a researcher. Whether you are a
sport psychologist, exercise scientist, psychotherapist, coach, or researcher,
or are in any other position in which you could be interested in offering
MSPE, it is important to recognize that a number of skill sets and knowledge
bases intersect in your role as an MSPE leader. Throughout this chapter, we
share what these skill sets are, review some of the unique challenges often
faced when working within the culture of athletics, and suggest strategies for
building the necessary competence to make sure MSPE participants get the
most out of their training. First, however, let us share our cautionary tale.

http://dx.doi.org/10.1037/0000048-014
Mindful Sport Performance Enhancement: Mental Training for Athletes and Coaches, by K. A. Kaufman,
C. R. Glass, and T. R. Pineau

A Cautionary Tale

After we had expanded MSPE from four to six sessions and made other significant modifications (described in Chapter 11), we were interested in examining empirically whether the program had been strengthened (Pineau, 2014). We targeted intact cross-country teams instead of using self-selected community samples as we had in previous studies. After getting institutional review board (IRB) approval, we were able to recruit two National Collegiate Athletic Association (NCAA) Division I teams to participate, with one team receiving MSPE and the other serving as a control. The team receiving MSPE was randomly split into two groups to see the effect of infusing even more self-compassion language into the exercises. Group leaders were our coauthors, Tim Pineau and Keith Kaufman.

A number of research-related considerations affected how this iteration of MSPE was carried out. To maintain the integrity of the program, the coach agreed to six weekly 90-minute sessions for his team, who were in-season at the time. Also, our contact with the team was limited to one introductory meeting, the six MSPE sessions, and times for data collection. Because only one time block on a single day of the week was available for both intervention groups, Tim and Keith traded off which of the two groups they led each week of the program to protect against facilitator effects. In addition, our IRB was concerned that having team coaches present at sessions could feel coercive to the athletes, so only the runners attended. With regard to recruitment, although there were benefits to working with intact teams (perhaps a more realistic reflection of how MSPE can be implemented), having the coach prescribe MSPE as part of regular-season training meant that the athletes had not independently expressed prior interest in learning about mindfulness, which may have impacted intrinsic motivation and commitment (see Chapter 12 for a discussion of the importance of these factors for MSPE participants).

Other, nonresearch factors also impacted how these groups were administered. Perhaps the most significant of these was the meeting space on the team's campus. Despite great efforts to secure a more appropriate location, the sessions were held in open-concourse areas of the university's large indoor arena. This loud, public setting resulted in frequent interruptions from the basketball team's practices and various individuals (e.g., custodial staff) walking through.

All of these factors combined to severely limit the effectiveness of MSPE with this team. Although the coaching staff accommodated our need for 90-minute meetings by replacing one afternoon practice each week with our training, they did not want the team to sacrifice any physical work, so an early-morning practice was added on the days of our meetings, leaving the athletes worn out by our late-afternoon sessions. In fact, several athletes noted in postworkshop feedback that the training could have been improved had it been held at a different time. Furthermore, although our attempts to maintain internal validity were methodologically sound by research standards, having Tim and Keith switch between the two intervention groups each week with no contact with the team outside of MSPE sessions made it harder for the athletes to develop a rapport with us as leaders, which likely detracted from their willingness to embrace MSPE. This lack of rapport manifested in the team's general lack of compliance with the home practice and, toward the end of the program, a few athletes even flatly refusing to participate in certain exercises. The icing on the proverbial cake was that, for budgetary reasons, the men's cross-country team was eliminated as a varsity sport at that university during the time the study was being conducted, which undoubtedly affected the athletes and their motivation for the training.

The absence of coach support similarly undercut the momentum the training could have generated among the runners. Coaches were largely unaware of the session content and home practice recommendations. They thus had no opportunity to integrate MSPE concepts or exercises into team practices and were unable to promote home practice accountability. Finally, the highly public space and near-constant interruption and distraction interfered with the participants' efforts to learn a challenging new set of mental skills.

It probably won't surprise you to learn that, at the end of the study, we found no significant changes in the runners who received MSPE and no significant differences between the intervention team and the control team. Although these results were disappointing, we realized in hindsight that the intervention really hadn't stood a chance because of the wall of resistance we had run into. Specifically, we had encountered some relatively common challenges, such as squeezing time into athletes' packed schedules, securing an appropriate space, cultivating a rapport that breeds trust, and receiving strong support from the coaching staff, which any outsiders trying to work in an athletic environment may face. The additional constraints imposed by our IRB and research design exacerbated these hurdles.

Rather than being a true test of the efficacy of MSPE, this study actually seemed to show us the impact of the (albeit well-intentioned) mistakes we had made. As reviewed earlier in this book, other research has been supportive of MSPE and mindfulness-based interventions for athletes in general, but despite the lack of significant findings, we consider this early effort among our most valuable in terms of what we learned. We hope that this story, and the advice in this chapter, will be an informative guide for best practice in conducting MSPE.

Recently, other authors researching mindfulness-based interventions for athletes have similarly written about their lessons learned from real-world experiences, so we know we're in good company. For instance, Wolanin and Gross (2016) offered a cogent discussion of the challenges faced in implementing the mindfulness–acceptance–commitment (MAC) approach with collegiate athletes (see Chapter 2 for a description of MAC). They included suggestions for presenting the theoretical rationale to athletic departments and coaches, dealing with time constraints, introducing athletes to mindfulness concepts, and coping with logistical issues. Also, F. R. Goodman and Kashdan (2015) detailed their experience training student–athletes in mindfulness, hoping to provide guidance on how such interventions can be delivered most effectively.

In the remainder of this chapter, we explore further some of the most important elements to consider when leading MSPE trainings, including having a thorough understanding of the nature of mindfulness, working with groups, sport performance and athletic culture, and ethical considerations when working with athletes.

Mindfulness Is as Mindfulness Does: The Importance of the Mindful Teacher

An oft-quoted piece of wisdom is that the best way to learn something is to teach it. However, that advice does not hold when it comes to mindfulness. In fact, many authors who address the qualifications of a mindfulness teacher emphasize the absolute necessity of a deep familiarity with mindfulness, gained only through a regular, personal practice (e.g., R. S. Crane et al., 2012; Felder, Dimidjian, & Segal, 2012; Kabat-Zinn, 2011; Segal, Williams, & Teasdale, 2002). This notion was emphasized heavily by author and mindfulness teacher Rezvan Ameli, who said in an interview (personal communication, October 10, 2015) that "I don't think anybody who's not a practitioner should teach mindfulness. Unless you have the internal experience, you will not understand the questions. You will not be able to provide people with a genuine response."

MSPE is a mindfulness-based intervention, so conceptual and experiential knowledge of mindfulness is essential to implementing the training most effectively. Having your own experiences with mindfulness is necessary, not only because it provides you with the insights to respond to questions but also because it allows you to actively model the curiosity, warmth, and openness that most mindfulness programs teach (Felder et al., 2012). Furthermore, being mindful may be important for work with athletes generally, even outside the context of providing a mindfulness-based intervention. For instance, D. E. Williams and Andersen (2012) stressed the importance of sport psychologists staying grounded in mindful practice, and Andersen and Mannion (2011) proposed how the Buddhist concepts of attachment, suffering, desire, and understandings of the self (or rather "no self") can be applied to training sport psychologists.

In addition, because each athlete's experience with mindfulness is personal, it is impossible to predict precisely what will come up in any given session, so actually being mindful gives group leaders the capacity to respond to any present-moment experience not merely with conceptual knowledge but with intuition that arises from "the spaciousness of *not-knowing*" (Kabat-Zinn, 2011, p. 297). Segal et al. (2002) summed up this idea well by saying, "If the [leaders] themselves are not mindful as they teach, the extent to which [participants] can learn mindfulness will be limited" (p. 56). Importantly this level of familiarity with mindfulness doesn't come from just taking a couple of classes or reading some literature on the subject.

Rezvan Ameli (personal communication, October 10, 2015) echoed this sentiment, stating that "without the challenge of developing your own practice, you will not be able to guide others in theirs." She further suggested that longer meditation retreats can be an important part of this development. Kabat-Zinn (2011) made a similar point when he said, "I personally consider the periodic sitting of relatively long (at least 7–10 days and occasionally much longer) teacher-led retreats to be an absolute necessity in the developing of one's own meditation practice, understanding, and effectiveness as a teacher" (p. 296).

Kabat-Zinn's reference to "teacher-led" alludes to another component of development as a mindfulness practitioner—having one's own experienced guide. Working with a teacher (or guru) is often encouraged by Buddhist practitioners (e.g., McDonald, 2005), with the terms *consultant* or *supervisor* appearing frequently in the more secularized psychology literature (e.g., Kabat-Zinn et al., 2014). Rezvan Ameli (personal communication, October 10, 2015) proposed that coteaching a mindfulness course with a more experienced colleague is an ideal way to develop one's teaching skills, and getting supervision is among the good-practice guidelines offered by several organizations involved in mindfulness teacher training (e.g., Kabat-Zinn et al., 2014; UK Network for Mindfulness-Based Teachers, 2011).

It is important to note that these recommendations regarding having extensive personal experience with mindfulness represent the highest possible bar for preparation, rather than a set of minimum requirements for MSPE leaders. For example, it is probably not necessary to have attended a meditation retreat to run an MSPE group, but we do believe it is extremely important for anyone planning to teach mindfulness to have some prior experience with this type of practice, ideally involving both formal and informal exercises. Honest self-assessment of one's readiness to teach others these concepts is crucial, and R. S. Crane and colleagues (2012) offered a detailed approach to making this determination. However, having personal experience with mindfulness is not the only ingredient in being an effective MSPE leader.

More Than the Sum of Its Parts: Working With Groups

Like many other mindfulness-based interventions, MSPE is designed to be delivered to a group of participants. Certainly, it is possible to teach these skills one-on-one, but important elements of the training (particularly the discussion components) may then be limited. Learning mindfulness skills can evoke disparate reactions, and receiving training in a group setting can allow participants to benefit from the experiences of their peers, expanding their understanding beyond what may be possible alone. As can be seen in the protocol (Chapters 4–9), MSPE encourages participation in group discussions to maximize this educational opportunity.

Having a shared experience and contributing to the growth of others represent two of the therapeutic factors (i.e., universality and altruism) that have been identified as making group therapy particularly effective (Yalom & Leszcz, 2005). Indeed, there seems to be something important about the very fact that most mindfulness-based interventions are designed to be delivered in a group format, as these kinds of group-level factors appear to contribute significantly to outcomes of group-based mindfulness interventions such as mindfulness-based stress reduction above and beyond the individual-level factors (e.g., meditating) present in these trainings (Imel, Baldwin, Bonus, & MacCoon, 2008). Facilitating these factors requires group leaders to have unique competencies (Riva, 2014), so perhaps not surprisingly mindfulness experts typically recommend that training leaders obtain this knowledge (e.g., Segal et al., 2002).

Because MSPE is not group therapy, MSPE leaders do not need to be psychotherapists. However, it is essential that they have an appreciation that any group, especially an intact team, will have its own unique dynamics that can impact how the training unfolds (F. R. Goodman & Kashdan, 2015). Thus, we advise MSPE leaders to have some prior experience managing a group of people, whether as a therapist, a coach, or an administrator, or in another relevant capacity. Educating oneself about basic principles of group dynamics could also involve reading on one's own or seeking out consultation or supervision from a more experienced practitioner.

An example from an MSPE training with a group of college athletes from mixed sports that Keith Kaufman and Tim Pineau co-led illustrates why this recommendation is necessary. In the fourth session of that training, the concept of limits was discussed. Although MSPE can help participants to recognize that many of their perceived limits are just that—perceptions—the point was made that sometimes the most self-compassionate decision in a given moment is to acknowledge a limit (e.g., pain that could be indicative of an injury) and then dwell there or step back, rather than trying to push through it.

One participant objected to this idea, claiming that her coach would never tolerate such behavior. The leaders attempted to explore what might have led her to that assumption, while reiterating the possible value of staying attuned to her body. However, this discussion only served to make her more agitated, and she began raising her voice, lamenting the implausibility of our point. Several other participants who were on her team and knew this coach nodded their heads in agreement, while other group members grew visibly uncomfortable with the anger being expressed.

This particular athlete had participated in several discussions to that point in the training, generally appearing engaged and cheerful. Recognizing the contrast from her previous demeanor and equipped with more experience leading groups than he had in the situation that led to the cautionary tale described previously, Tim decided to move away from the lesson he had been trying to impart and observed nonjudgmentally, "I've heard you make a number of comments over the past few weeks, but I've never seen you so fired up. What do you think is happening here?"

This shift from content to process immediately changed the tone of the discussion. When she responded, the agitation in this athlete's voice had disappeared. She was able to step back from her strong feelings in the moment and see how they were connected to something that had happened in the past. She revealed that she had fiercely battled back from an injury for which she had felt judged by her coaches and teammates and that she was holding on to more feelings about that experience than she had realized. Her disclosure helped other participants connect with their own injury experiences, and this conversation became a productive reference point in the remaining sessions (e.g., when we returned to the body scan in Session 6).

Tim's ability to use his skills as a group leader and work with this participant's resistance in a constructive, mindful way produced a powerful real-world example of how past experiences and associated predictions about the future can create perceptions of limits. This was, after all, the original teaching point. However, as anyone with experience managing groups can attest, no two groups are exactly alike. And when it comes to working with groups in the world of athletics, MSPE leaders would benefit from understanding some additional factors.

Know Your Audience: The Unique World of Athletics

The world of athletics has its own culture, within which every department, club, or team has its own distinct subculture (C. H. Brown, Gould, & Foster, 2005). Someone attempting to work in sport, especially as an athletics outsider, needs to be aware of the types of skills necessary to build rapport and operate effectively in that unique environment.

In general, athletes underutilize psychological services (Ferraro & Rush, 2000). They tend to be more open to these services when they are framed as targeting performance rather than personal issues (Wrisberg, Simpson, Loberg, Withycombe, & Reed, 2009), and certain demographic factors such as gender, age, sport played, and previous sport psychology experiences can also influence their receptivity (S. B. Martin, 2005; Wrisberg et al., 2009). Thus, MSPE leaders need to consider how best to nurture an alliance with any group or team they plan to work with.

It would be impossible to address every possible consideration in this chapter, but we offer some suggestions for working in athletics that are relevant for MSPE leaders. For instance, Henriksen, Larsen, Storm, and Ryom (2014) commented that an effective intervention for athletes should be holistic (i.e., incorporate skills that can be applied outside of sport), as athletes have complex identities that include roles and responsibilities far beyond the field of play (D. J. Brown et al., 2015). Others have also emphasized the importance of developing interventions for athletes with applications beyond just sports (Gould, Collins, Lauer, & Chung, 2007). We contend that when leaders draw connections to how MSPE can enhance daily functioning as well as performance (e.g., in relationships, school, work), the program is strengthened, as the potential benefits of mindfulness extend well beyond sport. As such, MSPE leaders should try to include real-world, nonsport examples of how to be more mindful.

However, clear links to sport should also be made (e.g., integrating mindfulness into practice routines). One way to enhance participants' awareness and understanding of this link is by considering the timing of the program. It is commonly recommended that sport psychology interventions occur in the off-season or preseason (e.g., Weinberg & Gould, 2015). Our experience has similarly taught us that the weeks directly leading up to a competitive season are an ideal time to provide MSPE. Participants can practice a new set of skills without the pressure of competitions and also have the opportunity to apply mindfulness to their performance shortly after the training, which may in turn reinforce their mindfulness practice.

Of course, timing is often determined by the availability of participants or by other restrictions (e.g., NCAA regulations for college teams), and we feel it is more important to adapt to the needs of the participants than to mandate a particular timeframe. In line with the need to recognize the practical realities that impact participants' lives, an effective intervention also needs to respect that athletes are embedded in an environment that includes many important figures (especially coaches), who should somehow be involved in the mental training. It may seem obvious, but it bears repeating that coach support is essential to weaving new mental skills into a practice routine.

Leaders should be aware that MSPE is designed to incorporate each of these principles, and it is important to encourage participants to execute their developing mindfulness skills both on and off the field of play. Pervasive sport-specific emphasis helps them learn to apply mindfulness directly to their training and competitions, while attention is also given to how this way of being can generalize to other daily activities. Although it is not an explicit part of the MSPE protocol, we have seen the power of coach involvement as well as the damage of its absence. We thus try to obtain coach support before conducting a training and, if possible, also include the coach in the group. We advise that other MSPE leaders do the same. Henriksen et al. (2014) shared this statement from an experienced Team Denmark (Denmark's organization for elite sport) sport psychologist regarding working with youth athletes:

> If the coach gives the impression it is unimportant, the athletes will not buy into it. And perhaps the most important way for a coach to show that sport psychology is important is to join the workshops, take an interest, be curious and ask questions. (p. 253)

As an example, in an MSPE training that Tim Pineau led for a team of female collegiate athletes, he was describing some basic mindfulness concepts and attempting to elicit from the group thoughts on how the concept of letting go could apply to their own performance. The athletes seemed reluctant to offer personal examples until their coach, who was present, chimed in, talking about her college career when she had trouble moving past mistakes. She then pointed out a few instances of when she had seen this same struggle in some of her players who were present. Those athletes all nodded in agreement, and then several team members, including ones who had not been named, shared examples of times when they couldn't let something go and how that impacted their performance. Without the coach being present, this conversation would likely have turned out quite differently.

In addition to these considerations pertaining to the intervention itself, it is important for MSPE leaders to get their foot in the door, so to speak, with any group they wish to work with. We suggest taking steps to build familiarity with participants beyond the session meetings. Attending practices, team meetings, and/or competitions can be great ways to get to know athletes a bit more and to allow them to get to know you. Such exposure is likely to enhance their receptivity to your services. Several authors have cited the importance of "hanging out" or getting "face time" with teams to build the rapport necessary to do effective work (Andersen, Van Raalte, & Brewer, 2001; Stapleton, Hankes, Hays, & Parham, 2010).

The benefits of establishing rapport have been shown in a variety of contexts, including working with athletes (Mannion & Andersen, 2015), delivering mindfulness interventions (Bowen & Kurz, 2012), and doing psychotherapy (D. J. Martin, Garske, & Davis, 2000). In addition, behaving mindfully while providing services has been linked to an enhanced therapeutic alliance (Hicks & Bien, 2008), a finding that certainly applies in sport, as Andersen (2012) suggested that being mindful when working with athletes builds strong therapeutic relationships with attunement (feeling connected and emotionally invested) and presence (nonjudgmentally being in the moment, observing verbal and nonverbal communication along with one's own internal changes). This is one reason why Mannion and Andersen (2015) stated their hope that any practitioners working with athletes would embrace mindfulness. Furthermore, the observations made when attending practices, meetings, or games can permit an MSPE group leader to bring in real-world examples from the participants' own experiences to highlight important concepts and drive home the relevance of the skills being taught.

The lack of rapport developed with the team of runners in our cautionary tale likely contributed to their resistance to and not benefitting from the program, and, in fact, several athletes suggested "being more involved with the athletes" and "overseeing more [team] practices" as ways to improve the training after its conclusion. We thus stress the importance of developing good rapport with the participants in MSPE trainings. Having an orientation meeting before the first session or attending some team gatherings (e.g., practices, games) can build familiarity and liking, potentially increasing openness to what is being offered.

Of course, just hanging out is not sufficient to ensure an effective working relationship with an MSPE group. To thrive in athletics, one also needs to be perceived as a credible and competent service provider. It is crucial to have knowledge of sport psychology to deliver this kind of training (Hack, 2005), and it can also be extremely helpful to display sport-specific knowledge (F. R. Goodman & Kashdan, 2015; Wrisberg et al., 2009). Every sport has its own ethos and terminology, and being conversant in the language makes it more likely that the participants will see how the skills you're teaching are relevant and worth learning.

The Sport Psychology Proficiency, created in 2003 by the American Psychological Association (APA) Division 47 (Society for Sport, Exercise and Performance Psychology), states explicitly that expert knowledge of the research within the field of sport and exercise sciences is a necessary criterion for the practice of sport psychology (APA, 2016). There are various ways to obtain such knowledge, with the most formal through the credentialing process done by the Association for Applied Sport Psychology (AASP). Even if you are knowledgeable about sport psychology, are fluent in the language of sport, have coach support, and develop a good rapport, there is still another valuable issue to weigh before leading an MSPE group: Is what you are doing consistent with ethical best practices?

Ethical Considerations When Working With Athletes

Athletics is a unique world, and so the ethical issues that arise when working with sport performers are equally unique (Andersen et al., 2001; Stapleton et al., 2010). Because we (the authors) are psychologists, our reference point is the APA's *Ethical*

Principles of Psychologists and Code of Conduct (APA, 2017). Although others interested in leading MSPE groups may not be in this field, these standards represent important topics to consider when working with those in athletics to ensure that any intervention is always implemented with the best interests of participants in mind. Many of APA's ethical standards are applicable in the domain of athletics (boundaries of competence, confidentiality, informed consent), and the general principles, particularly beneficence and nonmaleficence (i.e., do no harm), should always inform a provider's work. However, several authors have pointed out that, similar to military and rural settings, working in athletics may necessitate certain considerations that require acting in a way that can initially feel quite different from standard clinical practice (Aoyagi & Portenga, 2010; Stapleton et al., 2010).

Hankes (2012) indicated that the ethical concerns around multiple relationships and boundary issues constitute "the signature issue for psychologists who work in sport and performance arenas" (p. 55). With the importance of hanging out and developing rapport, having some degree of informal contact with athletes is practically essential to the work, and so maintaining a relatively rigid boundary as one might with a client receiving psychotherapy may be unrealistic. As a service provider becomes more accepted and valued, the opportunities to interact with athletes will likely increase in situations that may seem to have nothing to do with official work, such as on the bus to an away game or at team meals. It may be necessary to learn how to deliver services appropriately in these types of "catch as catch can" contexts (Andersen et al., 2001), which could involve some of what is traditionally regarded as boundary crossing and multiple relationships.

The situations in which these ethical issues can arise may seem relatively subtle or unproblematic, such as when providing MSPE to a team and then answering some questions about mindfulness one-on-one with a member of that team. However, other situations can prove more vexing. For example, Tim Pineau works at a university counseling center as a staff psychologist. His primary role is to provide psychological services to the university community, but he also consults with the athletic department, providing MSPE to some of the teams. As members of the student body, all athletes are eligible to go to the counseling center and may seek services to address a mental health issue of some kind (e.g., an eating disorder) that, although potentially relevant to their sport performance, would not be a focus of MSPE.

As a licensed clinical psychologist, Tim may be equipped to treat the mental health issue, but if that athlete is also attending an MSPE training, it may not be ethically appropriate for Tim to do so (Aoyagi & Portenga, 2010). Instead, it would be a good idea for the athlete to see a different clinician who does not occupy this dual role. Recognition of this foreseeable potential ethical dilemma led Tim to engage in proactive consultation with other counseling center staff about how such situations would be managed and to develop a protocol for making a full and clear disclosure to participants in his MSPE groups about his role at the counseling center.

Even though the risk of boundary crossings and multiple relationships may be part of being a mental health provider working in athletics, the previous example highlights that certain boundaries still must be maintained. There is a distinction between a boundary crossing and a boundary violation. Violations are more likely to have harmful repercussions, whereas crossings can simply be adaptations to accommodate a particular client (L. L. Glass, 2003). From this perspective, some boundary crossings and multiple relationships could actually be therapeutically indicated (Hines, Ader, Chang, & Rundell, 1998) and even beneficial (Zur & Lazarus, 2002). However, even though working within athletics can necessitate some deviations from traditional practice, it is imperative for practitioners to remain self-aware and self-regulating with their boundaries (Aoyagi & Portenga, 2010) and to have a thorough informed-consent process (Andersen et al., 2001; Hankes, 2012; Stapleton et al., 2010).

This brief discussion of ethics only scratches the surface of what is faced within sport psychology, as we are not addressing the particular issues that arise around confidentiality when one is delivering services to athletes on the sidelines rather than in an office, or the complications that come up around dual agency when a coach or an administrator, rather than athletes themselves, make the referral. Plus, we aren't exploring the additional ethical concerns that exist when conducting research with athletes (e.g., Harriss & Atkinson, 2013). Even so, we hope this section makes clear the essential point that one of the most important considerations when preparing to lead an MSPE group is being sure that the intervention is designed, presented, and implemented with participants' needs and best interests in mind.

Pulling It All Together: Tips for MSPE Leaders

When doing sport psychology work, you will always encounter factors outside of your control, despite your best intentions. For instance, the packed schedules of athletes at all levels may require an openness to nontraditional means of service delivery. Responding to these factors mindfully can be a wonderful way to go with the flow while protecting the interests of those you serve. Hopefully, you are taking from this chapter the understanding that factors within your control, such as attending an MSPE workshop or participating in formal MSPE training, can enhance the effectiveness of an intervention such as MSPE. But is it absolutely necessary to have gone on a meditation retreat, be a seasoned group therapist, or be a certified AASP consultant before you're ready to lead an MSPE training? We would say, probably not. However, it is necessary to engage in honest self-reflection about your previous experiences with mindfulness, groups, and sport, as well as to assess your competence to be an effective and ethical leader who can embody what it is to be a mindful sport performer.

Another important point concerns openness to seeking out supervision and consultation. This could include discussing your work with peers, coleading groups with a more experienced colleague, and/or developing a relationship with a mindfulness mentor or teacher. Having good support can help with developing all of the skill sets outlined in this chapter and will likely improve your ability to foster the integral aspects of MSPE implementation, including obtaining the buy-in of important key figures (e.g., coaches), maintaining a holistic focus regarding both sport and daily life, and establishing trusting relationships with your participants.

Finally, we encourage you to take a long-term perspective when providing MSPE. This tip really has two meanings. The first is about the nature of mindfulness practice. MSPE is an introduction to mindfulness in the context of sport and is intended to provide participants with the necessary foundation to establish an ongoing mindfulness practice that ideally will deepen and expand over time. As we've found in our own research, MSPE appears to create long-term benefits that continue to accrue even a year after the initial training ends (Thompson, Kaufman, De Petrillo, Glass, & Arnkoff, 2011). The second meaning is that influencing personal development and/or organizational culture may take a lot longer than 6 weeks. Patience, persistence, and flexibility are key, and MSPE leaders can facilitate the long-term development of athletes and coaches by finding ways to remain available for consultation after MSPE ends.

Before concluding this chapter, we want to note that these guidelines, while presented in the context of working with coaches and athletes, could also apply to the provision of MSPE when working with other types of performers. We explore this potential for broader applications of MSPE in the next chapter as we review the literature on existing mindfulness-based interventions for performing artists, noting important themes and future directions.

Performance Applications Beyond Sport

14

D anielle, now 18 years old, left home 3 years ago, sacrificing a more typical teenage life for the chance to pursue her dreams. She has trained since the age of 3, each year adding more and more hours of practice to her already busy days. High school fell by the wayside as she decided that she could always go back for a general equivalency degree but needed to seize the moment now because just one injury could end her career. After she moved in with three other teammates, Danielle's life started to revolve almost completely around her passion.

Struggling with tendinitis in her ankle, Danielle arrives at her physical therapist's office at 7:00 a.m. each day so that she can make it to practice on time. She knows that she has no choice but to continue training through her injury. As her teacher reminds the girls frequently, "Everyone is replaceable." The rest of Danielle's day is filled with grueling practice from 9 to 5, and she pushes through her pain and sore muscles to continue to improve.

Although lunchtime could be a relaxing point in her nonstop day, it serves as a period of anxiety for Danielle. She constantly compares her body with those of her teammates, convinced that she was not born with the ideal figure to pursue her dream. Danielle often skips meals and turns to cigarettes to suppress her appetite. Caught up in her own head, Danielle is convinced

http://dx.doi.org/10.1037/0000048-015
Mindful Sport Performance Enhancement: Mental Training for Athletes and Coaches, by K. A. Kaufman, C. R. Glass, and T. R. Pineau

that with every pound she loses, she is one step closer to the coveted leading position. The pressure of competition is never far from her mind.

Day in and day out, Danielle's life is highly routine, following the same rigorous schedule, but it's all worth it to her. When she steps out in front of the crowd, sometimes the world slows down and she is totally absorbed in the moment, knowing all of her hard work has prepared her for these few moments in the spotlight. But, at other times, Danielle's heart pounds and she feels so anxious that she thinks she's going to "lose it," recalling her falls in practice and fearing that she'll fall again with everyone watching.

At first glance, Danielle would appear to be a perfect candidate for mindful sport performance enhancement (MSPE), and maybe you wondered whether she was a gymnast or figure skater. Would it surprise you to learn that Danielle is actually a ballet dancer? The similarity of her story as a performing artist to those of many athletes strikes to the heart of significant changes taking place within the field of sport and exercise psychology. Many sport psychologists now consider themselves to be performance specialists and sport psychology to be a domain within performance psychology (Moyle, 2012). Reflecting this shift, Division 47 of the American Psychological Association (APA) voted in 2015 to expand its name from the Division of Exercise and Sport Psychology to the Society for Sport, Exercise and Performance Psychology.

Performance psychology refers to the "mental components of superior performance, in situations and performance domains where excellence is a central element" (Hays, 2012, p. 25). In addition to athletes, performing artists (including dancers, musicians, and actors), business executives, and those in high-risk professions (with lives on the line) also have to be "on" when they perform. As such, just as with athletes, they may also benefit from consultation or therapy when issues interfere with optimal performance.

In Danielle's case, parallels to the lives of many athletes are clear. She has devoted years of her life to the pursuit of excellence. Faced with extreme pressures to maintain peak performance, she has spent countless hours devoted to intense daily practice, fueled by a passion and motivation to be the best that has bordered, at times, on perfectionism. She has faced stiff competition when auditioning for positions and roles, which has produced anxiety similar to what athletes can face when competing. Although Danielle has been involved in dance since she was very young, she still sometimes experiences disruptive levels of stage fright when anticipating performing in front of an audience, with all eyes on her.

Sometimes, Danielle is unable to regulate her feelings to the extent that, when she has become upset about making errors, she has felt out of control, angry, and overwhelmed by her emotions. Her body being on public display has triggered an obsession with her weight and appearance that, quite possibly, has led to a diagnosable eating disorder. She has learned to endure a high degree of pain to perform day after day and has recovered from so many repetitive injuries that she has wondered whether she could regain a past level of performance or even continue her career. On a more positive note, Danielle also has experienced moments of pure joy, complete absorption, and effortlessness when dancing, or what we have already described as flow or being in the zone. As with athletes, dancers' careers are often short-lived due to injuries, and they experience chronic pain due to intense physical demands, separation from families while touring, social isolation resulting from intensive daily training, and limited career options (Moyle, 2012).

Although MSPE hasn't yet been studied in performance realms outside of sport, it and aspects of our FAME (flow, anxiety, mindfulness, and emotion regulation) profile (see Chapter 11) are applicable to performing artists such as Danielle. In this chapter, we make a case for why this is so by reviewing interventions and research on mindfulness approaches for performing artists such as musicians, dancers, and actors. Our hope is that highlighting the broader applicability of MSPE will inspire research on the program in other domains. We'll begin with a brief introduction to the emerging field of performance psychology.

Performance Psychology

In their seminal book on consulting for peak performance, Hays and Brown (2004) focused on factors common to any performance: being judged on proficiency, facing consequences for poor performance, needing strong coping skills for excellence, and bringing out skill and expertise at specific moments. Although everyone performs, some professions require performance in high-pressure contexts such as auditioning for career-defining roles, competing with the game on the line, or acting to save lives (Hays, 2009b). Performance psychology often focuses on such high-end performers, who strive to be the best they can be, often in intense circumstances (Terry, 2008). A range of psychological processes, including anxiety, concentration, awareness, emotion regulation, motivation, and self-efficacy, are critical (Hays, 2012).

Hays (2002) described four parallels between athletes and performing artists. First, mental aspects of performance are critical, and judgments about performance and intense competition can breed anxiety that, if not managed effectively, may disrupt crucial factors such as concentration. Second, developmental issues are prominent, given that competition begins in childhood, with an immense number of hours devoted to training. Third, there is a risk of shortened careers due to injuries or conditions exacerbated by constant repetitive motions. Fourth, the emphasis on appearance (e.g., thinness) can raise the risk for disordered eating.

Interviews with individuals across performance domains revealed interesting similarities (Hays & Brown, 2004). Regarding mental skills, "performers appear to achieve their optimal pre-performance state in a way similar to that of athletes" (p. 118), including a focus on routine and maintaining moment-to-moment attention. Also, physical arousal, performance demands, and the significance or uncertainty of the situation can contribute to stress, as the body "may be central to the performance itself" (p. 149). With regard to coping with stress, they mentioned the importance of staying focused on the present and letting go of the past (which sounds a lot like mindfulness). Finally, many performers emphasized concentration, and one dancer proposed that finding a way to center (in a meditative state) could be a valuable way to deal with stage fright.

These many similarities across performance realms suggest that interventions for athletes, such as MSPE, could be very applicable in other areas. Nordin-Bates (2012) argued that approaches from sport psychology can transfer successfully to dance, music, and theater, yet studies lag far behind on applications of psychological skills in the performing arts. Although applications outpace research for mindfulness interventions as well, a growing number of performance psychologists are introducing mindfulness, and an entire book now explores mindfulness and performance (Baltzell, 2016a). We provide in this chapter an overview of applications of mindfulness in the performing arts and highlight the many parallels between these approaches and MSPE, starting with the largest body of literature in this domain that focuses on mindfulness for musicians.

Mindfulness and Music

Greater attention is now being paid to principles of musical performance enhancement, with an emphasis on physical, psychological, and technical skills (see Williamon, 2004). Interviews with internationally renowned classical musicians have revealed that perceived keys to excellence include long-term involvement, deep commitment, ambitious goals, a strong sense of self, feelings of control, a positive attitude, enjoyment of playing, flexibility, and appropriate concentration both before and during performances (Talbot-Honeck & Orlick, 1998), each of which has also been identified as crucial in sport. Although mental training programs for musicians often draw from sport psychology (e.g., Clark & Williamon, 2011), mindfulness has been largely overlooked. Some of the approaches used, however, sound a lot like mindfulness.

APPROACHES FOR MUSICIANS
CONSISTENT WITH MINDFULNESS

The mindfulness-compatible inner-game methods for tennis described in Chapter 2 (Gallwey, 1974) were translated into applications for musicians (Green & Gallwey, 1986). In his introduction to this later book, Gallwey noted similarities between sports and music: people "play" both; both require discipline, hard work, and mastery over the human body; and both are performed before an audience. According to Green and Gallwey, the inner game for athletes and musicians alike involves reducing mental interference, self-consciousness, and self-judgment. Thus, they encouraged musicians to pay attention to what's happening without judgment or trying to do a task correctly, which requires accepting distractions and focusing attention on the present (e.g., what is seen, heard, felt, and known about the music). They suggested a number of exercises to help musicians let go (e.g., a body scan), along with ways to change action-based instructions to do things a certain way into awareness-based instructions to notice an experience.

Ristad (1982) spoke to the integration of mind and body and tricking our inner judges by giving ourselves permission to experience moment-by-moment awareness, without trying to perform as we "should" or to control feelings of anxiety. Mariam Gregorian (personal communication, February 29, 2016), an experienced violin teacher, shared some other ideas that she incorporates into instruction: that the aim of the performer is not to do an impressive job but to "be" the feeling of the music and to replace "make, do, try" with "notice and allow."

Jazz pianist Kenny Werner (1996) introduced a number of meditations in his "effortless" approach to music, which is based on acceptance and playing without thinking. He seeks to remove mental baggage and enhance self-compassion through detachment from the ego and letting go of the need to sound good. His meditations incorporate breathing, relaxation, letting go of the need to play well, filling the head and body with healing light, and affirmations. Examples of exercises he described are observing, while relaxed, as each fingertip is allowed to settle onto the keys one at a time and playing keys at random without trying, just observing.

In addition to performance anxiety, performance-related musculoskeletal disorders are prevalent in musicians. The Alexander Technique (AT), more recently popularized by Barlow (1973, 2001), was developed by F. M. Alexander in the early 20th century as a method of mind–body reeducation to enhance awareness of body alignment (Alexander, 1932). As described by a certified AT teacher (M. Naden, personal communication, July 16, 2015), the first of the three main principles of this technique is kinesthetic awareness of physical sensations, just noticing what is happening (such as tension patterns) with curiosity and without judgment. The second principle is inhibition of automatic reactions and usual habits, so that you can pause and choose if you want to do something differently. The final principle is redirecting your intention toward another choice and allowing new things to happen.

There are clear links between these principles and those of mindfulness. The AT helps musicians attend to what they are doing (e.g., how they are sitting and holding the instrument) and what their muscles and body are doing in space. They can thus be more "present" and fluid in their performances, adapt their bodies to release tension and make movement less effortful, and change postures that could put them at greater risk of repetitive-strain injury.

Although the AT is taught at major music conservatories, empirical support for it with musicians is mixed, with only one of three randomized controlled trials finding an improvement in musical performance (e.g., Valentine, Fitzgerald, Gorton, Hudson, & Symonds, 1995). A review of 12 mostly unpublished controlled studies found that respiratory function was not improved significantly by AT training (Klein, Bayard, & Wolf, 2014), although there were significant decreases in performance anxiety compared with no-treatment (but not active) controls.

MINDFULNESS AND MUSIC PERFORMANCE ANXIETY

Performance anxiety has been the main focus of mindfulness approaches for musicians. As with athletes, excessive anxiety can mentally and physically interfere with skilled action during auditions and concerts and may also hinder musicians from entering a flow state. Research has shown that performance anxiety was inversely correlated with both flow and self-confidence while playing or singing, as well as the ability to concentrate on the music (Kirchner, Bloom, & Skutnick-Henley, 2008).

Performance anxiety is a common reason why performers seek assistance from therapists or performance psychology consultants. As Hays (2009a) said, performing before an audience involves stressors inherent in presenting oneself; demonstrating a high level of skill while under close scrutiny and often in competition with others; and the expectation of control over memory, concentration, and coordination. She presented a case study of a musician, using both traditional mental skills techniques (e.g., cognitive restructuring, thought stopping) as well as approaches more consistent with (although not explicitly called) mindfulness: diaphragmatic breathing, catching the mind drifting off during practice sessions and gently bringing it back, practicing awareness of what was going on, and redirecting attention to aspects of the present moment.

Mindfulness may be a particularly effective way to cope with music performance anxiety, through its emphasis on metacognitive awareness and decentering, exposure to avoided thoughts and feelings, self-acceptance, and sustained attention to the task in the present moment (Farnsworth-Grodd & Cameron, 2013). These authors found significant inverse relationships between the mindfulness facet of acting with awareness and music performance anxiety. Some musicians already are aware of the benefits of meditation (Steptoe & Fidler, 1987), and an online survey found that 46% of singing teachers who had routinely experienced symptoms of performance anxiety reported that they used some form of meditation to diminish symptoms, with three quarters indicating that it was very effective (Taylor, 2001). Fortunately, a handful of mindfulness-based training programs have been developed or adapted for use with musicians, although empirical support to date comes mostly from unpublished dissertations.

MINDFULNESS PROGRAMS FOR MUSICIANS

Meditation-Based Approaches

On the basis of Kabat-Zinn's work, De Felice (2004) created a mindfulness meditation intervention for musical performance anxiety. This approach emphasizes observing thoughts and feelings nonjudgmentally, including muscle tension, and acknowledging, accepting, and letting go of them so that the mind can remain focused on the music. Staying in the moment this way during practice can allow for mastery of each measure, one at a time, without anticipation of later difficulties. Musicians also learn to be mindful in each second of a performance, experiencing and enjoying the richness of sound and bodily strength as music is created.

Also drawing from Kabat-Zinn, Oyan (2006) proposed that, to be fully mindful during the inevitable stress of a performance, one first must integrate mindfulness into music training and day-to-day life. As in MSPE, musicians are taught to become aware of thoughts and feelings without reacting to them. Body scan and walking meditation exercises are used to develop awareness of body sensations, which can help musicians let go of muscle tension and thus enhance musical expression and prevent common injuries. Mindful music practice exercises also have similarities to the MSPE sport meditation, as musicians learn to pay attention to their experience in the moment while engaging in core aspects of music performance (e.g., playing a scale slowly, then passages of music, and finally during regular practice and performance) while they let feelings of anxiety, self-conscious thoughts, and uncomfortable physical sensations come and go.

A program of guided attention practice (GAP) breathing meditation was created by Koen (2007) to help music students become fully present in the moment. GAP progresses through five stages: engaging the mind and body through breathing and long vocal tone exercises, observing thoughts coming and drifting away, journaling about the experience and enjoyment of this state of mind, introducing a special word into meditation to capture desired experience while playing (e.g., calm) and hearing the music in their minds, and finally extending this type of consciousness into practice sessions and performances. Music majors in Koen's class reported a greater ability to focus on and learn highly technical passages that had previously been obstacles, as well as a rediscovery of love for and personal meaning in their music.

Bruser (2011) described how meditation can help musicians settle their minds and notice muscle tension or if they're trying too hard and suggested ways to practice being more open by scanning the body and then focusing attention while playing or singing a single note. Playing slowly at first, musicians then increase speed while engaging in "peaceful effort." An exercise to decrease self-evaluation involves closing the eyes and reflecting on what first attracted them to their instrument as well as people who had been helpful or inspirational. After appreciating their own talent and hard work, musicians think of the audience as fellow human beings who are receptive to the music being given to them. Bruser suggested that this form of practice could also help actors become more expressive and spontaneous in their work.

In reflecting on how mindfulness can enhance the performance and well-being of musicians, Cornett-Murtada (2012) noted the importance of being able to stay focused in the present moment while performing, accepting each note without judgment, noticing mistakes or concerns with noncritical awareness, and refocusing attention back on the music. She suggested doing 10 minutes of daily meditation practice and provided an introductory breathing meditation exercise. Elliott (2010) recommended a similar regimen for singers, saying that although singers likely already know the importance of the breath, increasing nonjudgmental mindful awareness can weaken attachments to one specific aspect of experience (a hallmark of anxiety) and thus return attention to the present moment when worry-laden or judgmental thoughts are observed.

In an approach with a different group of music performers, D. Grant (2006) suggested applying mindfulness to the performance of conductors, proposing that the mental skills of selflessness (letting go of ego and control) and mindfulness are just as important as learning the requisite physical skills. When conductors focus on external results, such as how others receive their performance and that of the orchestra, self-consciousness, pressure, tension, and anxiety can result. Grant thus described a short breathing meditation that involves letting go of thoughts, allowing conductors to be more present with the music.

Empirical Support for Meditation-Based Programs

In one early study with a brief mindfulness intervention, college vocal students were given written instructions to practice a 3-minute taped awareness of breathing exercise for 6 weeks and were then asked to apply it prior to both a class performance and a music jury assessment before a panel of voice faculty (Deen, 1999). Those using the exercise had a significant reduction in performance anxiety compared with controls (although performance quality did not differ), and most reported that it helped them to relax and concentrate.

Chan (Zen) meditation has been introduced to help musicians cultivate mindfulness and concentration, enhance their experience in the moment, and decrease the influence of inner mental states and the external environment (Chang, Midlarsky, & Lin, 2003; Lin, Chang, Zemon, & Midlarsky, 2008). Each 75-minute class in this 8-week program includes meditation exercises such as yoga stretches and awareness of both the breath and thoughts. Musicians are taught to observe their flow of consciousness, accept the present moment, and see thoughts and feelings as passing events and not aspects of their selves or reflections of reality. Group discussion encourages sharing experiences practicing meditation, and daily practice (especially right before lessons and music practice) is encouraged. Music students did not experience significantly reduced music performance anxiety compared with randomized controls, but the meditation group showed significant pre–post change. Furthermore, qualitative feedback highlighted the value of meditation for both musical performances and practice as well as greater relaxation felt after hours of practice (Chang et al., 2003). Lin et al. (2008) found that musicians who learned Chan meditation, but not waiting-list controls, showed decreases in musical performance anxiety, although no improvement in the quality of musical performance was found.

Czajkowski and Greasley (2015) developed an 8-week mindfulness course for singers in the United Kingdom, which they characterized as akin to mindfulness-based stress reduction (MBSR) and mindfulness-based cognitive therapy. This class includes group discussions, lectures, exercises, 10-minute daily practices, and a resource website. The content and exercises were customized for singers, so that, for example, breathing awareness is linked to singing breaths, mindful yoga emphasizes movements useful for singers' posture, and body scans highlight awareness of those body regions used in singing. Additional emphasis is placed on dealing with judgment from others as well as self-criticism during performances. In a small, uncontrolled study with eight college voice majors, mindfulness increased (especially nonjudging of and nonreactivity to inner experience), but no statistical analyses were performed. Postprogram interviews revealed benefits of the program, particularly for breathing and awareness of muscle sensations and tonal quality, and practicing mindfulness before singing lessons appeared to help decrease stress and increase focus.

Yoga and Meditation

In a pilot study with professional musicians, Khalsa and Cope (2006) introduced an 8-week program that included daily Kripalu yoga sessions, a weekly yoga and group discussion session, and optional 30-minute meditation sessions (which half attended regularly). Significant improvements were found in performance anxiety compared with (nonrandomized) controls, while both groups showed significant increases in overall negative mood states but not in flow. Some participants who regularly attended meditation sessions thought this had the most important effect on their music performance.

Similarly, young-adult professional musicians who received a 2-month yoga and meditation program showed a trend toward decreased music performance anxiety and a significantly greater decline in anxiety, tension, depression, and anger compared with a control group (Khalsa, Shorter, Cope, Wyshak, & Sklar, 2009). Stern, Khalsa, and Hofmann (2012) introduced 14 one-hour Kripalu yoga classes (including breathing techniques and meditation) to music conservatory students, who decreased significantly in trait and music performance anxiety, at both posttest and follow-up. Finally, Khalsa, Butzer, Shorter, Reinhardt, and Cope (2013) extended this line of research to adolescent music students in a 6-week yoga program and found a significantly greater drop in music performance anxiety compared with controls.

Approaches Integrating the MAC Approach or Langerian Mindfulness

Steyn (2013) adapted the mindfulness–acceptance–commitment (MAC) approach (Gardner & Moore, 2007) for musicians, integrating it into a 7-week psychological skills training program to help musicians fully engage in performance despite experiencing negative thoughts and emotions. This program focuses on arousal management; present-moment concentration; awareness (through mindful breathing) and a winner's state of mind; changing perceptions of stress and becoming mindful in daily actions; applying imagery, goal setting, and mindfulness during music training sessions; and finding a balance between letting it happen through mindfulness and making it happen using other psychological skills. The college students who chose to be in the intervention group showed significant improvements in competitive state anxiety and mindfulness, but the nonrandomized control group did not.

Langer's (2000) mindfulness approach emphasizing mental flexibility has also been evaluated with musicians. In a study by Langer, Russel, and Eisenkraft (2009), college orchestra musicians played a piece after thinking about the finest performance they could remember and then played it again while giving new, subtle nuances to the performance (i.e., mindfully). The musicians rated their enjoyment of the performance more highly after playing mindfully, and audience members who expressed a preference preferred this one as well.

More recently, Patston (2016) proposed a mindful music pedagogy model for studio music teachers, which he called music instruction nondeficit (MIND). Rather than focusing on correcting errors, teachers can integrate aspects of mindfulness (both the acceptance focus of Eastern approaches and Langer's focus on novel stimuli and experience) into their pedagogical framework. The MIND model encourages teachers to help students intentionally notice what is working and savor that experience, observing and accepting each moment as music flows from and through them, while also noticing where there is room for improvement. For example, young children can notice the feel and sound of the instrument with a sense of curiosity, and mindfulness exercises such as a focus on the breath contribute to an interest in and enjoyment of making music. Adolescent musicians are encouraged to be mindfully aware in the moment and accept negative thoughts and feelings about their musical performance without judgment as well as actively notice new things. Aspects of the MAC approach are also incorporated through attention to students' commitment to action in support of their values and musical goals.

Mindfulness and Dance

Despite the parallels between mindfulness for athletes and dancers, whose bodies are their instruments (Hays, 2009a), far less has been written about mindfulness for dancers than for musicians. Mindfulness is compatible with a number of somatic movement practices that involve heightened sensory and motor awareness, so that movement can change in response to one's observed sensations. When used with dancers, somatic movement education can reduce the occurrence of and aid recovery from injuries, strengthen technique, enhance performance and expressiveness, and raise the likelihood of attaining a flow state (Eddy, 2009).

Most existing literature on mindfulness in dance does not address peak performance. Rather, the focus is on increasing mindfulness in the general population through movement-based courses such as Pilates (Caldwell, Harrison, Adams, Quin, & Greeson, 2010) or on integrating mindfulness into dance therapy. This type of therapy can be mindfulness-based or combine meditation with the use of dance or movement in treating issues such as cancer, trauma, chronic pain, substance abuse, depression, or severe mental illness (see Rappaport, 2013). For example, dancing mindfulness (Marich, 2015) incorporates spontaneous dancing to music as a mechanism for the practice of mindful awareness of the body, to enhance healing and recovery, develop nonjudgment and acceptance, and learn to let go.

We found only a few publications describing mindfulness programs to enhance the experiences and/or performance of dancers. Lefebvre Sell (2013) hypothesized that including mindfulness meditation could enhance the creative process of choreography and allow dancers to deal with distractions. She introduced four college dance students to principles and practices of sitting meditation, mindful moving, and yoga nidra during weekly 45-minute sessions and suggested strategies for daily meditation and informal mindfulness practice. Mindful moving involved staying in the present moment while walking with deliberate attention to the movement of the feet and legs (similar to what we do in MSPE) and later improvising dance movement. Moving in this way is associated with the full-immersion experience of a flow state.

A phenomenological study incorporated mindfulness into improvisational dance (Black, 2014). Including yoga and sitting meditation, this personal journey applied principles of nonattachment to choreography, preperformance improvisation, and performance in concert. Scores on a nonattachment weekly questionnaire increased over time during later practice.

Moyle (2016) presented a detailed description of a mindfulness–meditation (MM) training for university dance students, which was combined with other somatic-based approaches such as Pilates, yoga, and the AT to comprise a performance psychology intervention. This 9-week program, which has roots in acceptance and commitment therapy, was delivered as a 1-hour weekly class during the semester. Sessions included mindfulness of the breath, body, sounds, images, and emotions. Moyle later revised the program, cutting sessions to 45 minutes, increasing the number of walking meditations (including a silent walking meditation with a loving-kindness mantra), and holding some sessions outdoors.

The outcome of the MM training was evaluated with students in a university dance program, where teachers were invited to attend the weekly sessions in order to be able to incorporate what students were learning about mindfulness into their dance and academic theory courses (Moyle, 2016). Dancers indicated their level of mindfulness during each practice and kept a reflective journal. Results after the first year of the program showed no significant increases on a measure of mindful awareness and attention, although a qualitative measure of their level of awareness and understanding of applications of mindfulness revealed that students felt the MM program had led to performance and personal improvement. Several dancers spoke, for example, about the helpfulness of mindfulness for developing more focus and relaxation.

After the second year of the program, when dancers took MM as part of one large class, Moyle (2016) reported that mindful awareness decreased slightly, although results were inconclusive. She attributed this finding to logistical aspects of the study, such as the need for shorter and early morning sessions, alternating locations, and the fact that many dancers may not have preferred the walking meditation. However, qualitative feedback again indicated that some dancers derived positive outcomes such as being more focused and calm, and being more aware of the body and mental distraction while performing. In fact, almost 80% of dancers cited MM and other somatic-based practices as helpful to the development of dance technique.

Mindfulness and Acting

Performance psychologists have also turned their attention to the mental strategies used by professional actors. Interviews have revealed that athletes and actors share a focus on mental and physical preparation, preperformance routines, use of imagery, increasing confidence and energy, and constant evaluation of performance (Murphy & Orlick, 2006). However, very little has been written on applications of mindfulness for actors, even though Ellis-Jones (2013) drew compelling parallels between the present-moment concentration cultivated by mindfulness and the style of concentration used in method acting, in which actors focus on the sense memory of an emotional event from their lives. It may be useful to consider acting not as what an actor does but rather a process that happens, just like living mindfully by being open to and aware of thoughts, memories, body sensations, sounds, and feelings in the present moment.

ACTING APPROACHES CONSISTENT WITH MINDFULNESS

Several popular approaches to acting instruction incorporate principles of mindfulness but don't explicitly refer to them as such. For example, Anne Bogart's Viewpoints has become an important technique for directors to focus actors' awareness on aspects of performance and what's happening onstage (e.g., gestures, duration, tempo, spatial relationships) to encourage exploration (Herrington, 2000). Actors are moved out of their heads to be able to respond more instinctively, consistent with the concept of present-moment awareness.

Although more studies explore the AT for musicians than for actors, Alexander himself was a professional reciter who developed his approach after repeatedly losing his voice during public recitation. Chan (2008) even referred to the AT for actors as a mindfulness practice, emphasizing mindfulness in action. This technique allows actors to become aware of and attend to what they're doing with their bodies, such as how they sit, stand, move, and carry tension, and AT classes are required for drama students at some universities.

MEDITATION AND ACTING

Although we found no published research on the effectiveness of mindfulness programs for actors, many acting teachers incorporate mindfulness meditation into their work. For example, in an online post, a university acting teacher (Brody, 2014) said that she begins almost every class with a 10- to 20-minute meditation, followed by having actors stand and continue the state of meditation while moving. She has found that this state prevents self-consciousness and associated tension and anxiety, allowing for better attention and work. One actor described in an interview how mindfulness can "free you from the anxieties of performance" so that you can "open yourself to the possibilities of the moment instead of overlooking them by sticking rigidly to your ideas of how things should go" (McKenzie, 2015, p. 165).

An article wittily titled "Lights, Camera, Meditation" (Goguen-Hughes, 2011) reported on a conversation with the leader of a meditation-for-actors program. Because a key element in theater is awareness of the body, speech, thoughts, and space, this leader argued that meditation could enhance acting ability through greater self-awareness, spontaneity, and sensory awareness. He led training sessions ranging from half days to weeklong retreats as well as ongoing weekly classes, which included applications of mindfulness for practical situations such as preparation for rehearsals and auditions, coping with stage fright, and dealing with the successes and failures of an acting career.

Wallace (2013) similarly offered a meditation-for-actors program that met for 3 hours a week over 4 weeks. He suggested that meditation can strengthen concentration and calmness and included guided visualization meditations, exercises connecting to the breath, and instruction in loving kindness, concentration, and mindfulness.

One unpublished study used qualitative methods to look at the effects of an 8-week MBSR program on eight community theater actors' attitudes of acceptance and nonjudgment, letting go, and sense of individual empowerment (Barber, 2014). This program included 2½-hour weekly sessions plus a "day of mindfulness" in addition to up to 45 minutes a day of informal and formal mindfulness practice. Participants also received workbooks and audio recordings of exercises. Observations of sessions and semistructured interviews revealed that experiential awareness and expression developed through the MBSR program facilitated actors' empowerment, although difficulties in acceptance and letting go were also noted. Barber suggested that the benefits of mindfulness for actors could include better memorization, improvisational skills, self-awareness, role understanding, and thus the ability to integrate present-moment experiential awareness and expression while performing.

Mindfulness and Performance Beyond the Performing Arts

As Terry (2008) described, sport psychologists are expanding their practices to apply their expertise in other performance environments, such as organizational settings and the corporate world. Although such a review is beyond the scope of this chapter, the mindfulness movement has also extended to business (Brendel, 2015; Reb & Choi, 2014). Companies such as Aetna, General Mills, and Goldman Sachs are jumping on the mindfulness bandwagon by offering meditation training at work (Vallabh & Singhal, 2014), and a mindfulness-based program for workers in high-stress environments (e.g., military) seems promising (Stanley, 2014). Although controlled research lags behind (see, however, Shonin, Van Gordon, Dunn, Singh, & Griffiths, 2014, and reviews by Good et al., 2016, and Jamieson & Tuckey, 2016), numerous books on mindfulness in the workplace are appearing (e.g., Chaskalson, 2011; Reb & Atkins, 2015).

Conclusion and Future Directions

This is an exciting time to be a performance psychologist, especially one riding the wave of the mindfulness movement. An increasing number of athletes, as well as musicians, dancers, actors, and those in high-stress or high-stakes work environments, are now benefitting from mindfulness programs, and this surge of interest shows no sign of abating. The common factors of years of dedication and training, the experience of flow and pursuit of excellence, pressures to perform, grueling practice, stiff competition, performance anxiety, emotion dysregulation, body-image issues, and risk of pain and injury link together performing artists such as Danielle with athletes and other nonsport performers who experience similar joys and challenges. Thus, mindfulness-based interventions such as MSPE that were designed to enhance peak performance in sport, as well as our FAME profile, may be useful when working with others who perform.

The potential transferability of MSPE to other performance domains is highlighted by a number of prevalent themes seen throughout this chapter: (a) When mindfulness is introduced to performing artists, there is often a strong emphasis on training in present-moment awareness, which can be applied while performing to act with awareness and minimize being on autopilot. (b) A focus on acceptance encourages mindful performers to welcome "what is" and let go of mistakes without judgment. (c) As with MSPE, the majority of existing approaches introduce formal meditation exercises (e.g., mindfulness of the breath, body scan, yoga), in which performers practice becoming aware and letting go of thoughts and feelings as passing events, gently bringing attention back without judgment. (d) In the same way that we tailor MSPE to specific sports and move athletes from sedentary to motive mindfulness practice with opportunities to be mindful while engaging in the actions of their sport, many of the approaches in this chapter are customized for specific performers (e.g., a body scan that emphasizes awareness of the parts of the body used in singing) and involve focusing attention first while doing something very slowly in the performer's domain (e.g., playing or singing a single note, mindful moving) before increasing in speed. (e) These programs often include a focus on process rather than outcome, shifting from needing to make things happen to just letting them happen, and letting go of attachments both while practicing their art and during public performance.

We feel these parallels are quite striking, and yet there are relatively few empirical studies in support of the efficacy of mindfulness approaches for performance outside of athletics. Those that exist tend to focus on musicians, are mostly unpublished dissertations, and assess changes in negative emotions (anxiety, depression) rather than performance. Most outcome research in this area also consists of small, uncontrolled studies or those with nonrandomized or nonequivalent controls and fails to include measures of mindfulness or flow or to compare mindfulness with other psychological skills training approaches.

So where do we go from here? There are, without a doubt, a number of extremely promising developments in applying mindfulness with performers other than athletes. We predict that mindfulness interventions for performing artists will continue to increase exponentially over the coming years, hopefully with more applications to acting and dance as well as music. Adapting MSPE for other performance domains is thus an important future direction, and we have already begun discussions with drama faculty to design a future outcome study of MSPE with both undergraduate and graduate student actors.

As we have emphasized throughout this book, MSPE is intended to be customizable for any sport of interest, and similar adaptations can be made when working with performing artists. For instance, the rationale presented to participants in the first session could be tailored to include relevant examples from their domain, and the final applied (what we call "sport") meditation would incorporate core aspects (e.g., movements, gestures) of their performance. We recommend consulting with expert performing artists and teachers, even potential participants themselves, to gain an understanding of the specific culture of their world (see Pecen, Collins, & MacNamara, 2016) and for thoughts about how mindfulness can be incorporated into daily practice as well as public performance. Finally, just as coach support can be crucial to the success of MSPE, having the support of teachers and directors (ideally including them in the training too) will convey the message that learning mindfulness is to be taken seriously.

However, much more empirical evidence in support of the effectiveness of these approaches is necessary, with a focus on performance enhancement in addition to improvements in anxiety and psychological well-being. Answers are needed to questions about the mechanisms of change in mindfulness interventions, the exercises that work best for different types of performers, and how to customize programs to the demands of each performance area. Given that trainings differ in both the length and nature of home practice assigned, further research can additionally explore the optimum conditions for where and how future interventions should be conducted. The coming years will be exciting ones for the continued growth of the field of sport, exercise, and performance psychology, and it seems clear that the mindful revolution—and hopefully also MSPE—will play a key role.

CASE STUDIES IV

Case Study 1
John the Outfielder

15

W e think that a practical and engaging way to conclude this book is by sharing the respective journeys of two individual participants through mindful sport performance enhancement (MSPE) training. Rather than restating the session-by-session material that was already presented in Chapters 4 through 9, these final chapters (detailing the experiences of a collegiate baseball player and a collegiate basketball coach, respectively) focus on bringing to life what it is actually like to go through this program. Thus, what you will see are the reactions and reflections of these participants regarding what they encountered in and between each MSPE session, in their own words.

John's Background

John participated in a six-session MSPE training with a mixed group of athletes from seven different sports as part of an outcome study held on his campus during the fall of his junior year. All sessions were led by coauthors of this book, Keith Kaufman and Tim Pineau, with interviews conducted by Carol Glass before, during, and after the training (John's pre-MSPE interview took place on October 15, 2014, and is the source of the background information

http://dx.doi.org/10.1037/0000048-016
Mindful Sport Performance Enhancement: Mental Training for Athletes and Coaches, by K. A. Kaufman, C. R. Glass, and T. R. Pineau

reported here). To take part in this case study, John committed to attending each MSPE session; completing recommended home practice; filling out questionnaires before and right after the program; and engaging in recorded interviews prior to MSPE, after each session, and at the end of the school year. John later consented to go "on the record" to allow us to quote him by name in this chapter.

His baseball coach had recommended him for this case study because he knew John "loves the mental stuff," was the first player to inquire about mindfulness training after this opportunity had been announced, and was one of the hardest-working players on the team. When asked what he hoped to get out of this training, John replied, "mental calmness . . . on the field," which he thought would help with his focus. He was highly confident that if he worked hard in MSPE, his baseball performance would improve.

At the time of this case study, John was a 20-year-old junior, majoring in marketing, and the starting right fielder for his National Collegiate Athletic Association Division III team. His goal as a kid was to play college baseball, and his dreams evolved to getting drafted and playing professionally. He recognized that this was a "long shot" but said that maintaining such lofty goals is good for his motivation.

John started playing baseball when he was 5 years old. Although he enjoyed playing several sports as a kid, baseball emerged as his "true passion." He indicated particularly liking the competitive aspects of the game and being part of a team. John was proud of being named to leadership roles in baseball, serving as captain of his high school team during his senior year and recently as captain of his college team. He attributed receiving these distinctions to his work ethic and leadership skills, priding himself on "picking up" his teammates when they were down.

Because mental aspects make up "90% of the game," John took those aspects very seriously. As examples, he cited the importance of coping with failure, not getting too wrapped up in any single event, having fun, and staying "locked in on every pitch" while batting and in the field. The concept of being "in the zone" resonated with John, and he reflected on an instance when he was batting against a top team in the conference and he was "so locked in" and "everything slowed down." His vision and tracking the ball felt "perfect," as if "it was just me and the pitcher on the field."

John suggested that he is usually "pretty good at having a strong mental approach" while playing baseball. However, his mind can occasionally wander, and when he struggles mentally, he has observed that he can let self-doubts and fears of failure "creep into my mind." He labeled himself as a "perfectionist" who especially emphasizes preparation. Prior to MSPE, John had some exposure to sport psychology concepts through books on mental aspects of baseball, but outside of a few yoga classes, he had limited experience with mindfulness.

Session 1: Building Mindfulness Fundamentals

"I really enjoyed the session tonight!" John exclaimed during the interview shortly after his first MSPE session (personal communication, October 19, 2014).

[It] was very interesting, because it was something that I had never done before. . . . It's good to have . . . background in what the program is . . . like, and knowing that mindfulness is really going to be about focus. . . . The one theme that definitely came up the most tonight was "don't be judgmental." Whether it's after you mess up on a play in the field or make [some other] mistake, don't judge yourself. Just say, "it happened," and move on.

He expanded on his realization that mindfulness is about paying attention in a particular way. As John reported, baseball practice throughout the year can feel very "tedious" and repetitive. He felt that one benefit of the MSPE training would be improved focus during practice that could prevent his mind from getting lost in an "autopilot stage."

John continued by addressing the importance of staying in the present moment. Specifically, he noted that a worried mind that's "running a lot and . . . thinking about the end result or what happened before" can make an athlete "tired, mentally and physically." Therefore, John expected the training would lead to improved "mental toughness" and "stamina," both of which he believed would definitely "affect my athletic performance in a positive way."

The conversation then shifted to his reactions to the mindfulness exercises introduced in his first MSPE session. He was candid, stating that the candy exercise felt "very weird because it was something I never had done before." However, John saw potential benefits to practicing the style of awareness involved:

You can see how . . . slowing things down and really focusing on [a stimulus like] that can make a difference. A lot of things we do [involve going] on autopilot, so I thought it was very interesting to slow things down [with] . . . an everyday habit like eating. . . . Also, to get in touch with [my] senses, and really focus on using [my] senses.

John was particularly struck by the sitting meditation with a focus on the breath and linked that exercise to his experiences on the field. He acknowledged that, as athletes, when many players get nervous or tense they begin "breathing through [their] chest[s]." For this reason, John felt it important to improve his understanding of breathing to achieve more relaxation and focus while performing.

He readily picked up on how to respond to noticing a loss of focus during the breathing exercise. Specifically, John reported that he was able to "notice how my mind did wander" during the exercise and also how his "breathing did change" and "wouldn't be in the belly" any longer. He thought that because "you do it all the time," it was "harder to focus on breathing." Therefore, John explained, "I would have to remind myself to go back and focus, really lock in and focus . . . and connect with each breath."

It was impressive that John was already drawing connections between the MSPE exercises and his sport performance, as he used the same phrasing of "locking in" to the breath as he had earlier when describing what he tried to do during games at the plate or in the outfield. And he was clearly picking up on the main ideas conveyed in the first session, as he articulated the ways in which the core mindfulness concepts of awareness and acceptance were applicable to his play and how the training could address the detrimental effects of acting on autopilot. John sounded eager to practice the sitting meditation more during the week, but he spoke to the challenges of being "in that different mindset," requiring him to slow down and notice aspects of such familiar activities as eating and breathing, which he wasn't used to recognizing.

Session 2: Strengthening the Muscle of Attention

The discussion after John's second session of MSPE began with him sharing that it had been "a great week for [home] practice" (personal communication, October 26, 2014). As documented in his Daily Mindfulness Log, John had accessed the provided digital recordings and done the sitting meditation with a focus on the breath for 10 to 15 minutes each day. He described clear connections between his formal practice and the performance facilitator of relaxation.

> I thought the meditations this week were very relaxing. . . . It was actually a very busy week of schoolwork, so I . . . used it to take a break. When my mind was running a million different ways, I literally stepped back and did 10–15 minutes of the [sitting] meditation. That really helped clear my mind and relax me.

John was able to notice interesting changes in his formal practice during the week, seeing that mindfulness is about not only paying attention but also "not letting judgment get in the way." We've observed that participants are often self-critical at first when they struggle to stay focused on the breath, and, despite his recognition of the importance of nonjudgment, John was no different. Early in the week, when he found his mind had wandered, he "would get a little upset that I wasn't focused on breathing." But, by the end, John said he was "able to just ignore the judgment and move right back into my focus and concentration," something that felt like a big step to him. Also, as the week went on, he grew "a lot more comfortable with breathing through the belly. I started off the week with my hand over my belly to recognize that breathing pattern, and then, by the end of the week, it was something that came more [naturally]."

John also saw himself starting to apply mindfulness more informally to his daily activities, including baseball. Although, in many ways, it is advisable to introduce an intervention such as MSPE during the off-season or preseason, a limitation of that timing can be a delay in having opportunities to apply it to and learn from live competitive situations. In John's case, he began the training about 4 months before the start of his baseball season. However, team workouts were being held four times a week, so he did have some chances to bring mindfulness to meaningful baseball experiences. In addition, John noted that it actually might have been easier to practice these new skills because baseball was out of season. Not having the immediate pressure of competitions allowed him the space to just get more comfortable with the new skills. John said that, outside of baseball, he tried to seize opportunities to "focus on specific things that I [was] doing," such as brushing his teeth and eating.

The dialogue then shifted from his home practice to that day's session, and John reflected on the body scan exercise and a group discussion on expectations that had followed. He said the body scan "was very relaxing for my body, but, for my mind, it was tiring because I was using [it] to focus in on [the] different parts." He especially noticed sensations of tension in his shoulders and upper back, commenting that "I was just amazed that I could bring my mind to that part of my body and be able to recognize that. It was interesting to notice that and then just let it go." John connected the body scan to a visualization that he often does before a game, which he said helps him to focus on how he wants to perform.

He also appeared to enjoy and benefit from hearing the reactions of the other athletes in his group to the body scan. He said, "There were definitely different insights about the experience, so, in addition to what I thought about it, hearing someone else's reactions opened up a different way to look at it." Expectations emerged as a topic of focus in the group discussion, and John thought it was a "really good thing to recognize" that when "you're expecting something to feel some way, [it can take away from] that present moment." He identified how practicing letting go of such potential distractions and returning attention to the present in exercises such as the body scan "can really affect your performance [on the field]."

The insights John was conveying in this conversation are notable, as they suggest that he was digesting several of the main concepts presented in Session 2. For example, he addressed the roles of certain performance facilitators targeted in MSPE and the unique benefit associated with integrating awareness and acceptance. It was also evident that he was grasping the importance of the process of MSPE, speaking to his awareness of how his own experiences changed over time with repetition of the home practice and his appreciation for the instructive power of the experiences of others. We designed both the content and the structure of MSPE with careful intention, and it seemed that both were impacting John.

Session 3: Stretching the Body's Limits Mindfully

Following his third MSPE session, John (personal communication, November 2, 2014) indicated that, over the past week, he had practiced the breathing meditation without using the recording on 4 days, for 10 to 15 minutes per day, feeling it was effective and enjoyable. He offered that

> a big part of baseball, just like meditation, is getting my mind right. When my schedule started to be hectic, to be able to [do the breathing exercise] for 5, 10 minutes was a big part [of] clearing my mind and slowing me down [to] get me on track.

It was exciting to hear how John was branching beyond the recording, making the practice his own and seeing further parallels between his mental practice and baseball performances.

He described his body scan practice (done with the recording) as a bit more challenging for him. Because it was longer, he had a harder time keeping his attention focused and noticed his mind wandering to what he was going to do later that day. But, "for the most part, when my mind did wander, I was able to recognize that it wandered and bring it back."

Something that stood out on John's Daily Mindfulness Log for the week was his inclusion of two separate entries pertaining to the informal practice of mindfulness skills during batting practice. He elaborated on these entries, explaining that, while taking swings that week, he "tried to really just focus in on the task at hand and ignore all the things that I had to do, like studying for tests later on in the day." He seemed pleased that his mindfulness practice had already started to have an impact on his baseball performance, saying it was "a really cool thing to see how I could just focus my attention onto exactly what I was doing, and see how it paid off." By focusing this way, "things did seem to slow down for me," and he felt "more relaxed, more concentrated as I was practicing this week."

John shared that he had also continued expanding his informal practice outside of baseball. For example, he found himself "breathing through the belly . . . to just slow me down" when he noticed the presence of anxiety.

The conversation then shifted to John's biggest takeaways from Session 3; he spoke to the role of expectations of what an experience should or needs to be. He reported that

> the one thing that [is] coming up every week is staying in the present moment and getting rid of those judgments. It seems like we [make judgments] so much in our sport. . . . That's just a great concept that keeps popping up into my mind . . . that I have to work on. . . . [Keith] was saying how we use "should" and [how] that's like a judgment we make on ourselves, and I'm gonna try and avoid that [going forward] as an athlete.

Regarding the introduction of MSPE's mindful yoga, John said that he had some prior experience with yoga, and so found himself comfortable doing this exercise for the first time. He commented that his mind had wandered when trying yoga in the past, so it was "definitely different and interesting" to instead "really focus in on the muscle group that we were stretching." He especially liked the guidance from one of the group leaders to imagine "that you're breathing in and out through that muscle" when stretching it. Because he already had familiarity with yoga postures, John wasn't as concerned about whether he was doing them right (a common concern that can usurp attention among MSPE participants who are yoga novices), so "I was able to just focus on that present moment, and not if my foot was in the right place."

In addition, John observed some shifts in his ability to stay present while doing the expanded sitting meditation practice during this session. He said, "I just felt very present [with] what I was doing in that moment. . . . I guess I'm just doing the [sitting] meditation so many times now [that I've] become more comfortable with it."

John's statements following this session again seemed to reflect what he was integrating from the training. The impact of expectations is a prominent theme in MSPE and is a particular focus in Session 3. Although John didn't discuss this at great length, his apparent ability to put aside any expectations based on his previous experience with yoga allowed him to have an entirely new experience of the mindful yoga. Similarly, John was able to discern how his experience of the sitting meditation continued to change over time, which can happen only if a person stays open to the possibility that each repetition may be different from previous experiences. As such, John demonstrated that he was not just learning about mindfulness on an intellectual level but actually having the lived experience of being mindful.

Session 4: Embracing "What Is" in Stride

John (personal communication, November 9, 2014) had been sick in the week between his third and fourth MSPE sessions and felt the quality of his mindfulness practice was affected. He expressed specific disappointment at being unable to get in the informal mindfulness practice that he had planned for his batting sessions. Of course, this experience of thwarted plans, in itself, is an opportunity for informal mindfulness practice.

Even though his intended informal practice was stymied, John still observed some ways that MSPE was helping him in activities outside of his sport. He saw that his mind was "starting to just naturally go toward the things that I have learned through the workshop." For instance, during a flag football game with some friends, he misread one of the plays and got upset with himself. He recalled that "right away, I said to myself, 'recognize that it happened, move on and just focus on the next thing,' and that took my mind right off it."

Despite his illness, John was able to sustain his formal mindfulness practice. His log indicated that he had done 10 to 15 minutes of sitting meditation practice on 5 days. He was consistently doing sitting meditations without the recording and felt like this practice "has been one of the most helpful things for me." Sitting in the morning helped "get my day going," and practicing later in the day helped "relax me and [allow me to] take break times when I have a lot of school work."

John had trouble making time for the full mindful yoga routine but reported doing an abbreviated yoga practice twice, along with half a body scan on a different day. He continued enjoying the yoga practice he did, saying that it "relaxes my mind and helps me focus on the present moment of what I'm doing." John was pleased that he was increasingly able to "recognize that my mind is wandering" during formal mindfulness practice as well as baseball and weight lifting and could "bring my focus back to what I'm doing at that time."

Some concepts from Session 4 seemed to resonate with John, especially attachment to expectations. He noted how several participants cited the busyness of their weeks as a reason for not doing the home practice, which might reflect attachment to a mentality such as, "Oh, man, I *have* to fit it in this week" and probably won't lead to more practice. John said, "It's not really [about doing] it because you *have* to, it's being able to just do it of your own free will"—something that's hard to see when attached to how something has to be. Another example he recalled from the group discussion was how athletes can get attached to the concept of "if you do this, you're going to get this or that result," which can also interfere with how a process unfolds.

John was able to reflect on his own attachments present in his approach to baseball preparation and then expand this consideration to his life in general. He realized the attachment inherent in "the idea that if I don't put in [a certain amount of] work for games or I'm not doing [a particular thing] at practice, [then] . . . the [game] outcome is not going to be that great." He linked letting go of such an attachment to the importance of staying focused "in the present moment, not look[ing] behind me or into the future," which is true in and outside of baseball. John mused that people often "have this notion that if you do this or that, a lot [should] happen," and he saw the value in "just noticing that attachment and [then] focusing in on the present."

John did the walking meditation for the first time in this session and thought it was well liked by the group. He found it "very weird being able to really focus on each step" and remarked on how he had never paid such attention to walking. John said, "I could feel the pressure of my foot as it moved from my heel to the front of my foot" and found it interesting to be "able to step back and be aware of what I was doing, how I was walking, and what that felt like." By "stepping back off of that autopilot and being able to just focus on what I was doing . . . [I could] feel different and notice something different."

This conversation with John simultaneously highlighted his expanding understanding of mindfulness and the inevitable blind spots that arise when trying to embrace a new way of perceiving experience. He could notice the impact of attachments in others and during retrospective reflection in himself and yet appeared unaware that his own sense of disappointment when he could not practice during the week as expected was rooted in the very attachments he was describing. This dichotomy, which is common among new mindfulness practitioners, illustrates the power of unrecognized attachments, as well as the necessity of dedicated practice to develop the capacity for present-moment self-awareness.

Session 5: Embodying the Mindful Performer

John's Daily Mindfulness Log showed that in the week between his fourth and fifth MSPE sessions he had maintained his commitment to daily practice. For formal practice, he did the walking meditation three times and remarked, "I thought it was nice this week to add in the walking meditation . . . to recognize when your foot hits the ground, and really notice that you do so much [while walking] that you don't [ordinarily] get to recognize" (personal communication, November 16, 2014). John also did two brief sitting meditations. He did not, however, practice the yoga or body scan, which he attributed to leaving campus for a long weekend.

John was particularly enthusiastic about expanding his informal practice routines within baseball and thought that this practice might be what was helping him the most. He said,

> I have really been able to focus on my task at hand, like when I am hitting, and lock in. . . . I haven't [experienced] the sorts of outside distractions that I have in the past. I feel like the extra work that I have been putting in has been paying off so much.

John reported sharing some of these insights with his MSPE group that evening, giving them what he thought was an important example. After taking bad swings at the plate, at times he would think, "Man, I can't believe I just took a bad swing" or "Wow, I just looked really silly," a judgment that could throw off the rest of his at-bat. Now, though, he sees himself "being able to recognize that it was [a] bad [swing] and just move on from it, [which is] a huge part of success in baseball and everything [else] too."

John had some interesting reactions to what he learned in Session 5. He reflected on the idea of achieving through nonstriving, noting how expecting that "I should be perfect" at something can actually hurt performance. John had acknowledged to the group that he's tried to be "perfect" in baseball but recognized that "baseball is a game of failure. I'm going to have those failures and I am able to move on."

He also mentioned that there was group discussion of how MSPE can interface with visualization. The night before his games, John often spent about 20 minutes visualizing what he wanted to do the next day and was curious how that could fit with the idea of paying mindful attention. He said that the leaders had compared attention to a rubber band: "You can stretch it out [to the future with intention], but you . . . also [then] can pull it back in."

John's reaction to the sitting meditation with a focus on the breath, body, and sound was that the further expansion was "definitely needed," but, by the end of this longer exercise, "I almost felt my mind was fatiguing . . . so it was a little hard to focus." Afterward, when the participants learned the actual duration, he was surprised that he had underestimated the length. He said that he had made a "pretty cool connection" during the sport meditation, the ultimate application of MSPE skills to sport performance. Because John was in a group of mixed-sport athletes, present-moment anchors for the act of running had been chosen for this exercise. While running mindfully, John identified that he had been using "my breath as an anchor for a long time now. When I run, whether it's in practice or on my own, and I start to get tired, to ignore the pain and the feeling in my legs, I revert back to the breath and focus on breathing."

What was so striking about John's comments in this discussion following Session 5 was not just his growing comprehension of mindfulness or even his dedication to daily practice but that these developments appear to be so thoroughly informed by his lived experiences. John's understanding of nonstriving was not based solely on the explanation provided by an MSPE leader but also on his appreciation of how nonstriving was starting to shift his attitudes toward baseball. Similarly, the connection John made during the sport meditation was not only an intellectual "aha" moment but also an experiential one, in which he came to appreciate how even though mindfulness can be practiced intentionally (and at times effortfully), it can also emerge organically as one's natural inclination when facing unpleasant circumstances.

Session 6: Ending the Beginning

John's log showed that, over the final week of the training, his home practice had been quite varied. He did yoga a few times, a body scan, a 15-minute sitting meditation, three walking meditations, and what he identified as his "informal baseball meditation" during batting practice five times. John (personal communication, November 23, 2014) reported that he was still enjoying doing the sitting meditation and found that the best time for him was before bed. He fit in walking meditations while going to class and noted that it was feeling pretty comfortable and natural "to be really mindful and observe what I am doing."

John characterized his informal baseball meditation, which seemed to be an application of the sport meditation, as especially useful to him. He explained that he's started "really focus[ing] on what I am doing in the moment" while in the batting cage. He said he used to have a mindset of "having" to go to the batting cage to get swing work in, but his approach now is

> I am here, let me ignore everything else that I have going on in my day, whether it is something I have to look forward to in the future or something that I have in the past. Let me just lock in on what is going on right now and . . . bring myself to focus stronger in this present moment.

This shift in mindset, he stated, has "helped me to get the maximum benefit out of my workouts . . . and bring that focus to a higher level."

Session 6 of MSPE revisits the body scan, which gave John a chance to explore how his experience of it had evolved since its introduction in Session 2. He observed some clear differences, including that he felt much more comfortable, without concerns of whether he was "doing this right" or judging that "this feels uncomfortable and . . . weird." John also noted that "my focus is obviously a lot [stronger] than it was the first time" and it felt "a lot more fluid."

There is additional opportunity to reflect on experiences throughout the training in this session, and John shared his thoughts relating to attention and emotion regulation, in the context of both baseball and daily life.

> I noticed in games, when I am about to play, and at practice, I always want to be one step ahead. And so something [I've] usually [done] is think about the future too much. One thing I wanted to get out of this workshop . . . was really taking a step back and focusing on the present moment. . . . So, that is something that I got out of it, being able to work that into my [baseball] practice and

[also when] studying for a test; to not worry about the end result. Just worry about what I am doing in the moment, and that's been huge. Another thing that I have used in my daily life is, if I get a little bit nervous or anxious, I have been able to revert to breathing through the belly to really calm [myself] down. . . . I'm noticing that I'm able to slow down a little bit and bring my focus onto . . . what I am doing in the moment.

John's reflections at the conclusion of MSPE help to emphasize what we feel are some of the most important aspects of this training, namely, its flexibility and potential far-reaching impact. Without being given specific instructions on how to apply mindfulness in the batting cage, John was able to take the basic concepts he learned and create his own "baseball meditation." This kind of adaptability makes it more likely that a participant will find a mode of mindfulness practice that really works for him or her, which in turn increases the chances that mindfulness practice will shift from an assigned component of a 6-week program to a personally significant, intrinsically motivated, long-term practice. As for the far-reaching nature of the training, there are, of course, numerous approaches to sport performance enhancement, but what makes mindfulness unique is that its impact spreads well beyond the field of play. In our experience, many participants cite how mindfulness has improved their lives in other realms outside of sport, and John is no exception.

Postprogram Feedback

We typically invite comments from MSPE participants at the close of the training, and the responses we've received have helped us to improve the program over time. John was asked some of our common posttraining questions, and his answers are provided in the following paragraphs (personal communication, November 23, 2014).

What he liked the most about mindfulness training was becoming more focused and seeing improvements in his ability to bring "focus into the present." John attributed this shift primarily to doing the sitting meditation and felt it had "made me a better baseball player," particularly in the ability to better recognize what was going wrong when he was struggling and put "my full attention onto what I was doing." Both the walking meditation and doing informal mindfulness (especially in his sport) allowed him to step back out of autopilot and "opened up a part of my mind for me . . . not just for sports but in the other parts of my life too."

John described other ways that MSPE had benefitted him in baseball. He felt more "locked in" at the plate during batting practice. "I focused on my in-and-out breath to use my breath as an anchor, and it brought my full attention and control to my swings. I felt like I had a great workout compared to some of my other days." He also was aware that he was not thinking about the end result (e.g., driving an outside pitch to the opposite field) and instead was "able to just focus on my breath . . . [and] what I was doing at that moment," allowing him to calm down. Or, if he made a bad swing, he noticed "that I was focusing on the outcome rather than what is going on right there." John thought batting practice was an especially effective time to incorporate mindfulness practice "because when you hit in the game, you don't get many reps, but in batting practice, you can take so many reps to really drill the mindfulness in."

He also reported changes in his life outside of sport. For example, he had been a little nervous before a recent class presentation. But he paused and thought, "This is a perfect time for me to breathe through my belly and relax," permitting him to "[feel] extremely comfortable" and give a great talk.

The biggest hurdle John identified to building a home practice routine was "making the time to do the exercises" when things got busier with school work. He noted that time pressures also affected his focus during formal practice (e.g., the sitting meditations), when he would become aware of thoughts such as, "Do I really have the time to do this? I kind of want to rush through this so that I can get to the other things that I have to do." However, John found the sitting meditation calming and noted that "once I did the exercises, they reenergized me for the next thing I had to do."

Although he "definitely enjoyed the workshop, every session" and "got a lot out of it," John had one suggestion for improving MSPE. He recommended placing "more focus, from the beginning, on using [mindfulness] when practicing your sport, because that was [what] I found the most useful and helpful." John did indicate that he planned to continue incorporating mindfulness into his sport performances and day-to-day life beyond the end of MSPE, saying,

> I think the sitting meditation is something that I am definitely going to continue. The breathing was a huge part for me and I enjoyed the sitting meditation as a [way to bring] peace of mind. Maybe [I'll practice] twice, three times a week for 10–15 minutes when I get up in the morning or before I go to bed, [whenever] I have time. And [another] thing I am definitely going to [be] continuing is informal practice in my sport, staying in the present and focusing on what I am doing in the moment. I am excited to see how I can go from workouts on my own to incorporating this once we start with official practices.

Assessment

John completed the FAME (flow, anxiety, mindfulness, and emotion regulation) profile measures (described in Chapter 11) the week before his MSPE training began and again immediately after his last session. Figure 15.1 depicts John's pre- and postprogram z scores, calculated relative to published norms on the measures used. Fairly consistent with his anecdotal reports in the postsession discussions detailed previously, he showed a 13% rise in dispositional flow, with increases especially in the transformation of time and concentration on the task at hand aspects of flow. John displayed a 15% drop in sport anxiety, with his decrease in worry particularly notable. He showed the greatest

FIGURE 15.1

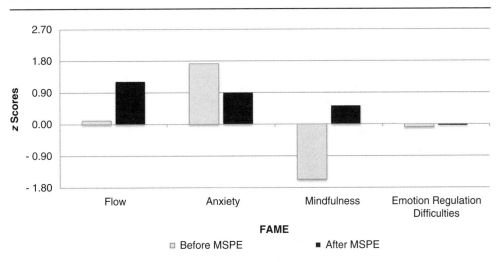

John's pre- and postprogram *z* scores (relative to published norms on each measure) for changes in flow, sport anxiety, mindfulness, and difficulties in emotion regulation. FAME = flow, anxiety, mindfulness, and emotion regulation.

improvement (30%) in mindfulness, with large increases in the facets of observing, describing, and nonreactivity to inner experience, and the least change in difficulties in emotion regulation (1%).

Follow-Up Interview

Approximately 5½ months after the end of his MSPE training, John participated in another interview (personal communication, May 7, 2015), this one focusing on how he had continued during the baseball season to incorporate the skills he had learned. When we spoke, his team had won eight of their last 10 regular-season games to, against the odds, qualify for their conference tournament. They had beaten the top-ranked team in their conference in the semifinals and were leaving for the championship games the day after this conversation. John had been sidelined with an injury for approximately 2 weeks but was able to return for the postseason.

We were eager to hear what kinds of changes John had noticed while practicing and competing and, not surprisingly, in line with his comments throughout the training, he talked about the importance of his mindfulness training for his attention and emotion regulation. He thought he was able to "center" himself better and was "just overall better focused. I've used the breathing techniques a lot this season to help me slow everything down" before at-bats and when games felt fast-paced. "[When] it literally feels like slow motion, that's when I know I'm in the zone."

He further went on to say, "Focusing in the present moment. I think that's definitely it." He had practiced this so often that it had become routine; "You just know to do it now. . . . [It] becomes so natural." For example, when feeling nervous before going to the plate or if he was on deck and noticing what the fans were saying, he was aware that he was "not focusing on the pitcher. I know that I'm not there at the present moment, so it's the first thing I do to bring myself back. . . . I use [the breathing] all the time." If he is feeling nervous in big situations, he said, "I'll definitely focus on my breathing and like I remember from [MSPE], 'your breath is your anchor,' use a little key word like that and go back to focus on my breathing. Feel my breath in, feel my breath out, and go up to the plate."

John also described finding visual anchors in the outfield before games and "focus[ing] my attention to that one point and bring[ing] myself together before the game," which is a great example of the MSPE performance facilitator referred to as forming key associations. For instance, he would stare at the 3 in the number delineating the distance to the fence, "and really focus on what the 3 looks like, where the curves are . . . really bring my focus to the present moment."

Though he had enjoyed quite a bit of success in the field, John spoke to experiencing some real challenges during the season, especially at the plate. When he'd struggled, John tried not to "let that bother me; I put it out of my head and move on." He gave some great examples demonstrating the benefits of mindfulness after having a bad at-bat or swing:

> I'll go into the outfield and pick up some grass and . . . I'll just throw it away and say 'It's gone, reset.' Or, when I step to the plate with my batting gloves and I take a bad swing, I'll step out of the box and use the physical anchor with my batting gloves, undo the Velcro and then back on, and will say 'I've cleared it, it's reset.' So, I guess just a quick memory and little triggers like that have definitely helped me to clear my mind. . . . By having those anchors and [letting go] of those feelings that you have, and thoughts that you have, that can prolong your moments of being in the zone.

Finally, we wanted to hear if John had noticed any changes in his life outside of sport and what his plans were to use mindfulness in the future. He had continued using breathing to slow himself down before class presentations and noted that, as a business major, he approaches business with the same competitive mindset he brings to baseball. He said that if he pursues plans to be an entrepreneur, he knows that many first businesses fail, so it will be important to maintain a mindful way of being to cope with such risk. Having skills to stay focused are a "big thing I have now that I will definitely use."

John shared that he intends to keep up a routine of sitting meditation and informal mindfulness over the next year and that he had seen several articles about how top companies are using mindfulness for their employees. Illustrating how much he had gleaned from his MSPE experience, John concluded by saying,

This is something that I'm definitely gonna take with me . . . when you know things are going good, you're playing the game in slow motion. I noticed last weekend at the beginning of the playoffs [for my team], it was the most mentally exhausted I've been. We had two 9-inning games, and my concentration was so high [even though] I was so tired. But mindfulness, paying attention to my muscles, noticing what's tight in my body. This was a great experience to have. I'm very appreciative of it and will take a lot of positive things out of it.

As a postscript, the day after this follow-up interview, John went 2 for 5 at the plate with an RBI (run batted in) in the first game of the conference finals, but the team fell 6 to 4. The entire season came down to the next game, in which John got 3 hits in 5 at-bats and scored 2 runs, helping his team to a 10–6 win. In the final game of the championship, he was 1 for 4 with 2 RBIs and 2 runs scored, and the team won the conference championship for only the third time in school history.

Case Study 2

Angie the Basketball Coach

16

A t the time of this case study, Angie was a 32-year-old assistant coach for a Division III collegiate women's basketball team and had already been in coaching for 11 years. She was also serving as an assistant athletic director at her university. The 6-week mindful sport performance enhancement (MSPE) training she attended included six other coaches (a mixture of head coaches and assistants) from her school, representing basketball, volleyball, baseball, and lacrosse, and was led by Keith Kaufman. To take part in this case study, Angie committed to attending all six MSPE sessions as well as completing recommended home practice, the FAME (flow, anxiety, mindfulness, and emotion regulation) profile measures, and recorded interviews (conducted by Carol Glass) both before the training and after each session. She later consented to go "on the record," allowing us to quote her by name in this chapter. (The pre-MSPE interview that was the source of her background information occurred on February 19, 2015.)

With the exception of a few yoga classes, Angie had little background in mental training but felt like she'd always been "pretty self-aware and emotionally steady." In her own playing career, confidence and drive had come somewhat naturally to her, but as a coach, Angie could now appreciate that "not everybody has the same approach to sports that I did." She

http://dx.doi.org/10.1037/0000048-017
Mindful Sport Performance Enhancement: Mental Training for Athletes and Coaches, by K. A. Kaufman, C. R. Glass, and T. R. Pineau

wondered how best to get her players to "redirect their emotions or mentality" when they missed shots and adopted a "body language of defeat." Angie's goal in signing up for MSPE was to "help myself so that I can help them," thereby building "mental toughness" among her players. Like John, she had high expectations for how she and ultimately her players would benefit.

Angie participated in multiple sports as a kid, moving toward specialization in basketball by seventh grade. She found basketball to be fun and challenging, discovered that she was good at it, and loved being a part of a team. Angie was recruited to play for a private high school, where she made the varsity team her freshman year, and then was a starter all 4 years in college.

After graduation, Angie got her first coaching job and quickly found that she loved it, especially "the X's and O's, the problem-solving pieces of it." She next moved to a different university, getting a master's degree while continuing to hone her coaching skills. Two years later, Angie was offered the head coaching position at a small Division III college. Getting a head coaching job had been a big goal, and although it was extremely demanding work, she learned a great deal. After her husband relocated for his work, Angie found her current assistant-coaching position. She conveyed a sense of pride that she "stuck with it" in a tough profession and said she greatly values her impact on the lives of the student–athletes she has coached.

Before starting MSPE, Angie was already fairly satisfied with her coaching performance, although she recognized that "I'm not Pat Summitt." She indicated feeling good about her knowledge of the game and tactical expertise, as well as her significant growth as a recruiter and team builder. Angie also viewed her focus during games as a strength, characterizing herself as someone who doesn't dwell much on mistakes because "if I'm going to be down about it, I can't pick my team back up from it. I have to pick myself up first." In addition, she said she puts tremendous "emotional and mental energy" into her job, trying to reframe any nervousness she feels as "excitement" or "good stress." Angie claimed that "I love being on the court and coaching [my players] . . . seeing them every day . . . seeing a little bit of growth."

She was familiar with the idea of being "in the zone" as a player and associated it with the ability to eliminate any distractions. When asked what finding the zone would be like as a coach, she struggled to pinpoint an answer because, in that role, one has "got to be thinking about 20 things at once" and yet still be very decisive.

Session 1: Building Mindfulness Fundamentals

"I really enjoyed it!" were the first words Angie said in the interview following her first MSPE session (personal communication, March 19, 2015). She was excited to become more aware of "the mental piece of it" and wondered if mindfulness would have helped her during her playing days.

One concept from the first session that struck a chord for her was nonjudgment, specifically, how getting wrapped up in reactions to events can deprive an athlete of control over a performance. She related this idea to her observation that student–athletes believing that "I'm having an off night" after missing the first few shots will often think they'll keep missing them. Angie recalled that, as a player, she "just did what I did and didn't think as much . . . and if I missed a shot, I didn't think twice about it." However, as a coach, if she could "put [herself] in the shoes of . . . our student–athletes where they do have those judgments when they miss a shot," she might better help them "let things pass through and not [get stuck in a] judgment." By stepping back from such judgments, they can see that "you're actually in control of the present, if you [let go of] the things that happened previously . . . that are not connected."

Angie expanded on her sense of how MSPE could facilitate an awareness of her players' experiences, which might be quite different from what hers had been, and how to teach them to play more mindfully. For instance, she recognized that her coaching decisions might be interpreted by her players differently than she intended, such as when "we take [a player] out of the game because maybe she has been in for 5 minutes, but she comes out and [thinks] 'What did I do wrong?'" The athlete may have done nothing wrong, but rather than "having each event be . . . its own, the mistake is to connect the events together [through assumption]." Having this awareness could allow her to understand how players can get "caught up in [such] thoughts" and then help them to "[re]focus on the moment . . . bring them back to paying attention with a purpose . . . at that time."

Angie also shared her initial thoughts on how MSPE could help her beyond coaching, sensing that she had more distractions and worries in her personal life than at work. She realized it would be helpful to remember that one negative event doesn't mean "everything in life is going wrong" and "that I can [only] control each moment in the present."

In terms of the mindfulness exercises done in the first session, Angie said she had no prior experience with any of them. She enjoyed the candy exercise, in particular becoming "aware of what your senses tell you about this one piece of candy," like it's an unknown object. Angie tried "to be much more curious about what I was looking at . . . the way it feels [and] smells." She found the sitting meditation with a focus on the breath "kind of relaxing, because I don't know the last time I was told to . . . just breathe!" Angie recalled some other coaches saying that they got distracted by the ticking clock and unrelated thoughts, yet she experienced that it was "fairly easy for me to just feel my stomach in and out, [to] focus on [the] inhale [and] exhale." At first, Angie had tried to "push all distractions to the side" and tell herself, "Okay, don't think of anything." As soon as she'd issued that internal command, however, she felt "like my breathing was a little heavier, . . . my heart beat . . . a little faster, because now, all of a sudden, there was something on my mind, and I could feel . . . more of my heart than my diaphragm."

The discussion after the sitting meditation helped her to better understand this experiential insight. Angie realized that she had been trying to tell herself "not to think of anything, instead of just plain [observing]" and remembered an example Keith had offered the group about how thought suppression can ironically backfire. "I was telling myself 'don't think of anything,' and that thought itself is exactly what

I thought of, so even though I didn't have other external thoughts [like] . . . 'What's for lunch,' I was just telling myself what to do."

Like John in the previous chapter, Angie was immediately able to generate real-world examples of the common mental pitfalls that mindfulness training can address, indicating that she too was readily able to take in and understand the concepts introduced in this first session. However, unlike with John, who emphasized the potential impact of mindfulness on his awareness and concentration, it seemed that the ideas of nonjudgmental acceptance and letting go resonated more with Angie. She quickly identified the ways in which holding on to judgments and assumptions impacted her athletes and how her own automatic efforts to control her internal states affected her experiences. This contrast between John and Angie reflects more than just their differing roles and responsibilities as an athlete and coach, respectively; it also highlights the complex and multifaceted nature of mindfulness training and the myriad ways in which people may benefit from embracing this new perspective.

Session 2: Strengthening the Muscle of Attention

The interview following Angie's second session of MSPE began with a discussion of her home practice over the past week (personal communication, March 26, 2015). According to her Daily Mindfulness Log, she had practiced most days, and it seemed she had done so with great enthusiasm. She had downloaded a recording of the breathing meditation to her phone and had made a plan to practice early in the morning after she woke up.

Although finding time for formal practice had not been a problem for Angie, she found that, unlike her experience in the first session, it had been "difficult to sit still, focus, listen and just *be* for even 10 minutes . . . 'cause, in my head, I was just thinking of what was on my agenda for the day and things that I needed to do." As she continued to practice over the week, however, it got easier. "I knew that if my mind wandered, the recording said it's okay, that's what minds do, and I could bring myself back to breathing." However, when she found her mind wandering again, "it really was kind of eye-opening to see how I just couldn't sit and just relax and breathe."

Angie expanded on the differences between her home practice and her first time doing the sitting meditation during Session 1, when it "[had been] relaxing and I could really just focus on the inhale and the exhale." In that session, she had been "prepared to . . . learn something new, and just focus[ed] on that," while, at home, it was harder to think, "okay, this is going to help me, this is my own mental practice." In our conversation, Angie appeared to be judging her home practice experience, concluding that it meant she did not "really have that mindfulness" and that she "definitely need[ed] to work" on it.

At this point, Angie wasn't fully aware of how these judgments, and their impact on her, were similar to the ones that she described seeing in her own athletes (e.g., when being taken out of a game) in the interview following Session 1. However, she appeared to be moving toward this awareness when she reflected on the parallels between physical and mental training and how both work best when a commitment is made to engage in regular, systematic workouts as a choice, not an obligation. For example, Angie said,

> Maybe I approached it as, "Okay, I set my alarm, this is what I have to do, this is my homework," and not "This is a part of my life, because I need to train my mind" [as], you know, an everyday occurrence. It was more like, and we talked about that today [in the second session], not approaching mindfulness as an assignment to do, but just as you would exercise every day, well why not exercise your mind every day?

Angie commented that there would always be busyness in her life, but perhaps she could become more mentally focused and aware if she's able to "just sit back [even for just] a minute a day and maybe start the day preparing my mind for what's going on and not focusing on the stuff that I have to do, but just . . . *being.*" She noted that, in her personal life as well as her coaching, "being more aware . . . makes your attitude a little bit more positive [and] more hopeful."

Angie also remarked that she particularly enjoyed the group discussions and learning from others' experiences. In Session 2, the discussion on present-moment attention had made an especially strong impact on her. She recounted how the coaches had highlighted the many distractions now available to them and their players, like "always having a cell phone, always multitasking . . . always [being] stimulated." So, in wanting today's student–athletes "to focus on just being at practice, we have to be aware that there could be 10 other things going on at the same time" and somehow be able to work with that. By recognizing this as the experience of her athletes, she seemed to become more aware of how her own ability to live mindfully in the face of so many potential distractions could affect her team, observing that if coaches can "live with it and still be aware of it [while staying] mindful of the moment and of how you can focus within that moment . . . we can teach our student–athletes to live with [it] too."

Although Angie was able to gain this significant insight about how MSPE could influence her coaching, it is important to note that she started the program during her team's off-season so was not immediately able to implement mindfulness strategies. Instead, she shared some ideas for how the mindfulness skills she was learning could be incorporated into her coaching going forward, hitting on the mental training paradox.

> If someone was to ask me or other coaches here if the mental side of being a student–athlete [is] important, we'd say, "Yes, it's very important." But then, why aren't we practicing it, and why wouldn't we make it more of a daily occurrence where it's not something you *have* to do, it's just a part of what you do?

Angie suggested that, just as there's a portion of practice when her players are working on ball handling, mindfulness training could be "part of what we do . . . just like weight lifting . . . just like eating healthy." Making this commitment as "part of their routine" could help the team to be more focused during practices and to "think about what we're doing at this [moment] instead of 'just go, go, go.'"

This conversation concluded with Angie describing her reactions to doing the MSPE body scan for the first time. "Yeah, that was hard," she laughed. Angie found that she had "started to daydream a little bit," thinking of other things, and was tuned in to the exercise but aware that she "definitely wasn't focused on following it." Although she would bring her attention back to the part of the body that Keith was referring to, she found her "mind wasn't on it for long" and didn't know if that was because she was "just in a really relaxed state, or I was tired, or just not good at focusing."

Just as with her home practice, Angie's comments about her body scan reflect an underlying assumption about what being mindful "should" feel like, and in her attempts to explain why her experience did not match her expectations, self-judgments arose. Similar to John's experience following Session 4, this may represent the common occurrence of participants' intellectual understanding of mindfulness outpacing their experiential understanding. However, far from being a bad outcome, the continued presence of expectations during mindfulness training is an essential part of the process. Although an important aspect of mindfulness practice is letting go of such expectations, this capacity does not develop overnight, and, in fact, it is in the experiencing of one's own expectations that the opportunity arises to see their impact and let them go.

Session 3: Stretching the Body's Limits Mindfully

Angie noticed some interesting changes as she continued to practice mindfulness between her second and third MSPE sessions (personal communication, April 9, 2015). When doing the body scan, she found that "it just kind of resonated with me more" and her mind seemed to wander less than it had in the session. Angie observed herself preferring it to the sitting meditation, saying it got easier to "concentrate more on the sensations of different body parts than the sitting and just breathing." She claimed it actually felt harder to be "motivated to . . . do the seated meditation," which she thought might relate to "having . . . an expectation of doing [it], rather than [an intrinsic] goal," a differentiation that had come up in a session discussion among the coaches.

It is very common for experiences of an exercise to evolve and for preferences to emerge over the course of MSPE, and participants are taught to recognize and understand such processes nonjudgmentally while also learning why a diversity of practice efforts (not just what comes easy) is important. Angie was thus invited to process her home practice observations further, and she remarked that

> I might have a thought, but [my attention] came back much easier to the body part that I was on [than it had when I first tried the scan]. . . . When I would be doing the breathing meditation, . . . my mind would wander and [I'd] think,

"I need to do all these things today," [and] it was harder to bring it back to [that] anchor. So, I think it was just a matter of bringing [my] mind back to something that . . . resonates with [me], or that [I could] attach [myself] to.

This notion of the body scan resonating more with Angie generated curiosity about her views on whether people in athletics might tend to connect more with bodily attentional anchors. "I was thinking about this today when we did the yoga exercise," Angie replied.

I always thought I was very in tune with my body. . . . Being an athlete, I notice my body getting stronger because I'm lifting weights, and I know . . . when my shot is off because my hand [made a particular movement] when I shot the ball. So, when we did the yoga, I loved it 'cause I . . . could give myself back to knowing what my body feels like and knowing okay, I'm going to do this stretch and I know how it's gonna feel, and enjoy that . . . sense of being in tune with my body.

Elaborating on the theme of bodily awareness, Angie talked more about her experience of really liking the mindful yoga in Session 3. Although some movements were difficult for her body, she enjoyed the physical challenge. "So, when I would stretch, even though it would hurt some of the time, it might sound weird, but I liked it, it felt good. It kept my mind on that stretch." Angie gave an interesting reply to what she did with the discomfort she noticed:

At one point, with my hamstrings, I was like, I just want to stand up right now, but even though I told myself I should stand up, I didn't. Because I'm stretching. I'm in *this* position, holding it. . . . Even though my mind told me, 'hey you're stretching enough,' I just stayed with it.

She then broadened this thinking to her everyday life, with ideas related to the MSPE performance facilitator of letting go. For instance, if she found herself in a bad mood because of something that had happened that day, she could alternatively be "more aware of what's happened . . . move through it, and let it go, like we talked about [being able to do] in the first session. Just let it be."

Angie also saw how expectations can influence performance, a main topic of focus in Session 3, sharing her takeaway that "if you have expectations that are conditional, they can create [excess] fear and tension and anxiety [when] trying to meet [them]." She speculated, if athletes have expectations, might these lead them to "fear that they are gonna make a mistake . . . that they are gonna place judgment on that, and think that they aren't any good because they didn't meet that expectation?" Angie went on to talk about how expectations can interface with goals in athletics, saying, "You want to compete and to win so you need to have some kind of goals," but it might be beneficial to view them as "more of a guideline [than a rule], so there aren't these [fears associated with] not meeting these goals."

She delved further into the coaching implications, wondering how coaches can use knowledge of how expectations function to best motivate their athletes. Angie thought that one aspect of mindfulness is "just being aware of what either you or your athletes are thinking when . . . performing. Are they fearful of expectations? Are they motivated toward [appropriate] goals?" For instance, if a player seems nervous or is worrying about whether she is doing the right thing on the court, it might help to offer encouragement to "just go out and play. Don't be so focused on the expectations, because, if they don't work out, you are going to react negatively." Coaches aren't usually expecting athletes to play perfectly, so "Can you go out and put in all of your effort and play much more freely instead of tight and constrained?"

As in the previous sessions, Angie was eager to look for ways in which MSPE could influence her coaching and her athletes, and she readily found them. These connections still seemed to reflect more of an intellectual than an experiential understanding of mindfulness. However, Angie's comments after the third session suggest the growing impact of her personal experiences in the training. She continued to observe discrepancies between her expectations of and experiences with mindfulness practice, but rather than feeling discouraged or frustrated, she approached these observations with curiosity. Maybe the most concrete example of the impact of this kind of openness was expressed in her reaction to the yoga, when she noticed herself reaching an uncomfortable limit, observing both her physical and mental reactions and making the choice to dwell at that limit rather than move away.

Angie was beginning to live an essential truth of mindfulness: Namely, as we emphasize throughout MSPE, mindfulness is not about changing our experiences so that we never feel discomfort. Rather, it is about allowing us to relate to discomfort, emotional or physical, in a new way that introduces a sense of freedom and choice, releasing us from the reflexive reactions born of our unrecognized expectations and attachments.

Session 4: Embracing "What Is" in Stride

In the week between Sessions 3 and 4, Angie's home practice regimen became increasingly diversified, incorporating mindfulness more informally into her daily life and emphasizing those formal exercises that she "enjoys" (personal communication, April 16, 2015). This choice is not uncommon, but observing judgments of the exercises themselves and attachments to these judgments, as Angie alluded to after the previous session, can be a valuable teaching point.

She had a lot to say about the mindful yoga, which she "really enjoyed" doing one day after work. In particular, she talked about how it "stretches your limits," in terms of both "how far can you stretch and how you feel." Keeping with this theme, she suggested it was interesting to approach the yoga as a physical challenge that she could overcome mentally. Angie remarked that she had previously scheduled time to work out, but "now I'm working my mind *and* body."

She'd kept practicing the body scan in the mornings before getting out of bed, but doing the sitting meditation remained a struggle for her. She was more aware of her judgment of this struggle, however, explaining how she saw herself thinking "Oh, I have to do it" and not wanting to have that kind of attitude toward the practice. It seemed that this awareness helped Angie to adapt and incorporate a focus on the breath into her informal practice. She reported developing a "new perspective" on how to approach high-stress situations, as evidenced by a time during the week when she was "getting very anxious" preparing for something that was coming up. "I just stopped thinking and breathed . . . and [I felt] my breathing . . . [which] was more useful to me than doing the [formal sitting] meditation."

Angie also talked about her experience doing the walking meditation in Session 4, and her reaction was a common one. She observed that it was "hard to go slow" and preferred when they started walking faster. More subtly, she noticed the importance of the stabilizer muscles when shifting from one foot to the other and how easy it was to lose her balance when walking slowly. In contrast, when walking fast, "it was just kind of a rhythm. . . . Part of me appreciated the fact that walking is really kind of hard and something that we learn how to do."

One other element that stood out to her in the fourth session was the continued emphasis on personalizing and diversifying a budding mindfulness practice. She connected with

> the idea of having [both] informal practice and formal practice, with the informal piece being your daily life and, at some point, just being really aware of what's your anchor. And, if your anchor at that point needs to be a breath, just to slow down. But, also [the importance of] putting time aside for 15 minutes, or that 40-minute yoga, where it's just specifically allotted for a formal mindfulness practice.

The diversification of Angie's practice over these initial weeks of MSPE brought with it a deepening of her understanding of mindfulness on a number of levels. She was not only learning about mindfulness concepts and coming to better understand the experience of being mindful but also developing a better understanding of *how* to practice mindfulness.

The importance of this how-to knowledge cannot be overstated. Angie's capacity to nonjudgmentally observe her own struggles with the sitting meditation allowed her to understand the importance of intrinsic motivation in a more personal and immediate way than any didactic lesson could ever teach. By letting go of a belief that focusing on the breath was just too challenging for her, she was able to tap into her intrinsic motivation for the mindfulness training generally and find a way to use the breath as part of her informal practice.

It was this shift of focus to her informal practice that allowed Angie to attain the insight reflected in her final comment about Session 4. Whether talking about formal or informal mindfulness practice, there is a way in which people can view both as necessarily different from their usual way of being. Underlying her comment seems to be the understanding that practicing mindfulness doesn't have to be separate from her usual experience but, in fact, can simply be anchoring her attention to the present throughout her daily life. This knowledge will, of course, be important for Angie to sustain her personal practice once MSPE concludes, but perhaps even more significantly, this knowledge will be essential for Angie when attempting to teach her athletes how to perform and live mindfully.

Session 5: Embodying the Mindful Performer

Following Session 5, Angie reported that making time to practice mindfulness outside the weekly meetings was becoming more routine for her (personal communication, April 23, 2015). She was still doing the body scan in bed after waking, noting that it helped her feel "mentally prepared . . . for the day." She also continued integrating her physical and mental training, finding it worked well to do the walking meditation or yoga after returning from her morning workout. She remarked,

> Working out my body, and then . . . working on [my] mind. . . . Getting a workout in meant, "Okay now I can do my [mindfulness] exercises." And, if I was thinking, "Oh, maybe I shouldn't work out today," it was like, "Oh, I should work out and then do my [mindfulness] exercises." So, [they] worked hand in hand. . . . I think what I'm getting to, the whole thing Keith is telling us, is how you make [mindfulness practice] a part of your day, not something that you *have* to do, but something that you just do.

In terms of her reactions to the MSPE exercises themselves, Angie indicated that she was especially enjoying the opportunities to be mindful while in motion. For instance, she liked the walking meditation because it was "active. . . . It's something that I do all the time, I walk." She felt it allowed her to "appreciate walking" more. While doing the yoga, she focused not on

> how far you can stretch in terms of muscularly, but how far [your] comfort level can stretch and you can stay focused. What does your mind do when it goes too far, can you bring it back to what you're doing, instead of thinking how hard it might feel? . . . I do like the physical exercises, that challenge, where I have to think about my body and how my body feels going through this, and just observe it, and then move on.

Angie further considered how she could apply to her coaching what she was learning through her mindfulness practice. She explained that, in sports, "it's the repetition of knowing how something feels," such as in a shooting drill if the ball comes off the hand wrong, to "recognize how it felt, make an adjustment, and move on." In other words, it's important to

> not just do the physical movements, but to mentally be aware of what it feels like. You know, how does it really feel to make that stretch, when you slide to the right? It's not only muscle memory, it's mental memory.

In saying this, Angie seemed to be highlighting a way she could implement the concentration and letting go performance facilitators.

She then shared an example of how she was able to incorporate informal mindfulness practice during the week, specifically the STOP technique (stop, take a few breaths, observe, proceed). One day after work she was out at dinner and was "having an emotional time." In the midst of her emotions, Angie attempted to "stop, at least acknowledge how I'm feeling at this moment, and then move on from it," allowing her to "just let it pass and not affect the rest of the night." This experience reiterated for her the power of staying present, as opposed to getting "stuck in the past, [or] flying into the future." This example also illustrates how Angie was strengthening her ability to accept her present-moment experience, and she elaborated on her understanding of acceptance as "it is what it is, and you let it go" to move on to the next moment.

Angie continued to explore the concept of acceptance in her reflections on the experience of the sport meditation introduced in Session 5. As with John's MSPE program, Angie's group included representatives from various sports, so running anchors were chosen for this highly applied exercise. She described her experience of the meditation as essentially "doing the body scan while we were running, thinking about the placement of your head over your shoulders, how it felt." She felt especially "in tune" with her hips, "thinking about how they are moving, and making my stride happen." Angie said she liked to run and was comfortable doing it, without "any judgments in terms of what people might think of my form."

The group discussion following the exercise was very interesting to her, especially hearing how some of the other coaches were less accepting of their experiences and judging themselves for how certain body parts (e.g., arms) were moving and might have looked to others. Those judgments had notably taken those coaches out of their present-moment experiences, yet Angie hadn't thought anything of how they'd been moving. It occurred to her that if "everyone is thinking about someone else looking at them, [ironically] the last thing they are gonna do is look and think about you!" She continued, "We're not always the center of what's going on that's making us so self-conscious. All these little things that you might worry about aren't as big of a deal as we make them out to be sometimes." In other words, her peers had been so concerned about how they looked that they missed the experience of running, and Angie had been so focused on what she was doing that she hadn't noticed anything about the other coaches and certainly hadn't judged them!

Angie then applied this realization to what she'd seen from her players. If someone misses a free throw, "the whole gym isn't going to be thinking about [her] missing that shot. . . . One little error isn't such the catastrophe [we] might be internally thinking it is." She saw that, as a coach, it might be useful to remember that others are self-conscious in ways she is not, and she can use her attunement to the situation to offer her players reassurance not to "worry about all these little things, make note of it . . . but then move on and enjoy the moment." This idea was something that Angie was excited to take from the training.

Angie hoped to get on the court sometime before the next session and apply the principles of the sport meditation to shooting a basketball. She was curious to really observe "the mechanics of it . . . while I'm shooting and dribbling and running up and down the floor." In this sincere interest to apply mindfulness to her own sport, the evolution of Angie's motivation for mindfulness practice is clear. The shift from "having" to practice to "wanting" to practice has been a prominent theme for Angie, and with each postsession interview it became more and more apparent that this balance had been shifting toward the latter.

This is exactly what we hope the MSPE training engenders in participants. Mindfulness is a nonstriving, process-oriented endeavor, yet many people who engage in a mindfulness-based intervention such as MSPE usually have a desired outcome in mind, for instance, to improve sport performance. However, as participants experientially explore mindfulness, they begin to see the value of mindfulness practice irrespective of the original outcome they had hoped for. Of course, Angie may be eager to apply the sport meditation to her shooting because she hopes that mindfulness will make her a better coach or player, but she is also expressing a genuine curiosity about what this well-learned activity will feel like when she does it mindfully, regardless of what this experience will produce. This curiosity, as well as her dedication to daily practice (both formal and informal), her active engagement with the in-session discussions, and her between-session reflections on the different aspects of MSPE, reflects the blossoming of Angie's personal, intrinsic intention to be mindful, which is, in itself, a key component of the practice.

Session 6: Ending the Beginning

The week before her sixth and final MSPE session was probably the hardest for Angie in terms of doing formal mindfulness practice (personal communication, April 30, 2015). The week before Session 5, she had been building the routine of doing her formal practice (e.g., walking meditation) after her morning physical workouts and "liked how that kind of flowed in terms of carving out some time and knowing that it's like routine, it's just part of the day." However, she had trouble figuring out how to similarly integrate the sport meditation. She chose to practice a running meditation on a treadmill, where, in the past, she typically listened to music. Some part of altering that experience "didn't quite click" for her. Angie decided that when she practiced it again, she would run around her neighborhood "and not have it associated with something that I already know in my head how it *should* be."

She continued to express a preference for the more movement-based formal practices such as the walking meditation and even the body scan, as opposed to the sitting meditation, because they have "more physical meat to it," allowing her to be "in tune with my body." Nonetheless, Angie did practice the sitting meditation and "got through it okay" but still felt like she was doing it "because I *had* to be doing it."

Next, Angie spoke about continuing her mindfulness practice after the end of the training, for both her coaching and her personal life. In general, she felt she had successfully personalized her practice and made it "a part of [her] daily life." She still had some lingering questions, however, about how to best utilize the skills she'd learned in her coaching. One element she emphasized was, when introducing something new, it's important "to make sure [it] works with [that] team." In Session 6, another coach had brought up staying in sync with the student–athletes and making adjustments when change is called for. For example, that particular coach had never played music at practice, finding it distracting, but his players expressed a desire for it and he saw that it could pump them up, which he wanted. This comment had spawned a broader discussion about how to best introduce mindfulness to players in a way they can receive, given how different it is from what they're used to doing in their sport.

Angie recalled pointedly asking Keith in the session for guidance on this issue, saying, "Okay, all of this is great, but I [don't] know how to get started [with my team]!" She wondered what coaches such as Phil Jackson had done when they first exposed their players to this type of training. Angie found Keith's suggestions reassuring because they helped her realize that "it doesn't have to be some big, clever production."

> Whether it's implementing it in a shooting drill, [saying to players] "be aware of how the ball is coming off your hand when you shoot," or if it's as Phil Jackson did, come off the court, and then 10 minutes before going into a film practice, spend this time just going into a sitting meditation. It doesn't have to feel like it's this huge challenge. Maybe doing this kind of thing on our own . . . is kind of challenging, but when you're in a group setting and it's carved into a day and a routine, it won't feel as if it's this big program-changing thing. It's going to be accepted a lot easier, I think.

She left Session 6 thinking that her challenge for the future was, "How do you take it a step further and implement it into a program? And then consistently do it yourself where it's something you can commit to and believe in?" This, of course, is a challenge for every MSPE participant at the conclusion of the training. But, even if she had some questions about her ability to move forward, Angie was already well on her way. What we hope to impart to all MSPE participants is that this training is just the beginning. It can be incredibly valuable to be exposed to mindfulness with the help of a teacher and with some instruction on how to begin a practice, but the only way to truly learn about mindfulness is to be mindful. In each postsession interview, it seemed that the most important lessons Angie was learning were not only from the content of the MSPE session but also from how her personal experiences informed her understanding of that content. And with continued practice, that understanding only deepens.

Postprogram Feedback

As John did, Angie shared her reactions to the program following Session 6. She first addressed what she liked the most about MSPE, highlighting the numerous opportunities for group discussion. In her days as a player it was "all kind of routine, it's muscle memory, I didn't think too much and I guess I wasn't mindful," so she came into the program wanting to hear "other people's perspectives, how they think when doing sports." She felt that hearing various viewpoints in the sessions raised new and important considerations when "evaluating and observing [her] players in practice." Also, she enjoyed learning about the "psychology and the science part" that underlies MSPE. Echoing what she'd said throughout the training, she preferred the exercises that "were more active," such as the walking and sport meditations, and planned to keep practicing the sport meditation to better integrate it into her daily routine.

In terms of applying what she'd learned to her coaching, she expressed a desire to be much more observant during team practices and to talk with her players to figure out "what is important in their own mindfulness." If they are "just showing up and going through the motions, [getting] frustrated if they miss a shot," Angie thought that perhaps she could "pay more attention to that body language or maybe even what they say to get them on a different track." For instance, she could say after a missed shot, "Okay, that was one shot, you let it go, but be aware of how is the ball coming off your hand. Are you jumping enough, are your legs into it?" Such feedback could build their awareness of the situation and what they could choose to do differently, without getting "caught up by the [reactions]." Angie thought that, when introducing her players to more formal mindfulness practices, it would be "helpful to have the recordings" and perhaps just give them "a little taste" of a body scan and breathing meditation, to see what is most helpful.

Regarding how MSPE might benefit her life outside of sport, Angie felt she already handled stressful situations at work pretty well but might benefit from mindfulness in other domains, such as when she judges herself for not communicating something as best as she could. After the training, she thought she was more "aware" of what happens in such situations, "more in tune with how I am feeling, and I'm just okay with how I am feeling. 'It is what it is,' that kind of idea." She offered the example of getting bad news from a friend that week. At first, she was taken aback, but she paused and considered that "it is what it is, there is nothing I can do about it. I can't change it, but what I can do is accept it and be there to help in the future."

Overall, Angie felt she had a very positive experience with the training. However, like all MSPE participants she faced challenges, and the one she shared is among the most common. Angie said it wasn't easy to consistently make the time for formal mindfulness practice. She noted that it was easier when she did her formal practice after her morning workout, but she didn't work out every day. Something that seemed to help, she said, was to "set a time" in advance, so that her mindfulness practice was not contingent upon her workouts.

Assessment

Angie completed the FAME measures the week before Session 1 and just after Session 6. Figure 16.1 depicts her pre- and postprogram z scores relative to published norms on each measure. She showed a 12% increase in dispositional flow, especially in the aspects of loss of self-consciousness, unambiguous feedback, concentration on

FIGURE 16.1

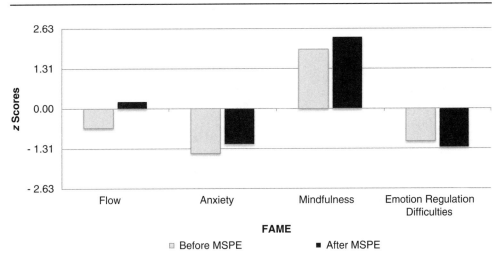

Angie's pre- and postprogram *z* scores (relative to published norms on each measure) for changes in flow, sport anxiety, mindfulness, and difficulties in emotion regulation. FAME = flow, anxiety, mindfulness, and emotion regulation.

the task at hand, and merging of action and awareness. Angie also demonstrated an increase in mindfulness (4%), to the greatest extent on the same facets as did John: observing, describing, and nonreactivity to inner experience. Although she improved in emotion regulation (7% decrease in difficulties), she demonstrated a 13% increase in sport anxiety in sport performance settings, which initially had been extremely low. In our experience, anxiety can sometimes go up in the short term when learning something new, such as mindfulness skills, and trying to figure out how best to implement it in a performance. In the interview following Session 6, Angie spoke extensively about how she still needs to determine the most effective way to bring mindfulness into her coaching and to her players, so perhaps that (understandable) uncertainty helps explain her sport anxiety increase.

References

Aherne, C., Moran, A. P., & Lonsdale, C. (2011). The effect of mindfulness training on athletes' flow: An initial investigation. *The Sport Psychologist, 25*, 177–189. http://dx.doi.org/10.1123/tsp.25.2.177

Alexander, F. M. (1932). *The use of the self*. New York, NY: Dutton.

Allen, M., Dietz, M., Blair, K. S., van Beek, M., Rees, G., Vestergaard-Poulsen, P., . . . Roepstorff, A. (2012). Cognitive-affective neural plasticity following active-controlled mindfulness intervention. *The Journal of Neuroscience, 32*, 15601–15610. http://dx.doi.org/10.1523/JNEUROSCI.2957-12.2012

Allen, M. S., Jones, M., McCarthy, P. J., Sheehan-Mansfield, S., & Sheffield, D. (2013). Emotions correlate with perceived mental effort and concentration disruption in adult sport performers. *European Journal of Sport Science, 13*, 697–706. http://dx.doi.org/10.1080/17461391.2013.771381

Ameli, R. (2014). *25 lessons in mindfulness: Now time for healthy living*. Washington, DC: American Psychological Association. http://dx.doi.org/10.1037/14257-000

Amemiya, R., Yusa, Y., & Sakairi, Y. (2015). Development of a mindfulness questionnaire for athletes. *Japanese Journal of Cognitive Therapy, 8*, 106–115.

American Psychological Association. (2017). *Ethical principles of psychologists and code of conduct* (2002, amended June 1, 2010 and January 1, 2017). Retrieved from http://www.apa.org/ethics/code/index.aspx

American Psychological Association, Division 47. (2016). *APA sport psychology proficiency*. Retrieved from http://www.apadivisions.org/division-47/about/sport-proficiency/index.aspx

American Psychological Association, Presidential Task Force on Evidence-Based Practice. (2006). Evidence-based practice in psychology. *American Psychologist, 61,* 271–285. http://dx.doi.org/10.1037/0003-066X.61.4.271

Andersen, M. B. (2012). Supervision and mindfulness in sport and performance psychology. In S. M. Murphy (Ed.), *The Oxford handbook of sport and performance psychology* (pp. 725–737). New York, NY: Oxford University Press. http://dx.doi.org/10.1093/oxfordhb/9780199731763.013.0039

Andersen, M. B., & Mannion, J. (2011). If you meet the Buddha on the football field, tackle him! In D. Gilbourne & M. B. Andersen (Eds.), *Critical essays in applied sport psychology* (pp. 173–192). Champaign, IL: Human Kinetics.

Andersen, M. B., Van Raalte, J. L., & Brewer, B. W. (2001). Sport psychology service delivery: Staying ethical while keeping loose. *Professional Psychology: Research and Practice, 32,* 12–18. http://dx.doi.org/10.1037/0735-7028.32.1.12

Anderson, R., Hanrahan, S. J., & Mallett, C. (2014). Investigating the optimal psychological state for peak performance in Australian elite athletes. *Journal of Applied Sport Psychology, 26,* 318–333. http://dx.doi.org/10.1080/10413200.2014.885915

Anshel, M. H., & Sutarso, T. (2010). Conceptualizing maladaptive sport perfectionism as a function of gender. *Journal of Clinical Sport Psychology, 4,* 263–281. http://dx.doi.org/10.1123/jcsp.4.4.263

Aoyagi, M. W., & Portenga, S. T. (2010). The role of positive ethics and virtues in the context of sport and performance psychology service delivery. *Professional Psychology: Research and Practice, 41,* 253–259. http://dx.doi.org/10.1037/a0019483

Armstrong, L. E., & VanHeest, J. L. (2002). The unknown mechanism of the overtraining syndrome: Clues from depression and psychoneuroimmunology. *Sports Medicine, 32,* 185–209. http://dx.doi.org/10.2165/00007256-200232030-00003

Ashcraft, M. H., & Kirk, E. P. (2001). The relationships among working memory, math anxiety, and performance. *Journal of Experimental Psychology: General, 130,* 224–237. http://dx.doi.org/10.1037/0096-3445.130.2.224

Athletes who meditate: Kobe Bryant & other sports stars who practice mindfulness. (2013, May 30). *The Huffington Post.* Retrieved from http://www.huffingtonpost.com/2013/05/30/athletes-who-meditate-kobe-bryant_n_3347089.html

A-Tjak, J. G., Davis, M. L., Morina, N., Powers, M. B., Smits, J. A., & Emmelkamp, P. M. (2015). A meta-analysis of the efficacy of acceptance and commitment therapy for clinically relevant mental and physical health problems. *Psychotherapy and Psychosomatics, 84,* 30–36. http://dx.doi.org/10.1159/000365764

Awh, E., Vogel, E. K., & Oh, S.-H. (2006). Interactions between attention and working memory. *Neuroscience, 139,* 201–208. http://dx.doi.org/10.1016/j.neuroscience.2005.08.023

Baddeley, A. (1992). Working memory. *Science, 255,* 556–559. http://dx.doi.org/10.1126/science.1736359

Baer, R. A. (Ed.). (2014). *Mindfulness-based treatment approaches: Clinician's guide to evidence base and applications* (2nd ed.). San Diego, CA: Elsevier Academic Press.

Baer, R. A., Smith, G. T., Hopkins, J., Krietemeyer, J., & Toney, L. (2006). Using self-report assessment methods to explore facets of mindfulness. *Assessment, 13,* 27–45. http://dx.doi.org/10.1177/1073191105283504

Baer, R. A., Smith, G. T., Lykins, E., Button, D., Krietemeyer, J., Sauer, S., . . . Williams, J. M. (2008). Construct validity of the five facet mindfulness questionnaire in meditating and nonmeditating samples. *Assessment, 15*, 329–342. http://dx.doi.org/10.1177/1073191107313003

Baltzell, A., Chipman, K., Hayden, L., & Bowman, C. (2015). Qualitative study of MMTS: Coaches' experience. *Journal of Multidisciplinary Research, 7*, 5–20.

Baltzell, A. L. (2011). *Living in the sweet spot: Preparing for performance in sport and life.* Morgantown, WV: Fitness Information Technology.

Baltzell, A. L. (Ed.). (2016a). *Mindfulness and performance.* New York, NY: Cambridge University Press. http://dx.doi.org/10.1017/CBO9781139871310

Baltzell, A. L. (2016b). Self-compassion, distress tolerance, and mindfulness in performance. In A. L. Baltzell (Ed.), *Mindfulness and performance* (pp. 53–77). New York, NY: Cambridge University Press. http://dx.doi.org/10.1017/CBO9781139871310.004

Baltzell, A. L., & Akhtar, V. L. (2014). Mindfulness meditation training for sport (MMTS) intervention: Impact of MMTS with division I female athletes. *Journal of Happiness and Well-Being, 2*, 160–173.

Baltzell, A. L., Caraballo, N., Chipman, K., & Hayden, L. (2014). A qualitative study of the mindfulness meditation training for sport (MMTS): Division I female soccer players' experience. *Journal of Clinical Sport Psychology, 8*, 221–244. http://dx.doi.org/10.1123/jcsp.2014-0030

Baltzell, A. L., & Summers, J. (2016). The future of mindfulness and performance across disciplines. In A. L. Baltzell (Ed.), *Mindfulness and performance* (pp. 515–541). New York, NY: Cambridge University Press. http://dx.doi.org/10.1017/CBO9781139871310.023

Banks, J. B., Welhaf, M. S., & Srour, A. (2015). The protective effects of brief mindfulness meditation training. *Consciousness and Cognition, 33*, 277–285. http://dx.doi.org/10.1016/j.concog.2015.01.016

Banks, S. J., Eddy, K. T., Angstadt, M., Nathan, P. J., & Phan, K. L. (2007). Amygdala-frontal connectivity during emotion regulation. *Social Cognitive and Affective Neuroscience, 2*, 303–312. http://dx.doi.org/10.1093/scan/nsm029

Barber, N. M. J. (2014). *Leading from within: A grounded theory of actors' empowerment through experiential phenomenology using mindfulness-based stress reduction* (Doctoral dissertation). Available from ProQuest Dissertations and Theses database. (UMI No. 3687605)

Bar-Eli, M., Plessner, H., & Raab, M. (2011). *Judgement, decision making and success in sport.* Chichester, England: Wiley-Blackwell. http://dx.doi.org/10.1002/9781119977032

Barlow, W. (1973). *The Alexander technique.* New York, NY: Knopf.

Barlow, W. (2001). *The Alexander Principle: How to use your body without stress.* London, England: Orion.

Baudouin, A., & Hawkins, D. (2002). A biomechanical review of factors affecting rowing performance. *British Journal of Sports Medicine, 36*, 396–402. http://dx.doi.org/10.1136/bjsm.36.6.396

Baumeister, R. F. (2002). Ego depletion and self-control failure: An energy model of the self's executive function. *Self and Identity, 1*, 129–136. http://dx.doi.org/10.1080/152988602317319302

Beedie, C. J., Terry, P. C., & Lane, A. M. (2000). The profile of mood states and athletic performance: Two meta-analyses. *Journal of Applied Sport Psychology, 12*, 49–68. http://dx.doi.org/10.1080/10413200008404213

Begley, I. (2014, October 13). Knicks take 'mindfulness training.' Retrieved from http://www.espn.com/new-york/nba/story/_/id/11694723/phil-jackson-new-york-knicks-taking-mindfulness-training

Benson, H. (1975). *The relaxation response.* New York, NY: Morrow.

Bernier, M., Thienot, E., Codron, R., & Fournier, J. F. (2009). Mindfulness and acceptance approaches in sport performance. *Journal of Clinical Sport Psychology, 3*, 320–333. http://dx.doi.org/10.1123/jcsp.3.4.320

Bernier, M., Thienot, E., Pelosse, E., & Fournier, J. F. (2014). Effects and underlying processes of a mindfulness-based intervention with young elite figure skaters: Two case studies. *The Sport Psychologist, 28*, 302–315. http://dx.doi.org/10.1123/tsp.2013-0006

Bertollo, M., Saltarelli, B., & Robazza, C. (2009). Mental preparation strategies of elite modern pentathletes. *Psychology of Sport and Exercise, 10*, 244–254. http://dx.doi.org/10.1016/j.psychsport.2008.09.003

Bijleveld, E., & Veling, H. (2014). Separating chokers from nonchokers: Predicting real-life tennis performance under pressure from behavioral tasks that tap into working memory functioning. *Journal of Sport and Exercise Psychology, 36*, 347–356. http://dx.doi.org/10.1123/jsep.2013-0051

Birrer, D., Röthlin, P., & Morgan, G. (2012). Mindfulness to enhance athletic performance: Theoretical considerations and possible impact mechanisms. *Mindfulness, 3*, 235–246. http://dx.doi.org/10.1007/s12671-012-0109-2

Bishop, S. R., Lau, M., Shapiro, S., Carlson, L., Anderson, N. D., Carmody, J., . . . Devins, G. (2004). Mindfulness: A proposed operational definition. *Clinical Psychology: Science and Practice, 11*, 230–241. http://dx.doi.org/10.1093/clipsy.bph077

Black, L. D. (2014). *[Sati] [Natya]/Mindfulness in movement: An investigation of practicing mindfulness in improvisational dance through the lens of non-attachment* (Master's thesis, University of Oregon). Retrieved from https://scholarsbank.uoregon.edu/xmlui/handle/1794/18746?show=full

Blackburn, E., & Epel, E. (2017). *The telomere effect: A revolutionary approach to living younger, healthier, longer.* New York, NY: Hachette Book Group.

Blythe, W. (2006). *To hate like this is to be happy forever: A thoroughly obsessive, intermittently uplifting, and occasionally unbiased account of the Duke–North Carolina basketball rivalry.* New York, NY: HarperCollins.

Bodner, T. E., & Langer, E. J. (2001, June). *Individual differences in mindfulness: The Mindfulness/Mindlessness Scale.* Toronto, Ontario, Canada: American Psychological Society.

Bohlmeijer, E., Prenger, R., Taal, E., & Cuijpers, P. (2010). The effects of mindfulness-based stress reduction therapy on mental health of adults with a chronic medical disease: A meta-analysis. *Journal of Psychosomatic Research, 68*, 539–544. http://dx.doi.org/10.1016/j.jpsychores.2009.10.005

Bois, J. E., Sarrazin, P. G., Southon, J., & Boiche, J. C. (2009). Psychological characteristics and their relation to performance in professional golfers. *The Sport Psychologist, 23*, 252–270. http://dx.doi.org/10.1123/tsp.23.2.252

Bond, F. W., Hayes, S. C., Baer, R. A., Carpenter, K. M., Guenole, N., Orcutt, H. K., . . . Zettle, R. D. (2011). Preliminary psychometric properties of the Acceptance and Action Questionnaire-II: A revised measure of psychological inflexibility and experiential avoidance. *Behavior Therapy, 42*, 676–688. http://dx.doi.org/10.1016/j.beth.2011.03.007

Bortoli, L., Bertollo, M., Hanin, Y., & Robazza, C. (2012). Striving for excellence: A multi-action plan intervention model for shooters. *Psychology of Sport and Exercise, 13*, 693–701. http://dx.doi.org/10.1016/j.psychsport.2012.04.006

Boutcher, S. H. (2008). Attentional processes and sport performance. In T. S. Horn (Ed.), *Advances in sport psychology* (3rd ed., pp. 325–338). Champaign, IL: Human Kinetics.

Bowen, S., & Kurz, A. S. (2012). Between-session practice and therapeutic alliance as predictors of mindfulness after mindfulness-based relapse prevention. *Journal of Clinical Psychology, 68*, 236–245. http://dx.doi.org/10.1002/jclp.20855

Boyce, B. (2015, November 26). NBA's winningest team guided by mindfulness and joy. *Mindful.* Retrieved from http://www.mindful.org/nbas-winningest-team-guided-by-mindfulness-and-joy

Brefczynski-Lewis, J. A., Lutz, A., Schaefer, H. S., Levinson, D. B., & Davidson, R. J. (2007). Neural correlates of attentional expertise in long-term meditation practitioners. *Proceedings of the National Academy of Sciences of the United States of America, 104*, 11483–11488. http://dx.doi.org/10.1073/pnas.0606552104

Breines, J. G., & Chen, S. (2012). Self-compassion increases self-improvement motivation. *Personality and Social Psychology Bulletin, 38*, 1133–1143. http://dx.doi.org/10.1177/0146167212445599

Brendel, D. (2015, February 11). There are risks to mindfulness at work. *Harvard Business Review.* Retrieved from https://hbr.org/2015/02/there-are-risks-to-mindfulness-at-work

Brody, J. (2014, February 19). Can mindfulness practice (specifically meditation) be used to enhance performance of actors/dancers/artists? [Blog post]. Retrieved from https://www.researchgate.net/post/Can_Mindfulness_Practice_specifically_meditation_be_used_to_enhance_performance_of_actors_dancers_artists

Brown, C. H., Gould, D., & Foster, S. (2005). A framework for developing contextual intelligence (CI). *The Sport Psychologist, 19*, 51–62. http://dx.doi.org/10.1123/tsp.19.1.51

Brown, D. J., Fletcher, D., Henry, I., Borrie, A., Emmett, J., Buzza, A., & Wombwell, S. (2015). A British university case study of the transitional experiences of student-athletes. *Psychology of Sport and Exercise, 21*, 78–90. http://dx.doi.org/10.1016/j.psychsport.2015.04.002

Brown, K. W. (2015). Mindfulness training to enhance positive functioning. In K. W. Brown, J. D. Creswell, & R. M. Ryan (Eds.), *Handbook of mindfulness: Theory, research, and practice* (pp. 311–325). New York, NY: Guilford Press.

Brown, K. W., Creswell, J. D., & Ryan, R. M. (Eds.). (2015). *Handbook of mindfulness: Theory, research, and practice.* New York, NY: Guilford Press.

Brown, K. W., & Ryan, R. M. (2003). The benefits of being present: Mindfulness and its role in psychological well-being. *Journal of Personality and Social Psychology, 84*, 822–848. http://dx.doi.org/10.1037/0022-3514.84.4.822

Bruser, M. (2011). Making music. In B. Boyce (Ed.), *The mindfulness revolution: Leading psychologists, scientists, artists, and meditation teachers on the power of mindfulness in daily life* (pp. 106–112). Boston, MA: Shambhala.

Buckworth, J., Dishman, R. K., O'Connor, P. J., & Tomporowski, P. D. (2013). *Exercise psychology* (2nd ed.). Champaign, IL: Human Kinetics.

Bull, S. J. (1991). Personal and situational influences on adherence to mental skills training. *Journal of Sport and Exercise Psychology, 13,* 121–132. http://dx.doi.org/10.1123/jsep.13.2.121

Burschka, J. M., Keune, P. M., Oy, U. H., Oschmann, P., & Kuhn, P. (2014). Mindfulness-based interventions in multiple sclerosis: Beneficial effects of Tai Chi on balance, coordination, fatigue and depression. *BMC Neurology, 14,* 165. http://dx.doi.org/10.1186/s12883-014-0165-4

Burt, J. (2009, October 28). Chelsea hope Bruno Demichelis' 'Mind Room' will produce results. *The Telegraph.* Retrieved from http://www.telegraph.co.uk/sport/football/teams/chelsea/6448101/Chelsea-hope-Bruno-Demicheliss-Mind-Room-will-produce-results.html

Caldwell, K., Harrison, M., Adams, M., Quin, R. H., & Greeson, J. (2010). Developing mindfulness in college students through movement-based courses: Effects on self-regulatory self-efficacy, mood, stress, and sleep quality. *Journal of American College Health, 58,* 433–442. http://dx.doi.org/10.1080/07448480903540481

Canucks sued by Italian sport psychologist over failed contract. (2013, March 9). Retrieved from http://www.cbc.ca/news/canada/british-columbia/canucks-sued-by-italian-sport-psychologist-over-failed-contract-1.1311587

Cardaciotto, L., Herbert, J. D., Forman, E. M., Moitra, E., & Farrow, V. (2008). The assessment of present-moment awareness and acceptance: The Philadelphia Mindfulness Scale. *Assessment, 15,* 204–223. http://dx.doi.org/10.1177/1073191107311467

Carmody, J. (2014). Eastern and western approaches to mindfulness: Similarities, differences, and clinical implications. In A. Ie, C. Ngnoumen, & E. Langer (Eds.), *The Wiley Blackwell handbook of mindfulness* (Vol. I, pp. 48–57). Chichester, England: Wiley. http://dx.doi.org/10.1002/9781118294895.ch3

Carmody, J., & Baer, R. A. (2008). Relationships between mindfulness practice and levels of mindfulness, medical and psychological symptoms and well-being in a mindfulness-based stress reduction program. *Journal of Behavioral Medicine, 31,* 23–33. http://dx.doi.org/10.1007/s10865-007-9130-7

Carraça, B., Serpa, S., Palmi, J., & Magalhães, C. (2015, July). *Mindfulness based stress reduction program (MBSR-SP) on elite soccer players: Psychological inflexibility versus acceptance.* Berlin, Germany: Association for Contextual Behavioral Science.

Cathcart, S., McGregor, M., & Groundwater, E. (2014). Mindfulness and flow in elite athletes. *Journal of Clinical Sport Psychology, 8,* 119–141. http://dx.doi.org/10.1123/jcsp.2014-0018

Cermakova, L., Moneta, G. B., & Spada, M. M. (2010). Dispositional flow as a mediator of the relationships between attentional control and approaches to studying during academic examination preparation. *Educational Psychology, 30,* 495–511. http://dx.doi.org/10.1080/01443411003777697

Chambers, R., Gullone, E., & Allen, N. B. (2009). Mindful emotion regulation: An integrative review. *Clinical Psychology Review*, *29*, 560–572. http://dx.doi.org/10.1016/j.cpr.2009.06.005

Chambers, R., Lo, B. C. Y., & Allen, N. B. (2008). The impact of intensive mindfulness training on attentional control, cognitive style, and affect. *Cognitive Therapy and Research*, *32*, 303–322. http://dx.doi.org/10.1007/s10608-007-9119-0

Chan, A. L. (2008, July 8). Actors swear by this mindful movement practice. Here's how *you* can benefit from it, too. *The Huffington Post*. Retrieved from http://www.huffingtonpost.com/2014/07/08/alexander-technique-everyday-life-mindfulness-movement-exercises_n_5521951.html

Chang, J. C., Midlarsky, E., & Lin, P. (2003). The effects of meditation on music performance anxiety. *Medical Problems of Performing Artists*, *18*, 126–130.

Chaskalson, M. (2011). *Mindful workplace: Developing resilient individuals and resonant organizations with MBSR*. Chichester, England: Wiley Blackwell. http://dx.doi.org/10.1002/9781119976974

Chavez, E. (2008). Flow in sport: A study of college athletes. *Imagination, Cognition and Personality*, *28*, 69–91. http://dx.doi.org/10.2190/IC.28.1.f

Chen, L. H., & Kee, Y. H. (2008). Gratitude and adolescent athletes' well-being. *Social Indicators Research*, *89*, 361–373. http://dx.doi.org/10.1007/s11205-008-9237-4

Chen, L. H., Kee, Y. H., & Tsai, Y. M. (2008). Relation of dispositional optimism with burnout among athletes. *Perceptual and Motor Skills*, *106*, 693–698. http://dx.doi.org/10.2466/pms.106.3.693-698

Chen, L. H., & Wu, C.-H. (2014). Gratitude enhances change in athletes' self-esteem: The moderating role of trust in coach. *Journal of Applied Sport Psychology*, *26*, 349–362. http://dx.doi.org/10.1080/10413200.2014.889255

Chiesa, A., Calati, R., & Serretti, A. (2011). Does mindfulness training improve cognitive abilities? A systematic review of neuropsychological findings. *Clinical Psychology Review*, *31*, 449–464. http://dx.doi.org/10.1016/j.cpr.2010.11.003

Chiesa, A., & Malinowski, P. (2011). Mindfulness-based approaches: Are they all the same? *Journal of Clinical Psychology*, *67*, 404–424. http://dx.doi.org/10.1002/jclp.20776

Chiesa, A., & Serretti, A. (2011). Mindfulness based cognitive therapy for psychiatric disorders: A systematic review and meta-analysis. *Psychiatry Research*, *187*, 441–453. http://dx.doi.org/10.1016/j.psychres.2010.08.011

Chiesa, A., & Serretti, A. (2014). Are mindfulness-based interventions effective for substance use disorders? A systematic review of the evidence. *Substance Use & Misuse*, *49*, 492–512. http://dx.doi.org/10.3109/10826084.2013.770027

Chong, Y. W., Kee, Y. H., & Chaturvedi, I. (2015). Effects of brief mindfulness induction on weakening habits: Evidence from a computer mouse control task. *Mindfulness*, *6*, 582–588. http://dx.doi.org/10.1007/s12671-014-0293-3

Chung, P. K., Si, G. Y., & Zhang, C. Q. (2013). 正念训练在运动竞技领域应用述评 [A review on the application of mindfulness-based interventions in sport field]. *Chinese Journal of Sports Medicine*, *32*, 65–74.

Clark, T., & Williamon, A. (2011). Evaluation of a mental skills training program for musicians. *Journal of Applied Sport Psychology*, *23*, 342–359. http://dx.doi.org/10.1080/10413200.2011.574676

Coffey, K. A., Hartman, M., & Fredrickson, B. L. (2010). Deconstructing mindfulness and constructing mental health: Understanding mindfulness and its mechanisms of action. *Mindfulness, 1*, 235–253. http://dx.doi.org/10.1007/s12671-010-0033-2

Cohen, E. E. A., Ejsmond-Frey, R., Knight, N., & Dunbar, R. I. M. (2010). Rowers' high: Behavioural synchrony is correlated with elevated pain thresholds. *Biology Letters, 6*, 106–108. http://dx.doi.org/10.1098/rsbl.2009.0670

Coker, C. A., & Mickle, A. (2000). Stability of the Iceberg Profile as a function of perceived difficulty in defeating an opponent. *Perceptual and Motor Skills, 90*, 1135–1138. http://dx.doi.org/10.2466/pms.2000.90.3c.1135

Cook, D. (2015, June 7). Float like a butterfly, play like a kid. *Times Free Press*. Retrieved from http://www.timesfreepress.com/news/opinion/columns/story/2015/jun/07/flobutterfly-play-kid/308320/

Cornett-Murtada, V. (2012, September). Nurturing the whole musician. *MTNA e-JOURNAL*, 15–28.

Cox, A. E., Ullrich-French, S., & French, B. F. (2016). Validity evidence for the state mindfulness scale for physical activity. *Measurement in Physical Education and Exercise Science, 20*, 38–49. http://dx.doi.org/10.1080/1091367X.2015.1089404

Crane, C., Crane, R. S., Eames, C., Fennell, M. J. V., Silverton, S., Williams, J. M. G., & Barnhofer, T. (2014). The effects of amount of home meditation practice in Mindfulness Based Cognitive Therapy on hazard of relapse to depression in the Staying Well after Depression Trial. *Behaviour Research and Therapy, 63*, 17–24. http://dx.doi.org/10.1016/j.brat.2014.08.015

Crane, R. S., Kuyken, W., Williams, J. M. G., Hastings, R. P., Cooper, L., & Fennell, M. J. V. (2012). Competence in teaching mindfulness-based courses: Concepts, development and assessment. *Mindfulness, 3*, 76–84. http://dx.doi.org/10.1007/s12671-011-0073-2

Creswell, J. D. (2017). Mindfulness interventions. *Annual Review of Psychology, 68*, 491–516. http://dx.doi.org/10.1146/annurev-psych-042716-051139

Crocker, P. R. E., Alderman, R. B., Murray, F., & Smith, R. (1988). Cognitive-affective stress management training with high performance youth volleyball players: Effects on affect, cognition, and performance. *Journal of Sport and Exercise Psychology, 10*, 448–460. http://dx.doi.org/10.1123/jsep.10.4.448

Csikszentmihalyi, M. (1990). *Flow: The psychology of optimal experience*. New York, NY: Harper & Row.

Csikszentmihalyi, M. (1996). *Creativity: Flow and the psychology of discovery and invention*. New York, NY: HarperCollins.

Czajkowski, A.-M. L., & Greasley, A. E. (2015). Mindfulness for singers: The effects of a targeted mindfulness course on learning vocal technique. *British Journal of Music Education, 32*, 211–233. http://dx.doi.org/10.1017/S0265051715000145

Dane, E. (2011). Paying attention to mindfulness and its effects on task performance in the workplace. *Journal of Management, 37*, 997–1018. http://dx.doi.org/10.1177/0149206310367948

Datu, J. A. (2013). Gratitude-based group intervention manual for college student-athletes. *International Journal of Research Studies in Psychology, 2*, 81–88. http://dx.doi.org/10.5861/ijrsp.2013.294

Davids, K., Hristoviski, R., Araújo, D., Balaque-Serre, N., Button, C., & Passos, P. (Eds.). (2014). *Complex systems in sport*. London, England: Routledge.

Davidson, R. J. (2002). Toward a biology of positive affect and compassion. In R. J. Davidson & A. Harrington (Eds.), *Visions of compassion: Western scientists and Tibetan Buddhists examine human nature* (pp. 107–130). New York, NY: Oxford University Press. http://dx.doi.org/10.1093/acprof:oso/9780195130430.003.0006

Davidson, R. J., Kabat-Zinn, J., Schumacher, J., Rosenkranz, M., Muller, D., Santorelli, S. F., . . . Sheridan, J. F. (2003). Alterations in brain and immune function produced by mindfulness meditation. *Psychosomatic Medicine, 65*, 564–570. http://dx.doi.org/10.1097/01.PSY.0000077505.67574.E3

Davis, D. M., & Hayes, J. A. (2011). What are the benefits of mindfulness? A practice review of psychotherapy-related research. *Psychotherapy, 48*, 198–208. http://dx.doi.org/10.1037/a0022062

deCharms, R. (1968). *Personal causation*. New York, NY: Academic Press.

Deci, E. L. (1972). The effects of contingent and noncontingent rewards and controls on intrinsic motivation. *Organizational Behavior and Human Performance, 8*, 217–229. http://dx.doi.org/10.1016/0030-5073(72)90047-5

Deci, E. L., & Ryan, R. M. (1985). *Intrinsic motivation and self-determination in human behavior*. New York, NY: Plenum. http://dx.doi.org/10.1007/978-1-4899-2271-7

Deen, D. R. (1999). *Awareness and breathing: Keys to the moderation of musical performance anxiety* (Doctoral dissertation). Available from ProQuest Dissertations and Theses database. (UMI No. 9957025)

De Felice, M. G. (2004). *Mindfulness meditation: A new tool for understanding and regulating musical performance anxiety. An affective neuroscientific perspective* (Doctoral dissertation). Available from ProQuest Dissertations and Theses database. (UMI No. 3125357)

Delehanty, H. (2014, December). The game changer. *Mindful*, 45–53.

Delehanty, H. (2016, February). Get in the zone: NBA meditation coach George Mumford on finding confidence within. *Mindful*, 46–55.

Den Hartigh, R. J. R., Cox, R. F. A., Gernigon, C., Van Yperen, N. W., & Van Geert, P. L. C. (2015). Pink noise in rowing ergometer performance and the role of skill level. *Motor Control, 19*, 355–369. http://dx.doi.org/10.1123/mc.2014-0071

De Petrillo, L. A., Kaufman, K. A., Glass, C. R., & Arnkoff, D. B. (2009). Mindfulness for long-distance runners: An open trial using mindful sport performance enhancement (MSPE). *Journal of Clinical Sport Psychology, 3*, 357–376. http://dx.doi.org/10.1123/jcsp.3.4.357

de Zoysa, N., Ruths, F. A., Walsh, J., & Hutton, J. (2014). Mindfulness based cognitive therapy for mental health professionals: A long-term qualitative follow-up study. *Mindfulness, 5*, 10–17. http://dx.doi.org/10.1007/s12671-012-0141-2

Diekhof, E. K., Geier, K., Falkai, P., & Gruber, O. (2011). Fear is only as deep as the mind allows: A coordinate-based meta-analysis of neuroimaging studies on the regulation of negative affect. *NeuroImage, 58*, 275–285. http://dx.doi.org/10.1016/j.neuroimage.2011.05.073

Dobkin, P. L., & Zhao, Q. (2011). Increased mindfulness—the active component of the mindfulness-based stress reduction program? *Complementary Therapies in Clinical Practice, 17*, 22–27. http://dx.doi.org/10.1016/j.ctcp.2010.03.002

Dormashev, Y. (2010). Flow experience explained on the grounds of an activity approach to attention. In B. Bruya (Ed.), *Effortless attention: A new perspective in the cognitive science of attention and action* (pp. 287–334). Cambridge, MA: MIT Press. http://dx.doi.org/10.7551/mitpress/9780262013840.003.0014

Dosil, J. (2006). Applied sport psychology: A new perspective. In J. Dosil (Ed.), *The sport psychologist's handbook* (pp. 3–17). Chichester, England: Wiley.

Dreyer, D. (2001, May 1). Physical running: Applying physics to your running form. *Running Times.* Retrieved from http://www.runnersworld.com/race-training/physical-running

Dreyer, D., & Dreyer, K. (2004). *ChiRunning: A revolutionary approach to effortless, injury-free running.* New York, NY: Simon & Schuster.

Duhigg, C. (2012). *The power of habit: Why we do what we do in life and business.* New York, NY: Random House.

Dupee, M., Werthner, P., & Forneris, T. (2015). A preliminary study on the relationship between athletes' ability to self-regulate and world ranking. *Biofeedback, 43,* 57–63. http://dx.doi.org/10.5298/1081-5937-43.2.01

Dweck, C. S. (2006). *Mindset: The new psychology of success: How we can learn to fulfill our potential.* New York, NY: Ballantine.

Eberth, J., & Sedlmeier, P. (2012). The effects of mindfulness meditation: A meta-analysis. *Mindfulness, 3,* 174–189. http://dx.doi.org/10.1007/s12671-012-0101-x

Eddy, M. (2009). A brief history of somatic practices and dance: Historical development of the field of somatic education and its relationship to dance. *Journal of Dance & Somatic Practices, 1,* 5–27. http://dx.doi.org/10.1386/jdsp.1.1.5_1

Elliott, M. (2010). Singing and mindfulness. *Journal of Singing: The Official Journal of the National Association of Teachers of Singing, 67,* 35–40.

Ellis-Jones, I. (2013, November 29). Mindfulness and method acting [Blog post]. Retrieved from http://ianellis-jones.blogspot.com/2013/11/mindfulness-and-method-acting.html

Embassy Row (Producer). (2015, January 27). *Men in blazers* [Audio podcast]. Retrieved from http://meninblazers.com

Englert, C., & Oudejans, R. R. D. (2014). Is choking under pressure a consequence of skill-focus or increased distractibility? Results from a tennis serve task. *Psychology, 5,* 1035–1043. http://dx.doi.org/10.4236/psych.2014.59116

Epstein, D. (2013). *The sports gene: Inside the science of extraordinary athletic performance.* New York, NY: Current.

Ericsson, K. A. (2006). The influence of experience and deliberate practice on the development of superior expert performance. In K. A. Ericsson, N. Charness, P. Feltovich, & R. R. Hoffman (Eds.), *Cambridge handbook of expertise and expert performance* (pp. 683–704). New York, NY: Cambridge University Press. http://dx.doi.org/10.1017/CBO9780511816796.038

Ericsson, K. A. (2013). Training history, deliberate practice and elite sports performance: An analysis in response to Tucker and Collins review—what makes champions? *British Journal of Sports Medicine, 47,* 533–535. http://dx.doi.org/10.1136/bjsports-2012-091767

Ericsson, K. A., Krampe, R. T., & Tesch-Römer, C. (1993). The role of deliberate practice in the acquisition of expert performance. *Psychological Review, 100,* 363–406. http://dx.doi.org/10.1037/0033-295X.100.3.363

Ewing, M. E., & Seefeldt, V. (1989). *Participation and attrition patterns in American agency-sponsored and interscholastic sports: An executive summary. Final report.* North Palm Beach, FL: Sporting Goods Manufacturers Association.

Eysenck, M. W., Derakshan, N., Santos, R., & Calvo, M. G. (2007). Anxiety and cognitive performance: Attentional control theory. *Emotion, 7,* 336–353. http://dx.doi.org/10.1037/1528-3542.7.2.336

Fan, J., McCandliss, B. D., Fossella, J., Flombaum, J. I., & Posner, M. I. (2005). The activation of attentional networks. *NeuroImage, 26,* 471–479. http://dx.doi.org/10.1016/j.neuroimage.2005.02.004

Farnsworth-Grodd, V. A., & Cameron, L. (2013). Mindfulness and the self-regulation of music performance anxiety. In A. Williamon & W. Goebl (Eds.), *Proceedings of the International Symposium on Performance Science* (pp. 317–322). Retrieved from http://www.performancescience.org/ISPS2013/Proceedings/Rows/074Paper_Farnsworth-Grodd.pdf

Fatemi, S. M., Ward, E. D., & Langer, E. J. (2016). Peak performance: Langerian mindfulness and flow. In A. L. Baltzell (Ed.), *Mindfulness and performance* (pp. 101–111). New York, NY: Cambridge University Press. http://dx.doi.org/10.1017/CBO9781139871310.006

Felder, J. N., Dimidjian, S., & Segal, Z. (2012). Collaboration in mindfulness-based cognitive therapy. *Journal of Clinical Psychology, 68,* 179–186. http://dx.doi.org/10.1002/jclp.21832

Ferguson, L. J., Kowalski, K. C., Mack, D. E., & Sabiston, C. M. (2014). Exploring self-compassion and eudaimonic well-being in young women athletes. *Journal of Sport and Exercise Psychology, 36,* 203–216. http://dx.doi.org/10.1123/jsep.2013-0096

Ferraro, T., & Rush, S. (2000). Why athletes resist sport psychology. *Athletic Insight: The Online Journal of Sport Psychology, 2,* 9–14.

Ferrell, M. D., Beach, R. L., Szeverenyi, N. M., Krch, M., & Fernhall, B. (2006). An fMRI analysis of neural activity during perceived zone-state performance. *Journal of Sport and Exercise Psychology, 28,* 421–433. http://dx.doi.org/10.1123/jsep.28.4.421

Fifer, A., Henschen, K., Gould, D., & Ravizza, K. (2008). What works when working with athletes. *The Sport Psychologist, 22,* 356–377. http://dx.doi.org/10.1123/tsp.22.3.356

Filimberti, A. E., Maffini, N., & Presti, G. (2013). ACT-ing sport: Un protocollo ACT per atleti [ACT-ing sport: An ACT protocol for athletes]. In P. Moderato & G. Presti (Eds.), *Cent'anni di comportamentismo. Dal manifesto di Watson alla teoria della mente, dalla BT all'ACT* (pp. 309–314). Milan, Italy: FrancoAngeli.

Filimberti, E., Maffini, N., & Presti, G. (2011, July). *ACTing Sport: A values-based protocol for training in sport.* Workshop presented at the Association for Contextual Behavioral Science World Conference IX, Parma, Italy.

Fitzgerald, M. (2010). *Run: The mind-body method of running by feel.* Boulder, CO: Velo Press.

Fox, K. C. R., Nijeboer, S., Dixon, M. L., Floman, J. L., Ellamil, M., Rumak, S. P., . . . Christoff, K. (2014). Is meditation associated with altered brain structure? A systematic review and meta-analysis of morphometric neuroimaging in meditation practitioners. *Neuroscience and Biobehavioral Reviews, 43,* 48–73. http://dx.doi.org/10.1016/j.neubiorev.2014.03.016

Franco, C. (2009). Modificación de los niveles de burnout y de personalidad resistente en un grupo de deportistas a través de un programa de conciencia plena (mindfulness) [Modifying burnout levels and resistant personality in a group of athletes using a mindfulness program]. *Anuario de Psicología, 40,* 377–390.

Fredrickson, B. L., Cohn, M. A., Coffey, K. A., Pek, J., & Finkel, S. M. (2008). Open hearts build lives: Positive emotions, induced through loving-kindness meditation, build consequential personal resources. *Journal of Personality and Social Psychology, 95,* 1045–1062. http://dx.doi.org/10.1037/a0013262

Fresco, D. M., Moore, M. T., van Dulmen, M. H., Segal, Z. V., Ma, S. H., Teasdale, J. D., & Williams, J. M. G. (2007). Initial psychometric properties of the experiences questionnaire: Validation of a self-report measure of decentering. *Behavior Therapy, 38,* 234–246. http://dx.doi.org/10.1016/j.beth.2006.08.003

Furley, P. A., & Memmert, D. (2012). Working memory capacity as controlled attention in tactical decision making. *Journal of Sport and Exercise Psychology, 34,* 322–344. http://dx.doi.org/10.1123/jsep.34.3.322

Furrer, P., Moen, F., & Firing, K. (2015, July 15). How mindfulness training may mediate stress, performance and burnout. *The Sport Journal.* Retrieved from http://thesportjournal.org/article/how-mindfulness-training-may-mediate-stress-performance-and-burnout

Futterman, M. (2015, January 27). The shrink on the Seattle Seahawks' sideline. *The Wall Street Journal.* Retrieved from https://www.wsj.com/articles/the-shrink-on-the-seattle-seahawks-sideline-1422402204

Gallwey, W. T. (1974). *The inner game of tennis.* New York, NY: Random House.

Gallwey, W. T. (1981). *The inner game of golf.* New York, NY: Random House.

Gallwey, W. T. (1997). *The inner game of tennis* (Rev. ed.). New York, NY: Random House.

Gantman, A. P., Gollwitzer, P. M., & Oettingen, G. (2014). Mindful mindlessness in goal pursuit. In A. Ie, C. T. Ngnoumen, & E. J. Langer (Eds.), *The Wiley Blackwell handbook of mindfulness* (Vol. 1, pp. 236–257). Chichester, England: Wiley Blackwell. http://dx.doi.org/10.1002/9781118294895.ch13

García, R. F., Villa, R. S., Cepeda, N. T., Cueto, E. G., & Montes, J. M. G. (2004). Efecto de la hipnosis y la terapia de aceptación y compromiso (ACT) en la mejora de la fuerza física en piragüistas [Effect of hypnosis and acceptance and commitment therapy (ACT) on physical performance in canoeists]. *International Journal of Clinical and Health Psychology, 4,* 481–493.

Gardner, F. L. (2016). Scientific advancements of mindfulness- and acceptance-based models in sport psychology: A decade in time, a seismic shift in philosophy and practice. In A. L. Baltzell (Ed.), *Mindfulness and performance* (pp. 127–152). New York, NY: Cambridge University Press.

Gardner, F. L., & Moore, Z. E. (2004). A mindfulness-acceptance-commitment-based approach to athletic performance enhancement: Theoretical considerations. *Behavior Therapy, 35*, 707–723. http://dx.doi.org/10.1016/S0005-7894(04)80016-9

Gardner, F. L., & Moore, Z. E. (2007). *The psychology of enhancing human performance: The mindfulness-acceptance-commitment (MAC) approach.* New York, NY: Springer.

Gaudiano, B. A. (2009). Ost's (2008) methodological comparison of clinical trials of acceptance and commitment therapy versus cognitive behavior therapy: Matching apples with oranges? *Behaviour Research and Therapy, 47*, 1066–1070. http://dx.doi.org/10.1016/j.brat.2009.07.020

Gazzaley, A., & Nobre, A. C. (2012). Top-down modulation: Bridging selective attention and working memory. *Trends in Cognitive Sciences, 16*, 129–135. http://dx.doi.org/10.1016/j.tics.2011.11.014

Gethin, R. (1998). *The foundations of Buddhism.* New York, NY: Oxford University Press.

Ghashghaei, H. T., Hilgetag, C. C., & Barbas, H. (2007). Sequence of information processing for emotions based on the anatomic dialogue between prefrontal cortex and amygdala. *NeuroImage, 34*, 905–923. http://dx.doi.org/10.1016/j.neuroimage.2006.09.046

Glass, C. R., Spears, C. A., Perskaudas, R., & Kaufman, K. A. (2016). *Mindful sport performance enhancement: Randomized controlled trial of a mental training program with collegiate athletes.* Manuscript submitted for publication.

Glass, L. L. (2003). The gray areas of boundary crossings and violations. *American Journal of Psychotherapy, 57*, 429–444.

Goguen-Hughes, L. (2011, January 17). Lights, camera, meditation. *Mindful.* Retrieved from http://www.mindful.org/lights-camera-meditation

Gonzalez, A. (2016, July 28). Off field, Heaney finds balance in meditation. Retrieved from http://m.mlb.com/news/article/192034884/angels-andrew-heaney-meditates-to-find-balance

Good, D. J., Lyddy, C. J., Glomb, T. M., Bono, J. E., Brown, K. W., Duffy, M. K., . . . Lazar, S. W. (2016). Contemplating mindfulness at work: An integrative review. *Journal of Management, 42*, 114–142. http://dx.doi.org/10.1177/0149206315617003

Goodger, K. I., & Jones, M. I. (2012). Burnout: A darker side to performance. In S. M. Murphy (Ed.), *The Oxford handbook of sport and performance psychology* (pp. 562–580). New York, NY: Oxford University Press.

Gooding, A., & Gardner, F. L. (2009). An investigation of the relationship between mindfulness, preshot routine, and basketball free throw percentage. *Journal of Clinical Sport Psychology, 3*, 303–319. http://dx.doi.org/10.1123/jcsp.3,4.303

Goodman, B. (2015, January/February). Mind games. *WebMD Magazine*, 60–63.

Goodman, F. R., & Kashdan, T. B. (2015). Behind the scenes of clinical research: Lessons from a mindfulness intervention with student-athletes. *The Behavior Therapist, 38*, 157–159.

Goodman, F. R., Kashdan, T. B., Mallard, T. T., & Schumann, M. (2014). A brief mindfulness and yoga intervention with an entire NCAA Division I athletic team: An initial investigation. *Psychology of Consciousness: Theory, Research, and Practice, 1*, 339–356. http://dx.doi.org/10.1037/cns0000022

Gordhamer, S. (2014, March 5). Mindfulness: The Seattle Seahawks' sports psychologist shares why it matters. *The Huffington Post.* Retrieved from http://www.huffingtonpost.com/soren-gordhamer/mindfulness-the-seattle-s_b_4815477.html

Gothe, N. P., & McAuley, E. (2015). Yoga and cognition: A meta-analysis of chronic and acute effects. *Psychosomatic Medicine, 77,* 784–797. http://dx.doi.org/10.1097/PSY.0000000000000218

Gotink, R. A., Chu, P., Busschbach, J. J. V., Benson, H., Fricchione, G. L., & Hunink, M. G. M. (2015). Standardised mindfulness-based interventions in healthcare: An overview of systematic reviews and meta-analyses of RCTs. *PLOS ONE, 10*(4), e0124344. http://dx.doi.org/10.1371/journal.pone.0124344

Gould, D., Collins, K., Lauer, L., & Chung, Y. C. (2007). Coaching life skills through football: A study of award winning high school coaches. *Journal of Applied Sport Psychology, 19,* 16–37. http://dx.doi.org/10.1080/10413200601113786

Goyal, M., Singh, S., Sibinga, E. M. S., Gould, N. F., Rowland-Seymour, A., Sharma, R., . . . Haythornthwaite, J. A. (2014). Meditation programs for psychological stress and well-being: A systematic review and meta-analysis. *JAMA Internal Medicine, 174,* 357–368. http://dx.doi.org/10.1001/jamainternmed.2013.13018

Grant, D. (2006, Fall). Zen in the art of conducting: Applying the principles of selflessness and mindfulness. *Canadian Winds,* 14–16.

Grant, J. A., Courtemanche, J., Duerden, E. G., Duncan, G. H., & Rainville, P. (2010). Cortical thickness and pain sensitivity in Zen meditators. *Emotion, 10,* 43–53. http://dx.doi.org/10.1037/a0018334

Grant, J. A., & Rainville, P. (2009). Pain sensitivity and analgesic effects of mindful states in Zen meditators: A cross-sectional study. *Psychosomatic Medicine, 71,* 106–114. http://dx.doi.org/10.1097/PSY.0b013e31818f52ee

Gratz, K. L., & Roemer, L. (2004). Multidimensional assessment of emotion regulation and dysregulation: Development, factor structure, and initial validation of the Difficulties in Emotion Regulation Scale. *Journal of Psychopathology and Behavioral Assessment, 26,* 41–54. http://dx.doi.org/10.1023/B:JOBA.0000007455.08539.94

Gratz, K. L., & Tull, M. T. (2010). Emotion regulation as a mechanism of change in acceptance- and mindfulness-based treatments. In R. A. Baer (Ed.), *Assessing mindfulness & acceptance processes in clients: Illuminating the theory & practice of change* (pp. 107–133). Oakland, CA: New Harbinger.

Gray, R. (2004). Attending to the execution of a complex sensorimotor skill: Expertise differences, choking, and slumps. *Journal of Experimental Psychology: Applied, 10,* 42–54. http://dx.doi.org/10.1037/1076-898X.10.1.42

Green, B., & Gallwey, W. T. (1986). *The inner game of music.* New York, NY: Doubleday.

Gregoire, C. (2014, February 4). Actually TIME, this is what the 'mindful revolution' really looks like. *The Huffington Post.* Retrieved from http://www.huffingtonpost.com/2014/02/04/this-is-proof-that-mindfu_n_4697734.html

Gross, M. B. (2014). *An empirical examination comparing the mindfulness-acceptance-commitment (MAC) approach and psychological skills training (PST) for the mental health and sport performance of student athletes* (Doctoral dissertation). Available from ProQuest Dissertations and Theses database. (UMI No. 3721717)

Gross, M., Gardner, F. L., & Autera, J. C. (2012, November). *Prevention for high school athletes: A pilot investigation of the mindfulness-acceptance-commitment approach.* National Harbor, MD: Association for Behavioral and Cognitive Therapies.

Gross, M., Moore, Z. E., Gardner, F. L., Wolanin, A. T., Pess, R., & Marks, D. R. (2016). An empirical examination comparing the mindfulness-acceptance-commitment (MAC) approach and Psychological Skills Training (PST) for the mental health and sport performance of female student athletes. *International Journal of Sport and Exercise Psychology.* http://dx.doi.org/10.1080/1612197X.2016.1250802

Grossman, L. (2011). *The magician king.* New York, NY: Viking.

Grow, J. C., Collins, S. E., Harrop, E. N., & Marlatt, G. A. (2015). Enactment of home practice following mindfulness-based relapse prevention and its association with substance-use outcomes. *Addictive Behaviors, 40*, 16–20. http://dx.doi.org/10.1016/j.addbeh.2014.07.030

Gu, J., Strauss, C., Bond, R., & Cavanagh, K. (2015). How do mindfulness-based cognitive therapy and mindfulness-based stress reduction improve mental health and wellbeing? A systematic review and meta-analysis of mediation studies. *Clinical Psychology Review, 37*, 1–12. http://dx.doi.org/10.1016/j.cpr.2015.01.006

Gustafsson, H., Skoog, T., Davis, P., Kenttä, G., & Haberl, P. (2015). Mindfulness and its relationship with perceived stress, affect, and burnout in elite junior athletes. *Journal of Clinical Sport Psychology, 9*, 263–281. http://dx.doi.org/10.1123/jcsp.2014-0051

Gutiérrez, O., Luciano, C., Rodríguez, M., & Fink, B. C. (2004). Comparison between an acceptance-based and a cognitive-control-based protocol for coping with pain. *Behavior Therapy, 35*, 767–783. http://dx.doi.org/10.1016/S0005-7894(04)80019-4

Haas, A. S., & Langer, E. J. (2014). Mindful attraction and synchronization: Mindfulness and regulation of interpersonal synchronicity. *NeuroQuantology: An Interdisciplinary Journal of Neuroscience and Quantum Physics, 12*, 21–34. http://dx.doi.org/10.14704/nq.2014.12.1.728

Haase, L., Kenttä, G., Hickman, S., Baltzell, A., & Paulus, M. (2016). Mindfulness training in elite athletes: mPeak with BMX cyclists. In A. L. Baltzell (Ed.), *Mindfulness and performance* (pp. 186–208). New York, NY: Cambridge University Press. http://dx.doi.org/10.1017/CBO9781139871310.010

Haase, L., May, A. C., Falahpour, M., Isakovic, S., Simmons, A. N., Hickman, S. D., . . . Paulus, M. P. (2015). A pilot study investigating changes in neural processing after mindfulness training in elite athletes. *Frontiers in Behavioral Neuroscience, 9*, 229. http://dx.doi.org/10.3389/fnbeh.2015.00229

Haberl, P. (2016). Mindfulness and the Olympic athlete—A personal journey. In A. L. Baltzell (Ed.), *Mindfulness and performance* (pp. 211–234). New York, NY: Cambridge University Press. http://dx.doi.org/10.1017/CBO9781139871310.011

Hack, B. (2005). Qualifications: Education and experience. In S. Murphy (Ed.), *The sport psych handbook* (pp. 293–304). Champaign, IL: Human Kinetics.

Hahn, J. U. (2004, August). The perfect form: Running better, from head to toe. *Runner's World.* Retrieved from http://www.runnersworld.com/running-tips/perfect-running-form

Hair, M., Renaud, K. V., & Ramsay, J. (2007). The influence of self-esteem and locus of control on perceived email-related stress. *Computers in Human Behavior, 23*, 2791–2803. http://dx.doi.org/10.1016/j.chb.2006.05.005

Hanin, Y. L. (Ed.). (2000a). *Emotions in sport.* Champaign, IL: Human Kinetics.

Hanin, Y. L. (2000b). Individual zones of optimal functioning (IZOF) model: Emotion-performance relationships in sport. In Y. L. Hanin (Ed.), *Emotions in sport* (pp. 65–89). Champaign, IL: Human Kinetics.

Hanin, Y. L. (2010). Coping with anxiety in sport. In A. R. Nicholls (Ed.), *Coping in sport: Theory, methods, and related constructs* (pp. 159–175). Hauppauge, NY: Nova Science.

Hankes, D. M. (2012). Sport and performance psychology: Ethical issues. In S. M. Murphy (Ed.), *The Oxford handbook of sport and performance psychology* (pp. 46–61). New York, NY: Oxford University Press.

Hanley, A. W., Warner, A. R., Dehili, V. M., Canto, A. I., & Garland, E. L. (2015). Washing dishes to wash the dishes: Brief instruction in an informal mindfulness practice. *Mindfulness, 6*, 1095–1103. http://dx.doi.org/10.1007/s12671-014-0360-9

Hanley, S. (1937). The sense of feel in golf. *The Journal of Health and Physical Education, 8*, 366–369.

Hardy, L., Jones, G., & Gould, D. (1996). *Understanding psychological preparation for sport: Theory and practice of elite performers.* Chichester, England: Wiley.

Harmison, R. J., & Casto, K. V. (2012). Optimal performance: Elite level performance in "the zone." In S. M. Murphy (Ed.), *The Oxford handbook of sport and performance psychology* (pp. 707–724). New York, NY: Oxford University Press. http://dx.doi.org/10.1093/oxfordhb/9780199731763.013.0038

Harris, R. (2009). *ACT made simple: An easy-to-read primer on acceptance and commitment therapy.* Oakland, CA: New Harbinger.

Harriss, D. J., & Atkinson, G. (2013). Ethical standards in sport and exercise science research: 2014 update. *International Journal of Sports Medicine, 34*, 1025–1028. http://dx.doi.org/10.1055/s-0033-1358756

Hasker, S. M. (2010). *Evaluation of the mindfulness-acceptance-commitment (MAC) approach for enhancing athletic performance* (Doctoral dissertation). Available from ProQuest Dissertations and Theses database. (UMI No. 3413164)

Hayes, S. C. (2005). *Get out of your mind & into your life: The new acceptance & commitment therapy.* Oakland, CA: New Harbinger.

Hayes, S. C., & Plumb, J. C. (2007). Mindfulness from the bottom up: Providing an inductive framework for understanding mindfulness processes and their application to human suffering. *Psychological Inquiry, 18*, 242–248. http://dx.doi.org/10.1080/10478400701598314

Hayes, S. C., & Shenk, C. (2004). Operationalizing mindfulness without unnecessary attachment. *Clinical Psychology: Science and Practice, 11*, 249–254. http://dx.doi.org/10.1093/clipsy.bph079

Hayes, S. C., Strosahl, K. D., & Wilson, K. G. (1999). *Acceptance and commitment therapy: An experiential approach to behavior change.* New York, NY: Guilford Press.

Hayes, S. C., Strosahl, K. D., & Wilson, K. G. (2011). *Acceptance and commitment therapy: The process and practice of mindful change* (2nd ed.). New York, NY: Guilford Press.

Hays, K. F. (2002). The enhancement of performance excellence among perform-ing artists. *Journal of Applied Sport Psychology, 14*, 299–312. http://dx.doi.org/10.1080/10413200290103572

Hays, K. F. (2009a). Performance anxiety. In K. F. Hays (Ed.), *Performance psychology in action: A casebook for working with athletes, performing artists, business leaders, and professionals in high-risk occupations* (pp. 101–120). Washington, DC: American Psy-chological Association. http://dx.doi.org/10.1037/11876-005

Hays, K. F. (Ed.). (2009b). *Performance psychology in action: A casebook for working with athletes, performing artists, business leaders, and professionals in high-risk occupa-tions*. Washington, DC: American Psychological Association. http://dx.doi.org/10.1037/11876-000

Hays, K. F. (2012). The psychology of performance in sport and other domains. In S. M. Murphy (Ed.), *The Oxford handbook of sport and performance psychology* (pp. 24–45). New York, NY: Oxford University Press. http://dx.doi.org/10.1093/oxfordhb/9780199731763.013.0002

Hays, K. F., & Brown, C. H. (2004). *You're on! Consulting for peak performance*. Washing-ton, DC: American Psychological Association. http://dx.doi.org/10.1037/10675-000

Heinz, K., Heidenreich, T., & Brand, R. (2010/2011). Entwicklung und effektüber-prüfung eines achtsamkeitsbasierten sportpsychologischen trainings zur aufmerksam-keits- und emotionsregulation [Development and outcome of a mindfulness-based sport psychological training for attention- and emotion regulation]. *BISp-Jahrbuch - Forschungsförderung*, 235–238.

Henriksen, K., Larsen, C. H., Storm, L. K., & Ryom, K. (2014). Sport psychology interventions with young athletes: The perspective of the sport psychology prac-titioner. *Journal of Clinical Sport Psychology, 8*, 245–260. http://dx.doi.org/10.1123/jcsp.2014-0033

Herbert, J. D., & Forman, E. M. (Eds.). (2010). *Acceptance and mindfulness in cognitive behavior therapy: Understanding and applying the new therapies*. New York, NY: Wiley.

Herrigel, E. (1953). *Zen in the art of archery*. New York, NY: Pantheon Books.

Herrington, J. (2000). Directing with the Viewpoints. *Theatre Topics, 10*, 155–168. http://dx.doi.org/10.1353/tt.2000.0014

Hicks, S. F., & Bien, T. (Eds.). (2008). *Mindfulness and the therapeutic relationship*. New York, NY: Guilford Press.

Hindman, R. K., Glass, C. R., Arnkoff, D. B., & Maron, D. D. (2015). A comparison of formal and informal mindfulness programs for stress reduction in university students. *Mindfulness, 6*, 873–884. http://dx.doi.org/10.1007/s12671-014-0331-1

Hines, A. H., Ader, D. N., Chang, A. S., & Rundell, J. R. (1998). Dual agency, dual relationships, boundary crossings, and associated boundary violations: A survey of military and civilian psychiatrists. *Military Medicine, 163*, 826–833.

Hodgins, H. S., & Adair, K. C. (2010). Attentional processes and meditation. *Conscious-ness and Cognition, 19*, 872–878. http://dx.doi.org/10.1016/j.concog.2010.04.002

Hölzel, B. K., Lazar, S. W., Gard, T., Schuman-Olivier, Z., Vago, D. R., & Ott, U. (2011). How does mindfulness meditation work? Proposing mechanisms of action from a conceptual and neural perspective. *Perspectives on Psychological Science, 6*, 537–559. http://dx.doi.org/10.1177/1745691611419671

Hölzel, B. K., & Ott, U. (2006). Relationships between meditation depth, absorption, meditation practice, and mindfulness: A latent variable approach. *Journal of Transpersonal Psychology, 38,* 179–199.

Hölzel, B. K., Ott, U., Hempel, H., Hackl, A., Wolf, K., Stark, R., & Vaitl, D. (2007). Differential engagement of anterior cingulate and adjacent medial frontal cortex in adept meditators and non-meditators. *Neuroscience Letters, 421,* 16–21. http://dx.doi.org/10.1016/j.neulet.2007.04.074

Hoyer, D., Glass, C. R., Spears, C. A., & Kaufman, K. A. (2016, April). *Mindful sport performance enhancement for Division III collegiate coaches: A pilot study.* Poster presented at the annual meeting of the Association for Applied Sport Psychology Mid-Atlantic Regional Conference, Philadelphia, PA.

Humphrey, J. H., Yow, D. A., & Bowden, W. W. (2000). *Stress in college athletics: Causes, consequences, coping.* Binghamton, NY: Haworth Press.

Hunt, C. A., Rietschel, J. C., Hatfield, B. D., & Iso-Ahola, S. E. (2013). A psychophysiological profile of winners and losers in sport competition. *Sport, Exercise, and Performance Psychology, 2,* 220–231. http://dx.doi.org/10.1037/a0031957

Ie, A., Ngnoumen, C. T., & Langer, E. J. (Eds.). (2014). *The Wiley Blackwell handbook of mindfulness.* Chichester, England: Wiley. http://dx.doi.org/10.1002/9781118294895

Imel, Z., Baldwin, S., Bonus, K., & MacCoon, D. (2008). Beyond the individual: Group effects in mindfulness-based stress reduction. *Psychotherapy Research, 18,* 735–742. http://dx.doi.org/10.1080/10503300802326038

Ivarsson, A., Johnson, U., Andersen, M. B., Fallby, J., & Altemyr, M. (2015). It pays to pay attention: A mindfulness-based program for injury prevention with soccer players. *Journal of Applied Sport Psychology, 27,* 319–334. http://dx.doi.org/10.1080/10413200.2015.1008072

Ivtzan, I., & Hart, R. (2016). Mindfulness scholarship and interventions: A review. In A. L. Baltzell (Ed.), *Mindfulness and performance* (pp. 3–28). New York, NY: Cambridge University Press. http://dx.doi.org/10.1017/CBO9781139871310.002

Jackson, P. (1995). *Sacred hoops: Spiritual lessons of a hardwood warrior.* New York, NY: Hyperion.

Jackson, P. (2013). *Eleven rings: The soul of success.* New York, NY: Penguin Books.

Jackson, S. A. (1992). Athletes in flow: A qualitative investigation of flow states in elite figure skaters. *Journal of Applied Sport Psychology, 4,* 161–180. http://dx.doi.org/10.1080/10413209208406459

Jackson, S. A. (1995). Factors influencing the occurrence of flow state in elite athletes. *Journal of Applied Sport Psychology, 7,* 138–166. http://dx.doi.org/10.1080/10413209508406962

Jackson, S. A. (1996). Toward a conceptual understanding of the flow experience in elite athletes. *Research Quarterly for Exercise and Sport, 67,* 76–90. http://dx.doi.org/10.1080/02701367.1996.10607928

Jackson, S. A. (2016). Flowing with mindfulness: Investigating the relationship between flow and mindfulness. In I. Ivtzan & T. Lomas (Eds.), *Mindfulness in positive psychology: The science of meditation and wellbeing* (pp. 141–155). New York, NY: Routledge.

Jackson, S. A., & Csikszentmihalyi, M. (1999). *Flow in sport*. Champaign, IL: Human Kinetics.

Jackson, S. A., & Eklund, R. C. (2002). Assessing flow in physical activity: The Flow State Scale-2 and Dispositional Flow Scale-2. *Journal of Sport and Exercise Psychology, 24*, 133–150. http://dx.doi.org/10.1123/jsep.24.2.133

Jackson, S. A., & Eklund, R. C. (2004). *The flow scales manual*. Morgantown, WV: Fitness Information Technology.

Jackson, S. A., Ford, S. K., Kimiecik, J. C., & Marsh, H. W. (1998). Psychological correlates of flow in sport. *Journal of Sport and Exercise Psychology, 20*, 358–378. http://dx.doi.org/10.1123/jsep.20.4.358

Jackson, S. A., & Kimiecik, J. C. (2008). The flow perspective of optimal experience in sport and physical activity. In T. Horn (Ed.), *Advances in sport psychology* (3rd ed., pp. 377–400). Champaign, IL: Human Kinetics.

Jackson, S. A., Thomas, P. R., Marsh, H. W., & Smethurst, C. J. (2001). Relationships between flow, self-concept, psychological skills, and performance. *Journal of Applied Sport Psychology, 13*, 129–153. http://dx.doi.org/10.1080/104132001753149865

Jamieson, S. D., & Tuckey, M. R. (2016). Mindfulness interventions in the workplace: A critique of the current state of the literature. *Journal of Occupational Health Psychology*. Advance online publication. http://dx.doi.org/10.1037/ocp0000048

Janelle, C. M. (1999). Ironic mental processes in sport: Implications for sport psychologists. *The Sport Psychologist, 13*, 201–220. http://dx.doi.org/10.1123/tsp.13.2.201

Janssen, L., Kan, C. C., Carpentier, P. J., Sizoo, B., Hepark, S., Grutters, J., . . . Speckens, A. E. M. (2015). Mindfulness based cognitive therapy versus treatment as usual in adults with attention deficit hyperactivity disorder (ADHD). *BMC Psychiatry, 15*, 216. http://dx.doi.org/10.1186/s12888-015-0591-x

Jekauc, D., & Kittler, C. (2015). Achtsamkeit im leistungssport [Mindfulness in top-level sports]. *Leistungssport, 45*(6), 19–23. Retrieved from https://www.researchgate.net/publication/286194277_Achtsamkeit_im_Leistungssport

Jensen, C. G., Vangkilde, S., Frokjaer, V., & Hasselbalch, S. G. (2012). Mindfulness training affects attention—or is it attentional effort? *Journal of Experimental Psychology: General, 141*, 106–123. http://dx.doi.org/10.1037/a0024931

Jha, A. P., Stanley, E. A., Kiyonaga, A., Wong, L., & Gelfand, L. (2010). Examining the protective effects of mindfulness training on working memory capacity and affective experience. *Emotion, 10*, 54–64. http://dx.doi.org/10.1037/a0018438

John, S., Verma, S. K., & Khanna, G. L. (2011). The effect of mindfulness meditation on HPA-axis in pre-competition stress in sports performance of elite shooters. *National Journal of Integrated Research in Medicine, 2*, 15–21.

Johnson, J. G. (2006). Cognitive modeling of decision making in sports. *Psychology of Sport and Exercise, 7*, 631–652. http://dx.doi.org/10.1016/j.psychsport.2006.03.009

Jones, G. (1995). More than just a game: Research developments and issues in competitive anxiety in sport. *British Journal of Psychology, 86*, 449–478. http://dx.doi.org/10.1111/j.2044-8295.1995.tb02565.x

Josefsson, T., & Broberg, A. (2011). Meditators and non-meditators on sustained and executive attentional performance. *Mental Health, Religion & Culture, 14*, 291–309. http://dx.doi.org/10.1080/13674670903578621

Jouper, J., & Gustafsson, H. (2013). Mindful recovery: A case study of a burned-out elite shooter. *The Sport Psychologist, 27*, 92–102. http://dx.doi.org/10.1123/tsp.27.1.92

Kabat-Zinn, J. (1982). An outpatient program in behavioral medicine for chronic pain patients based on the practice of mindfulness meditation: Theoretical considerations and preliminary results. *General Hospital Psychiatry, 4*, 33–47. http://dx.doi.org/10.1016/0163-8343(82)90026-3

Kabat-Zinn, J. (1990). *Full catastrophe living: Using the wisdom of your body and mind to face stress, pain, and illness*. New York, NY: Delta.

Kabat-Zinn, J. (1994). *Wherever you go, there you are: Mindfulness meditation in everyday life*. New York, NY: Hyperion.

Kabat-Zinn, J. (2003). Mindfulness-based interventions in context: Past, present, and future. *Clinical Psychology: Science and Practice, 10*, 144–156. http://dx.doi.org/10.1093/clipsy.bpg016

Kabat-Zinn, J. (2005a). *Coming to our senses: Healing ourselves and the world through mindfulness*. New York, NY: Hyperion.

Kabat-Zinn, J. (2005b). *Wherever you go, there you are: Mindfulness meditation in everyday life*. New York, NY: Hachette Book Group.

Kabat-Zinn, J. (2011). Some reflections on the origins of MBSR, skillful means, and the trouble with maps. *Contemporary Buddhism, 12*, 281–306. http://dx.doi.org/10.1080/14639947.2011.564844

Kabat-Zinn, J. (2012). *Mindfulness for beginners: Reclaiming the present moment—and your life*. Boulder, CO: Sounds True.

Kabat-Zinn, J., Beall, B., & Rippe, J. (1985, June). *A systematic mental training program based on mindfulness meditation to optimize performance in collegiate and Olympic rowers*. Poster session presented at the World Congress in Sport Psychology, Copenhagen, Denmark.

Kabat-Zinn, J., Lipworth, L., & Burney, R. (1985). The clinical use of mindfulness meditation for the self-regulation of chronic pain. *Journal of Behavioral Medicine, 8*, 163–190. http://dx.doi.org/10.1007/BF00845519

Kabat-Zinn, J., Lipworth, L., Burney, R., & Sellers, W. (1986). Four-year follow-up of a meditation-based program for the self-regulation of chronic pain: Treatment outcomes and compliance. *The Clinical Journal of Pain, 2*, 159–173. http://dx.doi.org/10.1097/00002508-198602030-00004

Kabat-Zinn, J., Santorelli, S. F., Blacker, M., Brantley, J., Meleo-Meyer, F., & Grossman, P., . . . Stahl, R. (2014). Training teachers to deliver mindfulness-based stress reduction: Principles and standards. *Mindfulness, 1*(2), 74–86.

Kageyama, N. (2014). Practicing self-compassion. *The Flutist Quarterly, 40*, 28–31.

Kaliman, P., Alvarez-López, M. J., Cosín-Tomás, M., Rosenkranz, M. A., Lutz, A., & Davidson, R. J. (2014). Rapid changes in histone deacetylases and inflammatory gene expression in expert meditators. *Psychoneuroendocrinology, 40*, 96–107. http://dx.doi.org/10.1016/j.psyneuen.2013.11.004

Kallapiran, K., Koo, S., Kirubakaran, R., & Hancock, K. (2015). Effectiveness of mindfulness in improving mental health symptoms of children and adolescents: A meta-analysis. *Child and Adolescent Mental Health, 20,* 182–194. http://dx.doi.org/10.1111/camh.12113

Kane, M. J., & Engle, R. W. (2003). Working-memory capacity and the control of attention: The contributions of goal neglect, response competition, and task set to Stroop interference. *Journal of Experimental Psychology: General, 132,* 47–70. http://dx.doi.org/10.1037/0096-3445.132.1.47

Kaufman, K. A., Glass, C. R., & Arnkoff, D. B. (2009). Evaluation of mindful sport performance enhancement (MSPE): A new approach to promote flow in athletes. *Journal of Clinical Sport Psychology, 3,* 334–356. http://dx.doi.org/10.1123/jcsp.3.4.334

Kee, Y. H., Chatzisarantis, N., Kong, P. W., Chow, J. Y., & Chen, L. H. (2012). Mindfulness, movement control, and attentional focus strategies: Effects of mindfulness on a postural balance task. *Journal of Sport and Exercise Psychology, 34,* 561–579. http://dx.doi.org/10.1123/jsep.34.5.561

Kee, Y. H., & Wang, C. K. J. (2008). Relationships between mindfulness, flow dispositions and mental skills adoption: A cluster analytic approach. *Psychology of Sport and Exercise, 9,* 393–411. http://dx.doi.org/10.1016/j.psychsport.2007.07.001

Keng, S.-L., Smoski, M. J., & Robins, C. J. (2011). Effects of mindfulness on psychological health: A review of empirical studies. *Clinical Psychology Review, 31,* 1041–1056. http://dx.doi.org/10.1016/j.cpr.2011.04.006

Kettunen, A., & Välimäki, V. (2014). *Acceptance and value-based psychological coaching intervention for elite female floorball players* (Master's thesis, University of Jyväskylä). Retrieved from https://jyx.jyu.fi/dspace/bitstream/handle/123456789/44346/URN%3ANBN%3Afi%3Ajyu-201409292891.pdf?sequence=1

Khalsa, S. B. S., Butzer, B., Shorter, S. M., Reinhardt, K. M., & Cope, S. (2013). Yoga reduces performance anxiety in adolescent musicians. *Alternative Therapies in Health and Medicine, 19*(2), 34–45.

Khalsa, S. B. S., & Cope, S. (2006). Effects of a yoga lifestyle intervention on performance-related characteristics of musicians: A preliminary study. *Medical Science Monitor, 12*(8), CR325–CR331.

Khalsa, S. B. S., Shorter, S. M., Cope, S., Wyshak, G., & Sklar, E. (2009). Yoga ameliorates performance anxiety and mood disturbance in young professional musicians. *Applied Psychophysiology and Biofeedback, 34,* 279–289. http://dx.doi.org/10.1007/s10484-009-9103-4

Khazan, O. (2014, February 7). How Olympians stay motivated. *The Atlantic.* Retrieved from https://www.theatlantic.com/health/archive/2014/02/how-olympians-stay-motivated/283643

Khoury, B., Lecomte, T., Fortin, G., Masse, M., Therien, P., Bouchard, V., . . . Hofmann, S. G. (2013). Mindfulness-based therapy: A comprehensive meta-analysis. *Clinical Psychology Review, 33,* 763–771. http://dx.doi.org/10.1016/j.cpr.2013.05.005

Khoury, B., Sharma, M., Rush, S. E., & Fournier, C. (2015). Mindfulness-based stress reduction for healthy individuals: A meta-analysis. *Journal of Psychosomatic Research, 78,* 519–528. http://dx.doi.org/10.1016/j.jpsychores.2015.03.009

Kirchner, J. M., Bloom, A. J., & Skutnick-Henley, P. (2008). The relationship between performance anxiety and flow. *Medical Problems of Performing Artists, 23*(2), 59–65.

Klein, S. D., Bayard, C., & Wolf, U. (2014). The Alexander Technique and musicians: A systematic review of controlled trials. *BMC Complementary and Alternative Medicine, 14*, 414. http://dx.doi.org/10.1186/1472-6882-14-414

Klinger, E., Barta, S. G., & Glas, R. A. (1981). Thought content and gap time in basketball. *Cognitive Therapy and Research, 5*, 109–114. http://dx.doi.org/10.1007/BF01172331

Koehn, S. (2013). Effects of confidence and anxiety on flow state in competition. *European Journal of Sport Science, 13*, 543–550. http://dx.doi.org/10.1080/17461391.2012.746731

Koen, B. (2007, June/July). Musical mastery and the meditative mind via the GAP—guided attention practice. *American Music Teacher*, 12–15.

Kondo, H., Osaka, N., & Osaka, M. (2004). Cooperation of the anterior cingulate cortex and dorsolateral prefrontal cortex for attention shifting. *NeuroImage, 23*, 670–679. http://dx.doi.org/10.1016/j.neuroimage.2004.06.014

Kuyken, W., Warren, F. C., Taylor, R. S., Whalley, B., Crane, C., Bondolfi, G., . . . Dalgleish, T. (2016). Efficacy of mindfulness-based cognitive therapy in prevention of depressive relapse: An individual patient data meta-analysis from randomized trials. *JAMA Psychiatry, 73*, 565–574. http://dx.doi.org/10.1001/jamapsychiatry.2016.0076

Kuyken, W., Watkins, E., Holden, E., White, K., Taylor, R. S., Byford, S., . . . Dalgleish, T. (2010). How does mindfulness-based cognitive therapy work? *Behaviour Research and Therapy, 48*, 1105–1112. http://dx.doi.org/10.1016/j.brat.2010.08.003

Lambert, C. (1998). *Mind over water.* New York, NY: Houghton Mifflin.

Lane, A. M., Beedie, C. J., Jones, M. V., Uphill, M., & Devonport, T. J. (2012). The BASES expert statement on emotion regulation in sport. *Journal of Sports Sciences, 30*, 1189–1195. http://dx.doi.org/10.1080/02640414.2012.693621

Lane, A. M., Devonport, T. J., & Beedie, C. J. (2012). Can anger and tension be helpful? Emotions associated with optimal performance. *Athletic Insight: The Online Journal of Sport Psychology, 4*, 187–197.

Langer, E. J. (1989). *Mindfulness.* Reading, MA: Addison Wesley.

Langer, E. J. (1997). *The power of mindful learning.* Cambridge, MA: Da Capo Press.

Langer, E. J. (2000). Mindful learning. *Current Directions in Psychological Science, 9*, 220–223. http://dx.doi.org/10.1111/1467-8721.00099

Langer, E. J. (2014). Mindfulness forward and back. In A. Ie, C. Ngnoumen, & E. Langer (Eds.), *The Wiley Blackwell handbook of mindfulness* (Vol. 1, pp. 7–20). Chichester, England: Wiley. http://dx.doi.org/10.1002/9781118294895.ch1

Langer, E., Russel, T., & Eisenkraft, N. (2009). Orchestral performance and the footprint of mindfulness. *Psychology of Music, 37*, 125–136. http://dx.doi.org/10.1177/0305735607086053

Lau, M. A., Bishop, S. R., Segal, Z. V., Buis, T., Anderson, N. D., Carlson, L., . . . Devins, G. (2006). The Toronto Mindfulness Scale: Development and validation. *Journal of Clinical Psychology, 62*, 1445–1467. http://dx.doi.org/10.1002/jclp.20326

Lay, B. S., Sparrow, W. A., Hughes, K. M., & O'Dwyer, N. J. (2002). Practice effects on coordination and control, metabolic energy expenditure, and muscle activation. *Human Movement Science, 21*, 807–830. http://dx.doi.org/10.1016/S0167-9457(02)00166-5

Lazar, S. W., Bush, G., Gollub, R. L., Fricchione, G. L., Khalsa, G., & Benson, H. (2000). Functional brain mapping of the relaxation response and meditation. *Neuroreport, 11*, 1581–1585. http://dx.doi.org/10.1097/00001756-200005150-00042

Lazarus, R. S. (2000). How emotions influence performance in competitive sports. *The Sport Psychologist, 14*, 229–252. http://dx.doi.org/10.1123/tsp.14.3.229

Ledesma, D., & Kumano, H. (2009). Mindfulness-based stress reduction and cancer: A meta-analysis. *Psycho-Oncology, 18*, 571–579. http://dx.doi.org/10.1002/pon.1400

Lee, K., & de Bondt, R. (2005). *Total archery*. Republic of Korea: Samick Sports.

Lefebvre Sell, N. (2013). *dharmakaya: An investigation into the impact of mindful meditation on dancers' creative processes in a choreographic environment* (Unpublished doctoral dissertation). Trinity Laban Conservatoire of Music and Dance/City University, London, England.

Lemyre, P., Treasure, D. C., & Roberts, G. C. (2006). Influence of variability in motivation and affect on elite athlete burnout susceptibility. *Journal of Sport and Exercise Psychology, 28*, 32–48. http://dx.doi.org/10.1123/jsep.28.1.32

Levin, M. E., Luoma, J. B., & Haeger, J. A. (2015). Decoupling as a mechanism of change in mindfulness and acceptance: A literature review. *Behavior Modification, 39*, 870–911. http://dx.doi.org/10.1177/0145445515603707

Lin, P., Chang, J., Zemon, V., & Midlarsky, E. (2008). Silent illumination: A study on Chan (Zen) meditation, anxiety, and musical performance quality. *Psychology of Music, 36*, 139–155. http://dx.doi.org/10.1177/0305735607080840

Little, L. M. (1998). *An experimental analysis of an acceptance-based performance enhancement intervention in a sports context* (Doctoral dissertation). Available from ProQuest Dissertations and Theses database. (UMI No. 9911760)

Little, L. M., & Simpson, T. L. (2000). An acceptance based performance enhancement intervention for collegiate athletes. In M. J. Dougher (Ed.), *Clinical behavior analysis* (pp. 231–244). Reno, NV: Context Press.

Liu, S., & Xu, S. (2013). 正念训练对射击运动心理训练的启示 [Implications of mindfulness training on psychological training in shooting events]. *Journal of Capital University of Physical Education and Sports, 25*, 455–458.

Longshore, K., & Sachs, M. (2015). Mindfulness training for coaches: A mixed-method exploratory study. *Journal of Clinical Sport Psychology, 9*, 116–137. http://dx.doi.org/10.1123/jcsp.2014-0038

Lumma, A.-L., Kok, B. E., & Singer, T. (2015). Is meditation always relaxing? Investigating heart rate, heart rate variability, experienced effort and likeability during training of three types of meditation. *International Journal of Psychophysiology, 97*, 38–45. http://dx.doi.org/10.1016/j.ijpsycho.2015.04.017

Lundgren, T. (2015, July). Evaluation of the effects of an ACT based intervention for ice hockey players: A randomized controlled trial. In B. Carraça (Chair), *ACT in sports: Enhancing performance and measuring sport-related psychological flexibility*. Berlin, Germany: Association for Contextual Behavioral Science.

Lynch, J., & Scott, W. (1999). *Running within: A guide to mastering the body-mind-spirit connection for ultimate training and racing*. Champaign, IL: Human Kinetics.

MacPherson, A. C., Collins, D., & Obhi, S. S. (2009). The importance of temporal structure and rhythm for the optimum performance of motor skills: A new focus for practitioners of sport psychology. *Journal of Applied Sport Psychology, 21*(Suppl. 1), 48–61. http://dx.doi.org/10.1080/10413200802595930

Mahoney, J., & Hanrahan, S. J. (2011). A brief educational intervention using acceptance and commitment therapy: Four injured athletes' experiences. *Journal of Clinical Sport Psychology, 5,* 252–273. http://dx.doi.org/10.1123/jcsp.5.3.252

Mann, D. T. Y., Williams, A. M., Ward, P., & Janelle, C. M. (2007). Perceptual-cognitive expertise in sport: A meta-analysis. *Journal of Sport and Exercise Psychology, 29,* 457–478. http://dx.doi.org/10.1123/jsep.29.4.457

Mannion, J., & Andersen, M. B. (2015). Mindfulness, therapeutic relationships, and neuroscience in applied exercise psychology. In M. B. Andersen & S. J. Hanrahan (Eds.), *Doing exercise psychology* (pp. 3–18). Champaign, IL: Human Kinetics.

Mannion, J., & Andersen, M. B. (2016). Interpersonal mindfulness for athletic coaches and other performance professionals. In A. L. Baltzell (Ed.), *Mindfulness and performance* (pp. 439–463). New York, NY: Cambridge University Press. http://dx.doi.org/10.1017/CBO9781139871310.020

Marcora, S. M., & Staiano, W. (2010). The limit to exercise tolerance in humans: Mind over muscle? *European Journal of Applied Physiology, 109,* 763–770. http://dx.doi.org/10.1007/s00421-010-1418-6

Mardon, N., Richards, H., & Martindale, A. (2016). The effect of mindfulness training on attention and performance in national-level swimmers: An exploratory investigation. *The Sport Psychologist, 30,* 131–140. http://dx.doi.org/10.1123/tsp.2014-0085

Marich, J. (2015). *Dancing mindfulness: A creative path to healing & transformation.* Woodstock, VT: Skylight Paths.

Marks, D. R. (2008). The Buddha's extra scoop: Neural correlates of mindfulness and clinical sport psychology. *Journal of Clinical Sport Psychology, 2,* 216–241. http://dx.doi.org/10.1123/jcsp.2.3.216

Martin, D. J., Garske, J. P., & Davis, M. K. (2000). Relation of the therapeutic alliance with outcome and other variables: A meta-analytic review. *Journal of Consulting and Clinical Psychology, 68,* 438–450. http://dx.doi.org/10.1037/0022-006X.68.3.438

Martin, S. B. (2005). High school and college athletes' attitudes toward sport psychology consulting. *Journal of Applied Sport Psychology, 17,* 127–139. http://dx.doi.org/10.1080/10413200590932434

McCabe, D. P., Roediger, H. L., III, McDaniel, M. A., Balota, D. A., & Hambrick, D. Z. (2010). The relationship between working memory capacity and executive functioning: Evidence for a common executive attention construct. *Neuropsychology, 24,* 222–243. http://dx.doi.org/10.1037/a0017619

McCarthy, P. J., Allen, M. S., & Jones, M. V. (2013). Emotions, cognitive interference, and concentration disruption in youth sport. *Journal of Sports Sciences, 31,* 505–515. http://dx.doi.org/10.1080/02640414.2012.738303

McDonald, K. (2005). *How to meditate: A practical guide* (2nd ed.). Somerville, MA: Wisdom.

McGinn, D. (2015, May 27). This mindfulness teacher gets results (just ask Kobe). *The Boston Globe.* Retrieved from https://www.bostonglobe.com/magazine/2015/05/27/

this-mindfulness-teacher-gets-results-just-ask-kobe/mMYGHRJSziVp4DLq2gAzcJ/
story.html

McKenzie, S. (2015). *Mindfulness at work: How to avoid stress, achieve more, and enjoy life!*
Pompton Plains, NJ: Career Press.

Memmert, D. (2007). Can creativity be improved by an attention-broadening training program? An exploratory study focusing on team sports. *Creativity Research
Journal, 19*, 281–291. http://dx.doi.org/10.1080/10400410701397420

Memmert, D. (2009). Pay attention! A review of visual attentional expertise in sport.
International Review of Sport and Exercise Psychology, 2, 119–138. http://dx.doi.org/
10.1080/17509840802641372

Memmert, D. (2011). Sports and creativity. In M. A. Runco & S. R. Pritzker (Eds.),
Encyclopedia of creativity (2nd ed., Vol. 2, pp. 373–378). San Diego, CA: Academic
Press. http://dx.doi.org/10.1016/B978-0-12-375038-9.00207-7

Memmert, D., & Furley, P. (2007). "I spy with my little eye!": Breadth of attention,
inattentional blindness, and tactical decision making in team sports. *Journal of Sport
and Exercise Psychology, 29*, 365–381. http://dx.doi.org/10.1123/jsep.29.3.365

Mikicin, M., & Kowalczyk, M. (2015). Audio-visual and autogenic relaxation alter
amplitude of alpha EEG band, causing improvements in mental work performance
in athletes. *Applied Psychophysiology and Biofeedback, 40*, 219–227. http://dx.doi.org/
10.1007/s10484-015-9290-0

Millar, S.-K., Oldham, A. R., & Renshaw, I. (2013). Interpersonal, intrapersonal,
extrapersonal? Qualitatively investigating coordinative couplings between rowers
in Olympic sculling. *Nonlinear Dynamics, Psychology, and Life Sciences, 17*, 425–443.

Miller, T. (2002). *Programmed to run.* Champaign, IL: Human Kinetics.

Mindfulness All-Party Parliamentary Group. (2015, October). *Mindful nation UK.*
Retrieved from http://www.themindfulnessinitiative.org.uk/images/reports/
Mindfulness-APPG-Report_Mindful-Nation-UK_Oct2015.pdf

Mipham, S. (2012). *Running with the mind of meditation: Lessons for training body and
mind.* New York, NY: Harmony Books.

Mistretta, E. G., Glass, C. R., Spears, C. A., Perskaudas, R., Kaufman, K. A., & Hoyer,
D. (2016). *Collegiate athletes' expectations and experiences of mindful sport performance
enhancement.* Manuscript submitted for publication.

Mistretta, E. G., Kaufman, K. A., Glass, C. R., & Spears, C. A. (2016, April). *Mindful
sport performance enhancement for high school athletes.* Poster presented at the annual
meeting of the Association for Applied Sport Psychology Mid-Atlantic Regional
Conference, Philadelphia, PA.

Mitchell, J., & Hassed, C. (2016). The mindful AFL player: Engagement, mobile
apps, and well-being. In A. L. Baltzell (Ed.), *Mindfulness and performance*
(pp. 268–299). New York, NY: Cambridge University Press. http://dx.doi.org/
10.1017/CBO9781139871310.013

Moghadam, M. S., Sayadi, E., Samimifar, M., & Moharer, A. (2013). Impact assessment of mindfulness techniques education on anxiety and sports performance in
badminton players Isfahan. *International Research Journal of Applied and Basic Sciences,
4*, 1170–1175.

Moore, A., & Malinowski, P. (2009). Meditation, mindfulness and cognitive flexibility. *Consciousness and Cognition, 18,* 176–186. http://dx.doi.org/10.1016/j.concog.2008.12.008

Moore, B. A. (2013). Propensity for experiencing flow: The roles of cognitive flexibility and mindfulness. *The Humanistic Psychologist, 41,* 319–332. http://dx.doi.org/10.1080/08873267.2013.820954

Moore, Z. E. (2009). Theoretical and empirical developments of the mindfulness-acceptance-commitment (MAC) approach to performance enhancement. *Journal of Clinical Sport Psychology, 3,* 291–302. http://dx.doi.org/10.1123/jcsp.3.4.291

Moore, Z. E. (2016). Mindfulness, emotion regulation, and performance. In A. L. Baltzell (Ed.), *Mindfulness and performance* (pp. 29–52). New York, NY: Cambridge University Press. http://dx.doi.org/10.1017/CBO9781139871310.003

Moore, Z. E., & Gardner, F. L. (2014). Mindfulness and performance. In A. Ie, C. T. Ngnoumen, & E. J. Langer (Eds.), *The Wiley Blackwell handbook of mindfulness* (Vol. II, pp. 986–1003). Chichester, England: Wiley. http://dx.doi.org/10.1002/9781118294895.ch51

Morgan, L. P. K., Graham, J. R., Hayes-Skelton, S. A., Orsillo, S. M., & Roemer, L. (2014). Relationships between amount of post-intervention mindfulness practice and follow-up outcome variables in an acceptance-based behavior therapy for generalized anxiety disorder: The importance of informal practice. *Journal of Contextual Behavioral Science, 3,* 173–178. http://dx.doi.org/10.1016/j.jcbs.2014.05.001

Morone, N. E., Lynch, C. S., Greco, C. M., Tindle, H. A., & Weiner, D. K. (2008). "I felt like a new person." The effects of mindfulness meditation on older adults with chronic pain: Qualitative narrative analysis of diary entries. *The Journal of Pain, 9,* 841–848. http://dx.doi.org/10.1016/j.jpain.2008.04.003

Mosewich, A. D., Crocker, P. R. E., Kowalski, K. C., & DeLongis, A. (2013). Applying self-compassion in sport: An intervention with women athletes. *Journal of Sport and Exercise Psychology, 35,* 514–524. http://dx.doi.org/10.1123/jsep.35.5.514

Mosewich, A. D., Kowalski, K. C., Sabiston, C. M., Sedgwick, W. A., & Tracy, J. L. (2011). Self-compassion: A potential resource for young women athletes. *Journal of Sport and Exercise Psychology, 33,* 103–123. http://dx.doi.org/10.1123/jsep.33.1.103

Moyle, G. M. (2012). Performance in the spotlight: Exploring psychology in the performing arts. *InPsych, 34*(6), 11–13.

Moyle, G. M. (2016). Mindfulness and dancers. In A. Baltzell (Ed.), *Mindfulness and performance* (pp. 367–388). New York, NY: Cambridge University Press. http://dx.doi.org/10.1017/CBO9781139871310.017

Mumford, G. (2015). *The mindful athlete: Secrets to pure performance.* Berkeley, CA: Parallax Press.

Murphy, M., & White, R. A. (1978). *The psychic side of sports.* Reading, MA: Addison-Wesley.

Murphy, T., & Orlick, T. (2006). Mental strategies of professional actors. *Journal of Excellence, 11,* 103–125.

Neff, K. D. (2003). Self-compassion: An alternative conceptualization of a healthy attitude toward oneself. *Self and Identity, 2,* 85–101. http://dx.doi.org/10.1080/15298860309032

Neporent, L. (2014, January 30). Seattle Seahawks will have 'ohm' team advantage: Head coach Pete Carroll encourages players to meditate. *ABC News*. Retrieved from http://abcnews.go.com/Health/seattle-seahawks-ohm-team-advantage/ story?id=21614481

Newell, S. (2001). *The golf instruction manual*. New York, NY: Dorling Kindersley.

Nhat Hanh, T. (1998). *The heart of the Buddha's teaching: Transforming suffering into peace, joy, and liberation*. New York, NY: Broadway Books.

Noakes, T. D. (2000). Physiological models to understand exercise fatigue and the adaptations that predict or enhance athletic performance. *Scandinavian Journal of Medicine & Science in Sports, 10*, 123–145. http://dx.doi.org/10.1034/ j.1600-0838.2000.010003123.x

Noakes, T. D. (2012). Fatigue is a brain-derived emotion that regulates the exercise behavior to ensure the protection of whole body homeostasis. *Frontiers in Physiology, 3*, 82. http://dx.doi.org/10.3389/fphys.2012.00082

Norcross, J. C., Pfund, R. A., & Prochaska, J. O. (2013). Psychotherapy in 2022: A Delphi poll on its future. *Professional Psychology: Research and Practice, 44*, 363–370. http://dx.doi.org/10.1037/a0034633

Nordin-Bates, S. M. (2012). Performance psychology in the performing arts. In S. M. Murphy (Ed.), *The Oxford handbook of sport and performance psychology* (pp. 81–114). New York, NY: Oxford University Press.

Noren, N. (2014, January 22). Taking notice of the hidden injury. *ESPN.com: OTL*. Retrieved from http://www.espn.com/espn/otl/story/_/id/10335925/ awareness-better-treatment-college-athletes-mental-health-begins-take-shape

O'Connor, E. (2016). *Pain tolerance in sport*. Retrieved from http://www. appliedsportpsych.org/resource-center/resources-for-athletes/pain-tolerance-in-sport

Orlick, T., & Partington, J. (1988). Mental links to excellence. *The Sport Psychologist, 2*, 105–130. http://dx.doi.org/10.1123/tsp.2.2.105

Ornish, D., Magbanua, M. J., Weidner, G., Weinberg, V., Kemp, C., Green, C., . . . Carroll, P. R. (2008). Changes in prostate gene expression in men undergoing an intensive nutrition and lifestyle intervention. *Proceedings of the National Academy of Sciences of the United States of America, 105*, 8369–8374. http://dx.doi.org/10.1073/ pnas.0803080105

Ostafin, B. D., Robinson, M. D., & Meiers, B. P. (Eds.). (2015). *Handbook of mindfulness and self-regulation*. New York, NY: Springer. http://dx.doi.org/10.1007/ 978-1-4939-2263-5

Ottoboni, G., Giusti, R., Gatta, A., Symes, E., & Tessari, A. (2014) Just do it: Embodied experiences improve Taekwondo athletes sport performance. *Sensoria: A Journal of Mind, Brain & Culture, 10*, 28–33.

Oyan, S. (2006). *Mindfulness meditation: Creative musical performance through awareness* (Doctoral dissertation). Available from ProQuest Dissertations and Theses database. (UMI No. 3208188)

Pal, G. K., Velkumary, S., & Madanmohan. (2004). Effect of short-term practice of breathing exercises on autonomic functions in normal human volunteers. *The Indian Journal of Medical Research, 120*, 115–121.

Partington, J., & Orlick, T. (1987). The sport psychology consultant: Olympic coaches' views. *The Sport Psychologist, 1*, 95–102. http://dx.doi.org/10.1123/tsp.1.2.95

Passmore, J., & Marianetti, O. (2007). The role of mindfulness in coaching. *The Coaching Psychologist, 3*, 131–137.

Patston, T. (2016). Mindfulness in music. In A. Baltzell (Ed.), *Mindfulness and performance* (pp. 412–436). New York, NY: Cambridge University Press. http://dx.doi.org/10.1017/CBO9781139871310.019

Pecen, E., Collins, D., & MacNamara, A. (2016). Music of the night: Performance practitioner considerations for enhancement work in music. *Sport, Exercise, and Performance Psychology, 5*, 377–395. http://dx.doi.org/10.1037/spy0000067

Perret, K. A. (2014). *Can acceptance and commitment therapy increase rehabilitation adherence for the treatment of sport injury?* (Doctoral dissertation). Available from ProQuest Dissertations and Theses database. (UMI No. 3636935)

Pickert, K. (2014, February 3). The mindful revolution: Finding peace in a stressed-out, digitally dependent culture may just be a matter of thinking differently. *TIME Magazine*, 40–46.

Pineau, T. R. (2014). *Effects of mindful sport performance enhancement (MSPE) on running performance and body image: Does self-compassion make a difference?* (Doctoral dissertation). Available from ProQuest Dissertations and Theses database. (UMI No. 364138).

Pineau, T. R. (2016). *Evaluation of mindful sport performance enhancement (MSPE) in a naturalistic university setting*. Manuscript in preparation.

Pineau, T. R., Glass, C. R., & Kaufman, K. A. (2012, July). *Sport anxiety and aspects of mindfulness in athletes: Implications for mindful sport performance enhancement (MSPE)*. Poster presented at the meeting of the Association for Contextual Behavioral Science, Washington, DC.

Pineau, T. R., Glass, C. R., & Kaufman, K. A. (2014). Mindfulness in sport performance. In A. Ie, C. T. Ngnoumen, & E. J. Langer (Eds.), *The Wiley Blackwell handbook of mindfulness* (Vol. II, pp. 1004–1033). Chichester, England: Wiley. http://dx.doi.org/10.1002/9781118294895.ch52

Pineau, T. R., Glass, C. R., Kaufman, K. A., & Bernal, D. R. (2014). Self- and team efficacy beliefs of rowers and their relation to mindfulness and flow. *Journal of Clinical Sport Psychology, 8*, 142–158. http://dx.doi.org/10.1123/jcsp.2014-0019

Pink, D. H. (2009). *Drive: The surprising truth about what motivates us*. New York, NY: Riverhead.

Plemmons, M. G. (2015). *Evaluation of the effectiveness of the mindfulness-acceptance-commitment (MAC) approach in recreational golfers* (Master's thesis, Appalachian State University). Retrieved from https://libres.uncg.edu/ir/asu/listing.aspx?id=18348

Posner, M. I., & Rothbart, M. K. (2007). Research on attention networks as a model for the integration of psychological science. *Annual Review of Psychology, 58*, 1–23. http://dx.doi.org/10.1146/annurev.psych.58.110405.085516

Powers, T. A., Koestner, R., Lacaille, N., Kwan, L., & Zuroff, D. C. (2009). Self-criticism, motivation, and goal progress of athletes and musicians: A prospective study. *Personality and Individual Differences, 47*, 279–283. http://dx.doi.org/10.1016/j.paid.2009.03.012

Premack, D. (1965). Reinforcement theory. In D. Levine (Ed.), *Nebraska symposium on motivation* (pp. 123–180). Lincoln, NE: University of Nebraska Press.

Privette, G. (1981). The phenomenology of peak performance in sports. *International Journal of Sport Psychology, 12,* 51–60.

Puff, R. (2014, February). How meditation won the super bowl. *Psychology Today.* Retrieved from https://www.psychologytoday.com/blog/meditation-modern-life/201402/how-meditation-won-the-super-bowl

Rappaport, L. (Ed.). (2013). *Mindfulness and the arts therapies: Theory and practice.* London, England: Jessica Kingsley.

Ravizza, K. (1977). Peak experiences in sport. *Journal of Humanistic Psychology, 17,* 35–40. http://dx.doi.org/10.1177/002216787701700404

Ravizza, K. (1995). A mental training approach to performance enhancement. In K. P. Henschen & W. F. Straub (Eds.), *Sport psychology: An analysis of athlete behavior* (3rd ed., pp. 35–44). Longmeadow, MA: Mouvement.

Ravizza, K. H. (2002). A philosophical construct: A framework for performance enhancement. *International Journal of Sport Psychology, 33,* 4–18.

Reb, J., & Atkins, P. W. G. (Eds.). (2015). *Mindfulness in organizations: Foundations, research, and applications.* Cambridge, England: Cambridge University Press. http://dx.doi.org/10.1017/CBO9781107587793

Reb, J., & Choi, E. (2014). Mindfulness in organizations. In N. N. Singh (Ed.), *Psychology of meditation* (pp. 279–309). New York, NY: NOVA Science.

Reed, K. (2013, November 14). Warped sports culture needs to change. *The Huffington Post.* Retrieved from http://www.huffingtonpost.com/ken-reed/warped-sports-culture-nee_b_4275163.html

Reis, N. A., Kowalski, K. C., Ferguson, L. J., Sabiston, C. M., Sedgwick, W. A., & Crocker, P. R. E. (2015). Self-compassion and women athletes' responses to emotionally difficult sport situations: An evaluation of a brief induction. *Psychology of Sport and Exercise, 16,* 18–25. http://dx.doi.org/10.1016/j.psychsport.2014.08.011

Reynolds, G. (2015, September 30). Does mindfulness make for a better athlete? *The New York Times.* Retrieved from https://well.blogs.nytimes.com/2015/09/30/does-mindfulness-make-for-a-better-athlete

Rheinberg, F., Vollmeyer, R., & Engeser, S. (2003). Die erfassung des flow-erlebens [The assessment of flow experience]. In J. Stiensmeier-Pelster & F. Rheinberg (Eds.), *Diagnostik von Motivation und selbstkonzept* (pp. 261–279). Göttingen, Germany: Hogrefe.

Rigby, C. S., Schultz, P. P., & Ryan, R. M. (2014). Mindfulness, interest-taking, and self-regulation: A self-determination theory perspective on the role of awareness in optimal functioning. In A. Ie, C. T. Ngnoumen, & E. J. Langer (Eds.), *The Wiley Blackwell handbook of mindfulness* (Vol. 1, pp. 216–235). Chichester, England: Wiley Blackwell. http://dx.doi.org/10.1002/9781118294895.ch12

Rippe, J., & Southmayd, W. (1986). *Sports performance factors.* New York, NY: Putnam.

Ristad, E. (1982). *A soprano on her head.* Moab, UT: Real People Press.

Riva, M. T. (2014). Supervision of group leaders. In J. L. DeLucia-Waack, C. R. Kalodner, & M. T. Riva (Eds.), *Handbook of group counseling and psychotherapy* (2nd ed., pp. 146–158). Thousand Oaks, CA: Sage.

Robazza, C., & Bortoli, L. (2003). Intensity, idiosyncratic content and functional impact of performance-related emotions in athletes. *Journal of Sports Sciences, 21,* 171–189. http://dx.doi.org/10.1080/0264041031000071065

Rodríguez, M. C., & Rodríguez, F. A. (2009). Efectos de la aplicación de la terapia de aceptación y compromiso sobre la conducta de evitación experiencial en competencia en jóvenes tenistas de la ciudad de Bogotá [Effects of application of the acceptance and commitment therapy on the behavior of experiential avoidance in competition in young tennis players in the city of Bogotá]. *Diversitas: Perspectivas en Psicología, 5,* 349–360. http://dx.doi.org/10.15332/s1794-9998.2009.0002.10

Roemer, L., & Orsillo, S. M. (2008). *Mindfulness- & acceptance-based behavioral therapies in practice.* New York, NY: Guilford Press.

Roenigk, A. (2013, August 21). Lotus pose on two. *ESPN The Magazine.* Retrieved from http://www.espn.com/nfl/story/_/id/9581925/seattle-seahawks-use-unusual-techniques-practice-espn-magazine

Ross, A., & Thomas, S. (2010). The health benefits of yoga and exercise: A review of comparison studies. *Journal of Alternative and Complementary Medicine, 16,* 3–12. http://dx.doi.org/10.1089/acm.2009.0044

Rotella, B. (2004). *The golfer's mind: Play to play great.* New York, NY: Free Press.

Röthlin, P., Birrer, D., Horvath, S., & grosse Holtforth, M. (2016). Psychological skills training and a mindfulness-based intervention to enhance functional athletic performance: Design of a randomized controlled trial using ambulatory assessment. *BMC Psychology, 4,* 39. http://dx.doi.org/10.1186/s40359-016-0147-y

Rush, I. R. (2014, March 17). Athletes using meditation to improve performance. *The Philadelphia Inquirer.* Retrieved from http://articles.philly.com

Ryan, T. (2012). *A mindful nation.* Carlsbad, CA: Hay House.

Salmon, P., Hanneman, S., & Harwood, B. (2010). Associative/dissociative cognitive strategies in sustained physical activity: Literature review and proposal for a mindfulness-based conceptual model. *The Sport Psychologist, 24,* 127–156. http://dx.doi.org/10.1123/tsp.24.2.127

Salmon, P. G., Santorelli, S. F., Sephton, S. E., & Kabat-Zinn, J. (2009). Intervention elements promoting adherence to mindfulness-based stress reduction (MBSR) programs in a clinical behavioral medicine setting. In S. A. Shumaker, J. K. Ockene, & K. A. Riekert (Eds.), *The handbook of health behavior change* (3rd ed., pp. 271–286). New York, NY: Springer.

Sandler, M., & Lee, J. (2015, July 1). Olympic medalist Deena Kastor shares 10 mindfulness tips for world record success, health and happiness. *The Huffington Post.* Retrieved from http://www.huffingtonpost.com/michael-sandler-and-jessica-lee/10-ways-runner-olympian-d_b_7649238.html

Sant, B. (2015). *The effect of mindfulness training on resilience in elite young athletes* (Master's Thesis, University of Edinburgh). Retrieved from http://www.academia.edu/18652111/MSc_Performance_Psychology_Thesis_The_Effect_of_Mindfulness_Training_on_Resilience_in_Elite_Young_Athletes

Santorelli, S. F. (1999). *Heal thy self: Lessons on mindfulness in medicine.* New York, NY: Bell Tower.

Sappington, R., & Longshore, K. (2015). Systematically reviewing the efficacy of mindfulness-based interventions for enhanced sport performance. *Journal of Clinical Sport Psychology, 9*, 232–262. http://dx.doi.org/10.1123/jcsp.2014-0017

Sauer, S., & Baer, R. A. (2010). Mindfulness and decentering as mechanisms of change in mindfulness- and acceptance-based interventions. In R. A. Baer (Ed.), *Assessing mindfulness & acceptance processes in clients: Illuminating the theory & practice of change* (pp. 25–45). Oakland, CA: New Harbinger.

Sauer, S., Walach, H., Schmidt, S., Hinterberger, T., Lynch, S., Büssing, A., & Kohls, N. (2013). Assessment of mindfulness: Review on state of the art. *Mindfulness, 4*, 3–17. http://dx.doi.org/10.1007/s12671-012-0122-5

Scarry, E. (1999). *Dreaming by the book.* New York, NY: Farrar Straus Giroux.

Schofield, T. P., Creswell, J. D., & Denson, T. F. (2015). Brief mindfulness induction reduces inattentional blindness. *Consciousness and Cognition, 37*, 63–70. http://dx.doi.org/10.1016/j.concog.2015.08.007

Schwanhausser, L. (2009). Application of the Mindfulness-Acceptance-Commitment (MAC) protocol with an adolescent springboard diver. *Journal of Clinical Sport Psychology, 3*, 377–395. http://dx.doi.org/10.1123/jcsp.3.4.377

Scott-Hamilton, J., & Schutte, N. S. (2016). The role of adherence in the effects of a mindfulness intervention for competitive athletes: Changes in mindfulness, flow, pessimism, and anxiety. *Journal of Clinical Sport Psychology, 10*, 99–117. http://dx.doi.org/10.1123/jcsp.2015-0020

Scott-Hamilton, J., Schutte, N. S., & Brown, R. F. (2016). Effects of a mindfulness intervention on sports-anxiety, pessimism, and flow in competitive cyclists. *Applied Psychology: Health and Well-Being, 8*, 85–103. http://dx.doi.org/10.1111/aphw.12063

Scott-Hamilton, J., Schutte, N. S., Moyle, G. M., & Brown, R. F. (2016). The relationships between mindfulness, sport anxiety, pessimistic attributions and flow in competitive cyclists. *International Journal of Sport Psychology, 47*, 103–121.

Sedlmeier, P., Eberth, J., Schwarz, M., Zimmermann, D., Haarig, F., Jaeger, S., & Kunze, S. (2012). The psychological effects of meditation: A meta-analysis. *Psychological Bulletin, 138*, 1139–1171. http://dx.doi.org/10.1037/a0028168

Segal, Z. V., Williams, J. M. G., & Teasdale, J. D. (2002). *Mindfulness-based cognitive therapy for depression: A new approach to preventing relapse.* New York, NY: Guilford Press.

Segal, Z. V., Williams, J. M. G., & Teasdale, J. D. (2012). *Mindfulness-based cognitive therapy for depression* (2nd ed.). New York, NY: Guilford Press.

Shapiro, S. L., Carlson, L. E., Astin, J. A., & Freedman, B. (2006). Mechanisms of mindfulness. *Journal of Clinical Psychology, 62*, 373–386. http://dx.doi.org/10.1002/jclp.20237

Sheldon, K. M., Prentice, M., & Halusic, M. (2015). The experiential incompatibility of mindfulness and flow absorption. *Social Psychological and Personality Science, 6*, 276–283. http://dx.doi.org/10.1177/1948550614555028

Shonin, E., Van Gordon, W., Dunn, T. J., Singh, N. N., & Griffiths, M. D. (2014). Meditation awareness training (MAT) for work-related wellbeing and job performance: A randomized controlled trial. *International Journal of Mental Health and Addiction, 12*, 806–823. http://dx.doi.org/10.1007/s11469-014-9513-2

Si, G., Lo, C.-H., & Zhang, C.-Q. (2016). Mindfulness training program for Chinese athletes and its effectiveness. In A. L. Baltzell (Ed.), *Mindfulness and performance* (pp. 235–267). New York, NY: Cambridge University Press. http://dx.doi.org/10.1017/CBO9781139871310.012

Siegel, D. J. (2007). *The mindful brain: Reflection and attunement in the cultivation of well-being.* New York, NY: Norton.

Silva, J. M. (1984a). Personality and sport performance: Controversy and challenge. In J. M. Silva & R. S. Weinberg (Eds.), *Psychological foundations of sport* (pp. 59–69). Champaign, IL: Human Kinetics.

Silva, J. M., III. (1984b). The status of sport psychology. *Journal of Physical Education, Recreation & Dance, 55,* 46–49. http://dx.doi.org/10.1080/07303084.1984.10630599

Silva, J. M. (2002). The evolution of sport psychology. In J. M. Silva & D. E. Stevens (Eds.), *Psychological foundations of sport* (pp. 1–26). Boston, MA: Allyn & Bacon.

Sime, W. E. (2003). Sport psychology applications of biofeedback and neurofeedback. In M. S. Schwartz & F. Andrasik (Eds.), *Biofeedback: A practitioner's guide* (3rd ed., pp. 560–588). New York, NY: Guilford Press.

Sinclair, G. D., & Sinclair, D. A. (1994). Developing reflective performers by integrating mental management skills with the learning process. *The Sport Psychologist, 8,* 13–27. http://dx.doi.org/10.1123/tsp.8.1.13

Slagter, H. A., Lutz, A., Greischar, L. L., Francis, A. D., Nieuwenhuis, S., Davis, J. M., & Davidson, R. J. (2007). Mental training affects distribution of limited brain resources. *PLoS Biology, 5,* e138. http://dx.doi.org/10.1371/journal.pbio.0050138

Smith, R. E., Smoll, F. L., Cumming, S. P., & Grossbard, J. R. (2006). Measurement of multidimensional sport performance anxiety in children and adults: The Sport Anxiety Scale-2. *Journal of Sport and Exercise Psychology, 28,* 479–501. http://dx.doi.org/10.1123/jsep.28.4.479

Solé, S., Carraça, B., Serpa, S., & Palmi, J. (2014). Aplicaciones del *mindfulness* (conciencia plena) en lesión deportiva [Mindfulness applications in sport injury]. *Revista de Psicología del Deporte, 23,* 501–508.

Speier, A. (2015, January 12). Red Sox create new behavioral health department. *Boston Globe.* Retrieved from https://www.bostonglobe.com/sports/2015/01/12/red-sox-create-new-behavioral-health-department/6XJfU2wnt0vw4N1ZvHtaFN/story.html

Sridharan, D., Levitin, D. J., & Menon, V. (2008). A critical role for the right fronto-insular cortex in switching between central-executive and default-mode networks. *Proceedings of the National Academy of Sciences of the United States of America, 105,* 12569–12574. http://dx.doi.org/10.1073/pnas.0800005105

Stahl, B., & Goldstein, E. (2010). *A mindfulness-based stress reduction workbook.* Oakland, CA: New Harbinger.

Standage, M., & Ryan, R. M. (2012). Self-determination theory and exercise motivation: Facilitating self-regulatory processes to support and maintain health and well-being. In G. C. Roberts & D. C. Treasure (Eds.), *Advances in motivation in sport and exercise* (3rd ed., pp. 233–270). Champaign, IL: Human Kinetics.

Stankovic, D. (2015). *Mindfulness meditation training for tennis players* (Doctoral dissertation). Available from ProQuest Dissertations and Theses database. (UMI No. 3708185)

Stanley, E. A. (2014). Mindfulness-based fitness training: An approach for enhancing performance and building resilience in high-stress contexts. In A. Ie, C. T. Ngnoumen, & E. J. Langer (Eds.), *The Wiley Blackwell handbook of mindfulness* (Vol. II, pp. 964–985). Chichester, England: Wiley. http://dx.doi.org/10.1002/9781118294895.ch50

Stanley, E. A., & Jha, P. (2009). Mind fitness: Improving operational effectiveness and building warrior resilience. *Joint Force Quarterly, 55*, 144–151.

Stapleton, A. B., Hankes, D. M., Hays, K. F., & Parham, W. D. (2010). Ethical dilemmas in sport psychology: A dialogue on the unique aspects impacting practice. *Professional Psychology: Research and Practice, 41*, 143–152. http://dx.doi.org/10.1037/a0017976

Steptoe, A., & Fidler, H. (1987). Stage fright in orchestral musicians: A study of cognitive and behavioural strategies in performance anxiety. *British Journal of Psychology, 78*, 241–249. http://dx.doi.org/10.1111/j.2044-8295.1987.tb02243.x

Stern, J. R. S., Khalsa, S. B. S., & Hofmann, S. G. (2012). A yoga intervention for music performance anxiety in conservatory students. *Medical Problems of Performing Artists, 27*, 123–128.

Steyn, M. H. (2013). *The impact of psychological skills and mindfulness training on the psychological well-being of undergraduate music students* (Unpublished master's thesis). University of Pretoria, South Africa. Retrieved from http://repository.up.ac.za/handle/2263/33367

Sun, S., Yao, Z., Wei, J., & Yu, R. (2015). Calm and smart? A selective review of meditation effects on decision making. *Frontiers in Psychology, 6*, 1059. http://dx.doi.org/10.3389/fpsyg.2015.01059

Sutton, J. (2007). Batting, habit and memory: The embodied mind and the nature of skill. *Sport in Society, 10*, 763–786. http://dx.doi.org/10.1080/17430430701442462

Swann, C., Keegan, R. J., Piggott, D., & Crust, L. (2012). A systematic review of the experience, occurrence, and controllability of flow states in elite sport. *Psychology of Sport and Exercise, 13*, 807–819. http://dx.doi.org/10.1016/j.psychsport.2012.05.006

Talbot-Honeck, C., & Orlick, T. (1998). The essence of excellence: Mental skills of top classical musicians. *Journal of Excellence, 1*, 61–75.

Tanay, G., & Bernstein, A. (2013). State Mindfulness Scale (SMS): Development and initial validation. *Psychological Assessment, 25*, 1286–1299. http://dx.doi.org/10.1037/a0034044

Tang, Y. Y., Hölzel, B. K., & Posner, M. I. (2015). The neuroscience of mindfulness meditation. *Nature Reviews Neuroscience, 16*, 213–225. http://dx.doi.org/10.1038/nrn3916

Tang, Y. Y., Rothbart, M. K., & Posner, M. I. (2012). Neural correlates of establishing, maintaining, and switching brain states. *Trends in Cognitive Sciences, 16*, 330–337. http://dx.doi.org/10.1016/j.tics.2012.05.001

Taylor, M. E. (2001). *Meditation as treatment for performance anxiety in singers* (Doctoral dissertation). Available from ProQuest Dissertations and Theses database. (UMI No. 3027382)

Terry, P. C. (2008). Performance psychology: Being the best, the best you can be, or just a little better? *InPsych, 30*(1), 8–11.

Thienot, E. (2013). *Mindfulness in elite athletes: Conceptualisation, measurement, and application* (Doctoral dissertation, University of Western Australia). Retrieved from http://research-repository.uwa.edu.au/files/3222049/Thienot_Emilie_2013.pdf

Thienot, E., Jackson, B., Dimmock, J., Grove, J. R., Bernier, M., & Fournier, J. F. (2014). Development and preliminary validation of the mindfulness inventory for sport. *Psychology of Sport and Exercise, 15,* 72–80. http://dx.doi.org/10.1016/j.psychsport.2013.10.003

Thompson, R. W., Kaufman, K. A., De Petrillo, L. A., Glass, C. R., & Arnkoff, D. B. (2011). One year follow-up of mindful sport performance enhancement (MSPE) for archers, golfers, and runners. *Journal of Clinical Sport Psychology, 5,* 99–116. http://dx.doi.org/10.1123/jcsp.5.2.99

Thoresen, C. E., & Mahoney, M. J. (1974). *Behavioral self-control.* New York, NY: Holt, Rinehart & Winston.

Toner, J., Montero, B. G., & Moran, A. (2015). The perils of automaticity. *Review of General Psychology, 19,* 431–442. http://dx.doi.org/10.1037/gpr0000054

Toner, J., & Moran, A. (2015). Enhancing performance proficiency at the expert level: Considering the role of 'somaesthetic awareness.' *Psychology of Sport and Exercise, 16,* 110–117. http://dx.doi.org/10.1016/j.psychsport.2014.07.006

True Athlete Project. (2015, November 17). "I feel like I'm floating in a cloud." *The True Athlete Project Newsletter,* p. 6.

UK Network for Mindfulness-Based Teachers. (2011). *Good practice guidelines for teaching mindfulness-based courses.* From http://mindfulnessteachersuk.org.uk/pdf/teacher-guidelines.pdf

Ungerleider, S. (2005). *Mental training for peak performance: Top athletes reveal the mind exercises they use to excel.* Emmaus, PA: Rodale.

Urry, H. L., van Reekum, C. M., Johnstone, T., Kalin, N. H., Thurow, M. E., Schaefer, H. S., . . . Davidson, R. J. (2006). Amygdala and ventromedial prefrontal cortex are inversely coupled during regulation of negative affect and predict the diurnal pattern of cortisol secretion among older adults. *The Journal of Neuroscience, 26,* 4415–4425. http://dx.doi.org/10.1523/JNEUROSCI.3215-05.2006

Valentine, E., Fitzgerald, D., Gorton, T., Hudson, J., & Symonds, E. (1995). The effect of lessons in the Alexander technique on music performance in high and low stress situations. *Psychology of Music, 23,* 129–141. http://dx.doi.org/10.1177/0305735695232002

Vallabh, P., & Singhal, M. (2014). Buddhism and decision making at individual, group and organizational levels. *Journal of Management Development, 33,* 763–775. http://dx.doi.org/10.1108/JMD-09-2013-0123

van den Hurk, P. A. M., Giommi, F., Gielen, S. C., Speckens, A. E. M., & Barendregt, H. P. (2010). Greater efficiency in attentional processing related to mindfulness meditation. *The Quarterly Journal of Experimental Psychology, 63,* 1168–1180. http://dx.doi.org/10.1080/17470210903249365

van Houten, R. (1998). *How to use prompts to initiate behavior* (2nd ed.). Austin, TX: Pro-Ed.

van Veen, V., & Carter, C. S. (2002). The anterior cingulate as a conflict monitor: fMRI and ERP studies. *Physiology & Behavior, 77*, 477–482. http://dx.doi.org/10.1016/S0031-9384(02)00930-7

Vast, R. L., Young, R. L., & Thomas, P. R. (2010). Emotions in sport: Perceived effects on attention, concentration, and performance. *Australian Psychologist, 45*, 132–140. http://dx.doi.org/10.1080/00050060903261538

Vealey, R. S. (2007). Mental skills training in sport. In G. Tenenbaum & R. Eklund (Eds.), *Handbook of sport psychology* (3rd ed., pp. 287–309). Hoboken, NJ: Wiley.

Vealey, R. S., & Perritt, N. C. (2015). Hardiness and optimism as predictors of the frequency of flow in collegiate athletes. *Journal of Sport Behavior, 38*, 321–338.

Veehof, M. M., Oskam, M.-J., Schreurs, K. M. G., & Bohlmeijer, E. T. (2011). Acceptance-based interventions for the treatment of chronic pain: A systematic review and meta-analysis. *Pain, 152*, 533–542. http://dx.doi.org/10.1016/j.pain.2010.11.002

Vettese, L. C., Toneatto, T., Stea, J. N., Nguyen, L., & Wang, J. J. (2009). Do mindfulness meditation participants do their homework? And does it make a difference? A review of the empirical evidence. *Journal of Cognitive Psychotherapy, 23*, 198–225. http://dx.doi.org/10.1891/0889-8391.23.3.198

Wagstaff, C. R. D. (2014). Emotion regulation and sport performance. *Journal of Sport and Exercise Psychology, 36*, 401–412. http://dx.doi.org/10.1123/jsep.2013-0257

Walker, B. S. (2013). Mindfulness and burnout among competitive adolescent tennis players. *South African Journal of Sports Medicine, 25*, 105–108. http://dx.doi.org/10.17159/2078-516X/2013/v25i4a344

Wallace, C. (2013, January 7). Introduction to meditation for actors (part 1) [Blog post]. Retrieved from http://www.backstage.com/advice-for-actors/backstage-experts/introduction-meditation-actors-part-1

Wegner, D. M. (1994). Ironic processes of mental control. *Psychological Review, 101*, 34–52. http://dx.doi.org/10.1037/0033-295X.101.1.34

Weinberg, R. S., & Gould, D. (2015). *Foundations of sport and exercise psychology* (6th ed.). Champaign, IL: Human Kinetics.

Wellcome Trust. (2011, December 22). Changes in London taxi drivers' brains driven by acquiring 'the Knowledge.' *ScienceDaily.* Retrieved from https://www.sciencedaily.com/releases/2011/12/111208125720.htm

Werner, K. (1996). *Effortless mastery: Liberating the master musician within.* New Albany, IN: Jamey Aebersold Jazz.

Wheeler, M. S., Arnkoff, D. B., & Glass, C. R. (2016). *The neuroscience of mindfulness: How mindfulness alters the brain and facilitates emotion regulation.* Manuscript submitted for publication.

Wicks, C. G. (2012). *Adolescent equestrienne athletes' experiences of mindfulness in competition* (Doctoral dissertation). Available from ProQuest Dissertations and Theses database. (UMI No. 3541461)

Willard, C., & Saltzman, A. (Eds.). (2015). *Teaching mindfulness skills to kids and teens.* New York, NY: Guilford Press.

Williamon, A. (Ed.). (2004). *Musical excellence: Strategies and techniques to enhance performance*. Oxford, England: Oxford University Press. http://dx.doi.org/10.1093/acprof:oso/9780198525356.001.0001

Williams, A. M., & Ford, P. R. (2008). Expertise and expert performance in sport. *International Review of Sport and Exercise Psychology, 1*, 4–18. http://dx.doi.org/10.1080/17509840701836867

Williams, D. E., & Andersen, M. B. (2012). Identity, wearing many hats, and boundary blurring: The mindful psychologist on the way to the Olympic and Paralympic games. *Journal of Sport Psychology in Action, 3*, 139–152. http://dx.doi.org/10.1080/21520704.2012.683090

Wisdom 2.0. (2016, March 4). *Mastering the mental game. Pete Carroll, Michael Gervais, Jon Kabat-Zinn. Wisdom 2.0 2016* [Video file]. Retrieved from https://www.youtube.com/watch?v=oUiCxse8zzA

Wittmann, M., & Schmidt, S. (2014). Mindfulness meditation and the experience of time. In S. Schmidt & H. Walach (Eds.), *Meditation—Neuroscientific approaches and philosophical implications* (pp. 199–209). Cham, Switzerland: Springer International. http://dx.doi.org/10.1007/978-3-319-01634-4_11

Wolanin, A. T. (2004). *Mindfulness-acceptance-commitment (MAC) based performance enhancement for Division I collegiate athletes: A preliminary investigation* (Doctoral dissertation). Available from ProQuest Dissertations and Theses database. (UMI No. 3139154)

Wolanin, A. T., & Gross, M. B. (2016). Mindfulness- and acceptance-based approaches with college student-athletes. In J. Block-Lerner & L. A. Cardaciotto (Eds.), *The mindfulness-informed educator: Building acceptance and psychological flexibility in higher education* (pp. 155–172). New York, NY: Routledge.

Wolanin, A., Gross, M., & Hong, E. (2015). Depression in athletes: Prevalence and risk factors. *Current Sports Medicine Reports, 14*, 56–60. http://dx.doi.org/10.1249/JSR.0000000000000123

Wolanin, A. T., & Schwanhausser, L. A. (2010). Psychological functioning as a moderator of the MAC approach to performance enhancement. *Journal of Clinical Sport Psychology, 4*, 312–322. http://dx.doi.org/10.1123/jcsp.4.4.312

Wood, A. M., Froh, J. J., & Geraghty, A. W. A. (2010). Gratitude and well-being: A review and theoretical integration. *Clinical Psychology Review, 30*, 890–905. http://dx.doi.org/10.1016/j.cpr.2010.03.005

Wrisberg, C. A., Simpson, D., Loberg, L. A., Withycombe, J. L., & Reed, A. (2009). NCAA Division-I student-athletes' receptivity to mental skills training by sport psychology consultants. *The Sport Psychologist, 23*, 470–486. http://dx.doi.org/10.1123/tsp.23.4.470

Wu, S.-D., & Lo, P.-C. (2008). Inward-attention meditation increases parasympathetic activity: A study based on heart rate variability. *Biomedical Research, 29*, 245–250. http://dx.doi.org/10.2220/biomedres.29.245

Wylie, M. S. (2015, January/February). The mindfulness explosion: The perils of mainstream acceptance. *Psychotherapy Networker*, 19–45.

Yalom, I., & Leszcz, M. (2005). *The theory and practice of group psychotherapy*. New York, NY: Basic Books.

Yang, S., & Zhang, Z. (2014). 正念认知干预训练对高水平运动员压力应对相关心理指标的影响 [Effect of mindfulness-based cognitive intervention on the stress-related psychological parameters of elite athletes]. *Chinese Journal of Sports Medicine, 33,* 214–223.

Yerkes, R. M., & Dodson, J. D. (1908). The relation of strength of stimulus to rapidity of habit formation. *The Journal of Comparative Neurology, 18,* 459–482. http://dx.doi.org/10.1002/cne.920180503

Young, D. C. (2005). Mens sana in corpore sano? Body and mind in ancient Greece. *The International Journal of the History of Sport, 22*(1), 22–41. http://dx.doi.org/10.1080/0952336052000314638

Young, J. A., & Pain, M. D. (1999). The zone: Evidence of a universal phenomenon for athletes across sports. *Athletic Insight: The Online Journal of Sport Psychology, 1*(3).

Zald, D. H. (2003). The human amygdala and the emotional evaluation of sensory stimuli. *Brain Research Reviews, 41,* 88–123. http://dx.doi.org/10.1016/S0165-0173(02)00248-5

Zeidan, F., Emerson, N. M., Farris, S. R., Ray, J. N., Jung, Y., McHaffie, J. G., & Coghill, R. C. (2015). Mindfulness meditation-based pain relief employs different neural mechanisms than placebo and sham mindfulness meditation-induced analgesia. *The Journal of Neuroscience, 35,* 15307–15325. http://dx.doi.org/10.1523/JNEUROSCI.2542-15.2015

Zeidan, F., Gordon, N. S., Merchant, J., & Goolkasian, P. (2010). The effects of brief mindfulness meditation training on experimentally induced pain. *The Journal of Pain, 11,* 199–209. http://dx.doi.org/10.1016/j.jpain.2009.07.015

Zeidan, F., Martucci, K. T., Kraft, R. A., Gordon, N. S., McHaffie, J. G., & Coghill, R. C. (2011). Brain mechanisms supporting the modulation of pain by mindfulness meditation. *The Journal of Neuroscience, 31,* 5540–5548. http://dx.doi.org/10.1523/JNEUROSCI.5791-10.2011

Zhang, C.-Q., Chung, P.-K., & Si, G. (2015). Assessing acceptance in mindfulness with direct-worded items: The development and initial validation of the athlete mindfulness questionnaire. *Journal of Sport and Health Science.* Advance online publication. http://dx.doi.org/10.1016/j.jshs.2015.09.010

Zhang, C.-Q., Chung, P.-K., Si, G., & Gucciardi, D. F. (2016). Measuring decentering as a unidimensional construct: The development and initial validation of the Decentering Scale for Sport. *Psychology of Sport and Exercise, 24,* 147–158. http://dx.doi.org/10.1016/j psychsport.2016.02.006

Zhang, C.-Q., Si, G., Duan, Y., Lyu, Y., Keatley, D. A., & Chan, D. K. C. (2016). The effects of mindfulness training on beginners' skill acquisition in dart throwing: A randomized controlled trial. *Psychology of Sport and Exercise, 22,* 279–285. http://dx.doi.org/10.1016/j.psychsport.2015.09.005

Zillmer, E. A., & Gigli, R. W. (2007). Clinical sport psychology in intercollegiate athletics. *Journal of Clinical Sport Psychology, 1,* 210–222. http://dx.doi.org/10.1123/jcsp.1.3.210

Zur, O., & Lazarus, A. A. (2002). Six arguments against dual relationships and their rebuttals. In A. A. Lazarus & O. Zur (Eds.), *Dual relationships and psychotherapy* (pp. 3–24). New York, NY: Springer.

Index

mindfulness-based stress reduction developed by, 4, 33–34
and mindfulness for musicians, 210
and mindful yoga, 95–96, 114
and motivation, 186
and muscle tension, 156
and raisin exercise, 69, 70
and reactions to meditation, 22
and research on mindfulness meditation with
athletes, 34, 36, 40
and sitting meditation, 72, 130
and teaching mindfulness, 4, 197
and walking meditation, 115
Kageyama, N., 161
Kashdan, T. B., 37, 195
Kastor, Deena, 32
Kaufman, Keith, 175, 198, 223, 239
Kaufman, Pamela, 96
Kerr, Steve, 32
Khalsa, S. B. S., 213
Khanna, G. L., 42
Knowledge, 17–18
Koen, B., 211
Kowalczyk, M., 155–156
Kowalski, K. C., 161
Krch, M., 58
Krzyzewski, Mike, 27

L

Langer, E. J., 29, 30, 213–214
Langer Mindfulness/Mindlessness Scale, 30
Lanning, Spencer, 11
Larsen, C. H., 199
Lee, K., 27
"Letting go," 84, 149–153
Levinson, D. B., 22, 51
Lin, P., 212
Long-distance runners, 165–167
Lonsdale, C., 41
Los Angeles Lakers, 24, 25, 28, 190
Lundgren, T., 38–39
Lutz, A., 22, 51
Lynch, J., 11

M

MAAS (Mindful Attention Awareness Scale), 30
MAC approach. *See* Mindfulness–acceptance–
commitment approach
MacPherson, A. C., 158
Maffini, N., 38–39
Magicians (Lev Grossman), 179–180
Mahoney, J., 39
Mallard, T. T., 37
Mannion, J., 196, 201
Marks, D. R., 22, 51, 56, 57, 59
Maron, David, 69
Mastery, 148, 186–188
May-Treanor, Misty, 32

MBCT. *See* Mindfulness-based cognitive therapy
MBSR. *See* Mindfulness-based stress reduction
McCarthy, P. J., 53
McGinn, D., 190
Meditation
and acting, 216–217
Chan, 212
and flow, 51
importance of, 25
mindfulness vs., 29
for musicians, 210–213
during running, 127–130
sitting, 75–75, 89–90, 105–107, 130–132
sport, 125–130, 138–139
stigma of, 22, 54, 67
use of anchors in, 125–127
walking, 115–118, 161, 210–211
Meditation training, 40–43
Memmert, D., 50
Mental cues, 160
Mental training
and attachment, 113
commitment to, 21–25
elements of, 13–15
introducing concepts of, 66
Mental training paradox, 11–26
and commitment to mental training, 21–25
and elements of mental training, 13–15
factors sustaining, 15–21
introducing concepts of, 66
and mindfulness as part of training routine,
25–26
puzzle of, 12
Metacognitive awareness, 210
Meuse, Barry, 18
Mikicin, M., 155–156
Millar, S.-K., 157
Miller, T., 69, 127
Mind–body connections, 97–98
Mindful Attention Awareness Scale (MAAS), 30
Mindful emotion regulation, 30
Mindful goal selection, 188
Mindfulness, 27–45, 49–50, 205–219
and acting, 215–217
assessment of, 30, 36
attention regulation as link between flow
and, 50–52
in baseball case study, 224–226
in basketball case study, 240–242
and dance, 214–215
defined, x, 29
emotion regulation as link between flow and,
52–54
foundations of, 33–36
future directions for research on sports and,
44–45
incompatibilities of flow and, 56–59
interventions for athletes based on, 36–43

About the Authors

Keith A. Kaufman, PhD, is a licensed clinical psychologist specializing in the mental training of athletes and others who wish to improve their health and performance. He has operated his own private practice since 2008, and currently has office locations in Washington, DC, and Fairfax, Virginia. He is also a research associate at The Catholic University of America (CUA), Washington, DC, where he codirects the Sport Psychology Lab and teaches undergraduate sport psychology. He codeveloped mindful sport performance enhancement (MSPE) and has coauthored two chapters on mindfulness and sport, along with writing or contributing to numerous articles on fitness, sport psychology, mindful sport performance, and dealing with athletic burnout and injury.

Dr. Kaufman obtained his bachelor of arts in both psychology and exercise & sport science from the University of North Carolina at Chapel Hill, where he received the Patrick F. Earey Award for the outstanding senior, Exercise & Sport Science major. He earned his doctorate from CUA and completed his predoctoral internship at Virginia Tech, training under the Athletic Department's in-house sport psychologist and receiving an American College Counseling Association special commendation for meritorious service following the 2007 shootings. He is a member of the American Psychological Association and the Association for Applied Sport Psychology, and can be contacted through his websites (http://www.KeithKaufmanPhD.com and http://www.MindfulCompetitor.com).

Carol R. Glass, PhD, is a professor of psychology at The Catholic University of America (CUA) in Washington, DC, where she is a faculty member in the PhD program in clinical psychology and received the James Dornan Memorial Undergraduate Educator of the Year Award in 2010. Her research interests include the role of cognition in anxiety, psychotherapy integration, and mindfulness and acceptance-based approaches to alleviate anxiety and stress and to promote peak performance. She codirects the Sport Psychology Lab at CUA, and is one of the developers of mindful sport performance enhancement (MSPE).

She is the author of more than 100 articles and chapters, as well as a coeditor of the book *Cognitive Assessment.* Additionally, she served on the editorial board of *Cognitive Therapy and Research* for over 20 years as well as on the editorial board of the *Journal of Psychotherapy Integration.* She is currently a member of the CUA Athletic Advisory Board.

Dr. Glass is a member of the Advisory Board (and former Steering Committee member) of the Society for the Exploration of Psychotherapy Integration and a Founding Fellow of the Academy of Cognitive Therapy. She is also a fellow of the American Psychological Association (Society of Clinical Psychology) and member of the Society for Sport, Exercise, & Performance Psychology and the Association for Applied Sport Psychology. She has over 30 years of experience as a practicing clinical psychologist in Washington, DC, and Bethesda, Maryland.

Timothy R. Pineau, PhD, is currently the outreach coordinator at the Marymount University Counseling Center in Arlington, Virginia, and he has a private practice in Washington, DC. Mindfulness is a cornerstone of his personal life and clinical work. As part of his work at Marymount, Dr. Pineau offers individual and group therapy, as well as drop-in sessions and workshops that emphasize mindfulness principles. He has coauthored two book chapters and a journal article on the topic of mindfulness and sports, and has spearheaded a research initiative at Marymount to examine the use of mindful sport performance enhancement (MSPE) with college sports teams. He also has taught courses in mindfulness and meditation and the history of psychology at The Catholic University of America (CUA), Washington, DC, and contributes to research in the CUA Sport Psychology Lab.

Dr. Pineau received his bachelor of science in clinical psychology, with a double major in philosophy, from Tufts University. He completed his doctoral training at CUA, which is where he joined his current coauthors in the Sport Psychology Lab and took the lead on expanding and enhancing MSPE into its present 6-week version. His more than a decade of experience in rowing (as a competitor and a coach) has been a significant influence on his work. Finally, he is a member of the American Psychological Association, American Group Psychotherapy Association, and Association for Applied Sport Psychology, and is a licensed clinical psychologist in both Virginia and Washington, DC.